Living with native title: the experiences of registered native title corporations

Living with native title: the experiences of registered native title corporations

Edited by
Toni Bauman, Lisa M Strelein and Jessica K Weir

First published in 2013 by AIATSIS Research Publications
Print edition published in 2014
Second edition 2017, reprinted 2024

© Australian Institute of Aboriginal and Torres Strait Islander Studies, 2013
© in individual chapters and updates as follows: Chapter 1, AIATSIS and Jessica Weir; Chapter 2, AIATSIS and Lara Wiseman; Chapter 3, AIATSIS; Chapter 4, AIATSIS and Hanz Spier; Chapter 5, AIATSIS and Jessica Weir; Chapter 6, Patrick Sullivan and John Hughes; Chapter 7, Paul Memmott and Peter Blackwood; Chapter 8, Manuchia Barcham and Francesca Merlan; Chapter 9, Ciaran O'Faircheallaigh

All rights reserved. Apart from any fair dealing for the purposes of private study, research, criticism or review, as permitted under the *Copyright Act 1968* (the Act), no part of this paper may be reproduced or transmitted in any form or by any means, electronic or mechanical, including photocopying, recording or by any information storage and retrieval system, without prior permission in writing from the publisher. The Act also allows a maximum of one chapter or 10 per cent of this paper, whichever is the greater, to be photocopied or distributed digitally by any educational institution for its educational purposes, provided that the educational institution (or body that administers it) has given a remuneration notice to Copyright Agency Limited (CAL) under the Act.

Australian Institute of Aboriginal and Torres Strait Islander Studies (AIATSIS)
GPO Box 553, Canberra ACT 2601
Phone: (61 2) 6246 1111
Fax: (61 2) 6261 4285
Email: research@aiatsis.gov.au
Web: www.aiatsis.gov.au

National Library of Australia Cataloguing-in-Publication entry:

Author:	Bauman, Toni, author.
Title:	Living with native title : the experiences of registered native title corporations / Toni Bauman, Lisa M Strelein and Jessica K Weir.
ISBN:	9781922102690 (pbk) 9781922102119 (ebook)
Subjects:	Native title (Australia) Land tenure--Law and legislation--Australia. Aboriginal Australians--Land tenure--Australia--Management. Land use--Law and legislation--Australia.
Other Authors/Contributors:	Strelein, Lisa, author. Weir, Jessica K., author. Australian Institute of Aboriginal and Torres Strait Islander Studies, issuing body.
Dewey Number:	346.940432

Typeset in 10.5/14.5 pt Plantin Std by Bookhouse, Sydney

Cover images: Barron Gorge National Park in Djabugay country (Photo: Hanz Spier); low tide, West Kimberley coast near Bidyadanga, Karajarri country (Photo: Jessica Weir); water tower, Bidyadanga, Karajarri country (Photo: Jessica Weir); Mer Island, Torres Strait (Photo: Lisa Strelein); Poruma Island, Torres Strait (Photo: Lisa Strelein); sandy tracks, Bidyadanga, Karajarri country (Photo: Jessica Weir).

AIATSIS acknowledges the funding support of the Department of the Prime Minister and Cabinet (PM&C).

Contents

List of figures	vii
List of tables	viii
Abbreviations and acronyms	ix
Notes on contributors	xii
Acknowledgments	xvii
Preface	xix

Chapter 1   Navigating complexity: living with native title   1
Toni Bauman, Lisa M Strelein and Jessica K Weir

Chapter 2   An overview of the Registered Native Title Bodies Corporate regime   27
Pamela Faye McGrath, Claire Stacey and Lara Wiseman

Chapter 3   Native Title Bodies Corporate in the Torres Strait: finding a place in the governance of a region   65
Lisa M Strelein

           Update: Torres Strait Native Title Bodies Corporate 2013   109
           Lisa M Strelein

Chapter 4   The Djabugay native title story: getting back in town   111
Toni Bauman

           Update: Djabugay Native Title Corporation 2013   142
           Hanz Spier

Chapter 5   Karajarri: native title and governance in the West Kimberley   147
Jessica K Weir

           Update: Karajarri Traditional Lands Association 2013   175
           Claire Stacey

Chapter 6	The Ord River Stage 2 Agreement and Miriuwung Gajerrong native title corporations *Patrick Sullivan*	181
	Update: Miriuwung Gajerrong Corporation and Registered Native Title Bodies Corporate 2013 *John Hughes*	208
Chapter 7	Managing mixed Indigenous land titles — Cape York case studies *Paul Memmott and Peter Blackwood*	217
	Update: Cape York Registered Native Title Bodies Corporate 2013 *Paul Memmott and Peter Blackwood*	248
Chapter 8	Working with Indigenous and western corporate structures — the Central Arrernte case *Manuhuia Barcham*	253
	Update: Lhere Artepe Registered Native Title Body Corporate 2013 *Francesca Merlan*	271
Chapter 9	Registered Native Title Bodies Corporate and mining agreements: capacities and structures *Ciaran O'Faircheallaigh*	275
	Update: Registered Native Title Bodies Corporate and mining agreements 2013 *Ciaran O'Faircheallaigh*	290
RNTBC selected reading list		293

List of figures

Figure 1.0:	Determinations and Native Title Prescribed Bodies Corporate, as at 31 March 2017	*facing page xx*
Figure 1.1:	Location of RNTBC case studies	3
Figure 3.1:	Native title determinations in the Torres Strait	68
Figure 3.2:	Misrepresenting native title: the Department of Natural Resources and Water's representation of native title as a layer of regulation, first meeting of PBCs of the Torres Strait, Waiben, December 2007	85
Figure 4.1:	Djabugay native title determination	112
Figure 5.1:	Karajarri native title determinations	148
Figure 6.1:	Miriuwung Gajerrong native title determinations	182
Figure 6.2:	Corporate structure of MG Corporation, 2006	187
Figure 6.3:	Corporate structure of MG Corporation, 2009	210
Figure 7.1:	Map of Queensland showing Coen and Wik regions (here labelled sub-regions) in relation to Cape York Land Council's Native Title Representative Body (NTRB) area	219
Figure 7.2:	Map of Wik and Wik Way Native Title Claim in the Wik region, as at 2013	225
Figure 7.3:	Map of existing and likely future Aboriginal land tenures in the Coen region, as at 2008	231
Figure 7.4:	Wik region model showing the proposed structural relationship between the Wik PBC and the Wik LSMA after the Chalco royalty flow allows a permanent RNTBC office to be established	235
Figure 7.5:	Coen region model illustrating the proposed Coen LSMA, a set of tribal PBCs which also serve as land trusts, and a set of four tribal corporations for day-to-day business in the Coen region. This would result from an amalgamation and rationalisation of all existing land owning corporations, RNTBCs (here labelled PBCs) and land trusts.	237
Figure 8.1:	Alice Springs native title determination	254

Figure 8.2: Lhere Artepe corporate structures, 2008   262
Figure 8.3: Lhere Artepe corporate structures, 2010   264
Figure 9.1: Possible structure for a 'mining agreement' RNTBC   284

List of tables

Table 2.1: Classification of PBCs under the CATSI Act   33
Table 2.2: Distribution of RNTBCs by state and size, June 2013   33
Table 2.3: Timeline of legislation, policy, case law and events relevant to RNTBCs   53
Table 3.1: Torres Strait Registered Native Title Bodies Corporate   98
Table 7.1: Model of harmonised rules for an RNTBC as trustee of a land trust   223
Table 7.2: Land trusts in the Coen region holding Aboriginal freehold land granted under the ALA, as at 2008   229
Table 7.3: Native title proceedings in the Coen region, as at 2008   229

Abbreviations and acronyms

ABN	Australian Business Number
ACA Act	*Aboriginal Councils and Associations Act 1976* (Cth)
ACHA	*Aboriginal Cultural Heritage Act 2003* (Qld)
ACNC	Australian Charities and Not-for-profits Commission
AGD	Attorney-General's Department
AGDSC	Attorney-General's Department Steering Committee
AGM	annual general meeting
AIATSIS	Australian Institute of Aboriginal and Torres Strait Islander Studies
ALA	*Aboriginal Land Act 1991* (Qld)
ALT	Aboriginal Lands Trust
ANU	Australian National University
ASEIA	Aboriginal Social and Economic Impact Assessment
ATNS	Agreements, Treaties and Negotiated Settlement Project
ATSI Act	*Aboriginal and Torres Strait Islander Act 2005* (Cth)
ATSIC	Aboriginal and Torres Strait Islander Commission
ATSISJC	Aboriginal and Torres Strait Islander Social Justice Commissioner
AusAID	Australian Government Overseas Aid Program
BADA	Buda:Dji Aboriginal Development Association Aboriginal Corporation
CAEPR	Centre for Aboriginal Economic Policy Research
CAT	Centre for Appropriate Technology
CATSI Act	*Corporations (Aboriginal and Torres Strait Islander) Act 2006* (Cth)
CBE	Coen Business Enterprises
CDC	Commercial Development Corporation
CDEP	Community Development Employment Program
CEO	Chief Executive Officer
Chalco	Aluminium Corporation of China Ltd
CLC	Central Land Council
CRAC	Coen Regional Aboriginal Corporation
CYLC	Cape York Land Council

DBDAC	Djabugay Business Development Aboriginal Corporation
DCT	Djabugay Country Tours
DEC	Department of Environment and Conservation (WA)
DERM	Department of Environment and Resource Management (Qld)
DNRM	Department of Natural Resources and Mines (Qld)
DNTAC	Djabugay Native Title Aboriginal Corporation
DOGIT	Deed of Grant in Trust Lands
DOTARS	Department of Transport and Regional Services (Qld)
DTAC	Djabugay Tribal Aboriginal Corporation
DTGAC	Djabugay Tour Guiding Aboriginal Corporation
EDU	Economic Development Unit
EPA	Queensland Government's Environmental Protection Agency, now DERM
FaHCSIA	Commonwealth Department of Families, Housing, Community, Services and Indigenous Affairs
FVTOC	Federation of Victorian Traditional Owner Corporations
HRSCATSIA	House of Representatives Standing Committee on Aboriginal and Torres Strait Islander Affairs
IBA	Indigenous Business Australia
ICA	Indigenous Commercial Arrangement
ICC	Indigenous Coordination Centre
ICDC	Indigenous Community Development Corporation
ILC	Indigenous Land Corporation
ILUA	Indigenous Land Use Agreement
IPA	Indigenous Protected Area
IWG	Interdepartmental Working Group
JWGILS	Joint Working Group on Indigenous Land Settlements
KDC	Kimberley Development Commission
KLC	Kimberley Land Council
KMKM	Koah Mantaka Kowrara Mona Mona Corporation
KTLA	Karajarri Traditional Lands Association
LNG	Liquefied Natural Gas
LSMA	Land and Sea Management Agency
MCA	Minerals Council of Australia
MG	Miriuwung Gajerrong (claims, people, corporation et cetera)
NCA	*Nature Conservation Act 1992* (Qld)
NEAC	Nyawarri Estate Aboriginal Corporation
NKAC	Nyangumarta Karajarri Aboriginal Corporation RNTBC
NNTC	National Native Title Council
NNTT	National Native Title Tribunal

NQLC	North Queensland Land Council
NT	Northern Territory
NTA	*Native Title Act 1993* (Cth)
NTG	Native Title Group
NTO	Native Title Office
NTP	Native Title Party
NTPC	Native Title Protection Conditions
NTRBs	Native Title Representative Bodies
NTRU	Native Title Research Unit
NTSPs	Native Title Service Providers
NTSV	Native Title Services Victoria
OES	Ord Enhancement Scheme
OFA	Ord Final Agreement
ORAC	Office of the Registrar of Aboriginal Corporations
ORATSIC	Office of the Registrar of Aboriginal and Torres Strait Islander Corporations
ORIC	Office of the Registrar of Indigenous Corporations
PBCs	Prescribed Bodies Corporate
PBI	public benevolent institution
PJCNT	Parliamentary Joint Committee on Native Title and the Aboriginal and Torres Strait Islander Land Account (formerly Land Fund)
PNG	Papua New Guinea
PZJA	Torres Strait Protected Zone Joint Authority
QIWG	Queensland Indigenous Working Group
QPWS	Queensland Parks and Wildlife Service
QRail	Queensland Rail
RNTBC	Registered Native Title Body Corporate
sDe	single Djabugay entity
SEWPaC	Department of Sustainability Environment, Water Populations and Community
SIA	social impact assessment
TRAWQ	acronym used for the Waiben suburbs of Tamwoy, Rose Hill, Aplin, Waiben and Quarantine
TSC	Torres Shire Council
TSILA	*Torres Strait Islander Land Act 1991* (Qld)
TSIRC	Torres Strait Islands Regional Council
TSRA	Torres Strait Regional Authority
Wik PBC	Ngan Aak Kunch Aboriginal Corporation
WoC	Working on Country

Notes on contributors

Dr Manuhuia Barcham is currently Chairman of the Hawke Group. Prior to this he was Foundation Director of the Centre for Indigenous Governance and Development at Massey University in New Zealand. He maintains an adjunct position at the Centre for Aboriginal Economic Policy Research (CAEPR) at the Australian National University (ANU). He is a member of the following Iwi (tribes) in New Zealand: Ngati Kahungunu, Te Arawa and Ngati Tuwharetoa.

Toni Bauman is a Senior Research Fellow in the Centre for Governance and Public Policy Research at AIATSIS. She is an anthropologist, mediator, facilitator and trainer who has published widely and made presentations to a range of national and international audiences. She has over 30 years experience in Indigenous matters including land and native title claims, agreement-making, decision-making and dispute management processes, joint management of protected areas, government policy, art and craft, program evaluation, feasibility studies and training, including governance training of Registered Native Title Bodies Corporate. Toni was the chief investigator for the Indigenous Facilitation and Mediation Project at AIATSIS and acted as adviser to the Federal Court project that produced the publication *Solid work you mob are doing: case studies in Indigenous dispute resolution and conflict management in Australia* (Federal Court of Australia, 2009). Toni is also a Director of Dodson, Bauman & Associates Pty Ltd, Legal and Anthropological Consultants.

Peter Blackwood is a consultant anthropologist based in Cairns. He has previously held positions as Senior Anthropologist with the Cape York Land Council and the Aboriginal Areas Protection Authority in Alice Springs. He has managed and undertaken research and been an expert witness on a number of statutory and native title land claims in Queensland, and has provided advice to Native Title Representative Bodies on the structuring of Aboriginal landholding corporations, particularly regarding representation, decision-making and conflict resolution. He has a background in Aboriginal cultural heritage recording and management and has been an anthropological adviser in negotiations over mining and other developments affecting Aboriginal landholders and site custodians in Queensland and the Northern Territory.

John Hughes commenced as Chief Executive Officer for the Miriuwung Gajerrong Corporation in Kununurra in February 2013. He previously held the positions of Senior Lawyer — Commercial at Indigenous Business Australia in Canberra, Legal Adviser and then Manager of the Mining and Major Projects Branch at the Northern Land Council in Darwin, Civil Lawyer at the then North Australian Aboriginal Legal Aid Service in Darwin, and was earlier in private practice in Perth. John holds a Bachelor of Jurisprudence and a Bachelor of Laws (University of Western Australia) and a Master of Laws in International Law (ANU).

Dr Pamela Faye McGrath is an anthropologist and Research Fellow in the Native Title Research Unit at AIATSIS. She has worked in native title for over a decade, initially as a researcher for representative bodies in Victoria and Western Australia. In 2010 she played a key role in establishing the ANU's Centre for Native Title Anthropology. Pam has a long-term research association with a Pilbara native title group that has seen her involved with every stage of the claim cycle, from registration to boundary mapping, connection inquiries, establishment of representative structures, heritage surveys, future act agreements and negotiations towards a consent determination. Pam has expertise in historical ethnography, colonial photography and intercultural sociality. Her PhD examined the photographic history of Ngaanyatjarra families in the Western Desert, and she has published on the practice of applied anthropology in Australia. Pam has been the Treasurer of the Australian Anthropological Society since 2009.

Professor Paul Memmott is an anthropologist and architect at the University of Queensland in the Institute for Social Science Research and at the School of Architecture, where he is also the Director of the Aboriginal Environments Research Centre. He has published widely, written many applied research reports and supervised numerous postgraduate students. One of his books, *Gunyah, Goondie + Wurley: Aboriginal Architecture of Australia* (University of Queensland Press, 2007), received three national book awards in 2008, including the Stanner Award from AIATSIS. He has been an expert witness on native title, land claims and other matters involving Indigenous people and the law since 1985 and has worked in Cape York and the Gulf of Carpentaria for many years.

Professor Francesca Merlan is as anthropologist who has been researching and teaching at the ANU since 1995. She has worked on a range of major land claim cases in the Northern Territory from the early 1980s onwards (Katherine Land Claim, Mataranka Land Claim, Elsey Station and Kakadu Stage 3 among others) and has also been involved in reviews of native title cases, as well as continuing academic research on a range of related topics in Northern Australia. She continues to research and write on social transformation in Papua New Guinea (Western Highlands) and in Europe. She is a recipient of an ARC Discovery Grant for research 2012–2015 on social diversity in Alice Springs.

Professor Ciaran O'Faircheallaigh works in the School of Government and International Relations at Griffith University, Brisbane. He has published numerous articles and books in the fields of public policy, resource economics and resources policy, negotiation, impact assessment and Indigenous studies. For over 15 years he has worked with Indigenous organisations on negotiation of mining agreements and has acted as an adviser and negotiator for the Cape York, Northern, Central, Yamatji and Kimberley land councils. He is currently advising the Kimberley Land Council on negotiations in relation to oil and gas development in the Kimberley, and the autonomous Bougainville Government in relation to the possible reopening of the Bougainville copper mine.

Hanz Spier was born in Holland and grew up in Amsterdam. Hanz studied in Deventer and graduated in Tropical Agriculture and Community Development. Before coming to Australia in 1993, he worked in India and Papua New Guinea in sustainable agriculture and community development projects. In Australia he managed Migrant Settlement Services (Centacare Cairns) for several years and worked with Indigenous communities in the Torres Strait Islands, Cape York and the Kuranda region. He has been involved with Djabugay since 1999 in various capacities. In 2007 Djabugay approached Hanz to assist with the rebuilding of their corporations and in the following year they recruited him as their Chief Executive Officer, a position he still holds.

Claire Stacey is a Project Manager in the Native Title Research Unit at AIATSIS. Claire has a background in community development and anthropology and has completed a Masters in Applied Anthropology and Participatory Development at the Australian National University, focusing on Indigenous community development and public policy. Claire has worked in the private, not-for-profit and government sectors and has experience working on community development projects in both urban and remote areas of Australia, as well as internationally. Claire has worked at AIATSIS since 2010 across a number of research projects focused on the post determination landscape for native title holders, including joint management, caring for country, climate change, community development and housing. Claire is now working with traditional owners through the Prescribed Bodies Corporate Support Project, which aims to support the growing number of native title holders to manage their traditional land and waters.

Dr Lisa M Strelein is the Director of Research at AIATSIS. She has degrees in Commerce and Law and her PhD thesis, completed at the ANU in 1998, examined Indigenous sovereignty and the common law. Lisa's research and publications have focused on the relationship between Indigenous peoples and the state, and the role of the courts in defining Indigenous peoples' rights. Her recent book *Compromised jurisprudence: native title cases since Mabo* (Aboriginal Studies Press, 2009) has been heralded by members of the judiciary and Indigenous community alike, and her work on taxation and corporate design has influenced recent debates on native title tax law. She maintains strong networks within the native title system, working in partnership with Native Title Representative Bodies and claimants as well as government departments. Lisa is an Adjunct Professor with the College of Law and National Centre for Indigenous Studies at the ANU.

Dr Patrick Sullivan is a political anthropologist whose work for Aboriginal organisations has involved practical research and advice on issues of land use and distribution, community control of community development, and governance institutions at the local and regional levels. He worked on native title claims following the High Court Mabo decision in 1992 and has been the Senior Anthropologist for the Kimberley Land Council, formulating anthropological and policy advice on local, national and international projects. He is the author of *Belonging together: dealing with the politics of disenchantment in Australian Indigenous policy* (Aboriginal Studies Press, 2011) and is an Adjunct Professor at the National Centre for Indigenous Studies at the ANU.

Dr Jessica K Weir was a Research Fellow in the Native Title Research Unit at AIATSIS from 2007 to 2012 and was part of the leadership team for the Prescribed Bodies Corporate Research and Resources Project. In 2011 she founded the AIATSIS Centre for Land and Water Research. She is the editor of *Country, native title and ecology* (ANU Epress, 2012) and the author of *Murray River Country: An ecological dialogue with traditional owners* (Aboriginal Studies Press, 2009). From 2012 to 2013 Jessica was a Senior Research Fellow in the Bushfire Cooperative Research Centre at the University of Canberra. In late 2013 she began a new position as Senior Research Fellow, Institute for Culture and Society, University of Western Sydney. Jessica is a founding member of the Ecological Humanities Group and a Visiting Fellow at the Fenner School of Environment and Society at the ANU.

Lara Wiseman worked in the Native Title Research Unit at AIATSIS from 2003 to 2012. Lara was a member of the Prescribed Bodies Corporate Research and Resources Project team, contributing to information resources, publications and workshops for and about PBCs. Lara previously worked as a Heritage Policy Officer with Aboriginal Affairs Victoria and as an anthropologist with the Aboriginal Areas Protection Authority in Alice Springs. She has an Honours Degree in Arts (Social

Sciences) and is completing a Master of Social Research at the ANU. Lara is now a member of the Family Dynamics and Policy Group at the university's Australian Demographic and Social Research Institute.

Acknowledgments

We wish to thank the former Department of Families, Housing, Community Services and Indigenous Affairs for sponsoring the Prescribed Bodies Corporate Research and Resources Project (2006–2009) and the Prescribed Bodies Corporate Support Project (2009–2012). We also thank the Minerals Council of Australia for their sponsorship of the Native Title Research Unit (NTRU) case study research action partnerships, and the Office of the Registrar of Indigenous Corporations for involvement as a research partner.

The editors acknowledge and thank the chapter authors for their contributions, and also direct readers to the acknowledgments that are made within chapters. The editors and other contributors also wish to thank the anonymous peer reviewers and those colleagues who provided comments on chapters. Any errors are of course our own responsibility.

We particularly wish to thank Christiane Keller, whose hard work and patience in editing numerous footnote changes and managing the book as a whole have been exceptional. We also thank her predecessors, Lydia Glick and Zoe Scanlon.

We acknowledge the commitment of native title holders, as members of Registered Native Title Bodies Corporate (RNTBCs) and first peoples of Australia, to holding and/or managing their native title and the major contributions they have made to the business of their RNTBCs, often under difficult circumstances. We wish to thank Native Title Representative Bodies, Native Title Service Providers and other networks of people and institutions across Australia for their support and participation in NTRU projects and their support of RNTBCs.

Preface

The case studies of Registered Native Title Bodies Corporate (RNTBCs) in this book arose from the PBC Research and Resources Project.[1] This was hosted by the Native Title Research Unit (NTRU) at AIATSIS from 2006 to 2009 to support the growing number of RNTBCs and to better understand the needs and aspirations of this growing sector. The project was funded by the Department of Families, Housing, Community Services and Indigenous Affairs (FaHCSIA), with additional sponsorship from the Minerals Council of Australia. Some aspects of the project were also carried out in partnership with the Office of the Registrar of Indigenous Corporations.

Central to the project was the building of research action partnerships with three case study RNTBCs from across Australia: the Karajarri Traditional Lands Association, south of Broome; the RNTBCs in the Torres Strait; and the Djabugay RNTBC in Kuranda in Far North Queensland. Funding from the Minerals Council of Australia supported strategic and operational planning assistance for the RNTBC partners.

The case study partnerships occurred alongside other research on issues of importance to RNTBCs, such as joint management, weeds management, climate change, carbon economies, governance, and tax and corporate structures. In the first year of the project, two workshops were held to identify the major issues facing RNTBCs and the impacts of these issues on RNTBC relationships with Native Title Representative Bodies and Native Title Service Providers. Over the life of the project two national meetings of RNTBCs were held, to which representatives of Commonwealth, state and territory government departments were invited to provide information about relevant funding programs. A series of meetings between representatives of Commonwealth departments were also held at AIATSIS to raise the profile of RNTBCs and discuss their assistance. Other research action activities included providing feedback on government policy and legal reform and building the profile of RNTBC issues at annual AIATSIS National Native Title Conferences.

The research and activities generated from the project are available on the NTRU webpages as workshop reports, newsletter articles and peer reviewed publications.

These are complemented by a range of internet resources to support current practice: national, state and territory funding and training guides for RNTBCs; a national statistical summary of RNTBCs; and web profiles for each RNTBC. The outcomes of the original project have been extended under a revised AIATSIS PBC Support Project, also funded by FaHCSIA, which has convened regional RNTBC meetings and ongoing national forums, established an RNTBC working group and website (http://www.nativetitle.org.au/), and is in the process of conducting a survey of RNTBCs.

The leadership that AIATSIS has demonstrated in informing RNTBC practice and policy was recognised in the 2006 Commonwealth review of Prescribed Bodies Corporate (PBCs), which referred to the role for AIATSIS in developing tools and resources for NTRBs.[2]

Materials, publications and further information from the PBC projects are available at http://www.aiatsis.gov.au/ntru/pbc.html.

Endnotes

1 When a native title corporation is registered with the National Native Title Tribunal following a native title determination by the Federal Court, it is referred to as a Registered Native Title Body Corporate (RNTBC). See Chapter 2 for further information about distinctions between PBCs and RNTBCs.
2 Attorney-General's Department Steering Committee (AGDSC), *Structures and processes of Prescribed Bodies Corporate*, 2006, Chapter 5.27, p. 16.

Figure 1.0 Determinations and Native Title Prescribed Bodies Corporate, as at 31 March 2017.

Map courtesy of the National Native Title Tribunal.

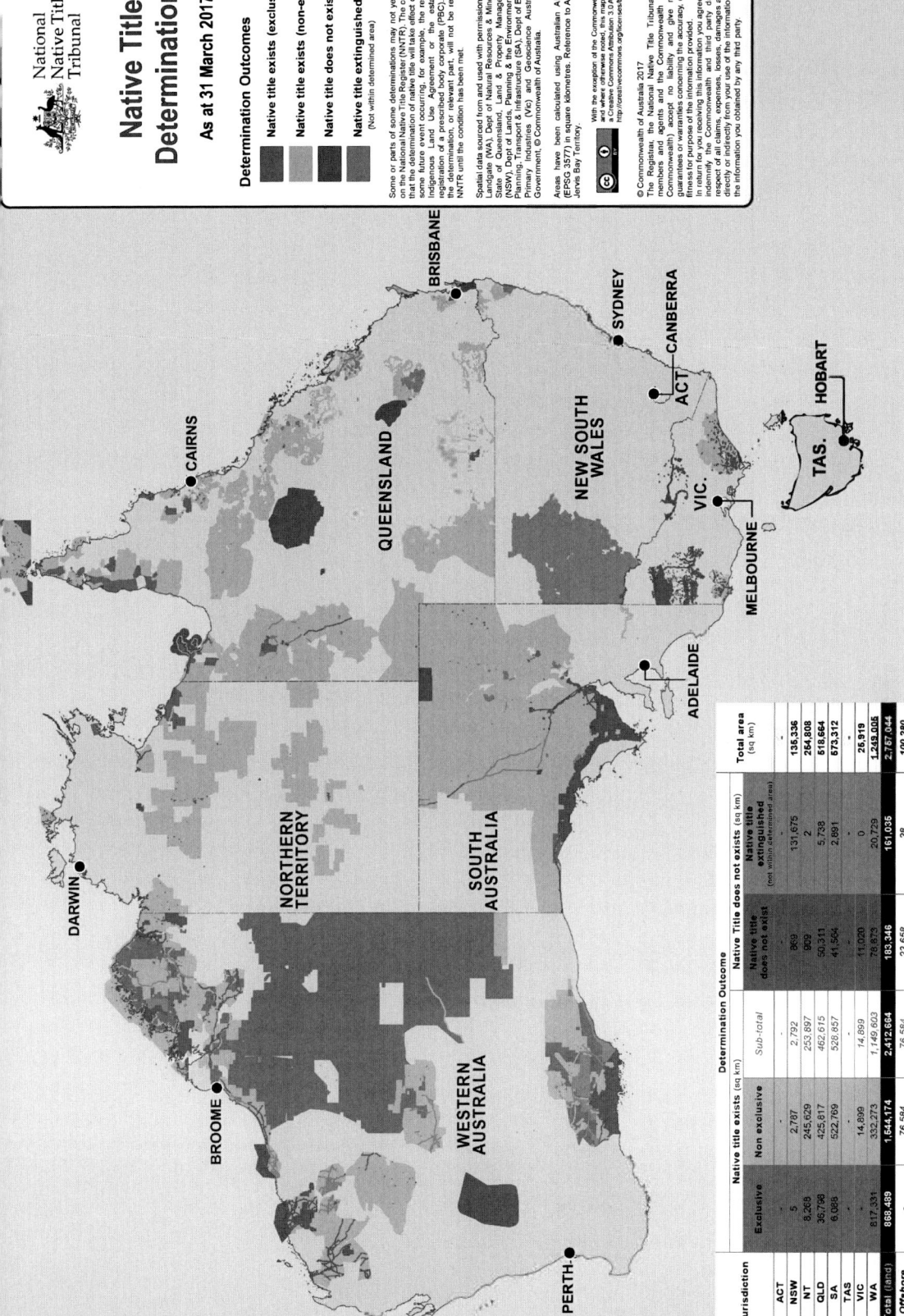

Chapter 1

Navigating complexity: living with native title

Toni Bauman, Lisa M Strelein and Jessica K Weir

Introduction

Relationships between Aboriginal and Torres Strait Islander peoples, as the Indigenous peoples of Australia, and the state underwent a seismic shift in 1992, when the High Court's *Mabo (No. 2)* decision acknowledged Indigenous peoples' pre-existing and continuing rights to their lands and waters as 'native title'.[1] The Commonwealth legislation that followed in 1993, the *Native Title Act 1993* (Cth) (NTA), created corporations that are charged with holding or managing as an agent these communal, group or individual rights and interests on behalf of native title holders.[2] This new corporate sector, underwritten by traditional laws and customs, is challenging legal, political and social institutions in Australia to be more responsive to Indigenous political, legal and cultural diversity. Accepting the enduring presence of this diversity within a modern nation state,[3] and moving beyond approaches that seek to ignore, marginalise, or discretely 'resolve' such diversity, is the required first step to building sustainable networks and institutions for native title governance.

There is significant tension between governments and native title holders about what is and what is not native title and what is and what is not reasonable support for the Registered Native Title Bodies Corporate (RNTBCs) prescribed by the NTA. There are many reasons for this tension, some arising from capacity constraints in the native title sector, whose focus is the lengthy court and agreement processes associated with the backlog of native title applications; others from the the diversity of government interests and agencies involved, including the distribution of functions across federal, state, territory and local government; and others still from conflicting views about the roles of RNTBCs.

For native title holders, recognition of traditional rights in country is often hard won, euphoric and highly symbolic. It creates the expectation of positive outcomes such as greater involvement in decision-making and an improvement in social and emotional wellbeing. The reality is that RNTBCs face a miasma of complex legal and political issues, competing demands, a lack of resources, and a great deal of uncertainty across the native title sector as to the meaning of the rights and interests of native title holders. Prescribing such a corporate sector without concomitant funding and other support is a policy failure that exasperates Indigenous peoples' governance bodies and leadership and frustrates all parties who have business with native title holders.

The existence of approximately 109 RNTBCs with rights and interests over around 20.7 per cent of Australia (see Figure 1.0: RNTBCs in Australia) demands a serious and systematic government response to ensure not only their sustainability but that of the native title sector.[4] RNTBCs play critical roles in the native title sector: as the holders and/or managers of native title, as access points for multiple parties with interests in native title lands and waters, and as readily identifiable representatives of traditional owners. They are also attractive as partners for broader policy priorities in areas as diverse as economic development, land management, health, housing and education.

Problems arising from different interpretations of RNTBC roles and functions and from a lack of funding are made worse by the impasse between federal, state and territory governments over responsibility for supporting these new corporations. There are exceptions, of course, where state and territory governments have supported RNTBCs in settling native title claims and making agreements; however, the vast majority of RNTBCs are struggling, often without government support, to meet the diverse expectations of both their own members and others.

The case studies in this book are drawn from Northern and Central Australia, where most RNTBCs are located (see Figure 1.1), and are contextualised in the following overview chapter. Northern and Central Australia are often typified as 'remote', but these case studies encompass the recognition of native title over significant regional towns and urban centres, as well as the experiences of RNTBCs in places with a long history of colonial settlement. The RNTBC experiences are presented from different disciplinary perspectives and complemented by updates written mostly in 2013. Four of the chapters are studies of particular RNTBCs, two present regional studies, and one explores the issues facing RNTBCs involved in mining agreements. Some of the RNTBCs participating in the case studies have received little or no funding for establishment and operation, while others have been party to large settlements worth millions of dollars — an exceptional experience in what is predominantly an under-resourced sector. Updates to the chapters offer the opportunity to consider how the diverse and uneven experiences of RNTBCs unfold over time.

This chapter introduces the structure of the book and outlines the case studies. It then highlights the key issues emerging from the case studies, as well as drawing on the lessons and findings of longer term AIATSIS research with RNTBCs, as outlined in the Preface. The chapter highlights the uncertainties and complexities faced not only by RNTBCs but also by other institutions engaged with the native title sector. The broad themes addressed are: the legal and conceptual framings of native title, including contestation over its meaning; the complexities of RNTBC governance, focusing on procedural issues and the need for RNTBCs to negotiate their roles as newcomers in local and regional governance; economic opportunities, risks and barriers; and RNTBC support needs and capacity issues.

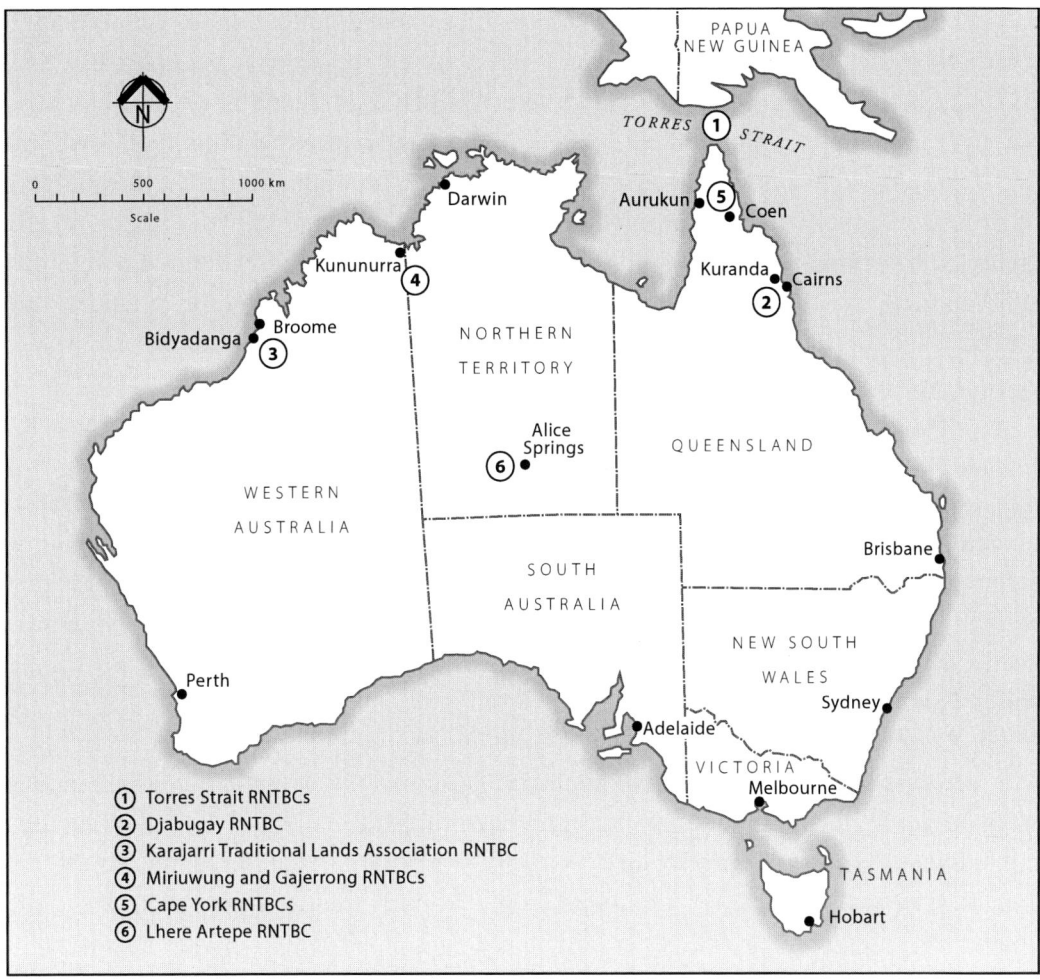

Figure 1.1 Location of RNTBC case studies. Map by Brenda Thornley for AIATSIS

The structure and content of the book

Chapter 2, by Pamela McGrath, Claire Stacey and Lara Wiseman, provides a demographic snapshot of RNTBCs, including their categorisation as small, medium or large under the *Corporations (Aboriginal and Torres Strait Islander) Act 2006* (Cth) (the CATSI Act).[5] An overview of the RNTBC regime summarises the numerous legislative and administrative reforms and consultations that have occurred since 2005 including changes to the NTA and the Native Title Prescribed Bodies Corporate Regulations 1999 (PBC Regulations) which apply to Registered Native Title Bodies Corporate.[6] Chapter 2 also highlights the diversity of RNTBCs and notes the range of aspirations they share. The chapter concludes with a discussion of moves to establish regional RNTBC working groups and some form of national advocacy and representation.

The following three chapters are case studies carried out as part of the AIATSIS research project described in the Preface and involving research action partnerships. In Chapter 3, Lisa Strelein considers the RNTBCs in the Torres Strait, whose native title includes inhabited and uninhabited islands on the border of Australia and Papua New Guinea. The chapter examines the attempts by native title holders to negotiate a place in the complex governance arrangements in the region in the face of changes to regional governance, including the establishment of a regional shire council and the disbanding of local island councils. The chapter considers the potential for native title management where native title is recognised over the entire lands and waters of a region.

Chapter 4, Toni Bauman's study of the Djabugay RNTBC in Kuranda in northern Queensland, highlights the challenges confronting many native title groups with non-exclusive possession native title over protected areas, in this instance Barron Gorge National Park. The chapter suggests the need to streamline governance arrangements for RNTBCs that emerge into a pre-existing complex of corporate structures. It also raises issues about the fragmentation of more inclusive native title groups as smaller subgroups assert exclusive interests over a specific area within the whole Djabugay estate.

In Chapter 5, Jessica Weir discusses the experiences of the Karajarri RNTBC, who are responsible for extensive exclusive possession native title holdings south of Broome, including the large Aboriginal community of Bidyadanga, as well as non-exclusive possession native title holdings over the pastoral leasehold lands that line the coast. This chapter examines how Karajarri people relate their RNTBC obligations to their other responsibilities; the role of RNTBCs in the provision of community infrastructure; and the way in which native title changes relationships between traditional owners and other residents in Aboriginal communities.

In Chapter 6, Patrick Sullivan discusses the first years of the implementation of the Ord Final Agreement (OFA) between Miriuwung and Gajerrong native title holders in the East Kimberley and the government of Western Australia. Internal corporate governance issues are central for the Yawooroong Miriuwung Gajerrong Yirrgeb Noong Dawang Aboriginal Corporation (MG Corporation) as the umbrella corporation for the two Miriuwung and Gajerrong RNTBCs. These include the incorporation of perceived traditional practices in governance structures and the barriers to taking advantage of economic opportunities arising from large-scale developments.

In Chapter 7, Paul Memmott and Peter Blackwood take a regional snapshot of the Wik and Coen areas of the Cape York Peninsula to highlight the challenge for RNTBCs of integrating and reconciling their newly recognised native title rights with pre-existing statutory tenures and traditional forms of ownership. They examine different forms of organisational design that might accommodate the multiple landholding types held by Aboriginal people in the region and recommend regional support organisations for RNTBCs.

In Chapter 8, Manuhuia Barcham examines how the Lhere Artepe RNTBC, representing its Central Arrernte members as native title holders of Alice Springs, has attempted to meet the challenges of establishing a governance structure that accounts for their cultural priorities while demonstrating legitimacy as the business partner of developers and governments. The chapter explains the location of the RNTBC in a group of corporations and trusts which aim to accommodate the interests of the three estate groups that make up the native title group and the commercial and social ventures to be undertaken.

In Chapter 9, the final case study of the book, Ciaran O'Faircheallaigh discusses the implementation and management challenges of mining agreements. Drawing on an unnamed confidential agreement, he identifies the types of rights and obligations RNTBCs are dealing with, the corporate structures that may be needed to manage them, and the capacities and skills required for success.

The case studies are accompanied by updates provided by their authors, RNTBC executives or researchers currently involved with the RNTBCs. Chapters 3 and 7 were updated by their authors, Lisa Strelein, and Paul Memmot and Peter Blackwood, providing further insight into the progression of RNTBC issues in the Torres Strait and Cape York. The chief executive officers of the Djabugay RNTBC and the MG Corporation, Hanz Spier and John Hughes, provided updates to Chapters 4 and 6 respectively, describing new economic and community development opportunities. Claire Stacey wrote the update for Chapter 5 about the Karajarri Traditional Lands Association to include new activities such as an additional native title determination and the declaration of an Indigenous Protected Area (IPA). Francesca Merlan updated Chapter 8, describing a number of challenges currently facing the Lhere Artepe RNTBC.

The case studies in this book are neither typical nor atypical. As Chapter 2 demonstrates, there is significant national diversity among RNTBCs but there are also critical shared priorities and challenges. Using the case studies as touchstones, the following discussion draws together our observations of the issues and trends that have emerged over the last seven years as the RNTBC sector has grown and taken shape. The book concludes with a selected reading list of RNTBC related publications.

RNTBC legal and conceptual framing

There is pervasive tension and misunderstanding in the native title sector about the meaning of native title. This extends to how native title is expressed and interpreted in different laws and policies, in matters such as economic development and land use planning, and more generally in day-to-day business by, and with, native title holders. It also extends to different interpretations of the roles of RNTBCs.

Administratively, the NTA prescribes the roles of RNTBCs in two parts: as the legal entity that holds and/or manages the native title rights and interests on behalf of native title holders, and as the corporate interface for third parties seeking access to native title territories.[7] However, these roles are subject to interpretation and often viewed differently by native title holders and other stakeholders. Some external parties, including in government, take a narrow view of the statutory obligations and other roles of RNTBCs, which is often underscored by their understandings of native title more generally. Accordingly, native title is encapsulated by its legal regime, which has imbued it with an inherent vulnerability rather than the enduring strength of the Indigenous connections to country on which it is based. For other external partners, native title is an anachronism that will eventually be extinguished once the land is allocated to a presumed 'more productive' purpose. For others still, as the Torres Strait case study reports, native title is misconceived as merely another layer of regulation.

To understand the purpose of RNTBCs, and of native title itself, it is also necessary to appreciate native title as a distinct part of an intercultural Australia.[8] Native title is a creature of both Indigenous and non-Indigenous laws and practice, and is recognised and managed as such. It also has a pivotal reference point external to common and statutory law in that it recognises rights and interests that are derived from and sustained by Indigenous societies and their laws and customs. The Indigenous cosmologies and ontologies underpinning these laws and customs have undergone transformations through their interactions with other world views and knowledge systems, to the extent that a profound syncretism has occurred.[9] However, the kinds of transformations and resulting complexities that are involved are poorly understood in the native title sector, where native title is often conceived as being located in an isolated Indigenous traditional domain and reduced to a 'finite thing', the unchanging attributes of which can be listed in ticked boxes.[10]

In contrast, many Indigenous peoples in Australia see native title as a set of relationships, viewed holistically, with implications for cultural, social and economic ties. For them native title, as Weiner has described, is a 'total social fact' which cannot be compartmentalised into distinct 'realms' of law and society.[11] Examples of the holistic approaches of native title holders to native title are found throughout the case studies, revealing how the protection and promotion of traditional laws and customs that give rise to native title rights to land and waters are inextricably linked with other social and emotional wellbeing and economic outcomes. Most, if not all, RNTBCs place a high priority on intergenerational transmission of cultural knowledge, including the involvement of youth in ceremonies and taking young and old people out on country together.[12] Djabugay place maintaining their culture and preserving their cultural and natural heritage alongside employment and economic development aspirations. Karajarri people note that formal RNTBC responsibilities are just one part of the work of their RNTBC, logically situated alongside other key Karajarri priorities such as their pastoral business and Karajarri Rangers. The Lhere Artepe case study contemplates the role of the RNTBC in facilitating traditional owner capacity to maintain the balance or wellbeing of the land and all those who live on it. Sullivan notes that the OFA is seen as redress for social and cultural as well as economic impacts of colonisation, with the Miriuwung and Gajerrong investing substantially in a charitable trust and community development programs that include employment, education, housing, health, family, youth and aged care services. O'Faircheallaigh reveals that all recent mining agreements have provisions for education, training and employment, which necessitate an RNTBC structure with the capability to deliver land and culture management, employment and business development, enterprises, community services and communication.

Native title clearly is not a mere regulatory or compliance mechanism for seeking land use approvals, and it is not only native title holders who think so. The 2006 federal government report on RNTBC roles and responsibilities (the PBC Report), for example, acknowledged that RNTBCs are likely to be engaged on issues that reflect their roles as traditional owners more broadly.[13] It identified such additional activities as 'town-planning, social harmony projects, cultural protocols, welcomes to country and interpretive and cultural signage', as well as economic development, but described these as secondary to the primary roles of RNTBCs as prescribed in the legislation.[14] Yet it is clear from the case studies that the report underestimated the demands placed on RNTBCs, both from their own membership and from other parties. In the Torres Strait RNTBC meetings described by Strelein a wide range of stakeholders sought the chance to consult with RNTBCs on a regional level on policy and legislative initiatives as well as about the design and implementation of government programs. In the mining project case study, O'Faircheallaigh reveals that providing advice on environmental and cultural heritage matters is an expected capacity of RNTBCs. While RNTBCs are generally motivated to provide this advice and take advantage of such work to look after and visit country, O'Faircheallaigh notes that these demanding responsibilities need to be recognised as RNTBC functions. The Karajarri case study and update demonstrates the key administrative and governance role of the RNTBC in the delivery of federal environmental programs.

The tensions over the different interpretations of native title and the roles of RNTBCs are also evident in the potential for native title to deliver economic outcomes for Indigenous peoples, including in land use planning and land management.

Expectations exist on all sides that native title will deliver economic returns, yet its economic potential has been severely curtailed by legal and policy parameters. The habitual (as well as discriminatory and unnecessary) configuration of native title rights and interests in determinations as personal, ceremonial and communal but not commercial is problematic.[15] This dichotomising of culture and commerce limits the benefits of native title in ways that do not reflect reality. In considering fishing enterprises in the Torres Strait case study, Strelein notes that the mundane aspects of native title, including commercial opportunities and economic activities, are inextricably tied up with and morally reinforce cultural and spiritual life. Similarly, culture and commerce are both essential to the activities of the Tjapukai Aboriginal Cultural Park, in the Djabugay case study.

The recognition of native title as exclusive or non-exclusive also has a number of implications for the types of rights and interests that can be asserted and exercised and for the eligibility of RNTBCs for government funding programs.[16] For exclusive possession native title holders, there is an overarching right to possession and to determine use of and access to the land and resources. As the Lhere Artepe case study demonstrates, non-exclusive native title recognition, although involving the partial extinguishment of native title rights, can provide authority and leverage to gain economic benefit, albeit not always to the satisfaction of the entire native title group. However, many jurisdictions have some way to go before they embrace the involvement of Indigenous groups with non-exclusive determinations in management and land use planning. Djabugay believe their non-exclusive possession native title, their Indigenous Land Use Agreement and the other multiple limitations of their native title determination have significantly impeded their enjoyment of native title.[17]

Even where there are exclusive native title determinations, examples in the Torres Strait demonstrate the failure of state and territory governments to acknowledge and accommodate native title in land use planning and management. This is an important economic and social infrastructure issue, since RNTBCs hold significant land and water interests and their key roles in negotiating and implementing agreements and facilitating economic and community development over large-scale development will only increase. Almost all new mining and resource developments require native title agreements, as O'Faircheallaigh explains in Chapter 9, yet many state and territory governments have not adjusted to take native title into account in their timescales and in planning critical pathways of development.

Neither have many state or territory governments addressed the issues which arise out of the myriad forms of tenure and land uses associated with native title settlements, such as freehold, conservation parks and reserves, and pastoral and agricultural leases. The Cape York case study estimates that the majority of Aboriginal-held land in this region will have at least two types of concurrent title, such as native title and Aboriginal freehold title under Queensland land rights legislation. The Cape York, Torres Strait and Karajarri case studies discuss the difficulties that also can arise when land tenures are overlaid and/or held by different holding entities, whether through historical circumstance or ongoing legislation. The Cape York study presents arguments for the alignment of tenure and ownership but recognises that this will be difficult when the tenures have different groups of beneficiaries and established histories.

While the recognition of native title, both as a general legal concept and in specific instances, is changing the legal and social landscape, the overall pace of RNTBCs' attempts to institutionalise and normalise native title has been slow. Nevertheless, as the practices of being a native title holder and of doing business with native title holders are being worked out, there are signs of change. There are, for example, sections of government and the private sector that appreciate RNTBCs as a valuable contact point for progressing their work with traditional owners and other community members, and as the deliverers of government services. The update to the MG Corporation case study demonstrates this.

As more people engage and become familiar with native title, Indigenous peoples will be required to engage more government and other third parties in dialogue about what native title means to them and how they see the roles of their RNTBCs. If cross-purposes and miscommunications persist, native title can be as disempowering as it can be empowering. However, there will always be multiple meanings and contestations; knowing and accepting the complexities and ambiguities of native title and learning to live with them is essential to navigating the RNTBC governance context.

RNTBC governance

No one doubts the need for effective governance, but determining exactly what that is for RNTBCs consumes significant attention in practice and policy discussions.[18] RNTBC governance is much more than compliance, tax, internal structures and accountabilities in the regulatory framework of the NTA, the PBC Regulations and the CATSI Act. It is also much more than the myriad state, territory and Commonwealth regulatory regimes that impact on the enjoyment of native title rights — from planning legislation to fishing regulations. The case studies in this book repeatedly highlight native title holders' expectation that recognition of and respect for their authority and responsibilities as traditional owners will be realised through their RNTBCs, and that RNTBCs will further their priorities in looking after and being on country.[19]

The case studies show it is critical for RNTBCs to have the governance capacity to respond to changing social, economic, political and cultural contexts, not least of which are changes to laws and customs and to the expectations and requirements of native title holders. They also demonstrate that a crucial component of RNTBC governance is the 'business of process' where emotional, procedural and substantive interests, including cultural beliefs and practices, impact on and give rise to each other.[20]

The 'business of process' refers to engagement, relationships, communication, decision-making and dispute management processes as RNTBCs negotiate and renegotiate their corporate governance arrangements and aspirations in ever-changing contexts. The concept suggests that governance is more than just the alignment of context and content, as has been mooted.[21] Rather, as Hunt and Smith have commented, it is also about:

> ...the evolving processes, relationships, institutions and structures by which a group of people, community or society organise themselves collectively to achieve the things that matter to them...In other words, governance is as much about people, power, and relationships as it is about formal structures, management and corporate technicalities. Indeed, the relational aspects of governance are often critical factors in effective performance.[22]

Thus the most significant but undervalued regulatory functions of RNTBCs involve the consultation, decision-making and dispute management processes they employ with native title holders[23] including in obtaining their free prior and informed consent.[24] Poor decision-making processes from which native title holders feel excluded inevitably lead to disputes. They also lead to a lack of support for the RNTBC from native title holders, other organisations and people in its community as well as from governments and industry. The nature of consultation and consent processes can significantly alter the ownership and sustainability of the outcome, as described in the Torres Strait example, where the directors of RNTBCs were left disgruntled by the consultations over changes to regional governance, which they felt did not involve them appropriately.

RNTBCs have to deal with many sources of conflict, including internal questions of native title group composition and eligibility for membership and benefits, which raise highly sensitive issues of identity. As in the Djabugay and Lhere Artepe case studies, many RNTBCs experience intra–native title group tensions over the distribution of benefits and the enjoyment of rights, and disputes about who speaks for particular areas. These include whether such matters are managed at the clan or subgroup level or by the broader group. Another common issue across RNTBCs, described in the Lhere Artepe case study, is balancing investments for the long-term benefit of the whole native title group against the significant short-term needs of individuals. O'Faircheallaigh notes that the capacity of RNTBCs to manage or diffuse tensions and conflicts over the allocation of benefits among groups or families is critical to the success of many mining agreements and projects.

RNTBCs are often established alongside existing local and regional Indigenous governance organisations that have been established for the benefit of the broader community. They provide formal representation for traditional owners as distinct interest groups often for the first time. In contrast, many Indigenous local governmental institutions have for decades exercised a level of self-government and service delivery: from early progress associations and welfare organisations, through collective ownership and self-management models, to general self-management and service organisations. As the Cape York study recognises, there can be conflicting priorities between organisations with similar jurisdictions when membership and governance are not aligned. RNTBCs must negotiate this governance space and, in some instances, compete for resources, as the broader community aspirations of the RNTBC and its members overlap with those of existing service organisations. The Karajarri case study shows how relationships with the community were transformed by the recognition of native title, creating conflict over jurisdiction and power struggles in what became a suspicious community environment. The Djabugay have resisted placing a native title claim over the Mona Mona Mission to avoid this kind of conflict.

Elsewhere, RNTBCs may be expected by the broader community to work for the benefit of or take responsibility for all Indigenous residents in their area. Through the Ord Enhancement Scheme, and charitable trust requirements, MG Corporation is expected to improve the wellbeing of not only native title holders but all Indigenous residents of the area. The Lhere Artepe RNTBC is expected to play a role in curbing the disruptive behaviour of all Aboriginal visitors to Arrernte country in Alice Springs as other organisations look to their traditional cultural authority to effect change — a significant challenge, as Merlan's update suggests.

Barcham discusses the 'cultural match' between Indigenous laws and customs and western law in the governance of the Lhere Artepe RNTBC. He refers to the work of the Harvard Project on American Indian Economic Development, which has defined cultural match as:

> ...the degree to which current governing institutions—the organization of authority, decision-making, dispute resolution, and the like that in fact are in place in Native nations—do or do not match that people's own ideas of what those rules should be, of how things should be done. Some...[Native nations] have carefully protected those older systems while modifying them when necessary, and use them to this day, maintaining a close link between their own, Indigenous political cultures and the formal institutions of day-to-day governance.[25]

However, 'cultural match' is not only about culture or transporting 'old' rules into contemporary contexts. The challenge for RNTBCs is to ensure the materialisation of the range of contemporary emotional, procedural and substantive interests in arriving at governing institutions that work without being constrained by what Merlan has referred to as a discourse of 'traditionalism'.[26] This discourse, which pervades the native title sector, confines traditions to the fixed and immutable, as if untouched by day-to-day negotiations. It means native title holders reflect back to governments and others the traditional profiles they believe they are expected to project. Indeed, this mirroring process is firmly ensconced in native title discourse, as traditional laws and customs provide the basis for the proof of native title in the first place.[27] The challenge for the Lhere Artepe RNTBC in making their protocols meaningful in the contemporary context is not so much a matter of 'cultural match' as it is the business of process. The processes required in making decisions about the protocols should pay close attention to how the emotional, procedural and substantive interests, including the cultural interests of native title holders, were identified, how the contemporary relevance of the protocols was explored and reality checked in relation to these interests, and how the protocols might be implemented.

RNTBCs need to maintain integrity while conducting the business of native title with a contemporary conceptualisation of 'traditional laws and customs' that is meaningful and works. However, as the Miriuwung and Gajerrong and Lhere Artepe case studies show, native title holders sometimes agree to governance arrangements that don't necessarily do this. The presumed clan-based bounded groups, such as *dawang* in the MG Corporation case and estate groups in Alice Springs, provide the bases for corporate structures and membership but do not necessarily reflect changing realities. In this vein, Sullivan argues against any attempt to codify traditional laws in membership rules and constitutions, and critiques the use of imagined traditional practices that are seen in isolation from the whole society.[28] Nevertheless, the Wik case study argues that the structure of the membership rules, which was pivotal to achieving and maintaining legitimacy, used elements of the local system of land tenure and decision-making as building blocks for the constitution of the corporation.[29]

It is not only cultural priorities and laws and customs that change as they are negotiated in contemporary contexts.[30] RNTBCs are also located in ever-changing social, political and economic contexts that include government legal and policy reforms, changing demographics and priorities of their members, the demands and scale of economic development, changing activities and associated needs, new future acts[31] and a changing marketplace. Climate change also is shifting the interaction between seasons, temperatures, species, water cycles, and ocean levels.[32]

RNTBCs need to adapt to these dynamic contexts, including in their planning strategies. Planning documents should be regularly revisited, strategically matching activities with changing capacities and priorities. For example, the Djabugay produced an online 'wiki-based roadmap', available only to those with a password, which is used and regularly updated.[33] The Karajarri RNTBC found that the absence of planning and policy protocols, such as for outstations, created stressful decision-making, and was likely to cause problems in the future and expose RNTBC executives to pressure from people with whom they have familial and cultural ties. As part of planning processes, RNTBCs may have to revisit previous agreements, as Strelein argues in the Torres Strait chapter, to enable the development of broader settlement packages that support the recognition and enjoyment of native title.

RNTBC corporate design must also accommodate social, cultural, political and economic change. Rule books should be living documents supported by meaningful business and strategic planning. The Lhere Artepe, Miriuwung and Gajerrong and the Djabugay have made a number of changes over the years to their corporate structures and rule books. Such changes may be necessary to align the governance of RNTBCs with that of related traditional owner corporations and trusts. In the case of MG Corporation, the RNTBCs were established in a complex of multiple corporations and trusts, some of which are prescribed in the OFA itself. For Djabugay, multiple corporations were already involved in ranger activity, a dance theatre and a theme park. Such complexity can create an excessive administrative burden and the potential for cooption by particular corporations, trusts or subgroups within the native title group. Complex corporate structures also can mean, as some of the case studies suggest, that native title holders are distanced from RNTBC activities and unable to understand them. The Djabugay, as a result of the planning process referred to above which produced the online 'wiki-based roadmap', have sought to minimise these risks in a number of ways, including by aligning the governance committees of their various corporations, having the same board for each corporation, holding meetings concurrently and nominating one body as the primary entity. While common practice has been to establish distinct corporate structures for particular functions, as the Lhere Artepe have done, with the aim of quaranting the risks associated with commercial ventures, O'Faircheallaigh suggests that specific purpose funds or trusts may be more appropriate. His study presents an argument for organisational design that is adaptable to the needs of agreement-making but is not driven solely by any particular agreement.

Given the complexity of RNTBC governance and the importance of effective engagement in accounting for it, good communication is a recurring theme in the case studies and updates. This is particularly challenging, as the Torres Strait case study shows, when RNTBCs have a substantial diaspora in a large and sometimes remote region and beyond. Effective communication is central to ensuring that RNTBCs are transparent and accountable to native title holders, governments, industry and other Indigenous people and organisations, and that the decisions of native title holders are informed by essential information in a comprehensible form. It is critical to building meaningful participatory community development, planning processes and partnerships, as the Djabugay case study discusses. It is also central to RNTBCs having their authority accepted by others as they seek respect for and recognition of their roles as custodians and promoters of traditional laws and customs — 'Ailan Kastom' as it is referred to in the Torres Strait.[34]

Yet this search for respect and recognition can be overshadowed by what RNTBCs see as 'over-governance'. As described in Chapter 2, many feel they continually play catch-up to government reform agendas and compliance requirements at the expense of their own priorities. In the Torres Strait case study, substantial changes to the *Torres Strait Islander Land Act 1991* (Qld) were introduced at the same time as the amalgamation of local government and alongside a two-year transition to the new CATSI Act. The resulting reform fatigue meant that there was little opportunity for RNTBCs to reflect or take a planned approach to the change.

The case studies demonstrate the corporate design challenges RNTBCs must meet and the complexities that arise when they join the broader Indigenous governance landscape. They highlight the need to account for the emotional, cultural, procedural and substantive interests of all parties involved including in decision-making processes about corporate design in the first instance. To achieve this, high quality and independent legal guidance and third-party facilitation may be required in what is a complex intercultural environment.

Given the lack of adequate funding for RNTBCs to purchase such assistance, it is not surprising that all are keen to identify economic development opportunities that will sustain them into the future. Such opportunities can only be realised with efficient and streamlined governance.[35]

Economic opportunities and risks

There are a range of ways in which RNTBCs may avail themselves of economic opportunities. The NTA provides important protection for native title by compelling third parties dealing with native title land to comply with the future act process to acquire validity for those dealings. Future act negotiations present opportunities for RNTBCs to leverage income and a role in the development activity. As discussed in the Miriuwung and Gajerrong and the mining agreement case studies, economic outcomes can be negotiated as part of a settlement, including as compensation for the loss and impairment of native title. Commercial activities may emerge from the investment and management of compensation funds, such as Lhere Artepe's Mount John development. In addition, native title holders can utilise their territories and pre-existing resources for commercial activities, as the Karajarri have done with a pastoral station, or enter into a joint venture with an investment partner such as Indigenous Business Australia (IBA), as Djabugay have done in the past. Business enterprises can be assisted by IBA or a range of other government programs.

However, securing sustainable economic futures for native title groups is not straightforward or easy, as the MG Corporation is aware, with its 10-year government funding period drawing to a close. Success also is determined by the market and the priorities of development parties and governments. Expectations can be raised and dashed, as the Wik in Cape York discovered when plans to mine bauxite were abandoned after years of negotiation. And the Miriuwung and Gajerrong found that many of the benefits negotiated under their agreement were at risk when the Western Australian government temporarily decided not to go ahead with the OFA.

Neither should the economic potential of native title lands be overstated or assessed uncritically. Native title recognition can occur on lands of low market value and economic potential, remote from markets. As discussed earlier in this chapter, commercial rights may not be recognised in native title determinations. Heavy regulation of resource use, such as minerals and water extraction and fishing, and of particular areas, such as waterways, nature reserves and protected areas, can impede economic opportunities. In the Torres Strait case study, the intensive non-Indigenous commercial fishing industry has effectively regulated away any native title fishery, although, as noted in the update, the recent recognition of the commercial value of a native title right to take resources provides a basis for assessing the extent of the impact of commercial licensing and exploitation on the economic potential of native title.[36]

Sustainable economic benefits also depend on the capacity of RNTBCs to manage development and to implement agreements and settlements. Implementation is not simply a matter of good practice; it can determine whether an agreement provides any benefit at all, as the effects of poor implementation go further than just missed opportunities. The Djabugay case study and update highlight the risks of not negotiating detailed co-management arrangements for protected areas and accompanying funding at the time of the determination, as their ILUA has now expired without any management agreement for the Barron Gorge National Park in place. O'Faircheallaigh points out how important is it when making mining agreements to invest in RNTBC capacity up front and to clearly define implementation requirements for appropriate and sufficient consultation, high quality advice, efficient adminstration and appropriate infrastructure. In agreement-making, such requirements are not always prioritised, identified effectively or matched by appropriate levels of resourcing.[37] Even relatively large-scale agreements such as the Miriuwung and Gajerrong OFA may not be sufficiently resourced to ensure that the benefits are realised and sustainable over the long term.

The social and cultural implications for native title holders in economic development activities are not always thoroughly explored or understood. RNTBCs are located in diverse economies where the demands of economic development and the priorities of native title holders may not always align, including the scale of economic development and plans for the future. While smaller enterprises such as cultural heritage work or running a kiosk may provide greater control for RNTBC members, they do not promise the financial benefits to the group as a whole that larger scale development may. However, as the MG Corporation and Lhere Artepe updates show, larger scale activities can strain the individual and organisational capabilities of the native title group and alienate native title holders who don't feel involved or informed. The Lhere Artepe case study describes the adoption of a long-term investment model that engages with risk for a greater return for the loss of their native title lands to development. Yet, as the Lhere Artepe update foreshadows, where native title holders do not understand the business machinations involved they may become distanced from RNTBC activities and not feel a sense of ownership of its decisions — that is, the line of sight between the interests of the common law native title holders and their corporation is lost.

This line of sight can also be lost when economic goals are pursued at the risk of other governance, social and cultural objectives. Such is the case in the future act scheme, where RNTBCs are largely unfunded. In responding to the external imperatives of developers, their workload can overwhelm the core priorities of the RNTBC and the native title group, which may lie, for example, in establishing structures to support good governance, as discussed in the Karajarri case study. There are similar observations of conflicting priorities in the MG Corporation update, as involvement in employment initiatives has occurred at the expense of the social and cultural objects in its Rule Book.[38] Even when economic development opportunities, such as tourism, appear to connect with RNTBC priorities to work on country and to have relatively low impacts, they can generate serious problems if not managed properly, particularly when the 'business of process' discussed earlier is not paid sufficient attention.

There will always be questions and uncertainty about managing economic development options and long-term intergenerational priorities and about sustaining RNTBC governance. Sullivan asks whether the benefits of the Miriuwung and Gajerrong OFA, however substantial, reflect the extent of the loss of native title lands to extinguishment. In all cases, the ongoing management and enjoyment of native title must be planned by applicants and governments concomitantly with native title application and determination processes, and the resources and capacity required for implementation must be carefully identified. Above all, successful economic development will depend on the capacity of RNTBCs to take opportunities that present themselves. To a significant degree this will be determined by whether an RNTBC has the resources and capacity to ensure even a basic level of functionality.

RNTBC funding, capacity and support

It is not surprising that the resourcing of RNTBCs has been a source of concern for well over a decade. To establish such an important corporate sector without a prescribed funding regime is a policy folly and failure. Leaving aside accusations that RNTBCs have been 'set up to fail',[39] working out the how and who of funding raises a number of challenging issues. Consider that: RNTBCs must be established for all native title lands in perpetuity; the NTA and RNTBCs were legislated by the federal government, but native title determinations and agreements fall within the ambit of state and territory jurisdiction over land and resource matters; and native title is a deeply divisive political issue, with its recognition in 1992 unsettling a status quo that had been beneficial to largely non-Indigenous interests. Expecting RNTBCs to individually resolve and overcome these issues is unrealistic.

The overview in Chapter 2 describes how a number of reports and recommendations have directed that RNTBCs be resourced to at least meet their core statutory responsibilities. Unless RNTBCs have significant resource extraction benefits or development opportunities on their determined lands, as do the two Miriuwung and Gajerrong RNTBCs serviced by MG Corporation and Lhere Artepe, few if any have the resources to fulfil their statutory responsibilities let alone meet the expectations of their native title groups and other parties. Instead, RNTBCs may need to rely on pro bono legal advice, as has been the case for the Wik in Cape York, or on the generosity of volunteer directors, who usually have multiple community responsibilities and sometimes paid employment from which they must take leave to attend meetings. Many RNTBCs, as is the case for the Wik in Cape York, have had no training for their governing committees, have no capacity to hold AGMs and have no Australian Business Number or bank account. Many draw on the office capacity of individual homes or other organisations, as Karajarri did with the local CDEP office and Mer Gedkem Le RNTBC in the Torres Strait did until recently in the Australian Quarantine and Inspection Service office. The build-up of paperwork and decisions to be made, and a lack of corporate memory, including lack of access to records of previous decisions, frustrates both RNTBCs and external stakeholders. Some have pieced together resources to keep afloat, such as the Karajarri have with their IPA funding. All native title holders face the same challenges and poor indicators that characterise Indigenous statistics across Australia, such as lack of education, poor housing, and premature morbidity.[40]

The federal government, as outlined in Chapter 2, provided some welcome funding for RNTBCs through the Department of Families, Housing, Community Services and Indigenous Affairs (FaHCSIA), which until the change of government in September 2013 was responsible for the funding of native title organisations.[41] However, the funding has been limited, not provided to all RNTBCs, and mostly for administrative and corporate compliance requirements. The Djabugay update demonstrates the importance of this funding, without which they would by now have used most of their limited funds received from elsewhere. Without designated funding to undertake their prescribed functions, the Djabugay, Karajarri, Torres Strait and Cape York RNTBCs note the difficulties associated with the ongoing employment of staff, an inability to plan and work towards long-term economic outcomes, and opportunities lost. There is some support for mediation, facilitation and governance training from the Office of the Registrar of Indigenous Corporations and the Aurora Project funded by FaHCSIA.[42] And AIATSIS has compiled toolkits and in the past has been funded by FaHCSIA to hold regional and national RNTBC meetings, as Chapter 2 discusses. Also at this national level, IBA recently established a Traditional Owner and Native Title Unit to work across agencies to achieve social and economic benefits, and Reconciliation Australia has produced a governance toolkit for Indigenous corporations.[43]

The PBC Report called on state and territory governments to take greater responsibility for RNTBCs,[44] and state and territory governments have provided limited assistance to some but not all RNTBCs, particularly with implementing agreements. However, the issue of prescribed RNTBC funding has not been addressed. The lack of coordinated service delivery to RNTBCs has left many uncertain about their future. Significantly, as the MG Corporation update shows, RNTBCs may be a state government's preferred provider of services such as employment and housing. This is also the case for land management services, such as those provided by the Karajarri Rangers, which make substantial contributions to Indigenous social and emotional wellbeing. Identifying and acknowledging the work that RNTBCs undertake for native title and broader policy objectives, including Closing the Gap outcomes,[45] is critical in getting governments to fund the establishment and operation of RNTBCs.

The risk that RNTBCs will be locked in an 'incapacity spiral' is high. They cannot build capacity through programs because funding partners are averse to investing in organisations that lack capacity. Agreement and program partners focus on how funds are managed, used and distributed and pay insufficient attention to the administrative burden of the agreements. There are numerous cases of missed opportunities where basic administrative capacity would have made a difference. The Wik case study has an example where revenue streams were available, particularly under Queensland's mandated exploration payments, but there was no capacity to issue an invoice. The absence of an office, as described in the Karajarri and Torres Strait case studies, impacts on RNTBC accessibility and relationships with members and the broader community. The Djabugay case study reports the 'relief' expressed by Queensland Government officials when the Djabugay finally established an office in Kuranda. For Djabugay, the opportunity of federal funding to support an office with staff capability had a noticeable impact. Not only could they reach existing goals; they could pursue new solicited and unsolicited opportunities and negotiate potentially beneficial partnerships. In the Karajarri case study, Weir surmises that a functioning RNTBC should be an investment in the sustainability of the agreement-making process, not a negotiated outcome of the agreement.

Capacity constraints are compounded by the challenging negotiations that RNTBCs are necessarily involved in and the high level of technical advice and assistance they require. Irrespective of their income, most need to seek advice on holding and/or managing native title, especially where extinguishment is a possibility, as well as on the management of assets and compensation funds to balance present and future entitlements and for land management issues. Because RNTBCs manage the often complex decision-making processes necessary for free, prior and informed consent there is also a need for facilitative expertise and assistance beyond the usual capabilities of RNTBCs.

Critically, only a few RNTBCs have sufficient funding and capacity to operate alone. Many get some form of support with future acts and governance issues from the Native Title Representative Bodies (NTRBs) or Native Title Service Providers (NTSPs) which ran their native title applications in the first instance. Some NTRBs and NTSPs have designated RNTBC support teams and many are considering ways to address the unique needs of RNTBCs, particularly in light of the current federal government review of native title organisations.[46]

However, while NTRBs and NTSPs are adjusting to the growing RNTBC sector, their own resources are stretched. They are often required to service large and sometimes remote areas and have to deal with native title applications still to be processed or yet to be filed. RNTBC needs are also increasing as the technical advice they require continues to compound and diversify. In seeking autonomy and self-government, many RNTBCs have described their future relationships with NTRBs and NTSPs as adjusting towards a relationship of interdependence and partnership.[47] Such partnerships could be brokered afresh to clarify the needs of both parties, to establish clear roles and responsibilities, and to set out transparent processes of accountability for accessing funding through NTRBs and NTSPs, which is the current requirement as set out in Chapter 2. Given the diversity of arrangements in the case studies in this book, the brokering of such partnerships should be on a case-by-case basis, with partnerships regularly revisited to account for changing needs and contexts.

Other regional or sub-regional solutions are being developed or mooted to meet RNTBC service needs. The Cape York case study suggests economies of scale in the form of regional or sub-regional services or trusts. Memmott and Blackwood describe this sub-regional distribution model as a centralised land management agency that could accommodate the needs of different groups within the region as well as allocating some benefits to the region as a whole. Smaller, less active RNTBCs could pool resources with larger RNTBCs where they exist to hire staff and skilled technical experts. Some funds could flow from the RNTBCs to such a body, where they are available through fee-for-service or compensation payments and from a range of government programs, though the constricted funding context for many RNTBCs would make it difficult for such models to be self-funding through RNTBC contributions. The model could gain efficiencies for external stakeholders in areas where RNTBCs are not very active and have little or no income or assets. Important elements of its success, as the Cape York study sets out, would be a history of cooperation, building on existing institutions, clear understanding among native title groups in the region about the use of resources coming into the organisation, and transparent rules on the distribution of benefits and the costs of administration. The need for such organisations and their make-up would be heavily context dependent. Where required, they could augment the services of NTRBs and NTSPs, and partnerships could be brokered between them, RNTBCs, NTRBs and NTSPs. However, under the current RNTBC funding guidelines there is no pathway for such sub-regional service providers to apply for funding.

There is much that governments can do to provide support for RNTBCs as a matter of urgency. For example, RNTBCs at AIATSIS national meetings have recommended that key federal departments each employ dedicated staff members who understand RNTBC structures and needs.[48] This approach could be mirrored in state and territory government departments, and the teams could work in whole-of-government coordinated approaches. They could simplify and facilitate access to existing government programs for RNTBCs, identify new funding programs and grants for RNTBCs as they arise, connect RNTBCs with contacts within other government departments, and develop policies and programs directed to the needs of RNTBCs.

The lack of resources and support for the basic functioning of RNTBCs remains a critical failure within the native title system. In Chapter 2 the authors report on the continued calls by many RNTBCs for greater representation at state, territory and national levels, reflecting their frustration that their needs, notwithstanding the valuable support provided by NTRBs and NTSPs, are not being adequately addressed. The legislative and policy drivers for effective RNTBC governance should be aimed at ensuring that RNTBCs are adequately resourced and appropriately structured and advised if they are to make informed decisions that have the best chance of sustainability. There is a high transaction cost if previous decisions must be changed. Providing basic support, funding and other assistance will have an accumulating benefit, ensuring not only that the native title system is working for RNTBCs but that it is providing greater certainty and development opportunities for all parties.

Conclusion

Given the ambiguities of native title and the complexities of communal interests held in perpetuity, state, territory and federal governments need to make policy innovations that will support native title holders in managing their land and carve out a role for RNTBCs in the governance of regions. Decision-making over land, water and town planning in particular requires a paradigm shift away from presumptions about the management of Crown waste lands to a collaborative approach that recognises Indigenous peoples' ownership and accommodates their law and custom relating to those lands. It might also take into account the increase in Indigenous involvement in environmental management and the relationship between being on country and achieving improved Closing the Gap outcomes such as Indigenous economic development and social and emotional wellbeing.[49]

There is an urgent need for a national, state and territory policy dialogue, involving local, state, territory and federal governments, NTRBs, NTSPs, RNTBCs and other stakeholders, about what it means to have native title recognised, how native title holders can build a sustainable future, and how they can all can work together to assist RNTBCs in achieving this. Discussions about 'settling' native title must focus not just on recognising rights in the present or compensating for the past but on reaching sustainable settlements. Such settlements should be negotiated not just in the context of the extinguishment or non-recognition of rights but in support of the recognition of rights.

The notion of a native title settlement in Australia needs to shift to a more ambitious level. As the WA Attorney-General commented, 'This requires a more expansive view of doing business than simply the future act procedures defined by the NTA.'[50] At this level, there would be opportunities for RNTBCs to form productive partnerships with governments and with the private and non-government sectors — for example, in providing environmental services and exercising local government jurisdiction — that actively involve native title holders in management decisions about their territories.

Most RNTBCs live a precarious existence, balancing uncertainty over funding against the incessant demands of third parties, carrying out consultations and negotiations, usually free of charge, while dealing with dire community and family circumstances. Many do not have sufficient resources to meet their statutory functions under the NTA and the CATSI Act. This is a critical failure within the native title system. It is poor policy for the Australian government to legislate a range of statutory functions for RNTBCs without providing appropriate resources. It may only be a matter of time before an RNTBC is taken to court for not consulting native title holders effectively over development proposals and not obtaining their free, prior and informed consent.

RNTBCs have already made a number of recommendations at national meetings, which should be seriously considered and implemented where appropriate.[51] One is that state and territory governments retrospectively review native title determinations to identify those that failed to provide for the effective enjoyment and exercise of native title rights and interests, and to then establish a revised settlement process for each such determination. Others repeat the issues raised in this chapter and throughout the book, including that governments should: view RNTBCs more broadly as vehicles to achieve a number of social outcomes and as legitimate stakeholders in the community; respect the sovereignty and independence of RNTBCs, recognising that RNTBCs are determined to become effective but disadvantaged at the outset through limited funding and assistance; support RNTBC state-based meetings followed by annual national meetings to measure changes; and address the fact that RNTBCs will exist in perpetuity and will require a secure resource base in addition to their land holdings rather than having to trade off their land to cover operational and compliance costs.

The case studies in this volume are illustrative snapshots in time, capturing the broad range of issues and experiences of RNTBCs across the country, both their uniqueness and their commonalities. It is clear that a reliance on only a narrow interpretation of the functions of RNTBCs is fundamentally inadequate for understanding and responding to the particular challenges facing this new corporate sector. Indeed, more than a misplaced ignorance it is a denial of the place of Indigenous peoples in the Australian state which was forged by the recognition of native title in *Mabo*: as first peoples, as law makers and as landowners. Native title is changing the legal and political fabric of the country, and the native title sector has been established to recognise something of great value to current and future generations. Embracing this new order is still a work in progress as governments come to terms with the need to adapt old ways and accommodate the existence of native title, to make reparation for past wrongs and to forge new partnerships that will be sustainable into the future.

Endnotes

1. *Mabo v Queensland [No. 2]* (1992) 175 CLR 1 (*Mabo (No. 2)*). We wish to thank Angus Frith for his comments on this chapter. Any errors are of course our own.
2. For a discussion of the difference between managing native title as a trustee RNTBC and managing native title as an agent RNTBC, see Chapter 2. See also the Native Title (Prescribed Bodies Corporate) Regulations 1999 (Cth)) (PBC Regulations), reg 6(1)(a).
3. For further discussion of the need for modern states to account for legal, political and cultural diversity see J Tully, *Strange multiplicity: constitutionalism in an age of diversity*, Cambridge University Press, Cambridge, New York, 2004.
4. See Chapter 2 for more RNTBC demographics.
5. The *Corporations (Aboriginal and Torres Strait Islander) Act 2006* (Cth) (CATSI Act), s 37.10, distinguishes between RNTBCs on the basis of their gross income, gross assets and number of employees, classifying them accordingly as small, medium or large corporations. The current numbers of RNTBCs by state and territory and size are provided in Table 2.2. More than three-quarters of all RNTBCs are small corporations, having an operating income per financial year of less than $100,000, and/or assets of less than $100,000, and/or five or fewer employees.
6. As Chapter 2 sets out, in making a native title determination the Federal Court requires the nomination of a body corporate to hold and manage (as trustee) or manage (as agent) the native title rights and interests. This must be incorporated under the *Corporations (Aboriginal and Torres Strait Islander) Act 2006* (CATSI Act). These corporations, often referred to as Prescribed Bodies Corporate or 'PBCs', are technically referred to as Registered Native Title Bodies Corporate (RNTBCs) once registered by the National Native Title Tribunal (NNTT) as required by the *Native Title Act 1993* (Cth) (NTA). It is at this point of registration that their statutory obligations under the NTA and the Native Title (Prescribed Bodies Corporate) Regulations 1999 (PBC Regulations) are triggered. See Chapter 2 for further detail.
7. See Attorney-General's Department Steering Committee (AGDSC), *Structures and processes of Prescribed Bodies Corporate*, Canberra, 2006, p. 6. This document, known as the 'PBC Report', is now located at the AIATSIS website (http://www.aiatsis.gov.au/ntru/docs/researchthemes/pbc/Guidelines2007.pdf, accessed 30 July 2013).

8   See M Hinkson & BR Smith, Introduction: conceptual moves towards an intercultural analysis, *Oceania*, vol. 75, no. 3, 2005, pp. 157–66.
9   BR Smith, '"Indigenous" and "scientific" knowledge in central Cape York Peninsula', in P Sillitoe (ed.), *Local science vs. global science: approaches to indigenous knowledge in international development*, Berghahn Books, New York, 2007, p. 77.
10 See T Bauman (ed.), 'Serendipity is not enough! State and territory connection processes' in T Bauman (ed.), *Dilemmas in applied native title anthropology*, AIATSIS, Canberra, 2010, pp. 137–41, and BR Smith and F Morphy, 'The social effects of native title: recognition, translation, coexistence' in BR Smith and F Morphy (eds), *The social effects of native title: recognition, translation, coexistence*, CAEPR Research Monograph, no. 27, ANU E Press, 2007, pp. 1–30.
11 JF Weiner, 'The law of the land: a review article', *The Australian Journal of Anthropology*, vol. 14, no. 1, 2003, p. 100.
12 See JK Weir (ed.), *Country, native title and ecology*, ANU Epress, Australian National University, Canberra, 2012, pp. i–xiv, 1–174.
13 AGDSC, above n 7, p. 10.
14 Ibid.
15 For further discussion see G Lauder & L Strelein, 'Native title and commercial fisheries: the Torres Strait Sea Claim', *Precedent*, Indigenous issue, no. 118, 2013.
16 The *Racial Discrimination Act 1975* (Cth) (RDA) extends protection from arbitrary extinguishment to native title, and the NTA, above n 6, s 11, declares invalid any act affecting native title that fails to go through the procedures under the NTA (that is, the appropriate future act process or Indigenous Land Use Agreement). See endnote 31 for further information about future acts.
17 For another powerful example, see M Riley, *Winning' native title: the experience of the Nharnuwangga, Wajarri and Ngarla People*, Land, Rights, Laws: Issues of Native Title, vol. 2, no. 19, 2002, pp. 2–5; and F Flanagan, *Pastoral access protocols: the corrosion of native title by contract*, Land, Rights, Laws: Issues of Native Title, vol. 2, no. 19, 2002, pp. 5–10.
18 Chapter 2 outlines a number of legal and administrative reform discussion papers and working group reports about native title benefits, the use of native title payments, what governments can do through native title settlement agreements to support sustainable economic outcomes, and taxation options. All the reports and discussions focus on the governance of native title organisations managing the benefits derived from agreements.
19 See Chapter 2, which brings together the aspirations of PBCs and RNTBCs expressed in various national meetings and inquiries.
20 T Bauman & R Williams, *The business of process: research issues in managing Indigenous decision making and disputes in land*, Research Report, no. 1, Indigenous Facilitation and Mediation Project, Native Title Research Unit, AIATSIS, Canberra, 2005. The relationships between emotional, procedural and substantive interests also have been described in terms of a satisfaction triangle in interest-based negotiation models developed by CDR Associates, Boulder, Colorado.
21 See M Grindle, 'Good enough governance: poverty reduction and reform in developing countries', *Governance—an International Journal of Policy and Administration*, vol. 17, no. 4, 2004, pp. 525–48.
22 DE Smith & J Hunt, 'Understanding Indigenous Australian governance: research, theory and representations', in J Hunt, DE Smith, S Garling & W Sanders (eds), *Contested governance: culture, power and institutions in Indigenous Australia*, CAEPR Research Monograph, no. 29, ANU Epress, Australian National University, Canberra, 2008, p. 9, http://epress.anu.edu.au/?p=97361, accessed 4 September 2013.

23 See PBC Regulations, above n 2, reg 8.
24 See United Nations, *United Nations Declaration on the Rights of Indigenous Peoples*, G.A. Res. 61/295, Annex, U.N. Doc. AIRES/61/295 (Sept. 13, 2007), article 10, United Nations webpage, http://www.un.org/esa/socdev/unpfii/documents/DRIPS_en.pdf, accessed 20 September 2013.
25 S Cornell, 'Economic development, governance, and what self-determination really means', Native Title Newsletter, no. 6, Native Title Research Unit, AIATSIS, Canberra, 2010, pp. 4–5, http://www.aiatsis.gov.au/ntru/docs/publications/newsletter/NOVDEC10.pdf, accessed 2 September 2013.
26 F Merlan, *Caging the rainbow: places, politics, and Aborigines in a north Australian town*, University of Hawai'i Press, Honolulu, 1998, pp. 231–7.
27 Ibid., p. 180; Bauman, above n 10.
28 See also D Martin, *Rethinking the design of Indigenous organisations: the need for strategic engagement*, CAEPR Discussion Paper, no. 248, CAEPR, Australian National University, Canberra, 2003, p. 10, http://hdl.handle.net/1885/41861, accessed 3 June 2013. He writes:

> The more that attempts are made to reflect the complexities and subtleties of the values and practices of indigenous people in formal corporate structures and processes — for example, regarding such matters as authority and decision-making, or the various forms of the typically labile indigenous groupings and sub-groupings — the more there is the risk that over time the formal corporate structures and processes will supplant the informal indigenous ones — a process of the 'juridification' of social relations.

See also DF Martin, T Bauman & J Neale, *Challenges for Australian native title anthropology: practice beyond the proof of connection*, AIATSIS Research Discussion Paper, no. 29, Native Title Research Unit, AIATSIS, Canberra, 2011, http://www.aiatsis.gov.au/research/documents/DP29NTRU2011.pdf, accessed 4 September 2013.
29 The national PBC meeting in 2007 devoted considerable time to discussing the design of RNTBCs and how or whether to incorporate traditional forms of decision-making into the corporate structure, with some seeing this as a way of acknowledging and thereby maintaining cultural practices. See LM Strelein & T Tran, *Native Title Representative Bodies and Prescribed Bodies Corporate: native title in a post determination environment*, Native Title Research Report, no. 2, Native Title Research Unit, AIATSIS, Canberra, 2007, pp. 11–13, http://www.aiatsis.gov.au/ntru/documents/PBCReport.pdf, accessed 29 July 2013.
30 T Bauman & G MacDonald, 'Concepts, hegemony, and analysis: unsettling native title anthropology', in T Bauman & G Macdonald (eds), *Unsettling anthropology: the demands of native title on worn concepts and changing lives*, AIATSIS, Canberra, 2011, pp. 1–15, http://www.aiatsis.gov.au/ntru/documents/UnsettlingAnthropology.pdf, accessed 4 September 2013. See also Bauman, above n 10.
31 As Chapter 2 describes, a future act is an act after 1 January 1994 (the date of the commencement of the NTA), above n 6, s 4(3)(b). Chapter 2 also outlines how a future act is an act which affects native title rights and interests and can include activities such as agriculture, mining exploration, public works, the grant of permits and licences and building public housing. Also as Chapter 2 sets out, the future act regime triggers a process of notification, consultation or the right to negotiate, dependent upon the level of impact that the activity will have, but does not guarantee the right to say no to any proposed act. See also Native Title Research Unit, *Native title resource guide: national*, Native Title Research Unit, AIATSIS, Canberra, 2010, p. 42, http://www.aiatsis.gov.au/ntru/docs/resources/NTRG/National2010.pdf, accessed 30 July 2013.
32 T Tran, LM Strelein, JK Weir, C Stacey & A Dwyer, *Native title and climate change: changes to country and culture, changes to climate: strengthening institutions for Indigenous resilience and adaptation*, National Climate Change Adaptation Research Facility, Gold Coast, 2013.

33 Bushwork Consultants, *Building Djabugay foundations: a wiki-based roadmap*, unpublished document, Bushwork Consultants and AIATSIS, 2008.
34 This need for respect and recognition is a key element of the Djabugay vision and was discussed at the second national RNTBC meeting in 2009, where participants complained that their role as cultural custodians and first nations was not respected, including by other Indigenous organisations. See T Bauman & C Ganesharajah, *Second National Meeting of Registered Native Title Bodies Corporate: issues and outcomes, Melbourne 2 June 2009*, Native Title Research Report, no. 2, Native Title Research Unit, AIATSIS, Canberra, 2009, p. 7.
35 Warren Mundine, the Executive Chairman of the Australian Indigenous Chamber of Commerce, recently commented that effective governance is essential for economic development. See W Mundine, 'Shooting an elephant: four giant steps', address to the Garma Festival corporate dinner, 2013, Australian Indigenous Chamber of Commerce webpage, p. 5, http://www.naccho.org.au/download/media-press-releases/2013-08%20Media%20Warren%20Mundine%20Speech-to-Garma-Festival%20August%202013.pdf, accessed 24 September 2013.
36 *Akiba on behalf of the Torres Strait Regional Seas Claim Group v Commonwealth of Australia* [2013] HCA 33 7 August 2013. For commentary on the decision see Lauder & Strelein, above n 15.
37 See also K Guest, *The promise of comprehensive native title settlements: the Burrup, MG-Ord and Wimmera agreements*, Research Discussion Paper, no. 27, Native Title Research Unit, AIATSIS, Canberra, 2009.
38 MG Corporation, *The Rule Book*, Yawoorroong Miriuwung Gajerrong Yirrgeb Noong Dawang Aboriginal Corporation (MG Corporation), Kununurra, 2009.
39 This is as Indigenous negotiators warned governments in the negotiations leading up to the NTA, above n 6, in the early 1990s. See M Dodson, 'Introduction: the limits of change', in T Bauman & L Glick (eds), *The limits of change: Mabo and native title 20 years on*, AIATSIS, Canberra, 2012, p. xix.
40 Steering Committee for the Review of Government Service Provision, *Overcoming Indigenous disadvantage: key indicators 2011*, Productivity Commission, Canberra, 2011, http://www.pc.gov.au/gsp/indigenous/key-indicators-2011, accessed 18 September 2013.
41 This responsibility has now been moved to the Department of the Prime Minister and Cabinet.
42 See also Aurora Project, 'PBC training and support', Aurora Project website, http://www.auroraproject.com.au/node/97#Results, accessed 19 September 2013.
43 Indigenous Business Australia website, http://www.iba.gov.au/, accessed 4 September 2013. See also Reconciliation Australia, Indigenous Governance Toolkit, http://governance.reconciliation.org.au/, accessed 24 September 2013.
44 AGDSC, above n 7, p. 6.
45 The Australian government has a 'Closing the Gap' policy aimed at addressing Indigenous disadvantage and achieving equity of health and life expectancy between Indigenous and non-Indigenous Australians within a generation (see the website of the Department Social Services (formerly the Department of Families, Housing, Community Services and Indigenous Affairs (FaHCSIA)), 'Closing the gap', http://www.fahcsia.gov.au/our-responsibilities/indigenous-australians/programs-services/closing-the-gap, accessed 19 September 2013). Partnerships and whole of government approaches are a critical part of this policy (see Australian Public Service Commission, *Connecting government: whole of government responses to Australia's priority challenges*, Commonwealth of Australia, Canberra, 2004).
46 Deloitte Access Economics, *Review of the roles and functions of native title organisations discussion paper*, Canberra, June 2013, https://www.deloitteaccesseconomics.com.au/uploads/File/DAE_NTOR%20Discussion%20Paper.pdf, accessed 31 July 2013.

47 PBCs at their first national meeting agreed that there is a need to develop formal understandings between PBCs and NTRBs/NTSPs which reflect their relationships as partners, establish clear roles and responsibilities, and set out transparent processes of accountability for accessing funding through NTRBs. T Bauman & T Tran, *First National Prescribed Bodies Corporate meeting: issues and outcomes, Canberra 11–13 April 2007*, Native Title Research Report, no. 3, Native Title Research Unit, AIATSIS, Canberra, 2007, p. 27, http://www.aiatsis.gov.au/ntru/docs/research-themes/pbc/PBCMeeting2007.pdf, accessed 27 June 2013.

48 Ibid.; Bauman & Ganesharajah, above n 34.

49 See D Smyth, *Indigenous land and sea management: a case study*, report prepared for the Australian Government Department of Sustainability, Environment, Water, Population and Communities on behalf of the State of the Environment 2011 Committee, Canberra, 2011, http://www.environment.gov.au/soe/2011/report/land/pubs/soe2011-supplementary-land-Indigenous-land-and-sea-management-case-study.pdf, accessed 20 March 2013; R Hill, PL Pert, J Davies, F Walsh, CJ Robinson & F Falco-Mammone, 'Indigenous land management in Australia: extent, scope, diversity, barriers and success factors', final draft, CSIRO, Canberra, 30 June 2012, p. 7; and JC Altman, G Buchanan & L Larsen, *The environmental significance of the Indigenous estate: natural resource management as economic development in remote Australia*, CAEPR Discussion Paper, no. 286, CAEPR, Australian National University, Canberra, 2007.

50 M Mischin, 'Keynote address', presentation at Native Title Conference for WA legal practitioners, Perth, 15 June 2013, http://www.dpc.wa.gov.au/lantu/MediaPublications/Documents/AG%20Speech%20notes%20-%20Legalwise%20Native%20Title%20Seminar%202013.pdf, accessed 4 September 2013.

51 Bauman & Tran, above n 47, pp. 39–40.

Chapter 2

An overview of the Registered Native Title Bodies Corporate regime

Pamela Faye McGrath, Claire Stacey and Lara Wiseman

Native title for me is from generation to generation. We always think and believe that we own the land, the water and the resources around us, under and above. This is native title for us. And when I mention resources, this includes sea rights. Native title is recognition of this to make the western society understand that we have a system in place and we have laws in place.

For me, native title doesn't mean the Native Title Act. You can amend the Native Title Act. Our law, Malo's lore, stays the same forever. I don't know when they actually amend that lore, I couldn't say that. It's the same from generation to generation, from time immemorial, that's what Eddie [Mabo] and the others would say.

Douglas Passi, Chair of Mer Gedkem Le (Torres Strait Islanders)
Corporation RNTBC[1]

Introduction

The *Native Title Act 1993* (Cth) (NTA)[2] sets out a framework and procedures for the holding and managing of native title which in practice has produced and perpetuated legal relationships of great complexity.[3] These bear little resemblance to the reality of native title as experienced by Aboriginal and Torres Strait Islander peoples.

When a group of Aboriginal or Torres Strait Islander people succeed in having their native title recognised in a Federal Court determination, they are required to nominate a body corporate to hold and manage (as trustee) or manage (as agent) their native title rights and interests.[4] These corporations are known as Prescribed Bodies Corporate (PBCs) because they have prescribed characteristics under the NTA, including that they are incorporated under the *Corporations (Aboriginal and Torres Strait Islander) Act 2006* (Cth) (the CATSI Act). Once registered by the National Native Title Tribunal (NNTT), as required by the NTA, they are technically known as Registered Native Title Bodies Corporate (RNTBCs).[5] It is at this point that their statutory obligations under the NTA and the Native Title (Prescribed Bodies Corporate) Regulations 1999 (PBC Regulations) are triggered.

The instruments that comprise the native title framework — primarily the NTA, the PBC Regulations and the CATSI Act — fulfil different functions. As Mantziaris and Martin have observed, many of the problems apparent in the operation of the native title system as a whole are generated at the point where such instruments interact.[6]

In some instances native title claim groups will create a new organisation whose sole purpose is to act as an RNTBC. Alternatively, they may nominate an existing corporation to become the RNTBC as long as it is already incorporated under the CATSI Act and complies with the provisions of the NTA. Importantly, it must have, among its purposes, the purpose of becoming an RNTBC.[7] Where native title groups have received financial settlements, RNTBCs may become part of a corporate structure which can include charitable and other trusts, companies and other Aboriginal or Torres Strait Islander corporations. Each of these may perform different or similar functions to achieve the objectives of the native title group. Some may be incorporated under the *Corporations Act 2001* (Cth) (Corporations Act) which applies to the broader Australian community. Adding further complexity to this corporate landscape are Aboriginal and Torres Strait Islander corporations (often referred to as 'native title corporations' or 'traditional owner corporations') that are not RNTBCs but have generated native title outcomes without having a native title determination. This may have occurred in various ways, including under other legislation such as the *Traditional Owner Settlement Act 2010* (Vic), through native title settlements such as the comprehensive South West Native Title Settlement for Noongar people in Western Australia[8] and through native title claimant groups entering into Indigenous Land Use Agreements (ILUAs).

There are many factors influencing the corporate design of an RNTBC, such as the social composition of a native title group, its decision-making processes, how the group intends to hold and/or manage native title rights and interests, the kinds of rights and interests that have been determined and the aspirations of native title holders. The design of the overall corporate structure in which an RNTBC may be located will also be influenced by factors such as the state or territory laws regulating the corporation's activities (planning or land management law, for example); the level of activity demanded of the group in dealing with mining, development, tourism, and pastoral/grazing, cultural, social and other activities; and available financial resources, economic opportunities and tax effectiveness. All these factors need to be weighed up when a particular group is considering its needs and aspirations, and its governance structures and practices.

Research to date suggests that recognised native title holders aspire to achieve a great deal through their RNTBCs. Since 2006, AIATSIS has conducted a number of workshops and consultations with RNTBCs and their representatives during which a range of aspirations have been identified.⁹ The vast majority of these ambitions relate to achieving independent decision-making around issues of land management, cultural heritage and community development. While priorities may differ between groups, a range of aspirations relating to both current activities and longer term ambitions have been consistently expressed. Very broadly, these fall into the following four categories:

1. Independence: RNTBCs seek more corporate independence in the management of their native title rights and interests.
2. Respect and recognition: RNTBCs seek greater levels of political recognition and respect for their traditional rights from other interest groups.
3. Caring for country, culture and people: RNTBCs aspire to use their native title rights to improve the social and cultural wellbeing of their members as well as the broader community.
4. Community development, service provision and economic development: RNTBCs want to use their native title rights to provide greater socio-economic security for their communities.[10]

The constraints RNTBCs face when pursuing these goals vary from organisation to organisation, but those most commonly reported include: a lack of human and financial resources; an over-reliance on the unpaid labour of their members; inadequate and poorly targeted training support; and ineffective mechanisms to deal with dispute resolution.[11] Other constraints are constantly changing policy environments, onerous and multiple reporting requirements and a lack of appropriate consultation. Above all, RNTBCs identify lack of access to funding, financial instability and longer term financial insecurity as issues preventing them from leveraging more opportunity from their native title rights.[12]

The framework in which RNTBCs operate has been designed with both native title and non–native title interests in mind. Almost 15 years ago the authors of the first comprehensive analysis of RNTBC law and policy, barrister Christos Mantziaris and anthropologist David Martin, argued that the regime was a 'confused response' to the communal character of native title.[13] Prescribing the establishment of a single perpetual legal entity in the form of a trust or agent was, they suggested, aimed at avoiding problems created by 'the ever-fluctuating membership of a group of natural persons lacking legal personalities'.[14] The design of the legislation was also influenced by concerns about the capacity of individual native title holders to control their RNTBCs and possible inconsistencies with racial discrimination laws.[15]

This chapter outlines the current legislative landscape and history of policy reform relating to the holding and/or managing of native title by RNTBCs. We provide a national snapshot of RNTBCs around the country, profiling their diversity in terms of location, size and the nature of their native title rights and interests. We then provide a short account of the evolution of the regime in which they operate, focusing on changes since 2005 in areas such as tax, future acts[16] and corporate governance. This account illustrates how legal and administrative reforms have occurred at a distance from the firsthand experience of RNTBCs, and have failed to address the systemic issue of chronic underfunding. We describe the challenges native title holders face in trying to balance competing demands with limited resources, and their struggles to meet legal compliance requirements as well as the expectations of their memberships. We set out what is known about the aspirations of RNTBCs and constraints on leveraging native title rights to achieve greater social and economic returns, and we highlight growing calls from RNTBCs for financial independence, self-determination and national and regional representation.

The diversity of RNTBCs

In 1997 a New South Wales corporation, Dunghutti, became the first PBC to be registered as an RNTBC.[17] As at 30 June 2013, the number of RNTBCs across Australia had grown to 109, arising from 181 successful determinations of native title.[18] There is considerable diversity in the location, size, assets and income of RNTBCs, as well as in the length of time they have been in operation, the nature of their native title determinations and the extent of their landholdings. Each RNTBC is a product of the unique cultural and socio-political context from which it has emerged, and a range of factors influence its corporate character and organisational capacities. These factors include the traditional laws and customs of the native title holders, the legal histories of their native title claims, their place in local Indigenous political landscapes and the legislative jurisdictional environments in which they are located.

The nature of rights determined

Native title has been recognised by the High Court as an intersection of Aboriginal and Torres Strait Islander peoples' traditional laws and customs with the common law.[19] The unique nature of native title rights and interests that emerges at this intersection has resisted analogies to other forms of property law.[20] When making a native title determination, the Federal Court recognises native title rights and interests as constituting either exclusive possession 'as against the world' or non-exclusive possession. Native title has been conceptualised as a 'bundle of rights' such as the right to exclude, the right to hunt and fish, or the right to make decisions about use of land and resources.[21] In non-exclusive native title determinations, the interests of the Crown and third parties with significant interests in the land, such as pastoralists, prevail over those of native title holders. Those rights that are not in conflict with the non-Indigenous rights and interests are not extinguished and form the remaining bundle of rights that native title holders continue to enjoy.[22] The nature of the rights and interests held or managed by RNTBCs has considerable bearing on the control that RNTBCs have over native title land and affects their potential to achieve the economic, social and cultural priorities of native title holders. Matthew Storey, CEO of Native Title Services Victoria (NTSV), commented, as quoted in the Aboriginal and Torres Strait Islander Social Justice Commissioner's (ATSISJC) *Native title report 2012*, that non-exclusive rights 'amount to little more than the rights enjoyed by the general public or the embellishment of existing statutory rights on third party owned pastoral leases' and that they are 'not a useful foundation for building economic development or showcasing self-determination'.[23]

Nationally, there is little difference between the total areas of land held under exclusive possession and non-exclusive possession native title determinations. The Centre for Aboriginal Economic Policy Research (CAEPR) calculates that, at the end of 2012, exclusive possession and non-exclusive possession native title determinations each occupied an area of approximately nine per cent of Australia, together covering 1,397,618 square kilometres or approximately 18.2 per cent of Australia's land mass.[24] In the six months following, this figure rose to 1,592,340 square kilometres or approximately 20.7 per cent of Australia.[25] With over 400 registered native title claims that collectively cover almost 40 per cent of Australia still in the system,[26] RNTBCs are set to become increasingly significant features of both the Indigenous corporate landscape and remote and regional governance more generally.[27]

Geographical distribution of RNTBCs

Most native title is recognised in areas away from where the majority of Australia's population lives.[28] It is estimated that less than 0.01 per cent (approximately 16,925 people) of the total Australian population (approximately 22 million people) live in an area where some form of native title rights has been recognised. In contrast, approximately 2.5 per cent of Australia's Indigenous population (approximately 16,500 of a population of 661,000) live on native title determined lands. The vast majority who live in areas where native title has been determined reside in places where land is held under exclusive possession (approximately 14,308 people). This includes where exclusive possession native title has been recognised over many of the Indigenous reserve and lands trust tenures which were historically established for the benefit of Indigenous peoples and which today remain home to many large discrete Aboriginal and Torres Strait Islander residential communities. However, the groups who hold or manage native title in remote areas also often have large diaspora populations.[29]

The uneven geographical distribution of RNTBCs across Australia (see Figure 1.0 following page xix and Table 2.2) reflects the irregular nature of historical dispossession as well as contemporary differences in the way native title groups, their representatives and successive state and territory governments have approached the resolution of native title claims in their various jurisdictions. Native title determinations are arrived at either by consent or litigation, and the approaches of state and territory governments vary in the degree of support or opposition they apply to the negotiation of consent determinations or to litigation procedures in the

Federal Court.[30] The majority of RNTBCs are located in remote or very remote regions where native title rights and interests have been recognised as exclusive possession and where native title groups have been more easily able to satisfy evidentiary requirements for proving native title.[31] Nevertheless, a number of groups in more densely settled areas of the country, such as Victoria, have achieved positive determinations and established RNTBCs, though most of these areas are subject to non-exclusive native title determinations.

As of June 2013, Queensland was home to 53 RNTBCs, almost half the national total. Nineteen of these are located in the Torres Strait, all of which were established in association with consent determinations following *Mabo (No. 2)*.[32] The resolution by consent of a number of claims in north Queensland has recently seen the establishment of 19 RNTBCs within the boundary of the North Queensland Land Council alone. With more determinations scheduled, this region now compares with the Torres Strait as containing the most RNTBCs in Queensland.

Although 27 RNTBCs have been established in Western Australia, at the time of writing no RNTBCs have been registered in the south-west of the state or in the Goldfields region surrounding Kalgoorlie and Esperance. Groups in both regions are in the process of negotiating native title outcomes, with the Goldfields on track to having a determination of native title in 2013 through the Ngadju claim.[33] Currently, the majority of RNTBCs in Western Australia are in the Kimberley, Pilbara and Western Desert regions.

While there are 13 RNTBCs in the Northern Territory, there are also 30 successful determinations for which an RNTBC is yet to be advised and which are technically categorised on the NNTT register as 'waiting on PBC'. This category is given to determinations where a PBC is still to be nominated. Other jurisdictions have few RNTBSs. Victoria, for example, has four and South Australia has nine, although no RNTBCs were registered in that state until 2007, 10 years after the first RNTBC was registered in Australia.[34] New South Wales has two RNTBCs, and no native title determinations have been made in either Tasmania or the Australian Capital Territory. These lower numbers may be due at least in part to the policy considerations of Native Title Representative Bodies in settling claims, such as the extinguishment of native title; assessments that native title will be difficult to prove; and preferences for building relationships prior to negotiating outcomes, as was the case in South Australia in the initial phase of native title, and for alternative agreement-making such as co-management of protected areas agreements and land grants, as is the case in Tasmania.[35]

Size classifications

The CATSI Act distinguishes between RNTBCs on the basis of their gross income, gross assets and number of employees, classifying them accordingly as small, medium or large corporations (see Table 2.1).[36] Native title rights and interests held by an

RNTBC are not considered when determining the value of the corporation's assets for reporting purposes.[37]

Table 2.1 Classification of PBCs under the CATSI Act

Has at least two of the below factors in a financial year:	Small	Medium	Large
· Consolidated gross operating income	<$100,000	$100,000–$5 million	>$5 million
· Consolidated gross assets	<$100,000	$100,000–$2.5 million	>$2.5 million
· Employees	<5	5–24	>24

Source: Office of the Registrar of Indigenous Corporations, 'Fact sheet corporation size and financial reporting', ORIC, Canberra, 2011, <http://www.oric.gov.au/html/publications/factsheets/Fact%20sheet_Corp-size-and-reporting_Jan2011_11_0012.pdf>, accessed 18 June 2013.

The current numbers of RNTBCs by state and territory and by size are provided in Table 2.2. More than three-quarters of all RNTBCs are small corporations, having an operating income per financial year of less than $100,000, and/or assets of less than $100,000, and/or five or fewer employees.[38] The figures are indicative of the lack of a stable funding provision for RNTBCs to support them to undertake their functions, particularly when they are first established.[39] By contrast, there are 17 medium and only three large corporations. The relative prosperity of these latter organisations can for the most part be attributed to substantial income derived from negotiated agreements with either a state or territory government or with private companies.

Table 2.2 Distribution of RNTBCs by region and size, June 2013[40]

	NSW	NT	QLD	TSI	SA	VIC	WA	Total (No.)	Total (%)
Small	1	11	31	19	6	1	19	88	81.48
Medium	1	1	4	0	3	3	5	17	15.74
Large	0	0	0	0	0	0	3	3	2.77
Total	2	13[1]	35	19	9	4	27	109[2]	100.00

1 The total number of RNTBCs in the Northern Territory at 30 June 2013 was 13; however, only 12 are incorporated under the CATSI Act. Injarnyala Aboriginal Corporation RNTBC was determined by the court and remains on the NNTT register of RNTBCs; however, it is not incorporated under the CATSI Act and therefore does not exist as an operating RNTBC.
2 This figure includes the total number of RNTBCs (109), which does not equal the total number of RNTBCs incorporated under the CATSI Act (108) (see note 1 above).
3 The Queensland figure does not include the Torres Strait Islands (TSI), which are listed separately.

Source: Office of the Registrar of Indigenous Corporations (ORIC), 'Public register', ORIC, Canberra, <www.oric.gov.au>, accessed 30 June 2013.

RNTBC members and directors

Under the PBC Regulations, members must either be members of the common law native title holding group or classes of person that the native title holders' consent to being members.[41] However, native title holders do not automatically become members of their RNTBC when a determination of native title is made. Each native title holder must make an application for membership to the corporation. An initial member list is provided when a corporation is registered with the Office of the Registrar of Indigenous Corporations (ORIC) and subsequent membership applications are made to the respective RNTBC.[42] An RNTBC will inevitably have fewer members than there are native title holders, and there may be a number of reasons for this. Membership may be limited by age requirements for joining, conditions of membership may be difficult to meet (such as attendance at an annual general meeting (AGM) or payment of an annual membership fee), or an RNTBC may have little capacity to promote and process membership applications.[43]

The governance and priorities of an RNTBC will in part be determined by their unique rule book or constitution established under the CATSI Act. This document outlines processes such as holding elections for directors, managing finances, membership requirements and making native title decisions.

At 30 June 2012, there were more than 760 directors across 100 RNTBCs nationally. The average number of directors per RNTBC is eight, but actual figures range from one to 23. An analysis of publicly available data held by ORIC shows that, aside from the Torres Strait region, the gender distribution of directors across RNTBCs is more or less equal. The average age of an RNTBC director is 51, with less than 20 per cent of directors under 40.[44] The demography of RNTBC directors and members is an area that warrants further research, particularly in light of the increasingly youthful age profile of Australia's Indigenous population[45] and related concerns of native title holders around the intergenerational transmission of cultural knowledge.

The statutory roles and responsibilities of RNTBCs

RNTBCs as conceived under the NTA are designed to serve two main purposes:

1. to promote, hold and manage (if a trustee) or manage (if an agent), and protect determined native title in accordance with the wishes of the broader native title holding group
2. to ensure certainty for governments and other parties with an interest in accessing or regulating native title lands and waters by providing a legal entity through which to conduct business with the native title holders.[46]

In carrying out their functions, RNTBCs are required to manage the native title rights of the common law holders (native title holders),[47] consult with and obtain their consent before doing acts that affect their native title rights and interests in relation to a range of matters, and hold and invest money as directed by them. The range of matters that an RNTBC is legislated to deal with includes but is not limited to future acts, ILUAs, native title agreements, and revision, compensation and future native title applications.[48]

Many RNTBCs are assisted in carrying out their functions to a greater or lesser degree by Native Title Representative Bodies (NTRBs) and Native Title Service Providers (NTSPs), of which there are currently 15 across Australia.[49] Most native title holders were represented and provided with substantial support by the NTRBs and NTSPs in realising their native title determinations. The legislative functions of NTRBs and NTSPs to assist native title holders in negotiating future acts and ILUAs, including resolving disputes, apply equally to RNTBCs and claimants. However, many RNTBCs have sought more diverse assistance and support in accessing programs and managing the implementation of agreements to achieve the aspirations identified above.

One of the first decisions native title holders must make about the character of their RNTBC is whether it will be a trustee or an agent.[50] The NTA gives the impression that this distinction is significant but it is primarily technical and the two are effectively equivalent for most purposes, with the functions of agents and of trustees set out in identical terms including around consent and consultation requirements. This removes one of the key distinctions that might otherwise exist between these two corporate forms, namely the capacity of a trustee to make decisions without the consent of beneficiaries.[51] At the time of writing, the numbers of agent and trustee RNTBCs nationally are about equal, although certain jurisdictions clearly favour one form over the other.[52] The intention of the drafters of the legislation was that all native title would be held in trust. However, Indigenous people argued that there may be illegality in effectively forcing native title holders to transfer their property to a corporate body. As a result, the default status was the agent model.[53]

As noted, RNTBCs are also required to be incorporated under the CATSI Act and hence must comply with its regulatory obligations. The CATSI Act includes specific provisions for RNTBCs, clarifying the duties of RNTBC directors, confirming their obligations under the NTA and addressing avoidance of conflict with normal corporate fiduciary obligations. The CATSI Act requires all RNTBCs to have the words 'registered native title body corporate' or the abbreviation 'RNTBC' as part of their name, in order to clearly identify to third parties that the corporation holds and/or manages native title rights and interests.[54]

Further, as landholders, RNTBCs may be required to perform functions under and/or navigate the impacts of a wide range of Commonwealth and state or territory legislation relating to matters such as land and water management; tenure issues; biodiversity and environmental protection; cultural heritage; and land use planning including town planning. RNTBC obligations may thus extend to activities such as managing and protecting cultural heritage sites; controlling feral pests and weeds; maintaining watercourses; establishing and maintaining firebreaks; and clearing and removing rubbish.[55]

RNTBC activities will be shaped to differing degrees by the broader social and economic context in which the native title group is located and outcomes from future act and ILUA negotiations. These might include activities involving economic and business development (e.g. cattle farming or cultural tourism); research partnerships; employment programs; cultural maintenance and revitalisation programs; community liaison functions; participation in local government; environmental management programs ('caring for country'); and health and education initiatives.[56] RNTBCs may also engage in political action towards achieving more self-determination and social and economic independence. As with other organisations within the rapidly expanding 'Indigenous sector', RNTBCs may grow to become both an expression of political identity and 'an appropriate modernisation strategy with the evolution of Aboriginal civil society'.[57]

The evolution of the RNTBC system

There is a pervasive sense among Indigenous stakeholders that native title groups have been the subjects of, rather than partners in, policy reform. The inevitable consequence has been piecemeal policy responses from federal, state and territory governments to address Indigenous disadvantage, which attempt to address old anxieties about governance and accountability as well as new ones relating to missed opportunities.

The legislative and policy environment that has created RNTBCs and which shapes and supports their operation is multi-jurisdictional. While it is federal law that laid the foundations for their creation through the NTA, much of the operation of RNTBCs is profoundly influenced by state and territory government approaches towards managing competing interests in land. The discussion that follows deals primarily with federal government reform agendas. Reviewing the history of individual state native title management regimes is beyond the capacity of this paper but is a subject worthy of further attention.[58]

Various aspects of the federal native title regime have been reviewed and changed since the enactment of the NTA in 1993. Much of the reform agenda appears to have been driven by emerging knowledge about the challenges RNTBCs face in attempting to navigate the various relationships and obligations created by the intersection of communally held native title rights with other Australian laws. But it has also been shaped by political expediency and concerns to reduce conflict and increase certainty for third parties with commercial interests in native title lands.[59]

One of the most significant gaps in the intersection of federal and state regimes is around funding. In 2001 the former Parliamentary Joint Committee on Native Title and the Aboriginal and Torres Strait Islander Land Fund recommended that RNTBCs receive adequate funding to perform their statutory functions and appropriate training to meet their statutory duties.[60] In 2002 the Aboriginal and Torres Strait Islander Commission (ATSIC) commissioned a comprehensive review of funding (the Rashid Report).⁶¹ The Rashid Report's authors assessed in considerable detail the costs associated with the establishment and registration of an RNTBC and the costs of performing their regulatory and statutory functions. They concluded that the lack of funding at that time resulted in RNTBCs that: 'on the most part, [are] essentially dysfunctional, have no infrastructure and are unlikely to be capable of meeting existing regulatory compliance requirements'.⁶² The Rashid Report advocated that NTRBs be given additional funding to assist native title holders to incorporate, nominate and register their RNTBC, and that RNTBCs be funded either directly or indirectly so that they had the capacity to meet their minimum regulatory compliance obligations and perform their statutory functions.⁶³

However, it was not until the number of RNTBCs had grown from 19 in 2002⁶⁴ to 40 in 2005 that major reforms to the RNTBC legislative, funding and policy environment were addressed at a federal level. By this time RNTBCs were beginning to organise on a larger scale and to demand more government assistance, reflecting a growing sense of the urgent need to attend to the 'post determination' environment which had received limited attention since the NTA was implemented in 1993.

A timeline showing major legislative and policy reform events that have impacted the functions and governance capacities of RNTBCs is in Table 2.3. These reforms include a number of inquiries and reports, various legislative changes to the NTA including significant amendments to the PBC Regulations, amendments to tax and charities legislation and the introduction of new legislation for Indigenous corporations (the CATSI Act referred to previously).

These reforms took place in the context of broader and significant changes to the processes by which the federal government consulted with Aboriginal and Torres Strait Islander peoples. In 2005 the federal government passed the *Aboriginal and Torres Strait Islander Commission Amendment Act 2005* (Cth) and abolished ATSIC. From 1990 ATSIC had been the peak representative body for Indigenous people in Australia, and with its demise they were left without a collective political voice to lobby for their interests.⁶⁵ The federal government began to look at alternative regional governance structures and the roles that NTRBs might play in that regard. However, there was little appetite for a strong Indigenous governance structure to replace ATSIC. In the absence of this national advocacy, in 2005 NTRBs and NTSPs established a peak body — the National Native Title Council (NNTC) — to represent their views and to promote the recognition and protection of native title. In 2010, after considerable national consultation and deliberation, the Congress of Australia's First Peoples (Congress) was established to provide national advocacy on Aboriginal and Torres Strait Islander issues. While RNTBCs may be represented by individuals on the boards or councils of NTRBs and NTSPs and can join as category 2 members of Congress as Aboriginal and Torres Strait Islander organisations (as of August 2013, four RNTBCs were organisational members),⁶⁶ RNTBCs have not had an advocacy body specifically representing their unique interests as native title holders at a national policy level.

Major changes to the native title regime that occurred under a conservative Liberal and National coalition government between 2005 and 2007 comprised five elements: consultation on measures to encourage the effective functioning of RNTBCs; an independent review of native title claims resolution processes; technical amendments to the NTA; measures to improve the effectiveness of NTRBs; and consultation with state and territory governments to promote and encourage more transparent resolution of native title issues.[67]

The initial stage of this process involved a review to assess the needs, functions and governance of RNTBCs and to identify strategies to support their effective operation. It was conducted by a Steering Committee chaired by the Attorney-General's Department (AGD) and comprised officers of the AGD, the Department of Family and Community Services (FaCS), as it was called at the time, and ORAC. In October 2006 the Steering Committee published a report entitled *Structures and processes of Prescribed Bodies Corporate* (the PBC Report).[68]

The PBC Report emphasised the crucial role of RNTBCs within the native title system, but observed that few were operating effectively. It also acknowledged that the level of resources available was not sufficient for RNTBCs to fulfil all the requirements imposed on them. The Steering Committee made 15 recommendations, including measures to improve the ability of RNTBCs to access funding from a range of government programs, authorise RNTBCs to recover costs reasonably incurred in performing specific functions at the request of third parties, and increase the flexibility of the statutory governance regime.[69]

The federal government accepted all the Steering Committee's recommendations and commenced implementation through a raft of administrative changes and legislative amendments.[70] The *Native Title Amendment Act 2007* (Cth) and the *Native Title (Technical Amendment) Act 2007* (Cth) subsequently came into effect on 1 July 2008. However, the changes also required amendments to the PBC Regulations, and a draft of the Native Title (Prescribed Body Corporate) Amendment Regulations 2010 was not released for comment until after a change of government in 2007.

The return of the Labor Party to government in 2007 saw continued attention to the efficiency of the native title system and RNTBCs in particular. Native title was declared to be critical to economic development and Closing the Gap policy initiatives aimed at addressing Indigenous disadvantage and achieving equity of health and life expectancy between Indigenous and non-Indigenous Australians within a generation.[71] An inadequate statutory framework, weak accountability arrangements and insufficient funding for NTRBs, NTSPs and RNTBCs were identified as impediments to realising Closing the Gap outcomes.[72] A Joint Working Group on Indigenous Land Settlements (JWGILS) was established to find ways to address these issues. Its membership comprised officers of AGD, the Department of Families, Housing, Community Services and Indigenous Affairs (FaHCSIA) and state and territory governments. The purview included an examination of complex native title taxation issues that had been lurking in the 'too hard basket' for nearly two decades.[73] At the same time as these complex legal and administrative reforms were taking place, RNTBCs were also required to adapt to new corporations legislation in the form of the CATSI Act.

While elements of reform have been welcomed by the native title sector, in his 2007 *Native title report*, the ATSISJC expressed concerns that the recognition and protection of native title was not central to the government's reform agenda.[74] The processes by which reforms have occurred have also been criticised. Three years later, when reflecting on the process, the commissioner concluded that during consultations for the Native Title Act Amendment Bill (No. 2) 2009 (Cth) the government did not allow sufficient time or opportunity for Aboriginal and Torres Strait Islander communities to participate and did not respond sufficiently to their concerns.[75]

At the time of writing, in August 2013, there are more reforms on the horizon. RNTBCs are subject to the latest in a series of policy reviews through the FaHCSIA Native Title Organisations Review, which contemplates a wide-scale examination of the roles, functions, governance and funding models of NTRBs and NTSPs and the RNTBCs they may service.[76] A bill to amend the NTA which, among other things, could significantly alter the legal test for 'good faith' negotiations was before the parliament but has now lapsed with the change of federal government in September 2013. The Australian Law Reform Commission is also conducting an extensive review of native title law, which was announced in June 2013 and will examine connection requirements and the authorisation of native title claims.[77]

Reforms to the PBC Regulations

The challenges RNTBCs face in meeting the corporate governance, regulatory and statutory demands in such complex and dynamic circumstances are confronting and ongoing. Some of the more significant elements of recent reforms to the system are outlined below.

As noted, several of the amendments to the NTA in 2007 required amendments to the PBC Regulations but they were not undertaken prior to a change of federal government in 2007. In order to progress them, in 2010 the government released a consultation draft of the Native Title (Prescribed Bodies Corporate) Amendment Regulations 2010 (the PBC Amendment Regulations) which addressed recommendations arising out of the PBC Report. In February 2012 the Native Title (Prescribed Bodies Corporate) Amendment Regulations 2011 were tabled in parliament.[78] Among other things, the amendments implemented key changes to consultation, certification and membership requirements, including making it possible for native title holders to elect non-member directors.[79] They also impacted how default corporations are determined and provided RNTBCs with the capacity to charge fees for service. Aspects of particular areas of reform are described in more detail below.

Consultation and certification

The NTA under s 58(d) provides for regulations requiring RNTBCs to consult and act in accordance with the directions and decisions of the common law holders in performing their functions. Such decisions relate only to native title matters, with the 2011 PBC Amendment Regulations[80] changing the PBC Regulations to define a native title decision as a decision '(a) to surrender native title rights and interests in relation to land or waters; or (b) to do, or agree to do, any other act that would affect native title rights and interests of the common law holders'.[81]

The 2011 PBC Amendment Regulations also amended the requirement that an RNTBC must 'consult with, and obtain the consent of' the native title group, to give RNTBCs the option of developing alternative consultation processes which must be included in their constitutions.[82] There are exceptions to this, with full consultation being mandated for native title decisions relating to actions such as: entering into an ILUA or a Right to Negotiate Agreement; extending the membership of the RNTBC beyond the native title group; and consenting to consultation processes, including alternative processes in the organisation's constitution.[83] This amendment was aimed at alleviating some of the burden of RNTBC governance by reducing costs, providing flexibility and supporting local decision-making processes and priorities.[84] The amendment is not without its critics, with some concerns raised about the possibility of this approach being strategically exploited by subsets of native title holders.[85] Additional amendments include a new regulation, 9(3), that allows for certificates providing evidence of standing authorisations to be prepared only once, rather than each time an RNTBC makes a decision in accordance with the authorisation.[86]

Determination of an existing RNTBC for a subsequent determination

The NTA and the PBC Regulations were amended to allow an existing RNTBC to be determined as the RNTBC for a subsequent determination of native title in circumstances where all the native title holders covered by the determinations agree.[87] If an existing RNTBC is determined for a subsequent determination it is required to retain its character as either trustee or agent, as it is not possible for the RNTBC to act as a trustee and agent at the same time.[88] This amendment was designed to relieve the burden that native title groups face when they are required to contribute to the operation and compliance of a second RNTBC and where it is likely they have limited resources to do so.

Non-native title holder membership

In a move not broadly supported by key Indigenous stakeholders, including the NNTC, the 1999 PBC Regulations were amended to allow non-native title holders to become members of RNTBCs provided that the native title group consents and that the requirement for a majority Indigenous membership, under the CATSI Act, is maintained. This measure was intended to 'assist in making the structure more representative of the broader community in which they live, and to increase the corporation's skill base'.[89]

Fees for service

The *Native Title Amendment (Technical Amendments) Act 2007* added s 60AB(1) to the NTA to provide for RNTBCs to charge third party fees for costs and disbursements, as described under new regulation 20 in the PBC Regulations. Costs are incurred in RNTBCs performing their statutory functions such as negotiating a future act agreement or an ILUA.[90] There is also provision to specify other functions for which a fee may be charged.[91] Beyond cost recovery the primary objective of this amendment was to create a potential funding stream for RNTBCs to support additional activities.

Default RNTBC

The original drafting of the NTA included provisions for the nomination of a PBC in circumstances where native title holders fail to do so. However, from the outset analysts identified these provisions as poorly drafted and in some cases inoperable, and calls were made for their amendment.[92]

Partly in response to these concerns, the revised PBC Regulations extend the definition of 'prescribed body corporate' to include the Indigenous Land Corporation (ILC). The ILC is a statutory body established under the *Land Fund and Indigenous Land Corporation (ATSIC Amendment) Act 1995* (Cth) following the *Mabo* decision to assist Indigenous people to acquire and manage land to achieve economic, environmental, social and cultural benefits.[93] This change to the PBC Regulations allows the Federal Court to appoint the ILC to operate as a default agent, for a defined period, in circumstances where an RNTBC has not been nominated by a native title group, or where an existing RNTBC is being wound up and no replacement has been found.[94] During this time it is expected that a PBC, or a new PBC, will be nominated. The Commonwealth Government identified the ILC as an appropriate candidate for this role on the basis that 'it has the organisational capacity and land management expertise to effectively represent the needs of native title groups'.[95] However, such sentiments were not universally accepted, as the ILC is not always seen in a favourable light, particularly by traditional owner groups in those regions where the ILC has large pastoral holdings and has not yet divested them to traditional owners.[96]

Reforms to taxation laws

Promoting the capacity for native title holders to make the most of the financial benefits derived from their unique rights and interests in land has been part of the government reform agenda for a number of years. Along with changes to the PBC Regulations, there has been extensive legislative review and change around native title and taxation payments. Between 2008 and 2010 the Commonwealth Government released a series of three discussion papers addressing these issues.

In December 2008 the government released *Optimising the benefits from native title agreements*,[97] which proposed a suite of reforms that would enable native title holders to optimise benefits received from mining and other agreements. Forty submissions were received in response to the paper, addressing issues such as transparency and workability of agreements, promotion of best practice, tax options and statutory schemes.[98]

Eighteen months later, FaHCSIA and AGD jointly released *Leading practice agreements: maximising outcomes from native title benefits*.[99] This paper proposed a number of measures designed to build the financial capacity and sustainability of RNTBCs as well as some austere governance measures. These included the capacity to appoint independent directors; enhanced transparency and accountability of directors to members;[100] an agreement review function; discretionary assessment of agreements; the development of a leading practice agreements toolkit;[101] and amendment of the NTA to streamline future act processes and clarify 'good faith' requirements.[102] Many submissions commented on the need for better resourcing of RNTBCs and for NTRBs and NTSPs to monitor and implement agreements. Concerns were also raised that consultation with Indigenous stakeholders about the proposed reforms had been inadequate, and that they prioritised government rather than native title holder aspirations.[103]

In the lead-up to an announcement about plans for a new mineral resource rent tax in July 2010, the Department of Treasury released a consultation paper on native title and taxation, *Native title, Indigenous economic development and tax* (May 2010).[104] It examined issues around the interaction of the income tax system and the native title management regime, and identified three possible areas of reform: income tax exemptions for payments under native title agreements; the creation of a new tax exempt entity, an Indigenous Community Fund; and a native title withholding tax.[105] The paper received 34 submissions that were, on the whole, supportive of the proposed changes. One of the central problems raised, however, was the difficulty of managing financial benefits from agreements through charitable trusts, a strategy commonly used by RNTBCs to avoid the uncertainty of tax treatment of native title payments.[106]

A joint submission by the Minerals Council of Australia (MCA) and the NNTC detailed a proposal for an Indigenous Community Development Corporation (ICDC), which was aimed at addressing this issue by providing an organisation that would have comparable tax exemptions as a charitable trust but be better able to support the aspirations of RNTBCs and native title groups. The proposal was aimed at:

- shifting the language away from concepts of charity to concepts of community and economic development;
- creating greater flexibility within the taxation system for community specific approaches to managing funds for socio-economic development;
- providing a structure that encourages intergenerational and sustainable benefits;
- creating capacity to maximise the delivery of economic and social dividends with minimal administrative burden; and
- recognising the unique multifaceted challenge of Indigenous disadvantage.[107]

In November 2012, the Tax Laws Amendment (2012 Measures No. 6) Bill 2012 was introduced into parliament, and in March 2013 the Department of Treasury established the Taxation of Native Title and Traditional Owner Benefits and Governance Working Group to examine the 'tax treatment of native title payments and how they can better benefit Indigenous communities now and into the future'. It was ostensibly aimed at examining the proposed ICDC and continuing governance concerns.[108]

The *Tax Laws Amendment (2012 Measures No. 6) Act 2012* (Cth) was passed in June 2013, giving certainty around the tax liabilities for native title agreements and ensuring that 'certain payments and benefits arising from native title agreements will not be subject to income tax and that certain capital gains from native title rights are not taxable'.[109] Part of the government's broader native title reform, these amendments were explicitly aimed at assisting Indigenous Australians to 'unlock the economic potential of their native title'.[110]

The Taxation of Native Title and Traditional Owner Benefits and Governance Working Group released its findings in a report in July 2013 and made a number of recommendations. They included support for the establishment of an ICDC like entity; an urgent recommendation to government to regulate private agents providing services to native title groups in future act negotiations; and amendments to the NTA to clarify that 'the native title holding community is the beneficial owner of funds generated by native title agreements, irrespective of the identity of the legal owner or possessor of those proceeds, and that the named applicant is in a fiduciary relationship to their native title holding group'.[111] The recommendations also included two proposals: one to establish under statute a trust to hold funds from native title agreements where there is no RNTBC, ICDC entity or other organisation appropriate to receive the funds, and the other for a process for the registration of s 31 native title future act agreements to be considered by the FaHCSIA Native Title Organisations Review.[112] The terms of this review have since been amended to incorporate two of these recommendations: the regulation of private agents (which was already referenced in part); and the creation of a statutory trust for holding native title agreement funds where a relevant organisation such as an RNTBC or ICDC like entity does not exist.[113]

The complexity of the issues facing the tax treatment of native title payments for RNTBCs and the rapid pace of legislative and policy review have limited the extent to which native title holders have been able to influence the outcomes of reform, particularly as it has been driven by bureaucracies in Canberra, both physically and ideologically remote from the areas where most RNTBCs are based.

Reforms to the not-for-profit sector

Alongside these reforms, a small number of RNTBCs have been subject to recent changes in the not-for-profit sector. The Australian Charities and Not-for-profits Commission (ACNC) was established in January 2013.[114] Five months later, in June 2013, new legislation was passed addressing the absence of a comprehensive definition of a charity under federal law.[115] The *Charities Act 2013* (Cth) amends the definition of 'charitable purpose' to account for RNTBCs, which previously could fail the public benefit test if directing benefits to people who were family members.[116] This could potentially widen the number of RNTBCs that can claim not-for-profit status.

The clarification of the tax treatment of native title and the definition of charitable entities provided by these legislative changes are significant moves towards enabling the financial viability of RNTBCs. The lengthy timeframes associated with reviewing and implementing these changes, however, along with the concerns raised about the inadequacy of consultation with Indigenous stakeholders, are indicative of the challenges that RNTBCs will continue to face as the Australian legislature incrementally wrestles with the accommodation of their unique characters and needs.

Reforms to the operation of future acts

Concurrent with positive reforms in the area of taxation and governance, other reforms have undermined the strength of the native title rights and interests that are the core of RNTBC business. The *Native Title Amendment Act (No. 1) 2010* (Cth) — specifically ss 24AA, 24AB, 24JAA, 222 and 253 — substantially weakened the rights of native title holders in the face of future acts relating to the provision of public infrastructure on native title lands. The apparent impetus for these amendments was the difficulties in administering the 2008 National Partnership Agreement on Remote Indigenous Housing (NPARIH), a 10-year, $5.5 billion Council of Australian Governments (COAG) partnership aimed at resolving chronic issues around poor housing conditions for Indigenous people in remote areas through public housing and infrastructure projects.[117] The operational timeframe of the new subdivision is linked to a sunset clause, which will expire at the end of the lifetime of the NPARIH in 2018. The amendments removed the potential for delays created by negotiations with native title parties. A number of submissions to the amendments strongly opposed these changes on the basis that they lacked an evidence base and failed to address a number of legal uncertainties. As with previous reforms, the government was also criticised for inadequate consultation and the absence of any critical review of the bureaucratic processes that contribute to delays in public housing provision.[118]

New corporate laws: the CATSI Act (2007)

In the midst of trying to come to terms with the various reforms outlined above, RNTBCs were also faced with changes to their corporate governance requirements. As noted previously, all RNTBCs are required to incorporate under the CATSI Act and to meet the corresponding Corporations (Aboriginal and Torres Strait Islander) Regulations 2007. The CATSI Act, which is administered by ORIC, commenced on 1 July 2007 and replaced the *Aboriginal Councils and Associations Act 1976* (Cth) (ACA Act).[119] Under transitional legislation, all ACA Act corporations had two years to make changes required under the new CATSI Act.[120] The CATSI Act was introduced to remedy the shortfalls of the ACA Act, which was outdated and inflexible in accommodating the corporate governance needs of Indigenous people.[121] The introduction of new corporate law in 2001 through the Corporations Act had made fundamental changes to regulation of corporations in Australia, and the CATSI Act aimed to bring corporate law for Indigenous corporations in line as much as possible with the Corporations Act — particularly where Indigenous corporations were subject to more regulation.[122] The CATSI Act is also a 'special measure' under the *Racial Discrimination Act 1975* (Cth) and a form of 'positive discrimination', as its objective is to enable 'Indigenous people to enjoy, on an equal basis with other Australians, the same legal facilities (and attendant socio-economic benefits) that incorporation can confer'.[123]

To assist RNTBCs with the transition, ORIC prepared documentation outlining proposed changes, one of the most welcome and significant of which was the scaling of reporting requirements to the size of the corporation as categorised in Table 2.1.[124] These changes reduce the administrative burden and reporting requirements for small and medium organisations, and bring reporting requirements in line with small corporations under the Corporations Act.[125] They also mean that the regulator, ORIC, has a much greater support and education role than under the ACA Act. The CATSI Act also adopted the concept of 'replaceable rules' which were introduced into the Corporations Act, providing more flexibility for corporations to create their own specific rules particularly around internal processes dealing with meetings, directors and membership.

Nevertheless, compliance with corporate requirements is significant under the CATSI Act, and many RNTBCs are not adequately resourced to meet their obligations under the Act.[126] The issue of support for compliance was raised in 2007 by both the ATSISJC and ORIC.[127]

State and territory legislative and policy reform

In addition to the Commonwealth reforms discussed above, there is an extraordinary number of other federal, state and territory laws and related policies that intersect with the native title regime which RNTBCs must potentially navigate and with which they must comply. Examples include cultural heritage protection and management acts; land use and planning acts; water acts; local government acts; land management and protection acts; mineral, energy and petroleum acts; title validation acts; and land rights acts.[128] Inevitably, many of these laws and policies regularly undergo changes as a result of review, reform and legislative amendment and this may have a profound impact on how RNTBCs go about their business.

The inconsistencies between various regimes can lead to frustrating delays and unwieldy complexities, particularly in the alignment of native title and state and territory government tenures. Some RNTBCs are seeking the divestment of leases held by state and territory governments on trust for the benefit of Aboriginal people through historical reserves systems such as the Aboriginal Lands Trusts (ALTs) in Western Australia and South Australia.[129] This can raise issues where the land is held in trust for Aboriginal people other than native title holders. In Queensland, changes have been made to the *Aboriginal Land Act 1991* (Qld) (ALA) so that RNTBCs can hold in trust inalienable freehold title over which native title rights and interests may also have been determined. Thus, native title rights and traditional rights as recognised by the ALA scheme may be held by a single legal entity.

Overall, however, the incompatibility of forms of tenure in which many areas of land can be divested to RNTBCs, with the character of communally held native title rights and interests, has delayed such alignments, and divestment may ultimately not be possible without new and innovative forms of tenure.[130]

Funding for native title corporations

The question of how RNTBCs should be funded to carry out their various obligations to native title holders, governments and non–native title interests is an ongoing concern. In particular there is considerable disagreement between the Commonwealth, states and territories about how the growing need for RNTBC funding should be addressed by the different levels of government. As noted in Table 2.2, the vast majority of RNTBCs fall into the 'small' category under the CATSI

Act, and have a gross operating income of less than $100,000 and limited capacity to self-fund activities.

As discussed previously, the importance of funding has been raised a number of times.[131] The history of RNTBC funding arrangements to date is characterised by reluctance on the part of the Commonwealth Government to deal directly with RNTBCs, preferring instead to provide nominal funds indirectly through NTRBs or NTSPs in line with one of the funding models in the Rashid Report. The 2006 PBC Report recommended that this resourcing be provided on application from RNTBCs through their representative NTRBs or NTSPs where possible, with direct funding to RNTBCs only being provided in exceptional circumstances.[132] In 2007 the then Department of Families, Housing, Community Services and Indigenous Affairs (FaHCSIA) released its *Guidelines for basic support funding for Prescribed Bodies Corporate (PBCs)*, inviting applications from RNTBCs and requiring an NTRB or NTSP to also administer the funding.[133] In the 2011–12 financial year, FaHCSIA provided almost $1.7 million to NTRBs and NTSPs to provide basic support to RNTBCs and some PBCs. This constitutes approximately two per cent of the total funding provided to NTRBs and NTSPs.[134]

In 2012, the ATSISJC sought feedback from NTRBs and NTSPs about the levels of funding and resources available to undertake their statutory functions and provide support to groups following a determination of native title. All who responded (nine of 15 organisations) expressed 'significant concerns' about RNTBC funding levels, especially in circumstances where a group does not have agreements with external stakeholders, such as mining companies, that provide an ongoing and substantial source of income.[135] Many groups cannot rely on such sources of income. While there are major resource extraction projects occurring in some remote and very remote areas, such as the Pilbara region of Western Australia, as a rule there are few mines situated on native title land and the majority of mining activity is located on land adjacent to Indigenous land holdings.[136] Other sources of income may be derived in exchange for the extinguishment of native title rights where native title determinations have been made in urban areas with significant development opportunities, such as by the Lhere Artepe RNTBC in Alice Springs in the Northern Territory and the Yawuru RNTBC in Broome in Western Australia. However, these kinds of opportunities are limited to a few RNTBCs.

The funding and support needs of RNTBCs will vary depending on a number of factors including the nature and extent of native title rights and interests, the remoteness of the determination area, the geographic dispersal of the native title holders, and the level and type of future act activity.[137] The cost of undertaking tasks such as convening AGMs can be enormous, particularly in remote and regional areas where membership is widely dispersed. While the location of RNTBCs in areas of relatively high future act activity may open up opportunities for agreements, responding to future act notifications can also place pressure on administrative capacities and resources. Many RNTBCs do not have the appropriate staff or infrastructure to support good administrative and governance practice and may be lacking the most basic facilities, such as computers, printers, phones and office space. In such circumstances RNTBCs may rely on the resources of other organisations, such as NTRBs and NTSPs, on local Indigenous councils and service providers or on the individual employers of their directors or members to carry out many aspects of their day-to-day business.[138] Few have the necessary resources to employ staff, and there is a heavy reliance on the volunteer contributions of directors and members to assist with administrative affairs. The few resources that are available may be spent responding to external requests at the expense of local priorities.

The PBC Report recommended that RNTBCs seek alternative funding through relevant Commonwealth, state and territory government programs, but many RNTBCs have struggled to access such support. Between 2006 and 2013, AIATSIS convened a series of workshops for RNTBCs, during which meetings were organised with a range of Commonwealth, state and territory government departments in order to raise awareness of RNTBC needs and identify suitable funding programs.[139] AIATSIS also convened a number of meetings of representatives of Commonwealth Government departments in Canberra to investigate the funding programs that might be available to RNTBCs. In both instances, the government representatives were often unaware of the existence of RNTBCs and the extent of RNTBC responsibilities. Moreover, it quickly became apparent that many of the programs that might be relevant to RNTBCs had eligibility criteria which RNTBCs could not meet. Some RNTBC members also expressed concerns that they lacked the capacity to complete the sometimes arduous application forms required to access funding programs.

There are potential opportunities for some RNTBCs to explore alternative income streams; for example, through conservation activities that are deemed environmental offsets under provisions of the *Environment Protection and Biodiversity Conservation Act 1999* (Cth). This avenue relates to matters of national significance, such as world or national heritage sites, threatened species and communities and wetlands of international importance designated under the Ramsar Convention and Commonwealth marine areas.[140] There are also potential income streams available through the federal Carbon Farming Initiative.[141] Making use of these opportunities, however, requires knowledge of the relevant policy regimes and the capacity to submit proposals for assessment, both of which are limiting factors for many RNTBCs.

RNTBCs made a number of conclusions relating to funding at the first national meeting of RNTBCs, convened by AIATSIS in Canberra in 2007. These included:

- the provision of funding directly to RNTBCs
- the need for additional funding for salaried positions within RNTBCs and to ensure that RNTBCs are not reliant on third party funding

- the provision of dedicated staff members within the AGD, FaHCSIA and ORIC who understand and can assist and support RNTBCs
- the role of FaHCSIA's Indigenous Coordination Centres in supporting and assisting RNTBCs
- the need for NTRBs to undertake regional RNTBC audits, organise RNTBC meetings and consider the development of memoranda of understanding with RNTBCs
- funding for AIATSIS to provide opportunities for RNTBC networking (including national meetings of RNTBCs), coordinate information and resources and develop RNTBC profiles.[142]

While RNTBCs have expressed a preference for direct funding, the 2013 FaHCSIA guidelines for funding of RNTBCs and PBCs generally encourage RNTBC funding applications to be made through their NTRB or NTSP and state that 'direct funding of PBC basic support is likely to be a rarity'.[143] The special circumstances warranting direct funding include: where the original native title claim was not handled by the NTRB or NTSP for the area; where there is a significant conflict of interest between the PBC and the NTRB or NTSP; or where there is demonstrated good governance and demonstrated ability to administer and account for funding.[144] The underlying assumption seems to be that RNTBCs attempting to access basic financial assistance through this scheme are unlikely to have the capacity to accountably administer their own affairs.

As of January 2013, FaHCSIA advised that no grants of direct funding to RNTBCs have been made since the program for basic support funding was introduced in 2007, and NTRBs and NTSPs have remained the primary administrators of federal government assistance.[145] While this arrangement may work for some RNTBCs, others have expressed concerns that channelling funding through NTRBs or NTSPs reinforces RNTBC dependence and undermines progress towards autonomy and self-governance.[146] This is particularly problematic for those RNTBCs in ongoing and long-term disputes with their NTRB or NTSP.

Funding arrangements for NTRBs, NTSPs and RNTBCs are currently being investigated as part of the FaHCSIA Native Title Organisations Review referred to previously.[147] During the period when ATSIC and subsequently the Office of Indigenous Policy Coordination (OIPC) had responsibility for NTRB Funding Agreements, these agreements limited NTRBs and NTSPs in providing support to RNTBCs in their day-to-day operations beyond the date of an RNTBC's first AGM, though a number of NTRBs and NTSPs continued to provide what support they could. This limitation was removed from the Funding Agreement in 2007[148] and most if not all NTRBs and NTSPs now invest in ongoing targeted advice and support to at least some RNTBCs.

The nature of NTRB and NTSP support varies from region to region, reflecting the diversity among NTRBs, NTSPs and RNTBCs. In many regions NTRB and NTSP staff members are listed as the ORIC contact officer for RNTBCs, a telling sign of the limited capacity that many RNTBCs have to manage their communications in the absence of paid staff. In addition to providing legal advice and assisting with the management of future acts, NTRBs and NTSPs may offer a range of support services for RNTBCs, including: building corporate governance and assisting with corporate compliance requirements; administering funding arrangements under Working on Country and Indigenous Protected Area programs and providing support for these activities; and assisting or taking on the primary role in negotiations between RNTBCs and respective state or territory governments. Nevertheless, the degree of assistance that NTRBs and NTSPs can provide to RNTBCs remains constrained by the priorities and functions of NTRBs and NTSPs, including claims resolution which is taken into account in FaHCSIA funding assessment processes.[149] This places RNTBCs and groups still in the process of establishing their native title effectively in competition for the same bucket of funding.

The terms of reference of the review include consideration of the nature of the assistance NTRBs and NTSPs currently provide to RNTBCs, making it clear that any recommendations for changes to existing arrangements cannot assume the availability of additional financial resources.[150] With no injection of new money into the system and with the number of RNTBCs across the country continuing to grow, it remains to be seen how effective any reforms initiated through this review will be in supporting native title holders to manage their native rights into the future. In the context of chronic underfunding of the native title system, the issue of financial compensation from native title claims (as circumscribed in s 51 of the NTA) is gaining increasing importance, and there have been ongoing calls for a compensation test case.[151] There is little likelihood that the workload of NTRBs and NTSPs in claims negotiation and litigation will ease quickly, particularly when an unknown quantum of compensation claims is factored in. In 2006 the Yulara compensation case failed largely because of issues relating to the proof of native title.[152] However, RNTBCs have already proven and hold and/or manage their native title, and a class action for compensation has been discussed. At the time of writing there is no precedent for compensation and the question of how native title will be valued by the courts in the future remains unanswered.

Towards a collective voice

A growing desire on the part of many RNTBCs for corporate independence and self-determination has resulted in efforts towards the establishment of a peak body to represent the collective interests of RNTBCs.[153] These efforts, which began in

2009 at the Second National Meeting of PBCs[154] and were renewed in 2011 and then at the 2013 National Native Title Conference in Alice Springs, have to date been hindered by the challenge RNTBCs face in establishing a mandate for this body in the absence of sufficient resources to bring together representatives from all RNTBCs. Additionally, any RNTBC representatives who may be nominated to sit on the proposed peak body face significant financial and capacity restraints, particularly in taking on additional responsibilities to those they already have for their own RNTBCs and for which, as noted, they often work in voluntary capacities.[155] One of the key priorities of an RNTBC peak body, as discussed in every RNTBC forum held at regional or national levels, is achieving a direct funding regime in future budgets, and this is seen as particularly important in the context of the Review of Native Title Organisations.

The NNTC is considering the unique position of RNTBCs as representatives of the first peoples of Australia and how RNTBCs fit into the governance of existing national Indigenous representative bodies. RNTBCs have identified emerging representative forums such as the Congress, established in 2010, as potentially playing a role in supporting their need for national representation, but Congress has yet to have any significant role in supporting the establishment of a peak body for RNTBCs.[156] Informal discussions at the 2013 National Native Title Conference between representatives of RNTBCs, the NNTC and Congress identified the gap that exists in the role of the NNTC and Congress in supporting RNTBC representation. At the conference a proposal was also presented for the establishment of an Assembly of First Nations and there was some discussion as to where such an assembly might sit in relation to Congress.[157]

Efforts towards regional representation also appear to be gaining traction. In Victoria the Federation of Victorian Traditional Owner Corporations (FVTOC) is being established with the assistance of NTSV to represent RNTBCs and other native title corporations when lobbying the Victorian state government.[158] In the Torres Strait, the Gur A Baradharaw Kod Torres Strait Sea and Land Council Torres Strait Islander Corporation has been formed to represent native title holders in the region. The first objective of this new organisation, as stated in its rule book, is to 'empower the native title holders and Native Title Bodies (RNTBCs) of the Torres Strait to fulfil their responsibilities to hold and manage their sea and lands in accordance with traditional law and custom'.[159]

Conclusion

These are very interesting days. It's a huge learning process for all involved. We have realised that to have your native title determined is not an end point, but a new starting point of a lot of hard work and responsibility.

Valerie Cooms, Quandamooka native title holder[160]

RNTBCs are an essential part of the native title system. Improving the operational capacities of the more than 100 unique RNTBCs that currently exist would contribute significantly to the extent to which native title holders are able to exercise their native title rights and interests, manage their traditional lands and waters and perform their statutory functions. Building corporate capacity also impacts on the land access needs of a variety of non–native title parties, including developers. In acting as agents of change towards 'closing the gap' of Indigenous disadvantage through investments into social, cultural and economic programs at a highly localised level, RNTBCs also have substantial but unrealised potential to be far more than just vehicles for the holding and/or managing of native title.[161]

And yet the legal and administrative reforms that have impacted RNTBCs over the past decade appear to have made little substantive difference to the capacity of native title holders to enjoy and benefit from their native title rights. Despite frequent reform over a number of years in key areas such as taxation, fees for services and governance structures, native title holders continue to express concern and frustration about the complexity of the regime and the ongoing and chronic lack of financial support. More change to which RNTBCs will have to adjust is expected with the change of federal government in the September 2013 elections and responsibilities for RNTBCs and their funding relocated to the Department of Prime Minister and Cabinet. Many RNTBCs find themselves pulled in multiple directions and under-resourced and unable to fully realise the priorities of their members or the expectations of other parties. Efforts to meet corporate compliance requirements often exhaust what little funding is available and many struggle to comply with imposed legislative and statutory responsibilities, significantly limiting their capacity to pursue other aspirations. Time spent managing the corporation is time not spent on country with family.

Processes for consultation over reforms have in many instances been criticised as inadequate, and the changes that have been imposed — some unwelcome — have done little to alleviate the problems created by the incommensurability of Indigenous and non-Indigenous systems of law.[162] In many respects native title remains a system that strains to reconcile seemingly incompatible interests. An ongoing tendency on the part of Commonwealth, state and territory governments to apply narrow interpretations of what native title is and how it should be managed limits the potential of what are unique native title rights and interests. Sectoral reforms have consistently failed to recognise that maximising the potential social and economic returns of native title rights requires a fundamental shift in the way governments engage with Australia's first peoples through RNTBCs.

Table 2.3 Timeline of legislation, policy, case law and events relevant to RNTBCs

1975	- *Racial Discrimination Act 1975* (Cth)
1976	- *Aboriginal Councils and Associations Act 1976* (Cth)
1984	- *Aboriginal and Torres Strait Islander Heritage Protection Act 1984* (Cth)
1989	- *Aboriginal and Torres Strait Islander Act 1989* (Cth)
1992	- *Mabo and Others v Queensland [No. 2]* (1992) 175 CLR 1
1993	- *Native Title Act 1993* (Cth)
1995	- *Land Fund and Indigenous Land Corporation (ATSIC Amendment) Act 1995* (Cth)
1996	- *Wik Peoples v Queensland* (1996) 187 CLR 1
1997	- Registration of the first RNTBC, Dunghutti Elders Council (Aboriginal Corporation) RNTBC
	- *Native Title Amendment (Tribunal Appointments) Act 1997* (Cth)
1998	- *Native Title Amendment Act 1998* (Cth)
1999	- Native Title (Prescribed Bodies Corporate) Regulations 1999
	- *Environment Protection and Biodiversity Conservation Act 1999* (Cth)
	- *Yanner v Eaton* [1999] HCA 53
2001	- Senate committee report, *Nineteenth report: second interim report for the s 206(d) inquiry – Indigenous Land Use Agreements,* released by the Parliamentary Joint Committee on Native Title and the Aboriginal and Torres Strait Islander Land Fund
	- *Commonwealth v Yarmirr* (2001) 208 CLR 1
2002	- Report to government, *Research project into the issue of funding of Registered Native Title Bodies Corporate*, released by the Aboriginal and Torres Strait Islander Commission (ATSIC) Native Title and Land Rights Centre
	- *Members of the Yorta Yorta Aboriginal Community v Victoria and Others* (2002) 214 CLR 422
	- *Western Australia v Ward on behalf of Miriuwung Gajerrong* [2002] HCA 28
2005	- *Aboriginal and Torres Strait Islander Commission Amendment Act 2005* (Cth)
2006	- Report to government, *Structures and processes of Prescribed Bodies Corporate,* released by the Attorney-General's Department Steering Committee (AGDSC)
	- *Corporations (Aboriginal and Torres Strait Islander) Act 2006* (Cth) (CATSI Act)
	- *Jango v Northern Territory of Australia* [2006] FCA
2007	- Corporations (Aboriginal and Torres Strait Islander) Regulations 2007
	- *Guidelines for basic support funding for Prescribed Bodies Corporate (PBCs),* released by the Department of Families, Housing, Community Services and Indigenous Affairs
	- *Native Title (Amendment) Act 2007* (Cth)
	- *Native Title (Technical Amendment) Act 2007* (Cth)
	- First National Meeting of RNTBCs held in Canberra
2008	- Discussion paper *Optimising the benefits of native title payments* released by the Joint Working Group on Indigenous Land Settlements
	- National Agreement, National Indigenous Reform Agreement (Closing the Gap), released by the Council of Australian Governments
2009	- Second National Meeting of RNTBCs held in Melbourne
	- *Native Title Amendment Act 2009* (Cth)
	- *Report to government, Native Title Payment Working Group Report* released by the Department of Families, Housing, Community Services and Indigenous Affairs
2010	- Discussion paper *Leading practice agreements: maximising outcomes from native title benefits* released by the Attorney-General's Department and the Department of Families, Housing, Community Services and Indigenous Affairs
	- Exposure draft 'Proposed amendment to enable the historical extinguishment of native title to be disregarded in certain circumstances' released by the Attorney-General's Department
	- Discussion paper *Native title, Indigenous economic development and tax* released by Treasury
	- *Native Title Amendment Act [No. 1] 2010* (Cth)
2011	- Native Title (Prescribed Bodies Corporate) Amendment Regulations 2011

2012	- Native Title Amendment Bill (2012)
	- Australian Charities and Not-for-profits Commission established
2013	- *Courts and Tribunals Legislation Amendment (Administration) Act 2013* (Cth)
	- Discussion paper *Review of the roles and functions of native title organisations* released by Deloitte Access Economics
	- Terms of reference, Review of the *Native Title Act 1993* (Cth), released by the Attorney-General's Department
	- *Tax Laws Amendment (2012 Measures No. 6) Act 2012* (Cth)
	- *Report to government, Taxation of Native Title and Traditional Owner Benefits and Governance Working Group: report to government* released by Treasury
	- *Charities Act 2013* (Cth)
	- *Akiba on behalf of the Torres Strait Regional Seas Claim Group v Commonwealth of Australia* [2013] HCA 33

Endnotes

1 Mer Gedkem Le (Torres Strait Islanders) Corporation RNTBC administers land on behalf of the Meriam people, who were recognised in the *Mabo* decision, *Mabo v Queensland [No. 2]* (1992) 175 CLR 1; G Lauder, 'Eyes and ears of the north: an interview with Douglas Passi, Chair of Mer Gedkem Le', *Native Title Newsletter*, no. 3, August 2012, AIATSIS, Canberra, pp. 5–6.

2 We wish to acknowledge that this chapter has been an NTRU collaboration and would like to thank Rob Powrie, Tran Tran and Nick Duff from the NTRU for their assistance, and David Martin and Angus Frith for reviewing the paper. We also wish to acknowledge extensive editorial advice and note that the authors are listed alphabetically. Any errors are of course our responsibility.

3 C Mantziaris & D Martin, *Native title corporations: a legal and anthropological analysis*, Federation Press, Sydney, 2000, p. 90.

4 When a positive native title determination is made, the court must 'at the same time as, or as soon as practicable after' make a determination about which corporation will fulfil this function, and whether it will be a trustee or agent. See *Native Title Act 1993* (Cth) (NTA), s 56(1).

5 The term Prescribed Body Corporate (PBC) derives from pt 2 div 6 of the NTA, which provides that a Prescribed Body Corporate must be determined to manage native title rights and interests. The Native Title (Prescribed Bodies Corporate) Regulations 1999 (PBC Regulations) prescribe the forms or types of bodies that may be nominated when a determination recognising native title has been made.

6 Mantziaris & Martin, above n 3, p. 90.

7 PBC Regulations, above n 5, reg 4(2)(a).

8 At time of writing, the Native Title Representative Body for the Noongar people, South West Aboriginal Land and Sea Council, is in negotiations with the Western Australian Government towards a settlement of their native title that will see them recognised as traditional owners but not as native title holders. Negotiations between the parties began in 2009 following a litigation that saw a judgment that recognised Noongar people's native title over the Perth metropolitan area overturned on appeal in April 2008; *Bodney v Bennell* [2008] FCAFC 63.

9 The first of these workshops was held in December 2006 and involved representatives from NTRBs and NTSPs to discuss issues around assisting native title claimants to establish an RNTBC. At this workshop participants reviewed the current legislative and policy context and examined various elements of RNTBC corporate design. See LM Strelein & T Tran, *Native*

Title Representative Bodies and Prescribed Bodies Corporate: native title in a post determination environment, Native Title Report, no. 2, Native Title Research Unit, AIATSIS, Canberra, 2007, pp. 4–6, 10–12, http://www.aiatsis.gov.au/ntru/documents/PBCReport.pdf, accessed 27 June 2013. Other meetings included: First National PBC Meeting, Canberra, April 2007; Second National PBC Meeting, Melbourne, June 2009; Torres Strait Regional PBC Workshops, 2007–09; Bardi Jawi Governance Project Workshop #1, Broome, May 2011; Balgo PBC Meeting, Western Australia, August 2011; Queensland PBC Meeting, Cairns, 25–27 October 2011; Victorian PBC Meeting, Melbourne, 13–14 December 2011; and South Australian PBC Meeting, Adelaide, 11–13 February 2012.

10 T Tran, C Stacey & PF McGrath, 'Background report on Prescribed Bodies Corporate aspirations', unpublished research report to Deloitte Access Economics for the FaHCSIA Review of Native Title Organisations, Native Title Research Unit, AIATSIS, Canberra, April 2013, p. 11.

11 Ibid., p. 12.

12 During national meetings of RNTBC representatives there have been repeated calls for more funds, and for those funds to be provided directly to RNTBCs, rather than being administered through NTRBs. See T Bauman & T Tran, *First National Prescribed Bodies Corporate meeting: issues and outcomes, Canberra 11–13 April 2007*, Native Title Research Report, no. 3, Native Title Research Unit, AIATSIS, Canberra, 2007, http://www.aiatsis.gov.au/ntru/docs/researchthemes/pbc/PBCMeeting2007.pdf, accessed 27 June 2013; T Bauman & C Ganesharajah, *Second National Meeting of Registered Native Title Bodies Corporate: issues and outcomes, Melbourne 2 June 2009*, Native Title Research Report, no. 2, Native Title Research Unit, AIATSIS, Canberra, 2009, pp. 8–9, http://aiatsis.gov.au/ntru/documents/PBCmeeting2009.pdf.

13 Mantziaris & Martin, above n 3, p. xviii.

14 Ibid., p. 90.

15 Ibid., p. xviii.

16 A future act is an act after 1 January 1994 (the date of the commencement of the NTA), above n 3, s 4(3)(b), which affects native title rights and interests. Future acts can include activities such as agriculture, mining exploration, public works, the grant of permits and licences and building public housing. Native title rights are protected under the future act regime, which triggers a process of notification, consultation or the right to negotiate, dependent upon the level of impact that the activity will have. The highest level of protection is the right to negotiate; however, this does not grant RNTBCs the right to veto a project or proposed activity from going ahead. Native Title Research Unit, *Native title resource guide: national*, Native Title Research Unit, AIATSIS, Canberra, 2010, p. 42, http://www.aiatsis.gov.au/ntru/docs/resources/NTRG/National2010.pdf, accessed 30 July 2013.

17 Allen Broomhead, NNTT, email to Claire Stacey, 16 March 2013.

18 Allen Broomhead, NNTT, email to Claire Stacey, 8 August 2013. For an up-to-date figure of RNTBCs, see Native Title Research Unit, 'Registered Native Title Bodies Corporate (RNTBC) summary', http://www.aiatsis.gov.au/ntru/docs/resources/issues/RNTBCsummary.pdf, accessed 22 August 2013. Note that in Queensland and Western Australia some RNTBCs relate to more than one native title determination and some determinations result in more than one RNTBC.

19 In *Fejo v Northern Territory of Australia* (1998) 195 CLR 96 at 128 [46], Chief Justice Gleeson and Justices Gaudron, McHugh, Gummow, Hayne and Callinan commented:

Native title has its origin in the traditional laws acknowledged and the customs observed by the indigenous people who possess the native title. Native title is neither an institution of the common law nor a form of common law tenure but it is recognised by the common law. There is, therefore, an intersection of traditional laws and customs with the common law. The underlying existence of the traditional laws and customs is a necessary pre-requisite for native title but their existence is not a sufficient basis for recognising native title. And yet the argument that a grant in fee simple does not extinguish, but merely suspends, native title is an argument that seeks to convert the fact of continued connection with the land into a right to maintain that connection.

20 R French, 'The role of the High Court in the recognition of native title', *Western Australian Law Review*, vol. 30, no. 2, 2002, p. 147.
21 For an explanation in the context of property law, see L Strelein, 'Conceptualising native title', *Sydney Law Review*, vol. 23, pp. 95–124.
22 See, *Western Australia v Ward on behalf of Miriuwung Gajerrong* [2002] HCA 28, and also LM Strelein, *Compromised jurisprudence: native title cases since Mabo*, Aboriginal Studies Press, Canberra, 2009.
23 Aboriginal and Torres Strait Islander Social Justice Commissioner (ATSISJC), *Native title report 2012*, Human Rights and Equal Opportunity Commission, Sydney, 2012, p. 106.
24 Actual figures are 682,334 square kilometres for non-exclusive holdings and 715,284 square kilometres for exclusive holdings. The vast majority of exclusive possession holdings are in Western Australia. JC Altman & F Markham, 'Values mapping Indigenous lands: an exploration of development possibilities', paper presented at the National Native Title Conference, Alice Springs, 3–5 June 2013, www.aiatsis.gov.au/ntru/documents/altmanmarkham.pdf, accessed 24 July 2013.
25 Sourced from National Native Title Tribunal (NNTT), 'Determinations and Native Title Prescribed Bodies Corporate map, 30 June 2013', http://www.nntt.gov.au/Mediation-and-agreement-making-services/Documents/Quarterly%20Maps/Determinations_and_PBCs_map.pdf, accessed 22 August 2013. There were also 32 determinations for which RNTBCs were yet to be advised.
26 Altman & Markham, above n 24.
27 BW Walker, D Porter & I Marsh, *Fixing the hole in Australia's heartland: how government needs to work in remote Australia*, Desert Knowledge Australia, Alice Springs, 2012, p. 90, http://www.desertknowledge.com.au/Files/Fixing-the-hole-in-Australia-s-Heartland.aspx, accessed 22 August 2013.
28 Exceptions to this include the litigated determinations of native title in Alice Springs (*Hayes v Northern Territory* [1999] FCA 1248; *Hayes v Northern Territory* [2000] FCA 671) and Broome (*Rubibi Community v State of Western Australia (No. 7)* [2006] FCA 459).
29 Altman & Markham, above n 24.
30 R Farrell, J Caitlin & T Bauman, 'Getting outcomes sooner: report on a native title connection workshop Barossa Valley July 2007', NNTT and AIATSIS, Canberra, 2010, http://www.aiatsis.gov.au/ntru/documents/GettingOutcomesSooner.pdf, accessed 19 August 2013.
31 These evidentiary requirements relate to the maintenance of traditional laws and customs under the NTA, above n 4, s 223 and the demonstration of connection to the land at sovereignty.
32 *Mabo (No. 2)*, above n 1.
33 N Duff, 'Ngadju win marks new era in the Goldfields', *Native Title Newsletter*, no. 4, Native Title Research Unit, AIATSIS, Canberra, 2013, p. 10, http://aiatsis.gov.au/ntru/documents/NativeTitleNewsletterApril13_ONLINE.pdf, accessed 23 August 2013.
34 In South Australia a state-wide approach to native title was adopted under the Agreements, Treaties and Negotiated Settlement Project (ATNS), *South Australian Indigenous Land Use Agreement (ILUA) statewide negotiations strategic plan 2006–2009*, ATNS, Melbourne, 2006, http://www.atns.net.au/agreement.asp?EntityID=5268, accessed 19 August 2013.
35 In New South Wales, many Aboriginal groups have opted to access land rights under the *Aboriginal Land Rights Act 1983* (NSW) rather than the NTA, given the impediments that many

Aboriginal groups in New South Wales face in meeting the connection requirements under the NTA.
36 *Corporations (Aboriginal and Torres Strait Islander) Act 2006* (Cth) (CATSI Act), s 37.10.
37 Ibid.
38 Office of the Registrar of Indigenous Corporations (ORIC), *Fact sheet: corporation size and financial reporting*, ORIC, Canberra, 2011.
39 ATSISJC, above n 23, p. 112.
40 Office of the Registrar of Indigenous Corporations (ORIC), 'Public register', ORIC, Canberra, www.oric.gov.au, accessed 30 June 2013.
41 PBC Regulations, above n 5, reg 4(2)(b) and (c). Reg 4(2)(d) also refers to the CATSI Act s 29.5 (and accompanying regulations) and contains an additional 'Indigeneity' requirement.
42 See Office of the Registrar of Indigenous Corporations (ORIC), *A guide to writing good governance rules*, ORIC, Canberra, 2008, p. 7, http://www.oric.gov.au/html/publications/ruleBook/ORIC-PBCs-guide_May11.pdf, accessed 30 July 2013.
43 Martin and Mantziaris also make the point that over time 'the internal composition of the native title group may evolve according to traditional law and custom in a manner not recognised in the corporate constitution's membership criteria'. Mantziaris & Martin, above n 3, p. 186.
44 G Buchanan, 'A preliminary demographic analysis of PBC directors: a basis for assessing demographic trends and implications for PBC governance', unpublished report, Native Title Research Unit, AIATSIS, Canberra, 2013, p. 13.
45 The 2011 Census indicated that 'the Aboriginal and Torres Strait Islander population had a younger age distribution than the non-Indigenous population, reflecting higher fertility and lower life expectancy. The median age (the age at which half the population is older and half the population is younger) for Aboriginal and Torres Strait Islander peoples was twenty-one years compared with thirty-seven years of age for non-Indigenous people', Australian Bureau of Statistics (ABS*), Census of population and housing — counts of Aboriginal and Torres Strait Islander Australians, 2011*, cat. no. 2075.0, ABS, Canberra, released 21 June 2012, http://www.abs.gov.au/ausstats/abs@.nsf/Lookup/2075.0main+features32011, accessed 8 August 2013.
46 Attorney-General's Department Steering Committee (AGDSC), *Structures and processes of Prescribed Bodies Corporate*, Canberra, 2006, p. 6. This document, known as the 'PBC Report', is now located on the AIATSIS website, http://www.aiatsis.gov.au/ntru/docs/researchthemes/pbc/Guidelines2007.pdf, accessed 30 July 2013.
47 The term 'common law holder' is equivalent to the term 'native title holder' and is defined under s 56(2)(a) of the NTA, above n 4.
48 The term 'future act' is defined under the NTA, above n 4, s 4(3)(b); area agreements are set out at NTA, above n 4, ss 24CA–24CL.
49 NTRBs are organisations appointed by the Minister for Families, Housing, Community Services and Indigenous Affairs under provisions in pt 11 of the NTA, above n 4, to perform the mandatory roles and functions set out in s 203B of the NTA. Section 203FE of the NTA also allows the Australian Government to fund a person or body to perform the functions of an NTRB without the recognition in pt 11 of the Act. This allows for NTSPs to provide services identified in s 203B. Most NTRBs are incorporated under the CATSI Act while NTSPs are usually incorporated under the Corporations Act.
50 Pt 2 div 6 of the NTA, above n 4, sets out the process for the determination of a PBC. See Mantziaris & Martin, above n 3, ch. 5 for a detailed discussion of trust and agency relationships.
51 Mantziaris & Martin, above n 3, p. 157.
52 As at 31 March 2013, 52 per cent of all RNTBCs nationally had opted to be trustees. However, there are noticeable jurisdictional preferences. For example, all RNTBCs in the Northern

Territory are agents, as are most in South Australia. In contrast, in Western Australia 24 of 25 RNTBCs act as trustees. Native Title Research Unit, above n 18.

53 It appears from *Hansard* that the original government proposal had been for all the mandated bodies corporate to hold the native title on trust, but in response to negotiations with 'the Aboriginal representatives', the government had agreed to allow native title holders the option of not having their rights and interests held on trust by a corporation. The Prime Minister of the day, Paul Keating, stated, 'There will still be a body corporate which will act as a representative body for native title holders'. Australia, House of Representatives, *Parliamentary debates*, 22 December 1993, p. 4541.

54 CATSI Act, above n 36, ss 85.1 and 633.5.

55 AGDSC, above n 46, pp. 8–9; N Duff & JK Weir, *Weeds and native title: law and assumption*, Rural Industries Research and Development Corporation (RIRDC) research report, RIRDC, Canberra, 2013.

56 T Bauman & T Tran, above n 12, pp. 7–12; T Tran, C Stacey & P McGrath, above n 10, pp. 11–12.

57 P Sullivan, *Belonging together: dealing with the politics of disenchantment in Australian Indigenous policy*, Aboriginal Studies Press, Canberra, 2011, p. 55.

58 For further analysis of the intersection of state and federal native title regimes, see LM Strelein & T Tran, 'Building Indigenous governance from native title: moving away from "fitting in" to creating a decolonised space', *Review of Constitutional Studies*, forthcoming. See also Farrell et al., above n 30, for an analysis of state and territory regimes in assessing native title connection requirements, though this analysis now requires updating.

59 D Ritter, *Contesting native title: from controversy to consensus in the struggle over Indigenous land rights*, Allen & Unwin, Crows Nest, NSW, 2009, pp. 172–6.

60 Parliamentary Joint Committee on Native Title and the Aboriginal and Torres Strait Islander Land Fund, *Nineteenth report: second interim report for the s.206(d) inquiry – Indigenous Land Use Agreements*, Parliament of Australia, Canberra 2001, http://www.aph.gov.au/Parliamentary_Business/Committees/Senate_Committees?url=ntlf_ctte/completed_inquiries/1999–02/report_19/report/contents.htm, accessed 5 August 2013.

61 M Rashid, D Martin, P Hunter & J Khatri, *Research project into the issue of funding of Registered Native Title Bodies Corporate* (known as the Rashid Report), Aboriginal and Torres Strait Islander Commission, Canberra, 2002.

62 Ibid., p. 4, Executive summary.

63 Ibid., p. 5, Executive summary. The report's authors proposed four possible funding models: direct; NTRB; regional RNTBC support centre; and regional RNTBC support centre special purpose corporations funding model. See report for details.

64 Ibid., p. 2, Executive summary. The Rashid Report noted that there could be at least 58 RNTBCs by the end of the 2005–06 financial year and 75 by the end of the 2007–08 financial year. However, there were only 45 RNTBCs by the end of 2006 and 54 by the end of 2007.

65 Agreements, Treaties and Negotiated Settlement Project (ATNS), 'Aboriginal and Torres Strait Islander Commission (ATSIC)', ANTS, Melbourne, http://www.atns.net.au/agreement.asp?EntityID=618, accessed 30 July 2013.

66 National Congress of Australia's First Peoples, *Congress member organisations*, http://nationalcongress.com.au/organisations/, accessed 22 August 2013.

67 See details about the reform process on the Attorney-General's Department website, 'Native title reform', http://www.ag.gov.au/www/agd/agd.nsf/Page/Indigenouslawandnativetitle_Nativetitle_2007NativeTitlereforms, accessed 6 June 2009.

68 AGDSC, above n 46.

69 Ibid., Recommendations, pp. 3–4.
70 Ibid. Recommendations 1–4, 9, 10, 12 and 14 did not require any legislative action. The *Native Title Amendment Act 2007* addresses recommendations 5 and 7, and the *Native Title Amendment (Technical Amendments) Act 2007* addresses recommendations 11 and 15. For a detailed analysis of the 2007 amendments see A Frith & A Foat, *The 2007 amendments to the* Native Title Act 1993 *(Cth): technical amendments or disturbing the balance of rights?*, Native Title Research Monograph, no.3, Native Title Research Unit, AIATSIS, Canberra, 2008, http://www.aiatsis.gov.au/ntru/docs/other/2007Amendments.pdf, accessed 25 September 2013.
71 The Closing the Gap initiative was announced in 2008 as a broad-scale policy strategy aimed at addressing Indigenous disadvantage in response to a recommendation made in the 2005 *Social justice report*. Closing the Gap targets are predominantly focused on health and education indicators, but include improving employment outcomes for Indigenous people. The approach focuses on six 'building blocks': early childhood; schooling; health; economic participation; healthy homes; safe communities; and governance and leadership. Department of Families, Housing, Community Services and Indigenous Affairs (FaHCSIA) website, 'Closing the gap', http://www.fahcsia.gov.au/our-responsibilities/indigenous-australians/programs-services/closing-the-gap, accessed 31 July 2013. Native title also featured in FaHCSIA's *Indigenous economic development strategy 2011–2018*, http://www.fahcsia.gov.au/sites/default/files/documents/09_2012/ieds_2011_2018.pdf, accessed 22 August 2013.
72 J Macklin, *Beyond Mabo: native title and closing the gap*, Mabo Lecture presented at James Cook University, Townsville, 21 May 2008, http://www.nswbar.asn.au/circulars/macklin.pdf, accessed 30 July 2013.
73 See LM Strelein, *Taxation of native title agreements*, Native Title Research Monograph, no. 1, Native Title Research Unit, AIATSIS, Canberra, 2008, http://www.aiatsis.gov.au/ntru/docs/researchthemes/developmenttax/taxation/TaxationAgreements.pdf, accessed 25 September 2013.
74 Aboriginal and Torres Strait Islander Social Justice Commissioner (ATSISJC), *Native title report 2007*, Human Rights and Equal Opportunity Commission, Sydney, 2008, p. 25, https://www.humanrights.gov.au/sites/default/files/content/social_justice/nt_report/ntreport07/pdf/ntr2007.pdf, accessed 25 September 2013.
75 Aboriginal and Torres Strait Islander Social Justice Commissioner (ATSISJC), *Native title report 2010*, Human Rights and Equal Opportunity Commission, Sydney, 2010, Chapter 3, https://www.humanrights.gov.au/publications/native-title-report-2010-chapter-3-consultation-cooperation-and-free-prior-and-informed, accessed 31 July 2013.
76 Department of Families, Housing, Community Services and Indigenous Affairs (FaHCSIA), 'Native Title Organisations Review', http://www.fahcsia.gov.au/our-responsibilities/indigenous-australians/programs-services/native-title-organisations-review-0, accessed 31 July 2013.
77 Attorney-General's Department (AGD), 'Australian Law Reform Commission native title inquiry', 2013, http://www.ag.gov.au/consultations/pages/AustralianLawReformCommissionnativetitleinquiry.aspx, accessed 19 August 2013.
78 Please note that the amendments changed from 2010 to 2011 because of the time delay in implementation.
79 Department of Families, Housing, Community Services and Indigenous Affairs (FaHCSIA), *Native Title (Prescribed Bodies Corporate) Amendment Regulations 2011 information sheet*, http://www.fahcsia.gov.au/sites/default/files/documents/08_2012/native_title_2011.pdf, accessed 31 July 2013.
80 Native Title (Prescribed Bodies Corporate) Amendment Regulations 2011 (No. 1), http://www.austlii.edu.au/au/legis/cth/num_reg/ntbcar20111n257o2011685.
81 Ibid., regs 3(1)(a) and 3(1)(b); AGDSC, above n 46, recommendation 5, p. 3.

82 Inserting an alternative consultation process into an RNTBC rulebook requires the consent of the native title group under new reg 8(1)(d), FaHCSIA, above n 79, pp. 2–3.
83 PBC Regulations, above n 5, reg 8(1)(b), (c) and (d); Explanatory Statement, Select Legislative Instrument 2011 No. 257, pp. 2–3.
84 FaHCSIA, above n 79, p. 3.
85 David Martin, email to Pam McGrath and Claire Stacey, 6 August 2013.
86 FaHCSIA, above n 79, p. 3.
87 See NTA, above n 4, ss 59A (1) and (2), and PBC Regulations, above n 5, reg 5.
88 FaHCSIA, above n 79, pp. 1–2.
89 AGDSC, above n 46, p. 22; National Native Title Council (NNTC), submission to the Senate Committee on Legal and Constitutional Affairs' inquiry into the Native Title Amendment (Technical Amendments) Bill 2007, NNTC, 2007, p. 4; see also Frith & Foat, above n 70, p. 89; AIATSIS, submission to FaHCSIA on the draft Native Title (Prescribed Bodies Corporate) Amendment Regulations 2010, AIATSIS, Canberra, 2010; Native Title (Prescribed Bodies Corporate) Amendment Regulations 2011 (the PBC Amendment Regulations).
90 See Minerals Council of Australia (MCA), submission to the Senate Committee on Legal and Constitutional Affairs' inquiry into the Native Title Amendment (Technical Amendments) Bill 2007, MCA, 2007, p. 2. The MCA argued that funding for core statutory functions should be provided by government.
91 New div 7 s 60AB(2) of the NTA, above n 4, provides for the PBC Regulations, under new reg 20, to specify other functions for which a fee may be charged. New section 60AC gives the Registrar of ORIC the authority to give an opinion, in writing, on whether a fee is one that the RNTBC may charge, in response to a written request, under new reg 21. The RNTBC and the third party are able to request a reconsideration of this opinion within a certain time period under new reg 23, and the registrar may request further information about the dispute, as outlined under new regs 24 and 25. A decision of this type by the registrar can be reviewed by the Administrative Appeals Tribunal, and the time period for a fee in dispute is set out under new reg 26. FaHCSIA, above n 79, pp. 5–6.
92 The NTA, above n 4, s 57(2)(c), states that 'if no prescribed body corporate is nominated in accordance with the request, the Federal Court must, in accordance with the regulations, determine which prescribed body corporate is to perform the functions'. See also Mantziaris & Martin, above n 3, p. 96.
93 The Indigenous Land Corporation (ILC) was established in 1995 under the *Land Fund and Indigenous Land Corporation (ATSIC Amendment) Act 1995* (Cth) as part of a Commonwealth Government response to the *Mabo* decision, which also included the NTA and the establishment of the NNTT. The ILC's role is to buy or manage land for providing economic, environment, social and/or cultural benefit to Indigenous people, particularly the many Indigenous people who are unlikely to benefit from the native title claims process. Indigenous Land Corporation, 'ILC at a glance', http://www.ilc.gov.au/About-Us, accessed 25 July 2013.
94 The FaHCSIA information sheet sets out these changes as 'new regulation 11 and ss 57(2)(c) and 60(b) of the NTA'; FaHCSIA, above n 79, p. 4.
95 Ibid.
96 P Sullivan, *Policy change and the Indigenous land corporation*, AIATSIS Research Discussion Paper, no. 25, AIATSIS, Canberra, 2009, http://www.aiatsis.gov.au/research/docs/dp/DP25.pdf.
97 Department of Families, Housing, Community Services and Indigenous Affairs (FaHCSIA), *Australian Government discussion paper: optimising benefits from native title agreements*, FaHCSIA, Canberra, 2008, http://www.fahcsia.gov.au/sites/default/files/documents/05_2012/native_title_discussion_paper_0.pdf, accessed 23 August 2013.

98 See, for example, Aboriginal and Torres Strait Islander Justice Commissioner, submission by the Aboriginal and Torres Strait Islander Social Justice Commissioner to the Australian Government's native title payments discussion paper, Australian Human Rights Commission, Sydney, 2009, http://www.humanrights.gov.au/native-title-payments-discussion-paper-optimising-benefits-native-title-agreements, accessed 6 November 2013; submission to the Optimising Native Title Benefits Review, Law Council of Australia, Sydney, 2009; Altman, JC & Jordan, K, *A brief commentary in response to the Australian Government discussion paper 'Optimising benefits from native title agreements' and the* Report of the Native Title Payments Working Group, CAEPR Topical Issue, no. 03/2009, Centre for Aboriginal Economic Policy Research, Australian National University, Canberra, 2009; Tax Institute, Optimising benefits from native title agreements, Tax Institute of Australia, Sydney, 2009.

99 J Macklin & R McClelland, *Leading practice agreements: maximising outcomes from native title benefits*, FaHCSIA, Canberra, 2010, http://www.fahcsia.gov.au/our-responsibilities/indigenous-australians/publications-articles/land-native-title/leading-practice-agreements-maximising-outcomes-from-native-title-benefits, accessed 8 July 2013.

100 Ibid., p. 6.

101 Ibid., pp. 8–11.

102 Ibid., pp. 12–14. The requirement in s 31 of the NTA, above n 4, to negotiate 'in good faith' is designed to ensure that proponents negotiate with native title groups with a view to reaching agreement. The right to negotiate provisions (subdiv P) amount only to a right to be consulted. Where future act negotiations break down, they can be referred to the NNTT for arbitration; see NTA, above n 4, s 27. However, to date the NNTT has decided in favour of native title applicants on only three occasions, the most recent, in 2011, in Western Australia where applicants did not want a number of mining leases to proceed because of the spiritual significance of the area. See *Weld Range Metals Limited/Western Australia/Ike Simpson and Others on behalf of Wajarri Yamatji* [2011] NNTTA 172.

103 A Cresswell & A Mooney, submission to the Treasury on the *Native title, Indigenous economic development and tax* consultation paper and *Leading practice agreements: maximising outcomes from native title benefits*, Reconciliation Australia, Canberra, December 2010, p. 11, http://www.treasury.gov.au/~/media/Treasury/Consultations%20and%20Reviews/2010/Native%20Title%20Indigenous%20Economic%20Development%20and%20Tax/Submissions/PDF/Reconciliation_Australia.ashx, accessed 31 July 2013.

104 Department of Treasury, *Native title, Indigenous economic development and tax* consultation paper, Department of Treasury, Canberra, 2010, http://www.treasury.gov.au/~/media/Treasury/Consultations%20and%20Reviews/2010/Native%20Title%20Indigenous%20Economic%20Development%20and%20Tax/Key%20Documents/PDF/CP_Native_Title_IED_and_Tax.ashx, accessed 1 August 2013.

105 Ibid.

106 Charitable trusts are limited by the restrictions placed on the use of a trust fund for charitable purposes, which does not always align with providing benefits to individuals related by blood (such as native title holders) and particularly where there are aspirations to use such funds to support the development of businesses. See, for example, Agreements, Treaties and Negotiated Settlement Project (ATNS), submission to Department of Treasury on Indigenous economic development and tax, ANTS, Melbourne, May 2001, p. 12, http://www.treasury.gov.au/~/media/Treasury/Consultations%20and%20Reviews/2010/Native%20Title%20Indigenous%20Economic%20Development%20and%20Tax/Submissions/PDF/ATNS.ashx, accessed 25 July.

107 Minerals Council of Australia (MCA), *Indigenous economic development from mining agreements: a response to the Treasury consultation paper* Native title, Indigenous economic development and

tax *and the Joint Attorney-General and Minister for Families, Housing, Community Services and Indigenous Affairs discussion paper* Leading practice agreements: maximising outcomes from native title benefits, MCA, November 2010, p. 14, http://www.treasury.gov.au/~/media/Treasury/Consultations%20and%20Reviews/2010/Native%20Title%20Indigenous%20Economic%20Development%20and%20Tax/Submissions/PDF/MCA.ashx, accessed 19 August 2013.

108 Attorney-General's Department (AGD), *Native title tax treatment to be examined*, media release, AGD 18 March 2013, http://www.attorneygeneral.gov.au/Mediareleases/Pages/2013/First%20quarter/18March2013-NativeTitletaxtreatmenttobeexamined.aspx, accessed 19 August 2013.

109 D Bradbury, J Macklin & M Dreyfus, *Native title amendments pass the parliament*, media release no. 118, 26 June 2013, D Bradbury website, http://ministers.treasury.gov.au/DisplayDocs.aspx?doc=pressreleases/2013/118.htm&pageID=003&min=djba&Year=&DocType=0, accessed 31 July 2013.

110 Ibid.

111 The Working Group noted that it supports the ICDC model for two main reasons:

First, an ICDC could be used by Indigenous communities to provide financial support for a wider range of community or economic development activities than is possible using other entities such as a charitable trust. It could contribute to developing the local Indigenous community by building local and regional businesses and social ventures that create flow-on economic and social development opportunities, particularly job creation. It could also encourage cooperative approaches in which holders of land-related payments can work as co-investors with governments and the private sector in delivering holistic regional development projects.

Department of Treasury, *Taxation of native title and traditional owner benefits and governance working group: report to government*, July 2013, http://www.treasury.gov.au/PublicationsAndMedia/Publications/2013/Taxation-of-Native-Title, accessed 19 August 2013.

112 Ibid., p. 6.

113 Kathryn Matthews, pers. comm. with PF McGrath and C Stacey, 14 August 2013.

114 Australian Charities and Not-for-profits Commission (ACNC), 'Not-for-profits (NFP) reform', http://www.acnc.gov.au/ACNC/About_ACNC/NFP_reforms/Reform_agenda/ACNC/Edu/NFP_Agenda.aspx, accessed 1 August 2013.

115 Explanatory memorandum, Charities Bill 2013 and Charities (Consequential Amendments and Transitional Provisions) Bill 2013, p. 5.

116 This was achieved by including the exception 'where the purpose of an entity that has land-rights related assets would fail a public benefit test solely because the entity directs benefits to indigenous Australians who are related, the purpose is treated as being for the public benefit'; ibid., p. 8.

117 C Stacey & J Fardin, *Housing on native title lands: responses to the housing amendments of the Native Title Act*, Land, Rights, Laws: Issues of Native Title, vol. 4, no. 6, AIATSIS, Canberra, 2011.

118 Ibid.

119 Formerly known as the Office of the Registrar of Aboriginal Corporations (ORAC), then the Office of the Registrar of Aboriginal and Torres Strait Islander Corporations (ORATSIC), and now Office of the Registrar of Indigenous Corporations (ORIC).

120 See *Corporations (Aboriginal and Torres Strait Islander) Consequential, Transitional and Other Measures Act 2006* (Cth).

121 Office of the Registrar of Indigenous Corporations (ORIC), 'Fact sheet: get in on the Act', http://www.oric.gov.au/html/publications/CATSI-Act/Get-in-on-the-Act_DLbooklet_Jan2010.pdf, accessed 19 August 2013.

122 Explanatory memorandum, Corporations (Aboriginal and Torres Strait Islander) Bill 2005, para 3.13, http://www.comlaw.gov.au/Details/C2005B00112/Explanatory%20Memorandum/Text, accessed 19 August 2013.
123 Ibid., para 3.14.
124 See CATSI Act, above n 36, pt 7.
125 Explanatory memorandum, above n 122, para 3.16.
126 In 2007, just under half (49 per cent) of all RNTBCs were not compliant. By October 2008 this number had fallen to 14.8 per cent. Anthony Bevan, Registrar of Indigenous Corporations, cited in Aboriginal and Torres Strait Islander Social Justice Commissioner (ATSISJC), *Native title report 2008*, Human Rights and Equal Opportunity Commission, Sydney, 2009, p. 40. As at 25 March 2011, eight of 77 RNTBCs (or 10 per cent) were listed as in breach of 2009–10 reporting requirements. Office of the Registrar of Aboriginal and Torres Strait Islander Corporations (ORIC), 'List of non-compliant corporations', http://www.oric.gov.au/html/List_non-compliant-corps_2011-03-25a.xls, accessed 3 April 2011.
127 ATSISJC, above n 126, pp. 40–1.
128 For example, at the time of writing at least five Australian jurisdictions were undertaking reviews of cultural heritage legislation to account for the emerging native title sector, including New South Wales, Victoria, Tasmania, Western Australia and South Australia.
129 E Wensing & J Taylor, *Secure tenure options for financing home ownership and economic development possibilities on Aboriginal land subject to native title: the case of Aboriginal Lands Trust reserve lands in Western Australia*, AIATSIS Research Discussion Paper, no. 31, AIATSIS, Canberra, 2012; and T Tran, LM Strelein, JK Weir, C Stacey, & A Dwyer, *Native title and climate change: changes to country and culture, changes to climate: strengthening institutions for Indigenous resilience and adaptation*, National Climate Change Adaptation Research Facility, Gold Coast, 2013.
130 Ibid.
131 Parliamentary Joint Committee on Native Title and the Aboriginal and Torres Strait Islander Land Fund, above n 60; Rashid Report, above n 61; AGDSC, above n 46.
132 AGDSC, above n 46.
133 Department of Families, Housing, Community Services and Indigenous Affairs (FaHCSIA), *Guidelines for basic support funding for Prescribed Bodies Corporate*, Land Programs Branch, Canberra, June 2013, p. 6, http://www.nativetitle.org.au/documents/FaHCSIA_PBCBasicSupportGuidelines2013.PDF, accessed 31 July 2013.
134 ATSISJC, above n 23, pp. 112–13.
135 Ibid., p. 112.
136 Altman & Markham, above n 24.
137 AGDSC, above n 46, p. 17.
138 ATSISJC, above n 23, p. 113
139 See above n 9.
140 M George, 'Making the black tape stick: environmental legislation & environmental offsets', presentation to the National Native Title Conference, Alice Springs, 4 June 2013, http://www.aiatsis.gov.au/ntru/documents/MelissaGeorge.pdf, accessed 31 July 2013.
141 Department of Industry, Innovation, Climate Change, Science, Research and Tertiary Education, 'Carbon farming initiative', http://www.climatechange.gov.au/reducing-carbon/carbon-farming-initiative, accessed 19 August 2013.
142 Bauman & Tran, above n 12, pp. xii–xiii, 39–40.
143 FaHCSIA, above n 133.
144 Ibid., p. 14.
145 Gina Howlett at FaHCSIA, pers. comm. with C Stacey, 19 February 2013.

146 Bauman & Tran, above n 12, p. x.
147 FaHCSIA, above n 76.
148 See Bauman & Tran, above n 12, p. 22. Although the limitation was removed from the Funding Agreement, a few NTRBs and NTSPs continued to think that it still existed.
149 NTRBs and NTSPs have the same powers and functions, as set out in s 203B of the NTA, above n 4. These include facilitation and preparation of native title claims, certification of applications for native title determinations and of the registrations of ILUAs, dispute resolution, notification of other claims and future acts, agreement-making, internal review and other functions conferred by the NTA or by any other law largely concerned with cooperation between NTRBs, consulting with Indigenous communities, and providing education to Indigenous communities on native title matters.
150 Deloitte Access Economics, *Review of the roles and functions of native title organisations discussion paper*, June 2013, Canberra, p. 25, https://www.deloitteaccesseconomics.com.au/uploads/File/DAE_NTOR%20Discussion%20Paper.pdf, accessed 31 July 2013.
151 Bauman & Ganesharajah, above n 12.
152 *Jango v Northern Territory of Australia* [2006] FCA 318.
153 Bauman & Ganesharajah, above n 12.
154 Ibid.
155 A half-day meeting prior to the conference was attended by 49 RNTBC representatives, representing 36 RNTBCs from Queensland, New South Wales, Victoria, South Australia, the Northern Territory and Western Australia; however, it was a much smaller scale than previous national meetings held in 2007 and 2009 due to a lack of funding to support a meeting and the increased costs of providing travel assistance to the growing number of RNTBCs.
156 At the time of writing only four RNTBCs were organisational members of Congress.
157 This was discussed following a conference presentation by Indigenous lawyer Tony McAvoy. T McAvoy, 'Building an assembly of first nations', presentation to the National Native Title Conference, convened by AIATSIS, Alice Springs, 3 June 2013.
158 See Native Title Services Victoria (NTSV), 'Prescribed Bodies Corporate', http://ntsv.com.au/prescribed-body-corporates/, accessed 28 July 2013.
159 Gur A Baradharaw Kod Torres Strait Sea and Land Council Torres Strait Islander Corporation, *Rule book*, Torres Strait Islander Corporation, Thursday Island, 2012, http://www.oric.gov.au/PrintCorporationSearch.aspx?corporationName=sea%20and%20land%20council&icn, accessed 8 July 2013.
160 M O'Rourke & V Cooms, 'Quandamooka native title determination', *Native Title Newsletter*, no. 4, July/August, AIATSIS, Canberra, 2011, p. 3, http://www.aiatsis.gov.au/ntru/docs/publications/newsletter/JulyAug11.pdf, accessed 8 August 2013, accessed 19 August 2013.
161 D Campbell & J Hunt, *Community development in Central Australia: broadening the benefits from land use agreements*, CAEPR Topical Issue, vol. 7, no. 201, CAEPR, ANU, Canberra, 2010.
162 The notion of 'incommensurability' between Indigenous and non-Indigenous systems of meaning in the context of native title management is explored further in Mantziaris & Martin, n 3, pp. 29–33.

Chapter 3

Native Title Bodies Corporate in the Torres Strait: finding a place in the governance of a region

Lisa M Strelein

Four brothers in individual canoes came from Tuger in Op Deudai (from what is now known as Irian Jaya). They were Malo, Sigai, Siu and Kolka. At Iama, the anchor on Sigai's canoe dragged and remained there forming the religion of Sigai. At Aurid, Kolka remained to form his own religion leaving Siu and Malo to travel on to Masig. At Masig, Siu remained and formed his cult. Malo travelled on and eventually arrived at Mer [where the religion of Malo began].

Tom Mosby[1]

This legend is one of many stories of the ancestral heroes who formed the cultures, religions and laws of the peoples who inhabit the more than 100 islands of the Torres Strait.[2] The legend of the four brothers reflects some of the complexity of social and political organisation within the Torres Strait, developed over 3000 years of habitation. The idea of who protects and enforces Ailan Kastom — the customary laws and traditions of the people of the region[3] — is of interest in the analysis of Torres Strait governance which this chapter undertakes. Consistent with the long-held vision of regional autonomy, all the institutions of governance, including their enabling instruments, purport to recognise and leave room for the exercise of Ailan Kastom, but they do not do so entirely. The dominant framework for decision-making for each of the many governance bodies that characterise Torres Strait governance emanates from 'western law' and is external to customary law. Between them, these institutions establish competing regimes which, in the end, can marginalise customary law because it is at the same time the responsibility of everybody and nobody.

The Torres Strait is the birthplace of native title, which was first recognised in Australian law in relation to the Meriam people's claim to title over their islands under Malo's law.[4] The Torres Strait has 19 Registered Native Title Bodies Corporate

(RNTBCs),[5] the bodies corporate required to be established under the *Native Title Act 1993* (Cth) (NTA) to hold and manage native title in trust or as agents of the native title holders.

This chapter examines the extent to which native title has changed or failed to change the geopolitics of the region. I examine the relationships between native title and the institutions of governance that cast a complex net over the people of the Torres Strait. I illustrate the tensions through a critical study of the key issues that have occupied RNTBCs in the Torres Strait over a number of years. I draw particular attention to the conflicts between RNTBCs and the Torres Strait Islands Regional Council (TSIRC), which was established in 2008 as the local government authority of the region, and the Torres Strait Regional Authority (TSRA), which is a unique Commonwealth authority administering programs in the region. The discussions centre on issues of tenure and representation against a backdrop of regional self-determination and self-government. I examine the options currently before the leaders of the Torres Strait to resolve the tensions, and I take into account that a much deeper examination of the meaning of native title and the struggle for autonomy is required to untangle the history of administration and to refocus the shared imperative to protect the unique culture, identity and sovereignty of the people.

The regular regional meetings of Torres Strait RNTBCs that occurred between 2007 and 2009 and the exchanges of RNTBC members with all levels of government at those meetings inform the discussion. Meetings took place on Waiben in December 2007; at Masig in April–May 2008; at Badu in March–April 2009; on Waiben from 15 to 19 June 2009; and on Mer in November 2009. The discussion also draws on reports from those meetings and associated discussions as well as ongoing discussions I have had with key landowners over a number of years. At the Masig meeting it was agreed that I should write a paper about these meetings and native title in the Torres Strait.[6]

A snapshot of the region

This section introduces the geography and history of the region. Individual islands have legal and political differences; some religious and philosophical traditions are shared across four 'clusters' of islands or nations; and similar laws and customs are shared across the whole of the Strait.[7] The cultural groupings of the four nations also reflect the geography of the region. The western islands of Mualgal, including Moa, Badu and Mabuiag, are the remains of the land bridge between Moegy Daudai (Papua New Guinea (PNG)) and the Koey Daudai (Cape York Peninsula) more than 8000 years ago. The islands feature weathered granite surrounded by mangroves, shallow seas and sandbanks. The large low-lying northern islands of Gudamaluigal, including Boigu, Dauan and Saibai with their swamps and mangroves, were formed by the deposit of silt into the Strait from the confluence of rivers in PNG. Kulkalgal, the central islands, include the habitable islands of Iama, Poruma, Warraber and Masig, as well as those no longer permanently inhabited, such as Tudu and Aurid and dozens of smaller islets and quays among the small low-lying coral islands. Meriam Mir, the eastern islands, are remnant volcanoes with rich fertile soils, the largest of which form the Mer group (Mer, Waier and Daur) and include Erub and Ugar, which enjoy rich vegetation. By far the greatest resource in the region is the sea, with its diversity of marine fauna (see Figure 3.1).[8]

Trade, particularly among the unfertile central islands and others, was extensive and required shared laws and customs relating to rights of passage and fishing. Traditional trading routes extended into PNG, across western Cape York and down the eastern seaboard.[9] The peoples of the Torres Strait have a close relationship with the Kaurareg, who hold native title over the inner islands of Ngurupai (Horn Island) and Muralug (Prince of Wales Island) and are traditional owners of Kiriri (Hammond Island) and Waiben (Thursday Island), the administration centre for the region.

The regional sea claim lodged by the Torres Strait Islander peoples in 2001 asserted a single identity and societal structure for the purposes of native title over the seas of the Torres Strait.[10] Ironically, this regional identity as a single society was rejected by the Commonwealth in its opposition to the sea claim despite the recognition of the distinct cultural identity of Torres Strait Islanders in Australian law and policy, including recognition of the Torres Strait flag as an official flag of Australia. This opposition is a reflection of the Commonwealth's interest in the seas and, in particular, the shipping lanes of the region.[11]

The Torres Strait, or more particularly the seas of the Torres Strait, was of interest to European mariners and explorers as early as 1569, with its existence confirmed in 1608 and reaffirmed by Cook in 1770. On 22 August 1770 the island of Tuined was renamed Possession Island and claimed for the British Crown. As an important passage from eastern Australia to Asia, the Strait has seen much naval traffic since the early 1800s despite the perils of the shallow seas which have wrecked many ships.[12]

By far the greatest cultural shift in the Torres Strait occurred when the London Missionary Society landed on Erub on 1 July 1871 and was welcomed by the warrior chief Dabad and paramount chief Amani.[13] The missionaries brought with them newly evangelised Pacific Islanders who acted as intermediaries. The Church of England established its first mission on Moa, and the date of the first Christian religious ceremony, 1 July 1871, is still celebrated annually by many in the region as 'the coming of the Light'.[14]

The presence of the church and influx of the Pacific Islanders, together with other nationalities involved in the early fishing industries, introduced new styles of song and dance and influenced the religion of the Torres Strait Islanders. The religions or hero cults, such as Kuiam (western islands), Waiet (Mabuiag and Mer), Gelam

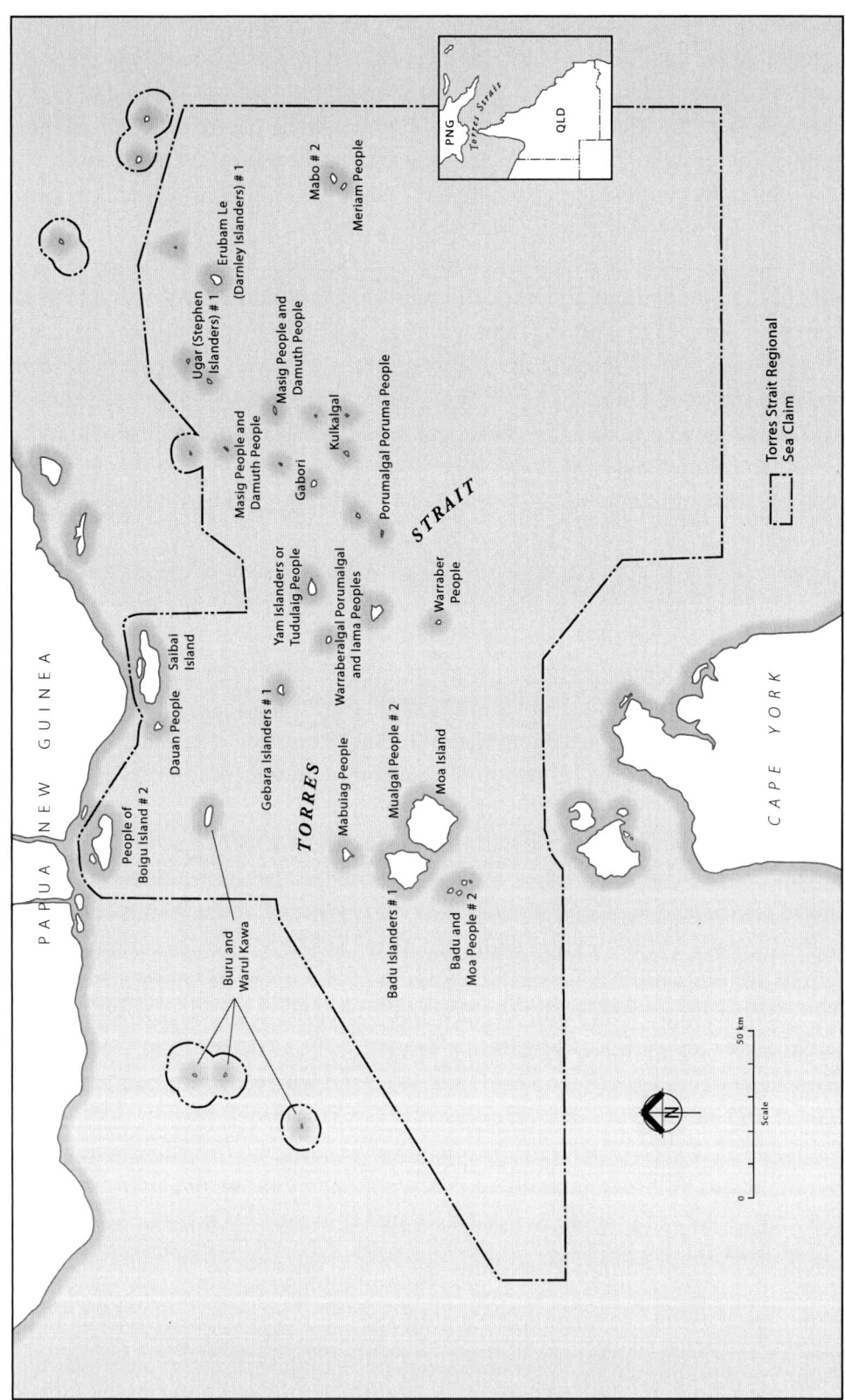

Figure 3.1 Native title determinations in the Torres Strait. National Native Title Tribunal (NNTT) 'short' names for determinations have been used in this map; for a full reference see Table 3.1. Map by Brenda Thornley for AIATSIS

(Moa and Mer) and Malo-Bomai (eastern islands), were displaced, and by the time the Cambridge Anthropological Expedition came through the Torres Strait in 1898, the region was predominantly Christian, although elements of the original religious traditions continued. Significantly, performance, ritual, laws and philosophies retained their importance and were shared with the researchers.[15]

The arrival of the Pacific Islander groups also had an influence on the language spoken in the Torres Strait, as did the later maritime community, particularly those involved with pearling. A blended pidgin emerged, which has become known as *umplatok* (Torres Strait Kriol), the predominant language now spoken in the Torres Strait. The traditional languages are still spoken but are considered endangered.[16] English only began to be widely spoken in the 1990s and is now the main language of education, while traditional language and cultural programs predominate in the Tagai school system in the region.[17]

The Torres Strait was 'annexed' to the colony of Queensland progressively (in 1872 and 1879) by executive order of the Queensland Colonial Secretary.[18] This incorporated a distinct cultural group into the history of Australian colonisation. The Queensland Government sought to administer the region through local inhabitants, appointing chiefs, or *mamooses*, who were often not the hereditary chiefs of the islands. From 1898 Administrator John Douglas instituted elected councils on each island, which also sat as island courts.[19] Douglas managed to exempt Torres Strait Islanders from the restrictive regime of the *Aboriginals Protection and Restriction on the Sale of Opium Act 1897* (Qld) until 1911, when the protector of Aborigines required all Torres Strait Islanders employed in the pearl shell industry to be taken under the permit system and their wages were retained. In 1936 the famed Maritime Strike saw Torres Strait fishermen bring the industry to a halt for weeks. A meeting of Torres Strait Councils at Masig in 1937 led to Torres Strait Islanders being distinguished from Aboriginal people, and local government and island courts were incorporated into the *Torres Strait Islanders Act 1939* (Qld).[20]

The laws and customs in relation to lands and waters, many of which trace back to the religious cults, remain a strong part of societal organisation and intellectual traditions of Torres Strait Islanders and form a system of laws and norms that continue to be observed throughout the region.[21] However, this system of law and custom is not predominantly a religious system, and in *Akiba* Justice Finn noted that 'the laws and customs of present concern are informed in quite some degree by considerations of utility and practicality'.[22] It is on the strength of these continuing laws and customs that the people of the Torres Strait have successfully asserted native title over almost all the land and sea of the region and secured a level of autonomy that is unique in Australia.

Governing institutions of the Torres Strait

Getano Lui Jnr, then Chair of the TSRA, once reflected that as Torres Strait Islanders, 'we are probably the most over consulted, over researched group of people in Australia… we are also over-governed'.[23] Overlaying the complex traditional social and political structures, the governance of the Torres Strait under Australian law is similarly multi-layered and complicated, integrating international, Commonwealth, state and local government regimes over Ailan Kastom, the Indigenous system of law and custom. This section introduces the all-important institutional framework for governance in the region. This multi-level regime, which has been described as 'beyond the normal tenets of federalism',[24] includes seven levels of governance for around 8000 people:

1. Torres Strait Protected Zone Joint Authority (PZJA)
2. Torres Strait Regional Authority (TSRA)
3. Australian Government
4. Queensland Government
5. Torres Strait Islands Regional Council (TSIRC) and Torres Shire Council (TSC)
6. Registered Native Title Bodies Corporate (RNTBCs)
7. Ailan Kastom.

Adding to this complexity, Will Sanders highlighted the importance of understanding the hybrid governance arrangements based on both Indigenous and resident status in the Torres Strait, especially in relation to the more densely populated inner islands (in particular, the seat of administration, Waiben) where the non-Indigenous population approaches 50 per cent.[25] At the 2011 Australian Census, the population of the Torres Strait Islands was 7489 (down from an estimated 8089 in 2006), of whom 5787 identified as Torres Strait Islander or as both Torres Strait Islander and Aboriginal (including 3610 living in the outer islands). The same census identified 46,826 Torres Strait Islanders residing outside the region.[26] This diaspora has an interest in more political autonomy for the Torres Strait for a variety of reasons and, importantly, many hold native title interests in the region as traditional landowners or as part of the broader common law native title holding group.[27]

The seven levels of governance outlined below illustrate the complex geopolitical landscape in which native title operates and through which the people of the Torres Strait have had to navigate a role for RNTBCs.

Torres Strait Protected Zone Joint Authority

At an international level the Torres Strait Treaty, a bilateral treaty between Australia and PNG, gives the PZJA authority over fishing activities in the Torres Strait.[28] The PZJA consists of the Commonwealth and state ministers and the Chair of the TSRA. The treaty contains express provisions for the protection and preservation of the interests of Indigenous inhabitants of the Torres Strait, including free movement and the pursuit of customary rights.[29] The role of the PZJA is significant because fishing is the largest industry in the Torres Strait — worth approximately $10.6 million per annum — although benefits flowing back to the Torres Strait are minimal.[30]

Torres Strait Regional Authority

The TSRA was established in 1994 as a model of regional autonomy alongside the regional councils and national representative structure of the Aboriginal and Torres Strait Islander Commission (ATSIC). Although ATSIC and the regional council structure were abolished in 2005, the TSRA survived. The TSRA describes itself as an elected arm and an administrative arm with its functions set out in the *Aboriginal and Torres Strait Islander Act 2005* (Cth) (ATSI Act).[31] These functions include, among others, the recognition and maintenance of Ailan Kastom of Torres Strait Islanders; formulation, implementation and monitoring of programs for Aboriginal people and Torres Strait Islanders living in the region; development of policy in the region; and the protection of cultural heritage.[32] The TSRA is also the Native Title Representative Body for the Torres Strait region and in this capacity exercises functions pursuant to div 3 of the NTA. These functions include facilitating claims for determinations of native title and for compensation, assisting native title holders in negotiations and consultations, and assisting the resolution of disputes within groups over claims or negotiations. The TSRA has its main offices on Waiben, and in 2012 had a budget of $56,338,000 and employed 127 staff.[33]

Australian Government

Like any other area in Australian territory, the Torres Strait is subject to Commonwealth laws unless provided otherwise (for example, by way of the Torres Strait Treaty). The TSRA performs most of the functions and programs of the Australian Government in the region. However, Commonwealth defence, immigration, customs and quarantine agencies also operate in the region, as well as Australia Post and Telstra. Taxation and social security matters also require Commonwealth agencies to have an interest in the region, though they do not necessarily have a strong presence. Regulatory bodies, particularly the Office of the Registrar of Indigenous Corporations (ORIC), which regulates the governance and compliance of bodies that have been incorporated under the *Corporations (Aboriginal and Torres Strait Islander) Act 2006* (CATSI Act), also have interests in the area. While the TSRA has a direct relationship with the Minister for Indigenous Affairs, the minister also receives advice on the TSRA and the region from the Department of Families, Housing, Community Services and Indigenous Affairs (FaHCSIA).[34]

Queensland Government

The Torres Strait is also subject to Queensland state laws. The Queensland Government is responsible for education, health, housing, infrastructure, policing and law enforcement. The state government owned energy company Ergon and retail outlet Island Board of Industry Services (IBIS) are monopoly providers. Importantly, Queensland property law also applies in the Torres Strait, primarily under the *Torres Strait Islander Land Act 1991* (Qld) (TSILA).

Torres Strait Islands Regional Council and Torres Shire Council

Local government has had an important place in the history of self-determination in the Torres Strait. Elected island councils were established in 1898, and in 1903 the TSC was formed to provide local administration. In most circumstances (except Mer), the island councils held statutory land rights tenure over the islands and all conducted community-based enterprises, owned community assets and coordinated or delivered most services and, as a result, most of the employment.[35] As landowners, the councils also granted permission to enter and conduct activities on the islands and surrounding waters. There were 16 island councils, one for each inhabited island. The island council chairs together formed the Island Coordinating Council, which in turn formed the TSRA Board.[36]

Under an amalgamation process in 2007, the island councils were replaced in March 2008 by individual councillors elected from each island community, who together form the TSIRC. The TSC remained,[37] having replaced the state government administrator in 1991 to form the local government for the inner islands, mainly Waiben, Ngurupai, Muralug and a small part of the northern peninsula area of Cape York. The members of the TSIRC (with the exception of the mayor) also formed the majority of the TSRA Board up until 2012, when the first elections were held for each organisation. The TSIRC includes 15 island communities and its administrative headquarters are located in Cairns and Waiben. Each councillor is supported by a three-person community forum, which also convenes as a land panel when land matters are to be discussed.[38] The community forum is responsible for meeting with the community to discuss issues relating to trust land, planning, the delivery of services and culture, but it has no decision-making power and councillors are not bound by its advice.

Under s 9 of the *Local Government Act 2009* (Qld), a local government has the power to 'do anything that is necessary or convenient for the good rule' of its local government area. Moreover, when exercising a power, a local government may *take account of* Torres Strait Island custom.[39] Under the previous legislation, local island councils' powers were defined somewhat more specifically as the 'good rule and government thereof *in accordance with* the customs and practices of the islanders concerned'.[40]

Registered Native Title Bodies Corporate

There are 19 RNTBCs in the Torres Strait—13 community island RNTBCs and six uninhabited island RNTBCs.[41] Their functions are set out in the NTA, in native title regulations and in their own constitutions (or rule books) under the CATSI Act. For example, the Mer Gedkem Le constitution contains specific reference to upholding the *Zogo* (custom) and *Malo ira Gelar* (Malo's law) 'for good governance, desired welfare status and ongoing progress of the Meriam people'. Others refer to ensuring that the interests and wellbeing of the people, including those of the individual common law holders of native title, are paramount. At the Masig meeting of RNTBCs in 2008, most RNTBCs were familiar with their rule books, but few were aware of the details of their determinations and the rights and interests recognised; that is, the rights and interests that they are obligated to manage and protect.

Ailan Kastom

Ailan Kastom emerges in the context of the TSRA, local government and RNTBCs' functions and responsibilities. However, none of these entities displace the separate operation of traditional laws and governance in the region. The native title determinations across the region recognise the continued operation of Ailan Kastom. In *Akiba* the claimants argued that foundational principles, such as descent, reciprocity and exchange, and territorial control gave rise to a complex system of rules that constitute the legal and social order of the Torres Strait.[42] The court repeatedly acknowledged the voluminous evidence of the continued operation of the laws and customs, including in areas of marriage and adoption, trade and property law.

Given the strength of the customary law, its fierce assertion by the TSRA on behalf of native title holders and its ready recognition by other levels of government, it is somewhat surprising to observe the lack of formal integration of these laws, and the rights and interests they convey, into the governance structure of the Torres Strait. The progressive realisation of native title over the islands and seas of the region has resulted in an uncomfortable geopolitical landscape littered with governance frameworks.

Native title in the Torres Strait

By 2005 nearly all the islands of the Torres Strait had been determined as native title lands. All the determinations are for exclusive possession,[43] and all were resolved by consent (with the exception of the original Meriam people's High Court case and the most recent regional sea claim discussed later in this chapter). The rights and interests recognised under most of the determinations include a very broad statement of the rights and interests enjoyed under native title, akin to those found in *Mabo (No. 2)*,[44] as the right to possession, occupation, use and enjoyment of all land in the determination area to the exclusion of all others.[45] Some determinations include a more detailed list of rights, such as Porumalgal, which includes rights to:

(a) live on the determination area;
(b) conserve, manage, use and enjoy the natural resources of the determination

area for the benefit of the common law holders including for social, cultural, economic, religious, spiritual, customary and traditional purposes;

(c) maintain, use and manage the determination area for the benefit of the common law holders, that is to:
   (i) maintain and protect sites of significance to the common law holders and other Aboriginal people, Papuans and Torres Strait Islanders on the determination area;
   (ii) inherit, dispose of or give native title rights and interests in the determination area to others, being members of the common law holders pursuant to their traditional laws and customs;
   (iii) decide who are the native title holders provided that such persons must be Torres Strait Islanders within the meaning of that term in the *Native Title Act 1993* (Cth);
   (iv) regulate among, and resolve disputes between, the common law holders in relation to the rights of possession, occupation, use and enjoyment of the determination area;
   (v) conduct social, religious, cultural and economic activities on the determination area; and

(d) make decisions about and to control the access to, and the use and enjoyment of, the determination area and its natural resources being animal, plant, fish and bird life found on or in the determination area from time to time and all water, clays and soils found on or below the surface of the determination area and all other matter comprising the determination area excluding minerals and petroleum and any other natural resources provided that these exclusions shall operate only to the extent to which native title has been extinguished or affected pursuant to laws of the Commonwealth and of the State of Queensland.[46]

All the consent determinations in the Torres Strait have the consent of the parties to the claim, including the state government. They are subject to the interests of the various levels of governments in the region but are expected to be:

> exercisable concurrently…but in those circumstances where they cannot be so exercised, the entitlements of the holders of the other interests may regulate, control, curtail, restrict, suspend or postpone the exercise of those native title rights and interests.[47]

Since the success of the *Mabo* case, the TSRA has focused on and been successful in establishing native title 'as against the world', with all but four claims resolved. Following the successful determinations over the islands, a region-wide sea claim, the Torres Strait Regional Sea Claim, has dominated the work of the TSRA Native

Title Office (NTO). In July 2010 Justice Finn of the Federal Court recognised native title rights and interests of Torres Strait Islanders over their seas, finding that, while the common law is unable to recognise exclusive rights over the seas, the Torres Strait Islanders nevertheless have rights to access, remain in and use their marine territories and all of their resources.[48] Finn J found that there is a single Torres Strait Islander society whose laws and customs are shared, although rights and interests are held at the community level.[49]

The successful assertion of native title reflects the continued observance and enforcement of traditional laws and customs in relation to land and waters. When I arrived in Poruma, the first outer island I visited in the Torres Strait, I was told a simple rule: 'never move a coconut'.[50] In the central islands, the coconut tree is a life source, providing food, drink, clothing and shelter. The trees take up to 40 years to grow and are therefore an investment for future generations. As Kris Lui Billy says, new coconuts are cultivated and placed to take root for this purpose:

> We collect the coconuts that fall from the trees and put them in piles underneath the tree or somewhere else. When these coconuts start to shoot, we often go and plant them either in our own area or in a place that everybody uses. This way there will be coconuts in the future. I myself have planted coconuts on our family's land, but also in places that everybody uses, such as Bet Island. If someone breaks down over there, they will have something to eat and to drink.[51]

Coconut trees likely belong to the traditional owners of a place and often mark boundaries of property, though the significance of laws and customs, ownership, trespass and sustainability has different manifestations across islands. When heading to Mer, I was warned not to touch anything. Everything belongs to the person on whose land you walk. I had heard this law when reading about the *Mabo* case — under Meriam law, Malo's law, the rule is stated as *tag mauki mauki, teter mauki mauki* ('keep your hands to yourself; do not touch the property of others').[52] The boundary markings, and this fundamental trespass law, were key elements in the evidence for the original *Mabo* case.

The other central tenet is one of reciprocity and balance. In the sea claim, Finn J recognised the normative framework of reciprocity operating in the Torres Strait but held that it was not recognised or protected by native title because it is a law in relation to persons, not a law 'in relation to land' as required by the NTA.[53] This point was the subject of cross appeal by the claimants. I am not convinced that the notion of reciprocity and balance is so easily separated from the laws and customs in relation to land and waters — property law itself is fundamentally premised not on regulating our relationships with things but on the relationships between people in relation to things.[54] Reciprocity and balance in relation to the environment, for example, regulates the use and distribution of resources. But perhaps consistent with his Honour's views in relation to commercial use of resources, once something is taken from the land or waters, its use and the regulation of that use is no longer a native title concern but a matter of the laws of the group with regard to social relations.

Regional meetings of Torres Strait RNTBCs

In response to a national meeting of RNTBCs in Canberra in 2007, AIATSIS was invited by the TSRA to facilitate a similar meeting at the regional level for Torres Strait RNTBCs. Only a few Torres Strait Islander representatives had attended the national meeting in light of the distinct funding and policy environment in the Torres Strait, and a regional meeting would enable more participation of RNTBCs on the islands in discussion tailored to their concerns. The first meeting, held on Waiben in December 2007, focused on regional particularities but had similar aims to those of the national meeting to:

- provide an opportunity for RNTBCs to meet and build networks
- provide RNTBCs with access to information about relevant funding and programs
- offer opportunities to develop relationships with relevant government agencies
- provide input into policy issues.[55]

The two issues that dominated the meeting and engaged significant energy from the RNTBCs and their legal representatives were, not surprisingly:

- the looming changes to the *Local Government Act 2009* (Qld) to amalgamate all the island councils in a single Torres Strait Islands Regional Council
- the changes to TSILA.[56]

Following that meeting, the RNTBCs of the region met regularly (at least twice each year) for the following three years, supported by additional funding from the TSRA. They met with the then Queensland Department of Environment and Resource Management, the then Commonwealth Department of Environment, Water, Heritage and the Arts,[57] the PZJA, ORIC, the Aboriginal and Torres Strait Islander Social Justice Commissioner (ATSISJC) and advisers to the Attorney-General, among others. They also met with representatives of various TSRA programs, including the Land and Sea Management Unit and the Economic Development Unit, and with the chair and native title portfolio holder of the TSRA Board. The meetings were also an important opportunity to gain information and discuss regional issues with the legal team from the TSRA NTO and the RNTBC Support Officer of TSRA, whose position was created to assist in building capacity among Torres Strait RNTBCs.

In addition to the aims described above, the group prioritised the need to talk among themselves about the challenges they were confronting, and the purpose of these meetings was reframed by the RNTBCs to focus on:

- empowerment of RNTBCs
- gaining and sharing knowledge and information
- developing understanding of native title
- building relationships
- having input into issues affecting native title.[58]

At the third meeting of the RNTBCs, on Badu in March 2009, the actions of the group coalesced around three core objectives:

- communication and education
- ownership of land
- representation.[59]

In the following sections I examine these core objectives and the related issues that have arisen for RNTBCs in the Torres Strait. The issues surrounding institutional arrangements and, importantly, the relationships between native title holders and the government have some unique characteristics in the Torres Strait that give rise to interesting questions of recognition, accommodation and integration of traditional laws and customs. I begin, though, with the issue of capacity, which underpins all other issues and is common to many RNTBCs around the country.

Organisational capacity

RNTBCs in the Torres Strait, like many of their counterparts on the mainland, continue to seek basic functionality in terms of resourcing and access to advice and support. They are expected under the Native Title Prescribed Bodies Corporate Regulations 1999 (PBC Regulations) to operate independently and be responsive to the needs of governments and others seeking access to their lands, but are without the resources to do so. Moreover, they are expected to mediate the interests of common law native title holders in relation to any proposed activity that may affect their native title rights and interests. Corporate compliance responsibilities also overburden RNTBCs in the Torres Strait, most of which are trustee corporations under the CATSI Act. Compliance with even the most minimal reporting obligations, including annual general meetings (AGMs), has been a challenge for most RNTBCs in the region, particularly those uninhabited island RNTBCs whose membership is spread across a number of island communities.

A major task for the TSRA RNTBC Support Officer was to assist RNTBCs to transition to new constitutions in accordance with the requirements of the CATSI Act. Most, if not all, RNTBCs have now participated in ORIC training, which provides a framework for good board governance and regulatory compliance.[60] But the corporate capacity of Torres Strait RNTBCs — their ability to undertake the 'business' of being an RNTBC — remains low. Presently, most Torres Strait RNTBCs operate out of someone's home or workplace — hence, one of the most pressing concerns for the RNTBCs has been basic functionality; that is, an office or corporate presence in the community and the capacity to engage with external demands and the internal expectations of the RNTBCs. This glaring need was amplified by the weight of issues on the agenda of the regional meetings that required urgent attention.

At the Waiben meeting a number of participants expressed frustration that previous regional traditional owner meetings had made resolutions and recommendations that governments had failed to act on. For example, it was noted that the Ngalpun Malu Kaimelan Gasaman Cultural Maritime Summit hosted by TRAWQ[61] Community Council in March 2001 made 22 resolutions,[62] few of which were perceived to have been implemented. The stark reality was reiterated that when an action was proposed at RNTBC meetings, no one else was going to action it or resource the group to do it.

A key foundational principle for the meetings, then, was that in order for things to change, the group needed to focus on action plans for RNTBCs to assert their own self-management, without reliance on intervention from any level of government. This development of specific actions and allocating responsibilities for carry through was a hallmark of the meetings. With the limited support that could be provided by the TSRA RNTBC Support Officer and legal advice from the TSRA NTO, immediate action needed to be taken where possible, either at the meetings themselves or referred to smaller working groups. However, despite the willingness and enthusiasm of the chairs and governing bodies of the RNTBCs, the lack of corporate capacity limited their ability to progress issues between meetings.

The TSRA has made some attempts to specifically fund RNTBCs over the years. Initially it tried to mirror the approach of the Commonwealth on the mainland in relation to RNTBC support, or lack thereof; that is, that RNTBCs would not receive Commonwealth funding for organisational needs or statutory functions.[63] However, this TSRA policy position was a somewhat simplistic and outdated 'adoption' of the mainland policy, which was ostensibly based around the allocation of funding to and prioritisation of native title claims resolution within NTRBs — in the Torres Strait only four claims remain unresolved.

Over the period of the regional meetings, the TSRA did reallocate resources from other programs to provide support and capacity building which was focused on the meetings, governance and other training, but until 2011 there was no funding directly available for their operations. A 2010–11 internal review of the TSRA's support for native title bodies resulted in a change of policy to allow a small amount of direct funding to RNTBCs for operational costs.[64] Through this funding, the TSRA assisted RNTBCs to establish bank accounts and obtain email addresses. Each RNTBC received a multi-function office machine (phone/fax and printer/copier) but a donation of two computers per RNTBC from a pro bono law firm was hindered by bureaucratic problems.

While the fact remains that there is no specific Commonwealth program funding for RNTBCs, FaHCSIA — the department responsible for NTRBs and RNTBCs — has set aside a portion of native title program funding for mainland RNTBCs. These RNTBCs can now apply for up to $100,000 each year (although normally for no more than $50,000). The total cost of the program is around $2 million per annum.[65] If the TSRA was to mirror this approach, RNTBC funding in the Torres Strait alone would equal this amount given the number of RNTBCs. Yet the TSRA (like FaHCSIA) has received no additional funding to support such a program.

Other sources of revenue perhaps more common on the mainland, such as mining and exploration agreements, have been unavailable to Torres Strait RNTBCs, although this may change with the recognition of sea rights in the Torres Strait Regional Sea Claim. Some small-scale agreements made by RNTBCs with developers such as Ergon Energy have resulted in 38 Indigenous Land Use Agreements (ILUAs) in the region, particularly for telecommunications and power.[66] The implications of the new infrastructure provisions under s 24JAA of the NTA may further exacerbate this low activity base if the Queensland and Commonwealth governments apply to expedite the process under the NTA to undermine the minimal negotiating power available to native title groups.[67] But, with an Ergon Energy lease yielding perhaps $30,000 over 30 years, the financial benefits are limited.

New provisions that allow RNTBCs to charge fees for their services in relation to native title obligations[68] might provide some RNTBCs in the Torres Strait with some revenue. To respond specifically to and take advantage of these new rules the TSRA piloted a toolkit for establishing RNTBCs as, in effect, small businesses. The toolkit covers issues such as the development of a fee structure, service charter, foundational (establishment) budget, invoicing and recordkeeping. Mer Gedkem Le piloted the toolkit and found the process both enlightening and empowering, and sought to institute much of the practice with support from a small business development specialist and the TSRA RNTBC Support Officer. Mer Gedkem Le hosted the fifth meeting of RNTBCs on Mer in November 2009 under its new framework and the model was shared with the other RNTBCs, including one-on-one sessions with an adviser. However, the current low level of activity for Torres Strait RNTBCs may provide limited opportunities to operationalise these practices.

Nevertheless, this small business / fee-for-service model is important in the Torres Strait given the size of the RNTBCs and the way some of the customary practices affect distribution of compensation, which may require monies to be paid directly to the traditional landowners affected by any future acts. However, the extent to which RNTBCs can build communal wealth in order to draw funds for their operations is severely inhibited. The biggest challenge in implementing a fee-for-service model lies in changing the expectations of those wishing to deal with RNTBCs, particularly government agencies accustomed to receiving free services from RNTBCs.[69]

Some RNTBCs have looked at diversifying their roles in order to cross-subsidise their native title functions. The *Torres Strait Islander Cultural Heritage Act 2003* (Qld) which was under review in 2009 as part of a regular review cycle, presented one such option. At the Masig meeting, the Department of Natural Resources and Water (later the Department of Environment and Resource Management) invited RNTBCs to apply to become the registered cultural heritage bodies for their areas. With the lure of automatic start-up funding of $10,000 and opportunities for project funding, a number of RNTBCs took up this option, though the funding turned out to be illusory.[70] A number of roles relating to cultural heritage management are clearly sympathetic with the RNTBCs' native title / land management roles.

On the same principle of cross-subsidisation, RNTBCs in the Torres Strait often talk about establishing or taking over community enterprises to support the RNTBC and the community.[71] However, the relationship between RNTBCs and such enterprises is vexed. ORIC training and leading practice advice has suggested for some time that commercial activity should be kept separate (in a separate corporate entity) from native title holding activities, yet the limited resources within many Torres Strait Island communities may make multiple corporate structures difficult to sustain.

Even in the context of the more commonly accepted forms of cross-subsidisation or diversification of funding, such as land management programs, there is a challenge in overcoming the 'incapacity spiral'. In 2004 Ron Day, then Chairman of the Mer Island Council, reflected on the difficulties of establishing and maintaining a functioning RNTBC, saying that RNTBCs inhibit economic and community development.[72] At the same time, Councillor Day was publicly criticised by the RNTBC chair for failing to support the Mer Gedkem Le RNTBC.

Despite all these shortcomings, slowly RNTBCs have begun to establish a presence on the islands. Mer Gedkem Le included provision for offices in negotiations with the Department of Education over a new school site. Similarly, Masigalgal negotiated permanent office space as part of an agreement to build a new town hall, and Badulgal negotiated with the council for shared office space and staff. Ugar Gedkem Le took advantage of training programs to appoint someone to a part-time clerical position.[73]

Experience elsewhere, and common sense, would suggest that an office and corporate personality for RNTBCs would not only assist external stakeholders in accessing RNTBCs, but would also alleviate internal tensions between the RNTBC and the community of native title holders.[74] It would also give the community a place to ask questions, seek information and lodge complaints. Moreover, it would physically integrate RNTBCs into communities. Staffing is also seen as crucial if RNTBCs are to effectively carry out their responsibilities as landholders and native title managers.

RNTBCs have no corporate track record of grant management, let alone of running an enterprise, and are therefore assumed to have no capacity to administer a grant or program; but without these opportunities they will never develop the capacity. Partnerships are the key to overcoming this cycle; but here, too, there is reluctance to direct funding and administrative responsibility to RNTBC partners. If one partner is completely incapacitated, conflict is almost inevitable. The presumption of incapacity, however, belies the experience of the native title holding community, as a whole, with community enterprise and self-government activities.

With overlapping territorial jurisdiction among governing institutions in the Torres Strait, coordination and communication is critical. It is imperative that RNTBCs in the Torres Strait have access to resources to give effect to their roles within the region.

Communication and education

Discussions at the RNTBC meetings identified a breakdown in communication and relations with other governing bodies in the Torres Strait and a lack of shared understanding of appropriate protocols, the rights and responsibilities of RNTBCs and their appropriate roles in the governance of the Torres Strait, particularly in the wake of the amalgamation of the island councils in March 2008.

At the Badu meeting of the Torres Strait RNTBCs, there seemed to be a concern among RNTBCs that their communities in some instances had developed an unhealthy distrust of native title. RNTBCs were seen as either holding up developments, wanting 'compensation', wanting something for nothing or representing a push for power by a few. The lack of RNTBC capacity exacerbates this problem, but so do the practices and expectations of the TSRA, the TSIRC and the Queensland Government. RNTBCs have often been consulted as part of a 'community consultation', with no opportunity for native title obligations, interests and concerns to be addressed directly. RNTBCs must seek legal advice on most issues due to the complexity of their own responsibilities, powers and rights. Taking into account the complexity of rights and responsibilities for land management and administration in the region, this inevitably creates delays. Tensions are exacerbated by the fact that RNTBCs, quite legitimately and necessarily, seek compensation for new projects, often on behalf of the particular traditional landowner affected by a future act. However, the TSIRC and Queensland departments have been reluctant to pay compensation or other payments and benefits for community infrastructure.[75]

The lack of RNTBC organisational capacity and the level of respect shown to RNTBCs by the governing institutions on the islands combine to impact, in some instances, the relationship between the RNTBC and the community of native title holders. The successful claiming of native title and handing down of each determination has been a source of community pride and celebration, but the operationalising of native title on the ground has not always enjoyed the same level of community support. When expectations of RNTBCs are not met, there is frustration on all sides.

To address the breakdown in communication, RNTBCs at the Badu meeting placed a high priority on education and awareness-raising for the RNTBC office holders, native title holders and the broader community.

Ownership of land

While exclusive possession native title exists over all the islands of the Torres Strait, the inhabited islands also have statutory land rights tenure — the Deed of Grant in Trust (DOGIT) (with the exception of Mer).[76] The DOGITs were originally held by the island councils in trust for the benefit of the Torres Strait Islander inhabitants. In 2007, at the same time as the establishment of the TSIRC was announced,[77] the Queensland Government began to re-examine its legislative regime for Indigenous-held land in the state to respond to the recognition of coexisting native title rights.

As a result of the amalgamation, the DOGITs are now held by the TSIRC. The misalignment of exclusive possession native title and DOGIT trusteeship is problematic because it vests land management responsibilities in two entities at one time. Even more problematic is the fact that the land ownership occurs at different levels of abstraction. When the island councils were amalgamated to form a single regional council, the land titles, assets and enterprises of the councils transferred to the new TSIRC. There was no consultation with the RNTBCs about the transfer and no consideration of the impact of such transfers on the enjoyment of native title. There was also no consultation with the community about the transfer of the DOGITs, as required by the TSILA.[78]

The TSILA provides for certain lands to be transferred to Torres Strait Islander communities, including DOGITs, reserves and available Crown land. One positive change to the TSILA in 2008 was to allow the minister to transfer land to an RNTBC.[79] This was a response to complications in relation to the resolution of broader land settlements where a separate land trust would have to be established to receive the land transfer meant as part of the native title settlement.[80] The automatic transfer on amalgamation did not allow for processes under the TSILA to be followed and options for transfer to be considered. This effectively required retrospective negotiations.

However, while these positive provisions were being discussed, there was also a policy imperative to facilitate government access to native title lands also held under the TSILA, in particular for infrastructure development and private ownership. In 2007 the Queensland Government began consultation on amendments to the TSILA, designed to:

- encourage home ownership and provide leases for public housing
- provide more certainty of tenure in townships and assist the transfer process for DOGIT land areas outside townships

- encourage economic development in Indigenous communities
- facilitate the construction of public infrastructure.

As a result, the amendments provided for:

- long-term lease options (up to 99 years) for Indigenous land for residential purposes, public housing, commercial purposes or public infrastructure
- the ability to gazette certain lands as non-transferable under the TSILA
- the introduction of expedited compulsory acquisition powers.[81]

These changes would have a significant impact on the interests of native title holders on the islands and, although a round of 'consultations' occurred between February and April 2009 including presentations by the Queensland Government to the RNTBC meetings in Masig and Waiben, concerns were raised by the TSRA NTO and RNTBC participants about the inadequacy of the consultation process. The NTO and RNTBCs were critical of the Queensland Government's presumption that consultation with the TSIRC was sufficient; indeed, there was no guarantee that the TSIRC would consult with the island communities or the RNTBCs in particular. The RNTBCs argued that there was a presumption of reliance on a governance structure (the island councils) that no longer existed.[82]

The impact of this process on the legitimacy (if not legality) of agreements entered into prior to the amalgamation is troubling to some. One RNTBC office holder expressed concern about the agreements signed between the previous island council and the RNTBC with consent of the elders, as they did not anticipate that the council would disappear and the assets and enterprises of the island would be transferred to a regional body.

At the regional meetings of RNTBCs it was clearly expressed that all DOGITs should be transferred to the RNTBCs or first offered to RNTBCs for consultation on the appropriate outcome. The Queensland Government also seemed to presume this to be the best option. Indeed, the TSILA is structured with this presumption in mind. As a result, it allows for an RNTBC to hold transferred land on behalf of the whole community. Nevertheless, the minister, in deciding whether to transfer land to the RNTBC, may have regard as to whether any Torres Strait Islanders particularly concerned with the land (other than native title holders) may be adversely affected by the transfer. Negotiations towards the transfer of lands under DOGITs have begun, in the first instance focusing on Badulgal. However, this transfer alone could take more than two years to settle; and while it might be expected that this case will establish some precedents and processes, the timeframe may still be unsatisfying for RNTBCs and the island communities.

The strong desires of RNTBCs notwithstanding, the transfer of DOGIT lands or other land titles should not be undertaken lightly or uncritically, since the TSIRC currently undertakes additional responsibilities and there are potentially significant financial implications for RNTBCs. As landowners, s 46 of the TSILA imposes various obligations in relation to the management and maintenance of trust lands and improvements, including pest and weed control, as well as requirements for the development of a plan of management and financial accountability requirements. There is a risk of RNTBCs taking over responsibilities of land ownership without access to resources to discharge their responsibilities and attend to related matters. Any transfer of title should also include an agreement to fund these activities; funding should follow function. However, the funding provided to TSIRC is provided under the Queensland Local Government Grants Commission.[83] The grants are a financial contribution (in lieu of rates) to meet general operating costs, such as staff salaries and other administrative needs incurred by shire councils in the provision of essential services and community policing, including financial administration. RNTBCs are not currently recognised as municipal bodies, so the same arrangement cannot be made automatically; hence another form of funding agreement may be required. Such an agreement would also need to take into account additional costs associated with the nature of the transfer; for example, the potential imposition of land taxes and insurance (again as a consequence of land not being held by a municipal government).

The related issue of whether RNTBCs should take on the previously community-owned enterprises and assets is even more uncertain. There is some concern about taking on the land ownership without the income provided by community economic enterprises, particularly in light of the fact that RNTBCs are not resourced to carry out their functions. The decisions left for the communities in the wake of these changes are difficult. The RNTBCs have not developed a corporate capacity, although the communities themselves have experience with local self-administration. Moreover, there is still unwillingness on the part of the TSIRC to invest in the capacity of RNTBCs by transferring substantial assets and commercial enterprises.

Land tenure and Indigenous title

At the regional meetings it was important to ensure that the information being conveyed to the group was accurate and provided from a native title and Torres Strait perspective. At a number of meetings there was concern that government presenters were not sufficiently prepared (for example, in researching the tenure structure in the region). The provision of inaccurate information to RNTBCs significantly impacts the kinds of decisions they might make and the long-term sustainability of the decisions. Of even more concern, however, was the explanation of policy based on the firm belief of governments, in this case the Queensland Government, that native title is non-proprietary.[84] Moreover, there is a presumption on the part of many governments that any void or absence of Crown tenure must be filled.

At the first meeting on Waiben, I was appalled by the graphic description given by the state government representative of the relationship between native title and what he described as 'real' tenures. In Figure 3.2, adapted from a diagram drawn on a whiteboard, the 'real tenures', such as freehold, leasehold and DOGIT, were regarded as ownership of the land. Native title, in contrast, was presented as a 'layer of regulation', much like land planning regulation or environmental regulation. These regulations, it was said, limit the way traditional owners can exercise their rights as the owners of land.

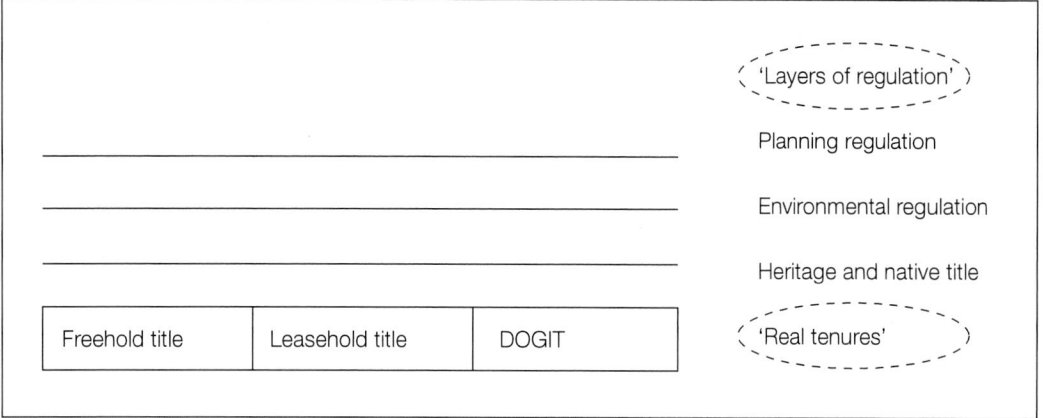

Figure 3.2 Misrepresenting native title: the Department of Natural Resources and Water's representation of native title as a layer of regulation, first meeting of PBCs of the Torres Strait, Waiben, December 2007

To represent native title in this way is not only disrespectful to native title holders as traditional owners of land whose proprietary claim on the land has been recognised to have survived colonisation, it is also legally misleading. It suggests that native title can coexist as a regulatory layer over freehold or leasehold land, which, presently, it cannot. It suggests that DOGIT and leasehold are somehow similar in their effect on native title, which they are not. This idea was repeated in a subsequent discussion of the TSILA review that purported to 'allow' and encourage native title holders to apply for a grant of a 99-year lease from the DOGIT so that they finally 'own their own land'.[85]

It is technically true that native title is not tenure under English property law traditions. But native title has been deliberately described as unique under Australian law to avoid limiting or pigeonholing native title according to English common law notions. Importantly, in *Akiba* Finn J recognised that, within the communal native title, a system of tenure exists under traditional law and custom.[86] That is, Ailan Kastom determines the allocation and transmission of rights and interests over defined areas. Yet, the system of governing interests in land in the Torres Strait has not moved to accommodate traditional ownership rights and, instead, has maintained a level of competition between the two systems of property.

To this end, in the Torres Strait and across Australia there is pressure to 'resolve tenure', which is usually shorthand for replacing (or 'overlaying') native title with something more familiar to the Australian property system. This contradicts the whole point of the *Mabo* decision, by which native title was intended to recognise the right of Indigenous peoples to inherit their property and by which Indigenous systems of property were not to be discriminated against in favour of common law understandings. The High Court founded the recognition of native title on the concepts of 'justice and human rights (especially equality before the law)'.[87] But this principle of equality is lost in practice and is a frustration to native title holders. Dan Mosby, Chair of Kulkalgal RNTBC, explained: 'I see DOGIT and native title as being on the same level, not one on top of the other, not native title underneath DOGIT.'[88]

If we cannot find the space within our legal system for recognised native title to operate effectively then it is imperative that the statutory title be aligned with native title. The resources that may flow from the alignment of native title and DOGIT are a significant consideration. Few government agencies currently pay rent or lease payments to RNTBCs in the Torres Strait region. The Queensland Government introduced a policy in 2009 prescribing that all government agencies on Indigenous land should pay a reasonable rent. However, the conflict in land ownership and management responsibilities creates confusion as to who is entitled to receive the rent. Indeed, in the case of Mer, until recently the state government itself could claim to receive the payments as trustees (beneficial title holders) of the state government reserve. If the title to the lands is transferred to an RNTBC (or, indeed, is withdrawn), the RNTBC will clearly be the owner of land under the *Land Act 1994* (Qld). In accordance with s 63(2), the owner of land can charge 'appropriate rent'. However, proposals for transfer of DOGIT lands have sought to exclude town areas where many services will be located.

In *Mabo*, the High Court declared that Murray Island was not Crown land within the meaning of s 5 of the *Land Act 1962* (Qld). It held that the trustee's rights under the reserve do not include the 'power to interfere with the rights and interests in land possessed…under native title'.[89] Statutory land rights and reserves held for the benefit of Aboriginal and Torres Strait Islander peoples have been held to be consistent with, and even protective of, native title. Nevertheless the duality of 'ownership' creates significant issues in the exercise of rights and makes decisions about access and use of land difficult.

A community forum was held on Mer Island in April 2009 to discuss the TSILA reforms and the potential for Mer to be granted a Torres Strait Islander Land Tenure under the new Act, which would replace the existing reserve. The meeting illustrated the tensions when tenure reform is discussed. The last remaining applicant from the *Mabo* case, Fr Passi, sat with the other senior members of the community, dressed in formal attire, and heard from the Queensland Department of Environment and

Resource Management that the Meriam Le did not actually 'own' their land. It was stated that in 1912 the Crown declared the Murray Islands to be a reserve 'for the use of the Aboriginal inhabitants of the state'.[90] Under Australian law, then, the State of Queensland owns the beneficial title in the land of Mer as the trustee.

It was evident that those at the meeting were quietly outraged by the suggestion that they did not own their land. They questioned why they had gone to the High Court in *Mabo*. The High Court had said that they owned their land. An immediate intention was that the reserve should be revoked rather than transferred as trust land.[91] Interestingly, the departmental officer present could not conceive of land without tenure, where only native title operated. The department undertook to consider the implications of native title existing without tenure. As at December 2011 Mer Gedkem Le was still awaiting a final response to the request, but discussions have progressed.[92]

Native title occurs elsewhere in Australia without another class of tenure overlaying it, though the understanding of native title as anything but 'unallocated' Crown land persists. Still, post-*Mabo*, state and territory governments have been slow to understand the distinction and to adjust their behaviour from that of beneficial owners to mere radical title holders.

The privileging of non-Indigenous title and the inherent limitations that have been entrenched in native title make it attractive to apply a stronger tenure over native title. Somewhere along the line our obligation not to discriminate and to avoid boxing native title into a common law tenure has provided the foundation for just the kind of discrimination that was said to be unjustified in *Mabo*. To ask Indigenous people to give up their traditional tenure (finally now recognised in Australian law) for one of 'our' tenures is not only racially discriminatory but also a failure of imagination. In *Mabo*, Justices Gaudron and Deane commented that the English common law inherited by Australia may have to adjust and accommodate Indigenous title.[93] But we have made little effort to do so. Any tenure reform in the Torres Strait must support the continued operation of customary title and the allocation of traditional ownership rights recognised through native title, rather than undermine them. And the role of RNTBCs in mediating this alignment must be recognised.

Representation: clarifying institutional roles and relationships

In 2007 and 2008 the externally imposed changes in the local government arrangements created, or perhaps revealed, significant conflict in the roles and responsibilities in decision-making in the region at an institutional level. At the same time, the proposed amendments to the TSILA placed native title at the centre of policy development. But native title has been given no place in the legal and political framework of the Torres Strait and has not been used to give traditional laws and customs or rights and interests any more strength. This section looks at conflicts between the governing institutions and the options to resolve the issues of excessive governance. Disputes or differences of opinion between leaders of the community are likely to reflect badly on RNTBCs because, like elsewhere in Australia, they are seen as the latecomers to already deeply embedded governance arrangements. They are adding a layer of complexity that is poorly understood, despite the fact that the role of the RNTBC should reflect a role that traditional landowners have asserted all along. The section also examines the notion of *gud pasin*, or 'the proper way' (or Torres Strait Island way), of doing things.

At the RNTBC meetings, it was clear that the experience of each RNTBC was different: some were relied on or deferred to by island councils and the TSRA, and others were ignored. All were inadequately resourced and all were poorly understood in terms of their decision-making roles (by the RNTBC itself, the native title holding group, the TSRA and local councils). Jack Billy, then Chair of Porumalgal, explained:

> My struggle with the PBC is this: after the determination I try to understand the giving of rights, what are my rights. Who am I?...native title [does] not even feed into government decision-making... To my understanding I don't understand where native title is fitting. I am a native boy, I understand myself. But when it comes to business, I don't see native title being recognised.[94]

To a large extent the pre-existing governance structures of the island councils and TSRA remained unchanged by the recognition of native title. This may suggest that the traditional decision-making structure informed the administration of local government on the islands, as the island councils enjoyed a high degree of legitimacy, both because they were steeped in the history of the struggle for self-government in the region and because the close proximity of decision-making to the community helped build consensus around directions and decisions of the councils. Some RNTBCs enjoyed strong relationships with the island councils. Others, though, experienced a decline in the relationship during the relatively short period over which the meetings were held. Arguably this could be explained simply by the change to the TSIRC, but it may also have been a result of RNTBCs increasingly fulfilling their consultation roles in processes such as those prescribed under the TSILA, which had raised the profile and self-awareness of the RNTBCs and created competition between RNTBCs and the island councils for authority and resources. Whatever the case, the island councils appear to have fulfilled an important function in providing decision-making close to each island community. With the amalgamation of the island councils, and the elevation of local government to the regional level, decisions are no longer made at the community level, or if they are it is by the administrative arm — the island manager — who potentially wields considerable power.[95]

The recognition of exclusive possession native title by consent, together with changes to regional governance, has challenged existing decision-making structures and processes. In the Torres Strait the courts and the respondent parties accepted that a DOGIT, under Queensland land rights legislation, does not extinguish native title and is, indeed, consistent with and protects native title.[96] Exclusive possession native title includes the right to make decisions in relation to who accesses the land, and the use and management of the land, including for economic purposes, and as we have seen, at least some RNTBCs were beginning to assert this right. At the same time, most decision-making in the Torres Strait continued to be exercised by the TSRA or the TSIRC, with the latter also holding the land in trust.

There was apparent concern at the meetings, even among the TSIRC regional councillors themselves, that the new model did not carry the same degree of legitimacy as the island councils once had, and that it placed too much power in a 'faceless bureaucracy' based in Cairns. Councillor Ron Day described the TSIRC as the creation of a 'regional monster'.[97]

On Masig in April 2008 the RNTBCs worked to articulate their concerns with the TSRA and TSIRC through a role-mapping exercise to identify their views of the respective responsibilities of the TSRA, TSIRC, TSC and the individual RNTBCs.[98] The exercise was revealing in that, despite the momentary frustration, there was a shared understanding of the spheres of responsibilities relevant to each of the bodies. The TSIRC and TSC were acknowledged as having responsibility for providing public services — the classic 'roads, rates and rubbish' jurisdictions of local government — but the RNTBCs viewed cultural issues as needing to be referred to them. They proposed that RNTBCs had a primary responsibility for the maintenance and promotion of the Ailan Kastom that underpins native title. They argued that, as representatives of the traditional landowners, RNTBCs should have primary responsibility for providing permissions for access to land and sea.

At the same time, RNTBCs also acknowledged that they had competing responsibilities for providing access, with the TSIRC as holder of the DOGITs. Overlapping responsibilities can cause structural competition; for example, the establishment of land panels under the *Local Government Act 2009* (Qld) which are charged with providing 'consent' to major works is inconsistent with the legal responsibly of RNTBCs to negotiate over acts affecting native title. Nevertheless, the need to transfer the DOGITs back to the community level has received general support from the TSIRC and the Queensland Government.

The TSRA, on the other hand, was perceived as primarily a funding body to provide grants and to auspice projects, but also as a first point of contact for people from outside the Torres Strait. However, there was concern that the TSRA should refer relevant matters to RNTBCs and support them to undertake projects and activities rather than undertaking them itself.[99]

What was not adequately explored was whether the group at the meeting believed that the TSRA and the TSIRC should uphold or be bound by Ailan Kastom.

Alignment and overlap

The vision of RNTBCs as trustees for landowners and keepers of law and custom is consistent with their position under common law. However, the regional autonomy model of the Torres Strait envisages that the TSRA, TSC and the TSIRC have functions that relate to the protection and promotion of law and custom. There are questions as to the appropriateness of them having a role in applying and enforcing traditional law and custom, as well as their capability to uphold law and custom if their representation is determined by residence and democratic election and not by traditional ownership. Their statutory discretion to take into account Ailan Kastom is not the same as making decisions in accordance with those customs. However, in a region where the vast majority of the population comprises Torres Strait Islander people, how can any institution of governance have legitimacy if it does not operate consistently with traditional law and custom? As Torres Strait Islanders themselves, how can members of governing bodies not take traditional law and custom into account?

This is an interesting issue in the Torres Strait for students of Indigenous self-determination. Is the TSRA an Indigenous body? Is the TSIRC an Indigenous body? The question for me, then, as an outside observer of the governance of the Torres Strait, is how the traditional laws or Ailan Kastom are incorporated into the decision-making processes of the TSRA and TSIRC, particularly in their formal structures, and where does native title fit in the system? Among the TSRA's goals are those relating to law, custom and land, but they sit alongside other goals for better quality health and services and economic and environmental sustainability. Goals relating to Ailan Kastom and land are to:

- gain recognition of our rights, customs and identity as Indigenous peoples... [and]
- assert native title to land and waters of the Torres Strait region.[100]

The ATSI Act envisages broad self-administration of the region by the TSRA. The inception of the TSRA was seen as a step towards autonomy and self-government for Torres Strait Islanders.[101] Indeed, previous Australian Government reports to international human rights bodies (under the International Covenant on Civil and Political Rights and the International Covenant on Economic, Social and Cultural Rights) identified the TSRA as an example of the recognition and promotion of Article 1, the right to self-determination.[102] However, over the past decade, the TSRA has come to be seen by some as simply the Australian Government presence in the Torres Strait rather than a vehicle for self-government, particularly as it has operated under the threat of dissolution since the demise of ATSIC.[103] As a result, while the TSRA's functions under the ATSI Act include the protection and promotion of Ailan

Kastom, the majority of its day-to-day functions centre on the provision of funding and services to the Aboriginal and Torres Strait Islander people of the region.

It is interesting to note that the new vision for the TSRA differs from the previous vision in that it does not expressly mention Ailan Kastom.[104] However, the TSRA retains the express statutory function under the ATSI Act[105] in relation to recognising and protecting Ailan Kastom and must not disregard Aboriginal law and custom. Nevertheless, without a greater level of autonomy and self-government, the TSRA has no law-making power that would enable it to entrench or enforce Ailan Kastom as the law of the land, despite the existence of native title. The overlaying of Australian property law, and in particular the TSILA and DOGITs, effectively suffocates native title as a system of property law. The question of who enforces Ailan Kastom was discussed at the fourth meeting on Waiben in June 2009, and the result is that the responsibility rests with both everyone and no one.

I do not mean to presume conflict — indeed, multiple governing structures can operate in one locality and for one polity as long as roles are defined, the scope of autonomy is understood, and communication and coordination are clear.[106] In the Torres Strait, however, there seems general consensus that there is excess governance in the system. The following sections explore a number of ways in which this issue of excessive governance and overlapping or conflicting roles could be resolved. One is to continue to support the existing institutions but, as mentioned, improve coordination and communication (for example, through protocols and agreements).

The second solution proposed is to provide equitable resourcing to each of the component parts; that is, specifically to transfer resources from the TSRA and TSIRC to the native title sector in the form of a sea and land council. None of these proposals would reduce the number of governance structures of the Torres Strait. The third possibility is to consider these issues in the context of proposals for more autonomy and territory status for the Torres Strait.

Gud pasin

At Masig the key notion of *gud pasin* was at the heart of the discussion about the frustration over the relationship with other bodies and the need for better protocols. Previously, Jack Billy had explained this with reference to my own research:

> We must know the information from government before they come here. What is their business here? Like your letter, I know what you are here to talk about, I can show other people and they know, they don't ask, 'Why that woman is here?', 'Why she is talking to Jack Billy?' They can come and talk to you. Not like that boat that anchored here. I asked him, 'Who said you can work here?' He said, 'The regional council.' They are not the boss of this island! You need to tell us before you come to work on this island. There is Ailan way and there is government way — you need to do both.[107]

In the context of the sea claim, *gud pasin* was described as a customary obligation of courtesy and proper behaviour, as explained by Kris Lui Billy:

Gud pasin means that we show respect for other people, particularly elders… *Gud pasin* means that we show respect for the property of other people. We don't take fruit from other people's gardens. We don't go to an island that we don't know very well, and act like it's our home island, for example, by going straight out to fish on the home reef or other places close to the island. We don't do these things without telling people from the island what we are doing.[108]

This notion of courtesy is concomitant with a fierce belief in the sanctity of territory. Justice Finn chose to contrast *gud pasin* with the 'pre-sovereign propensity to kill strangers who arrive unexpectedly'.[109] From the evidence before the court in the sea claim, Finn J noted that there were numerous instances where 'reasonable, measured and lawful steps' had been taken to protest objectionable conduct and breaches of *gud pasin* by others.[110] In the same vein, in a number of discussions at the RNTBC meetings there were instances when RNTBC chairs or others felt the need to turn away visitors to the islands who had arrived without permission or consultation with the RNTBC. Obviously, such action is not always well received by other governing institutions and is not always understood or accepted by the community.

What *gud pasin* means in terms of accessing islands was discussed at the 2008 Masig meeting, and while it was recognised that each island may have its own protocols and rules, there are certain shared principles, which include:

- Torres Strait traditions and customs have worked over time and are bound by kinship, *kwod* and protocols.
- Ailan Kastom applies in the Torres Strait and must be respected at all times.
- Native title holders should be recognised as the holders/authority of Ailan Kastom.
- Only Torres Strait Islanders know how to do our business and how to solve our problems — business must be done the proper way with adequate time given for sharing information with PBCs members and communities and between PBCs in order to make important decisions.
- The authority and rights of native title holders and PBCs must be recognised and respected at all times.[111]

The Badu meeting considered the example of PNG nationals who seek permission to conduct 'traditional visits'. These permits, like other decisions about access, are routinely made by the island manager. Some of the RNTBC participants argued that decisions about what constitutes tradition, like those concerning land use and planning and access, such as the PNG requests, should fall within the ambit of the RNTBCs as the representative (agent or trustee) for the native title holders. Others such as Francis Nai, Chair of Masigalgal RNTBC did not share this frustration over the relationship with the regional councillor and island manager. He said:

> The council knows who the traditional landowners are and respect that role. They understand that they are visitors and while they call themselves Yorke Islanders, they are not Masigalgal. The council carries out activities, but they seek the approval of the PBC. The relationship works very well.[112]

The TSRA now provides consultation protocols for government agencies in an effort to improve awareness of the scope of RNTBC authority and expectations. However, the protocol relies on good will and a commitment to observe traditional customs — as does the arrangement to which Pastor Nai refers — rather than being formally reflected in the design of the governing structures.

The need for a re-evaluation of the leadership and institutional roles within the Torres Strait was recognised at the Badu meeting by TSRA chair Toshi Kris and native title portfolio holder Donald Banu. Subsequently a meeting between the TSRA Board, and TSIRC and RNTBC chairs took place on Waiben in June 2009. The participants committed to develop a memorandum of understanding (MOU) between the key governance bodies to resolve the roles of each and establish a relationship of mutual respect.[113] Although the process has stalled, the RNTBCs remain committed to it.[114]

At the meeting, the group created a shared history timeline of governance and self-determination in the region, which was later published by AIATSIS as an educational resource.[115] The timeline illustrates the impact of imposed structures of governance on the leadership of the Torres Strait, none of which wholly represents the aspirations of the region for self-government. The structural tendency towards competition created by the overlapping governance of organisations can undermine the goodwill of the leaders in the Torres Strait group, which is only exacerbated by the imbalance of resources.

A Torres Strait sea and land council

Over the two years of the meetings, the idea of a peak RNTBC body, in part 'incorporating' the regional meetings, took hold. The proposal for a new regional body, conceived as a sea and land council, responded to a perceived inflexibility of the existing institutions and their inability to accommodate RNTBCs and traditional land ownership within the regional governing framework. The envisaged structure differed somewhat from an earlier proposal that emerged from the Cultural Maritime Summit in 2001.[116] There, it was proposed as primarily a political advocacy body, modelled on the established land councils on the mainland, such as the North Queensland and Cape York land councils. In contrast, the peak body proposed at the Torres Strait RNTBC meetings represented a clear intention to transfer the functions at least of the TSRA NTO/NTRB (itself six staff and a $1.6 million operating budget in 2009–10) and eventually of the TSRA Land and Sea Management Unit, largely funded through the Australian Government's Caring for Country programs. The ranger program administered by the unit received funding upward of $11,289,500 per annum over five years.[117]

The TSRA moved towards accepting the idea of a new body as a necessary development to avoid the growing conflict between the TSRA and the legal interests of the RNTBCs. To this end, the TSRA (through its NTO) made a submission to the Commonwealth review of native title funding which contemplated the emergence of a regional traditional owner body.[118] A review of the NTRB status of the TSRA is due to take place in the lead-up to re-recognition by the minister in 2013.

Importantly, with so many RNTBCs in the region, and many such as Porumalgal or Ugar Ged Kem Le supported by very small populations, it is unlikely that all RNTBCs will have the capacity to administer some of the larger government programs, particularly those under the Caring for our Country programs. On the mainland a number of RNTBCs administer programs on their own, such as the Australian Government's Indigenous Protected Areas program managed by Gunditj Mirring RNTBC (Gunditjmara) and Jabalbina RNTBC (Eastern Kuku Yalanji). Others are administered by the NTRB; for example, the ranger programs on the Wellesley Islands administered through the Carpentaria Land Council, and Karajarri Rangers administered through the Kimberley Land Council. It would be considered highly unusual on mainland Australia for such programs to be administered through a government agency or local government body. Indeed, projects under this program are specifically designed to be administered by an Indigenous non-government organisation.

The benefit of an RNTBC peak body, as with any peak body, would be its ability to respond and have input into policy and program development in the region. The RNTBC meetings, held once or twice a year, are simply insufficient to address the consultation needs of RNTBCs. If whole-of-community consultations were embedded in a culture of governance in the Torres Strait and if they reflected Ailan Kastom, such a peak body could monitor the structural engagement and involvement of native title holders in decisions that impact the rights and interests of native title holders. The issue with this proposal of course is that it increases rather than decreases the number of 'governing' institutions in the region.

Territory status: efficiency and effectiveness in governance?

In our region, we disagree about many things, and we speak our minds frankly. But we have no disagreement about land rights, sea rights, who we are, the fact that we are a distinct people, and that we wish to govern ourselves.

Getano Lui Jnr[119]

The TSRA is unique as a model of Indigenous self-government in Australia, although Torres Strait Islanders have repeatedly called for a greater degree of autonomy and self-government in the region.[120] A full exploration of this history of governance in the Torres Strait and the autonomy debates are outside the scope of this paper, but they are an essential backdrop to discussions of the place of native title in the region.[121]

In response to calls from then TSRA chair, Getano Lui Jnr, the then minister, Senator John Herron, referred the issue of Torres Strait autonomy to the House of Representatives Standing Committee on Aboriginal and Torres Strait Islander Affairs (HRSCATSIA).[122] This was received as a major milestone for the course of the Torres Strait. The 1997 HRSCATSIA report proposed a model of autonomy for the region that would combine the Commonwealth (TSRA) and state bodies (then the Island Coordinating Council), though notably retaining the island councils. The model contains some interesting potential contradictions between representative government based on residence rather than on 'any cultural basis' such as traditional ownership, while seeking to at least imbue the structure with Torres Strait cultural authority.[123] To overcome this, the committee proposed separation between an elected regional assembly and a 'cultural council', or forum of elders (although it does not ascribe any particular roles or accountabilities between the two).[124]

The suggested model adopted by the Bamaga Accord in 2001,[125] argued for a regional assembly of 21 members directly elected by and from the residents of the distinct communities of the Torres Strait and northern peninsula area, with a separate, directly elected chairperson and an executive of six members representing the six clusters of communities. The model, which combines state and local government responsibilities, is not unique; indeed, the Torres Strait model drew heavily on Norfolk Island, with the Australian Capital Territory (ACT) providing another example. Interestingly, both Norfolk Island and the ACT have their own distinctive property law jurisdictions, which are unique in Australia because of their absence of freehold.

In its submission to the committee's inquiry, the Centre for Aboriginal Policy Research (CAEPR) suggested that it is useful to distinguish between political and economic autonomy, the two of which may or may not be linked.[126] So far the calls for autonomy have focused mostly on political autonomy and the full gamut of political outcomes, including independent nation-statehood, although most discussions focus on a high level of regional self-government short of secession from the Australian state. Some of this preference is no doubt related to the risks of the northern border, but it also relates to concerns over the economic and social dependency on Australia.[127] For example, Ned David, Chair of Iama Mura Mabaigal Torres Strait Islander Corporation and coordinator of the Greater Autonomy Taskforce which ran from 1997 to 2000, expressed caution in relation to responsibility for the delivery of education and health services.[128]

The TSIRC, TSC and TSRA have consulted on the basis of previous deliberations, through the Bamaga Accord specifically. They have stated that they do not wish to reinvent the wheel. To achieve this, though, they have put native title to one side. They have deliberately labelled native title as an externally imposed regime that would continue unchanged by more autonomy in the Torres Strait. TSIRC Councillor Ron Day has commented that native title has been hijacked:

> It has been more than twenty years since the High Court's decision in our favour. Since then, I believe…we were once again overpowered by a foreign legal blanket of native title legislation…[and] jeopardising once again in this modern time and era our struggle to proceed with resurrecting the spirit of sovereignty amongst the people.[129]

In comparison, Reverend Bon argued, 'We want Territorial status immediately as all the Torres Strait is looking now for greater responsibility in the areas of land, native titles and sea rights.'[130] In 1976, in his call for autonomy, Eddie Mabo said:

> We Islanders ought to look closely at Australian laws and Australia's attitude toward us… I know several people have stated to me that independence of the Torres Strait Islands is not necessary. However, I think independence should be accepted as a long-term policy. We are a people of unique identity and we should work towards an ultimate goal of independence.[131]

Mabo argued that the Commonwealth should negotiate an arrangement for an autonomous region, including exclusive rights over the seas. He reiterated these ideas at the land rights conference in Townsville in 1981,[132] and it was this vision for autonomy that fuelled the fight for native title in the courts.

Then Queensland Premier Anna Bligh gave support to the idea of autonomy and a separate territory,[133] although, echoing the cautions of Ned David and CAEPR, she warned of the implications for the withdrawal of Queensland services. Any movement towards more autonomy should also have property law and native title clearly on the agenda. The integration of traditional ownership rights needs to be considered in the context of regional governance if existing overlap and tension are to be managed.

Conclusion: renegotiating native title in the Torres Strait

> *When truth confronts you, there is once again a shift in paradigm… You therefore challenge the status quo and start looking at new possibilities to create your future. Then we are in a position to consolidate and institutionalise the changes we create.*
>
> Gabriel Bani[134]

The issues presented in the Torres Strait case study reflect many of the same challenges confronting small RNTBCs on the mainland, yet the TSRA is often excluded from policy and funding decisions at the Commonwealth level because of its semi-autonomous operation. Discussion about RNTBCs must include the Torres Strait. While the number of RNTBCs nationally continues to rise, Torres Strait RNTBCs still constitute a significant percentage — currently around 20 per cent of all RNTBCs. They also represent an important group of RNTBCs that are unable to benefit from large-scale development. Nevertheless, they are recognised landowners of a significant geopolitical region. The opportunities for native title to facilitate long-term wellbeing of the common law native title holders in the Torres Strait should be given due consideration in native title policy decision-making.

RNTBCs have been inserted into the breach between traditional landowners and the 'community' governance decisions, and their role necessarily involves internal dynamics. RNTBCs are not merely the external contact point for parties wanting access to native title lands or to acquire an interest in the area. Nor are RNTBCs simply trustees for a series of private interests in land: they must also manage the communal title in a manner that accords with and allows space for the operation of traditional laws and customs. Indeed, some Torres Strait RNTBCs find dispute resolution and arbitration within the group their primary activity.[135] The recognition of traditional laws in relation to property does not freeze property rights at the point sovereignty was asserted, or even at the point the determination of native title is made.[136] Within any society, the distribution of property to individuals is mediated against community needs for shared resources. The duality of navigating the private interests of individual landholders and the communal title to the islands as a whole requires the RNTBCs to play a mediating as well as representative role. The necessity of renegotiating proprietary interests within the group to accommodate community infrastructure requirements involves an essentially governmental function. There is a need for more recognition and understanding of this aspect of RNTBC activity.

When I first travelled to the Torres Strait in 2007, native title had been recognised for 15 years. No doubt I had expectations that this would provide a model for the recognition of native title and its integration into the governance of regions. The failure to incorporate native title and RNTBCs into the institutional governance of the Torres Strait has risked embedding a conflict between RNTBCs and the local council structure. While day-to-day decisions might be made by the TSRA or TSIRC, decisions that require the council or others to go through the future act process can be frustrated if the RNTBCs do not have the same capacity to respond. The idea that an intermediary such as the sea and land council is required to negotiate the interests of traditional owners with the governing bodies of the region may reflect the absence of an effective and independent dispute management body that has traditional authority but no vested interest in the outcome. It may also further reveal that self-government in the Torres Strait is incomplete, with an unsuccessful alignment of existing institutions with traditional decision-making regarding rights and interests.

The Commonwealth and state governments have recognised the value in negotiating broader land settlements that augment and support the recognition of native title.[137] The JWGILS Guidelines for Best Practice has similarly structured its directives based on this principle of practical and sustainable outcomes. The focus of the guidelines is the benefits that can be achieved through broader land settlements and regional settlements:

> Government parties should recognise and acknowledge that all stakeholders can benefit from an agreed broader land settlement. This can contribute to improved relationships and a shared commitment to achieving high quality outcomes.[138]

There is a need to revisit this issue of broader land settlements in the Torres Strait. Consent determinations in and of themselves provide no implementation plan for what is essentially only part of a settlement or agreement in relation to native title. Neither do DOGIT land transfers have adequate implementation processes. There are no negotiated or agreed understandings of how the ongoing relationship between native title holders and other governance bodies will be managed or how the relative roles and responsibilities or rights and interests will be affected by the recognition of native title and exercised into the future. The Torres Strait Islander native title groups have not had the benefit of the acquired knowledge that has led to this policy shift towards broader settlements. In light of this, the Queensland and Commonwealth governments need to revisit the idea of 'settlement' of native title in the Torres Strait to better support the TSRA and RNTBCs in effectively administering native title as part of the regional governance structure. Such a settlement should be framed against the need for rationalised governance and more autonomy, and should not be fearful of examining the potential for Ailan Kastom and native title to play a greater role within the legal framework. It should ensure that the issue of capacity that plagues RNTBCs and the issue of legitimacy that confronts the TSIRC are addressed, and the lessons of past imposed structures do not go unheeded.

Table 3.1 Torres Strait Registered Native Title Bodies Corporate

Determination (NNTT) short name	Case reference	Islands included in determination	TSI RNTBCs
Badu and Moa People #2	Nona and Manas v Queensland [2006] FCA 412	Parts of Badu Island	Badu Ar Mua Migi Lagal (TSI) Corporation
Dauan People	Dauan People v Queensland [2000] FCA 1064	Dauan Island	Dauanalgaw (TSI) Corporation
Erubam Le (Darnley Islanders) # 1	Mye on behalf of Erubam Le v State of Queensland [2004] FCA 1573	Erub (Darnley) Island	Erubam Le Traditional Land and Sea Owners (TSI) Corporation

Determination (NNTT) short name	Case reference	Islands included in determination	TSI RNTBCs
Garboi	*Lota Warria on behalf of the Poruma & Masig Peoples v State of Queensland & Ors* (2005) 223 ALR 62; [2005] FCA 1117	Garboi (Arden) Island	Garboi (TSI) Corporation
Gebara Islanders # 1	*Newie on behalf of the Gebaralgal v Queensland* [2004] FCA 1577	Gebar Island	Gebaralgal (TSI) Corporation
Mabuiag People	*Mabuiag People v State of Queensland* [2000] FCA 106	Mabuiag Island	Goemulgaw (TSI) Corporation
Kulkalgal	*Warria on behalf of the Kulkalgal v Queensland* [2004] FCA 1572	Aureed Island	Kulkalgal (TSI) Corporation
Yam Islanders, or Tudulaig People	*David on behalf of the Iama People and Tudulaig v Queensland* [2004] FCA 1576	Iama (Yam), Zagai and Tudu islands, Cap Islet	Magani Lagaugal (TSI) Corporation
People of Boigu Island # 2	*Gibuma on behalf of the Boigu People v Queensland* [2004] FCA 1575	Buru (Turnagain) and Waral Kawa (Deliverance) islands, Kerr Islet, Turu Cay	Malu Ki'ai (TSI) Corporation
Buru and Warul Kawa	*Victor Nona, John Whop, Pili Waigana, Nelson Gibuma and Phillip Bigie on behalf of the Saibai, Dauan, Mabuiag, Badu and Boigu Peoples v The State of Queensland and Ors* [2005] FCA 1118	Boigu Island	Maluilgal (TSI) Corporation
Masig People and Damuth People	*Masig People v Queensland* [2000] FCA 1067	Masig (Yorke) Island	Masigalgal (TSI) Corporation
Mabo (No. 2) and Meriam People	*Mabo v Queensland* [1992] HCA 23; (1992) 175 CLR 1 and *Passi v Queensland* [2001] FCA 697	Mer, Waier and Dauar islands	Mer Gedkem Le (TSI) Corporation
Moa Island and Mualgal # 2	*Mualgal People v Queensland* [1999] FCA 157 and *Manas v Queensland* [2006] FCA 413	Moa Island and other islands	Mualgal (TSI) Corporation
Badu Islanders # 1	*Nona on behalf of the Badulgal v Queensland* [2004] FCA 1578	Parts of Badu Island	Mura Badulgal (TSI) Corporation
Porumalgal Poruma People	*Poruma People v Queensland* [2000] FCA 1066	Poruma, Uttu and Yarpar islands	Porumalgal (TSI) Corporation
Saibai Island	*Saibai People v Queensland* [1999] FCA 158	Saibai and three other islands	Saibai Mura Buway (TSI) Corporation
Ugar (Stephens Islanders # 1)	*Stephen on behalf of the Ugar People v Queensland* [2004] FCA 1574	Ugar (Stephens) and Campbell islands, Pearce Cay	Ugar Kem Le Ged Zeuber Er Kep Le (TSI) Corporation

Determination (NNTT) short name	Case reference	Islands included in determination	TSI RNTBCs
Warraberalgal, Porumalgal and Iama Peoples	*Thaiday & Ors on behalf of the Warraber, Poruma and Iama Peoples v Queensland* [2005] FCA 1116	Sassie Island	Wakeyama (TSI) Corporation
Warraber People	*Poruma People v Queensland* [2000] FCA 1066	Warraber, Ulu, Bara and Miggi-Maituin islands	Warraberalgal (TSI) Corporation
Torres Strait Regional Sea Claim	*Commonwealth of Australia v Akiba on behalf of the Torres Strait Islanders of the Regional Seas Claim Group* [2012] FCAFC 25 (Appeal) and *Akiba on behalf of the Torres Strait Islanders of the Regional Sea Claim Group v State of Queensland (No 2)* [2010] FCA 643	Does not include islands but see Figure 3.1	RNTBC not yet determined

* uninhabited island RNTBC

Source: Table created using the Torres Strait Regional Authority's 'Prescribed Bodies Corporate directory', November 2012 (www.tsra.gov.au/data/assets/pdf_file/0018/2493/DOC12-009710-PBC-Support-and-Contact-information.pdf) and the AIATSIS web resource 'Native title corporations: PBC profiles', August 2013 (http://www.nativetitle.org.au/index.html)

Endnotes

1 T Mosby, 'Bepo Time', in T Mosby (ed.), *Ilan Pasin: Torres Strait art (this is our way)*, Cairns Regional Gallery, Cairns, 1998, p. 31, citing George Collingrod, *Discovery of Australia*, Golden Press, Gladesville, 1983, p. 26. See also AC Haddon, *Reports of the Cambridge Anthropological Expedition to Torres Straits*, vol. i: general ethnography, Cambridge University Press, Cambridge, 1935, p. 385. The hero cult of the four brothers is most important to the central and eastern islands of the Torres Strait.

2 I dedicate this chapter to the memory of James Bon. I would like to acknowledge the chairs of the Native Title Bodies (NTBs) of the Torres Strait and the support of the Torres Strait Regional Authority (TSRA) and staff of the Native Title Office (NTO) for inviting me to participate in their meetings between 2007 and 2009 and for their ongoing discussions since then. I would particularly like to thank the board of Mer Gedkem Le and the chairperson, Doug Passi, and the Chair of Porumalgal, Pastor Jack Billy, who hosted additional visits to their islands to deepen my understanding of the issues confronting Registered Native Title Bodies Corporate (RNTBCs) in the Torres Strait.

3 *Aboriginal and Torres Strait Islander Act 2005* (Cth) (ATSI Act), s 4, defines Ailan Kastom as 'the body of customs, traditions, observances and beliefs of some or all of the Torres Strait Islanders'.

4 *Mabo v Queensland [No. 2]* (1992) 175 CLR 1 (*Mabo (No. 2)*).

5 Although local Torres Strait Islanders mostly refer to NTBs or to Prescribed Bodies Corporate (PBCs), the term RNTBC is used to keep in line with the other chapters in this volume.

6 Torres Strait Regional Authority (TSRA), 'Proceedings of Torres Strait PBC Workshop: Masig Island, 28–30 April 2008', unpublished document, 2008, resolution no. 8, TSRA, Thursday Island.

7 *Akiba on behalf of the Torres Strait Islanders of the Regional Seas Claim Group v State of Queensland (No. 2)* [2010] FCA 643, (*Akiba*) [488–90]. The relationship between land custom at the community, cluster and whole of Torres Strait society levels is explored in great depth in the sea claim determination.
8 See MJ Carter, 'North of the cape and south of the fly: the archaeology of settlement and subsistence on the Murray Islands Eastern Torres Strait', unpublished PhD thesis, James Cook University, 2004. See also F Loban, 'Ngalpun Adhabth a Goeygayil Bangal (Our sea, our future): an examination of the Torres Strait Protected Zone Joint Authority principles and Torres Strait Islander needs and aspirations for the Torres Strait fisheries, from a Torres Strait perspective', unpublished MA thesis, James Cook University, 2007, p. 20.
9 J Beckett, *Torres Strait Islander custom and colonialism,* Cambridge University Press, Cambridge, 1987, pp. 27–8; also S Mullins, *Torres Strait: a history of colonial occupation and culture contact 1864–1897,* Central Queensland University Press, Rockhampton, 1995.
10 *Akiba*, above n 7.
11 The Commonwealth had appealed to the Full Court of the Federal Court in this matter, *Commonwealth of Australia v Akiba on behalf of the Torres Strait Islanders of the Regional Seas Claim Group* [2012] FCAFC 25
12 See, for example, M Flinders, *A voyage to Terra Australis,* Nicol, London, 1814.
13 Warrior chief is head of the fighters; paramount chief is head of the chiefs. See T Mosby, 'Religion is strong because there is nothing necessarily to compensate the spirit', in Mosby, above n 1, p. 64.
14 A Shnukal, 'Torres Strait Islanders', in M Brändle (ed.), *Multicultural Queensland 2001: 100 years, 100 communities, a century of contributions,* Department of Premier and Cabinet, Brisbane, 2001, p. 5. See also H Lawrence, 'Dance and music in the Torres Strait', in Mosby, above n 1, p. 54. The London Missionary Society ministered in the Torres Strait from 1871 to 1915, when they handed the responsibility to the Church of England.
15 The Cambridge Anthropological Expedition 1898 & AC Haddon, *Reports of the Cambridge Anthropological Expedition to Torres Straits,* vol. iv, Cambridge University Press, Cambridge, 1912.
16 Meriam Mir comes from the eastern islands and the family of Kala Lagaw Ya dialects from the western islands, see E Bani, 'Language structures', in Mosby, above n 1, p. 50. See also E Bani, *The language situation in the Torres Strait,* Australian Institute of Aboriginal Studies, Canberra, 1976.
17 The Tagai State College is named after the stars of Tagai, a system of constellations that move across the skies of the Torres Strait and form the basis of the shared beliefs and traditions of the peoples of the region. The school is a 'constellation of campuses that aspires to a fusion of academic rigour, identity, culture, history and community', see https://tagaisc.eq.edu.au/Ourschool/Missionandvalues/Pages/Missionandvalues.aspx, accessed 4 June 2013.
18 European settlement in Torres Strait began with the establishment of the bêche-de-mer and pearl shell fisheries in the 1870s. Earlier trading in tortoiseshell is recorded as early as the 1830s and Indigenous trade in artefacts and seagoing vessels had a long history prior to this.
19 The Cambridge Anthropological Expedition 1898 & AC Haddon, *Reports of the Cambridge Anthropological Expedition to Torres Straits,* vol. v, Cambridge University Press, Cambridge, 1904, pp. 264–5.
20 Beckett, above 9, p. 54; see also N Sharp, *Torres Strait Islands: a great cultural refusal. The meaning of the Maritime Strike of 1936,* LaTrobe University, Bundaroo, Vic, 1980; and SJ Kehoe-Forutan, *Torres Strait independence: a chronicle of events,* Research Report no. 1, Department of Geographical Sciences, University of Queensland, St Lucia, 1988.

21 The active transfer of knowledge of laws and customs was noted in *Akiba*, above n 7, [152]; [317]; [310–14] among others. Regarding Malo's law and Murray Islands, see N Sharp, *No ordinary judgment: Mabo, the Murray Islanders' land case*, Aboriginal Studies Press, Canberra, p. 7. For the continuity of intellectual traditions see Rehoboth Torres Strait Islander Symposium, *Zenadth Kes: I, Torres Strait Islander*, Rehoboth Torres Strait Islander Symposium, Thursday Island, 2009.
22 *Akiba*, above n 7, [3].
23 G Lui, 'Self-government in the Torres Strait Islands' in C Fletcher (ed.) *Aboriginal self-determination in Australia*, Aboriginal Studies Press, Canberra, 1994, pp. 125–6.
24 LR O'Donnell, 'The Torres Strait: a case study analysis in multi-level governance', unpublished PhD thesis, Griffith University, November 2006, p. 5.
25 W Sanders, 'Reshaping governance in Torres Strait: the Torres Strait Regional Authority and beyond', *Australian Journal of Political Science*, vol. 30, no. 3, November 1995, pp. 500–24.
26 Australian Bureau of Statistics (ABS), http://www.censusdata.abs.gov.au/census_services/getproduct/census/2011/quickstat/IREG307?opendocument&navpos=220, accessed 11 June 2013. For a historical comparison see J Taylor & WS Arthur, *Patterns and trends in the spatial diffusion of the Torres Strait Islander population*, CAEPR Discussion Paper, no. 25, CAEPR, Australian National University, Canberra, 1992.
27 JC Altman, WS Arthur & W Sanders, *Towards greater autonomy for the Torres Strait: political and economic dimensions*, CAEPR Discussion Paper, no. 121, CAEPR, Australian National University, Canberra, 1996, p. 6, http://caepr.anu.edu.au/sites/default/files/Publications/DP/1996_DP121.pdf, accessed 13 June 2013; referring to the 1994 National Aboriginal and Torres Strait Islander Survey (NATSIS) as discussed in WS Arthur, 'Torres Strait Islanders', in JC Altman & J Taylor (eds) *The 1994 National Aboriginal and Torres Strait Survey: findings and future prospects*, CAEPR Research Monograph, no. 11, CAEPR, Australian National University, Canberra, 1996.
28 The Torres Strait Treaty establishes the international border between Papua New Guinea and Australia by specifying seabed and fisheries boundaries, and also by presenting a framework for the management of the area. The protected zone is defined in the Treaty between Australia and the Independent State of Papua New Guinea Concerning Sovereignty and Maritime Boundaries in the Area between the Two Countries, Including the Area Known as Torres Strait, and Related Matters, opened for signature 18 December 1978, 1985 ATS 4 (entered into force 15 February 1985), given effect in Australian domestic law by the *Torres Strait Treaty (Miscellaneous Amendments) Act 1984* (Cth).
29 Ibid., articles 10, 11 and 12. See also *Torres Strait Fisheries Act 1984* (Cth). For general reference see Aboriginal and Torres Strait Islander Social Justice Commissioner (ATSISJC), *Native title report 2000*, Human Rights and Equal Opportunity Commission, Sydney, 2000, p. 92.
30 This is primarily due to the major component, the prawn fishery, being wholly non-Indigenous owned from outside the region. While the PZJA has an Indigenous Traditional Fishers Advisory Committee, the management of the fisheries lies primarily with the TSRA. See JC Altman, WS Arthur & HJ Bek, *Indigenous participation in the commercial fisheries in the Torres Strait: a preliminary discussion*, CAEPR Discussion Paper, no. 73, CAEPR, Australian National University, Canberra, 1994, and Loban, above n 8.
31 The TSRA is established and performs functions pursuant to ss 142 and 142A of the ATSI Act, above n 3.
32 Ibid., s 142A.
33 Torres Strait Regional Authority (TSRA), *Annual report 2009–10*, TSRA, Thursday Island, 2011, http://www.tsra.gov.au/__data/assets/pdf_file/0017/1718/AR_2010–2011_Full.PDF, accessed 4 June 2013.

34 At the time of writing the Torres Strait and TSRA are part of the responsibilities of the Indigenous Programs Branch within the Department of Families, Housing, Community Services and Indigenous Affairs (FaHCSIA).
35 In 2007–08, the TSRA was allocated $33,618,148 for the Community Development Employment Program (CDEP), supporting 1750 participants in 19 communities (including Seisia and Bamaga) almost entirely through local government. Activities included: council and CDEP administration; fuel depots; public transport; landscaping; landcare and environment management programs fostered by the TSRA's Land and Sea Management Unit; recycling; contract cleaning; hydroponics; cemetery maintenance; road and drainage construction and maintenance; nursery projects; livestock management; an abattoir; stevedoring; mechanical workshops; tourism and hospitality; community policing; women, youth, culture and church projects; work experience as teachers' aides and health care assistants; fishing; seafood processing and marketing; takeaway enterprises; a supermarket and other retail outlets; construction and maintenance of buildings; a quarry; sea walls; levee banks; screen-printing, art and crafts; child care; and broadcasting. Torres Strait Regional Authority (TSRA) 'Community, development, employment', http://www.tsra.gov.au/the-tsra/community-development-employment--training.aspx, accessed 1 December 2009. In 2009 the TSRA introduced a new Torres Strait Development Plan 2009–13, the fourth since its establishment. Torres Strait Regional Authority (TSRA) 'Torres Strait development plan', http://www.tsra.gov.au/the-tsra/development-plan, accessed 2 July 2013.
36 Bamaga and Seisia communities on the Cape York Peninsula are Torres Strait Islander settlements. For further details of all the inhabited communities, see Torres Shire Council, 'About the shire', http://www.torres.qld.gov.au/about-the-shire, accessed 4 June 2013.
37 The *Local Government Amendment Act 2007* (Qld), and the *Local Government and Other Legislation (Indigenous Regional Councils) Amendment Act 2007* (Qld).
38 *Local Government Act 2009* (Qld), s 87. The minister can establish a community forum for any Indigenous Regional Council or Indigenous Regional Council division, with a minimum of three but no more than seven members.
39 Ibid., s 9(3) (emphasis added).
40 Ibid., s 87. The minister can establish a community forum for any Indigenous Regional Council or Indigenous Regional Council division, with a minimum of three but no more than seven members.
41 There are only three claims remaining over land — Zuizin, Naghir and Warral/Ului. The Raine Island claim has been discontinued with an Indigenous Land Use Agreement (ILUA) now in place. These numbers do not include the Kaurareg RNTBC, which holds title on behalf of the Aboriginal traditional owners of the inner islands. The Kaurareg people are culturally distinct from Torres Strait Islander peoples.
42 *Akiba*, above n 7, [179].
43 Subject to various third party interests, including various public and private infrastructure leases.
44 *Mabo (No. 2)*, above n 4.
45 For example, *Manas v State of Queensland* [2006] FCA 413. Note provisos in relation to non-exclusive rights in water and use of resources in water.
46 *Poruma People v State of Queensland* [2000] FCA 1066.
47 See, for example, *Masig People v State of Queensland* [2000] FCA 1067, [5].
48 The common law will not recognise a native title right to control use by others due to the international obligations of free passage and navigations and the public right to fish: see *Commonwealth v Yarmirr* (2001) 208 CLR 1. The judgment recognised the right to take resources for any purpose, including for trade and commerce, although noting that native title holders were bound by regulatory regimes for licensing, for example, of commercial fishing.

49 While the Commonwealth appealed the decision, the matter of a single society for the purposes of the sea claim was not disturbed, see *Commonwealth of Australia v Akiba on behalf of the Torres Strait Islanders of the Regional Seas Claim Group* [2012] FCAFC 25.
50 Jack Billy, Chair of Porumalgal (Torres Strait Islanders) Corporation (RNTBC), interview with the author, Poruma, 4 April 2009. Poruma is also known as 'Coconut Island'.
51 Kris Lui Billy, evidence in the sea claim, see *Akiba*, above n 7, [241].
52 Eddie Mabo quoted in Sharp, above n 20, p. 63.
53 *Akiba*, above n 7, [509].
54 F Cohen, 'Dialogue on private property', *Rutgers Law Review* 357, 1954. See *Yanner v Eaton* (1999) 201 CLR 351.
55 TSRA, above n 6.
56 Ibid.
57 These departments are now the Queensland departments of Environment and Heritage Protection and Natural Resources and Mines, and the Commonwealth Department of the Environment.
58 Torres Strait Regional Authority (TSRA), 'Proceedings of Torres Strait PBC workshop, Thursday Island, 4–6 December 2007', unpublished report, TSRA, Thursday Island 2007, pp. 10–11.
59 Torres Strait Regional Authority (TSRA), 'Torres Strait PBC meeting (no.3), Badu: Resolutions recommendations and actions', unpublished report, TSRA, 2007.
60 The Office of the Registrar of Indigenous Corporations, which administers the CATSI Act, provided governance training in the region in 2008 and held a 'transition workshop' for RNTBCs in January 2009. However, advice from the Office on new constitutions (or 'rule books') was confusing, and in some instances legally inaccurate, leaving draft new rule books unworkable.
61 An acronym used for the Waiben suburbs of Tamwoy, Rose Hill, Aplin, Waiben and Quarantine.
62 Tamwoy, Rose Hill, Aplin, Waiben and Quarantine Community Council (TRAWQ), 'Ngalpun Malu Kaimelan Gasaman Cultural Maritime Summit', unpublished document, TRAWQ, Thursday Island, 2001.
63 The Commonwealth policy is contained in Department of Families, Housing, Community Services and Indigenous Affairs (FaHCSIA), *Guidelines for support of Prescribed Bodies Corporate (PBCs)*, FaHCSIA, Canberra, 2009, [4.1].
64 D Banu & K Whitton, 'Towards autonomous and self-sustaining Prescribed Bodies Corporate — an overview of TSRA's Capacity Building Project', presented at the Native Title Conference 2011, Brisbane, 1–3 June 2011.
65 FaHCSIA, above n 63, [4.6]. These guidelines do not expressly exclude Torres Strait RNTBCs from applying but in practice the program does not extend beyond the mainland, consistent with the main native title program funding administered by FaHCSIA.
66 As of 4 June 2013. See Native Title Tribunal website, http://www.nntt.gov.au/Pages/Search.aspx?k=ilua ergon energy, accessed 4 June 2013.
67 Section 24JAA does not require the right to negotiate for housing and infrastructure developments. For a full discussion of the s 24JAA amendments see J Weir, ch. 4 in this volume.
68 *Native Title Act 1993* (Cth) (NTA), s 60AB; Native Title (Prescribed Bodies Corporate) Amendment Regulations 2011, para 4, regs 19–26.
69 M Rumler & S Marjanac, 'Normalisation, administrative practice and native title', paper presented to the Native Title Conference 2010: People, Place, Power, Canberra, 1–3 June 2010.
70 TSRA, above n 6.
71 Community-owned enterprises are familiar in the Strait, as seen in relation to those enterprises formerly owned by the island councils (now by the TSIRC), but also harking back to the first island-owned boats.
72 R Day, 'Ten years since *Mabo* — native title at Mer', *Journal of Indigenous Policy*, no. 45, 2004.

73 Torres Strait Regional Authority (TSRA), 'Proceedings of the 5th meeting of Torres Strait PBCs, Mer Island, November 2009', unpublished document, TSRA, Thursday Island, 2009.
74 See also T Bauman, ch. 5 in this volume.
75 These issues were discussed by Rumler & Marjanac, above n 69.
76 The Meriam Le rejected the offer of Deed of Grant in Trust (DOGIT) in the 1980s and was the only island to do so. As a result, however, a state reserve stayed in place over Murray Island.
77 As a result of the establishment of the TSIRC, the Island Coordinating Council disbanded in March 2008.
78 The Badu community challenged the transfer and received a consent order to require the state to consult. The transfer may also have constituted an illegal future act. Following consultations, in February 2009 the state announced that the title would not be transferred to the RNTBC but to a public company established to take back community-owned enterprises. The Badu Ar Mua Migi Lagal (Torres Strait Islanders) Corporation, the local RNTBC, objected and negotiations have ensued to resolve the issue at the community level.
79 *Torres Strait Islander Land Act 1991* (Qld) (TSILA), s 25A.
80 See, for example, the Eastern Kuku Yalanji settlement, Jabalbina Yalanji Aboriginal Corporation website, http://www.jabalbina.com.au/intro.html, accessed 12 June 2013.
81 See TSILA, above n 79, ss 13B, 37–37N and 38.
82 TSRA, above n 6, p. 29. The government reaffirmed the primary role of RNTBCs as landholders in such consultations and committed to engaging directly with RNTBCs in the future.
83 Prior to the amalgamation, the funding for councils in the Torres Strait was provided under the State Government Financial Aid Fund Program, which provided recurrent grants to councils established under the *Local Government (Community Governance Areas) Act 2004* and the *Community Services (Torres Strait) Act 1984*.
84 Compare *Mabo v Queensland [No. 1]* (1988) 166 CLR 186 and *Western Australia v Ward* (2002) 213 CLR 1. In both cases the impact of the *Racial Discrimination Act 1975* (Cth) (RDA) was discussed in relation to native title. The courts have clearly stated that in native title, while it is unique under the law, Indigenous peoples should not be discriminated against in regard to the right to own and inherit property. As such, native title should be treated the same as other similar property rights under Australian law. Failure to do so could result in a breach of the RDA.
85 TSRA, above n 6, pp. 13–14.
86 *Akiba*, above n 7, [260].
87 *Mabo (No. 2)*, above n 4, p. 30, per Brennan J, also p. 58.
88 Dan Mosby, Chair, Kulkalgal RNTBC, pers. comm., Badu Island, 31 March 2009.
89 *Mabo (No.2)*, above n 4, [97] per Brennan J.
90 Reserve no. R380, under s 180(1) *Land Act 1910* (Qld) continued as a reserve for 'Aboriginal purposes' under the *Land Act 1962* (Qld) and *Land Act 1994* (Qld). The trusteeship is held by the Director of Aboriginal and Islander Affairs.
91 Correspondence to this effect was sent to the minister from Mer Gedkem Le on 28 August 2009.
92 J Bon, 'From freezer to freedom — a short history of infrastructure on Murray Island post Mabo', paper presented at the Native Title Conference 2010: People Place Power, Canberra, 1–3 June 2010.
93 *Mabo (No. 2)*, above n 4, p. 180, per Deane and Gaudron JJ.
94 Billy, above n 50.
95 Ibid.
96 For example, see *Manas*, above n 45, *Poruma People*, above n 46 or *Masig People*, above n 47.

97 R Day, 'After Mabo, what?', in Rehoboth, above n 21, p. 36.
98 The RNTBCs identified a gap in representation at the regional governance level in the protection of the rights and interests of traditional landowners and native title holders that required a new regional body. At that stage the group was not ready to articulate the exact nature of such a regional body — whether it should be a peak body for RNTBCs, an advocacy land and sea council, the sea claim PBC, a new NTRB or some combination of those.
99 TSRA, above n 6, Table 1: Role mapping.
100 Department of Families, Housing, Community Services and Indigenous Affairs website, 'Torres Strait Regional Authority', http://www.fahcsia.gov.au/our-responsibilities/indigenous-australians/programs-services/communities-regions/torres-strait-regional-authority, accessed 1 July 2013.
101 G Lui (Jnr), 'Self-government in the Torres Strait Islands', in C Fletcher (ed.) *Aboriginal self-determination in Australia*, Aboriginal Studies Press, Canberra, 1994, pp. 125–30.
102 At p. 55, Australia's 2007 report refers back to the comprehensive third report by the Australian Government, Attorney-General's Department (AGD), *Australia's third report under the International Covenant on Civil and Political Rights*, AGD, Barton, ACT, 1998, p. 9. More recent reports refer to Australia's support for the Declaration on the Rights of Indigenous Peoples, which of course includes the right to self-determination. See AGD webpage, 'Universal Periodic Review — National Report Part III — Promotion and Protection of Human Rights', http://www.ag.gov.au/RightsAndProtections/HumanRights/UniversalPeriodicReview/Pages/UniversalPeriodicReviewNationalReportPartIIIPromotionandProtectionofHumanRights.aspx, accessed 4 July 2013.
103 TSRA, above n 6.
104 Previously 'To empower our people to determine their own affairs based on our unique Ailan Kastom bilong Torres Strait from which we draw our unity and strength', in Torres Strait Regional Authority (TSRA), *Annual report 2007–08*, TSRA, Thursday Island, 2008, p. v, http://www.tsra.gov.au/__data/assets/pdf_file/0016/1735/anrep0708.pdf, accessed 12 June 2013.
105 ATSI Act, above n 3.
106 See, for example, Australian Public Service Commission, *Connecting government: whole of government responses to Australia's priority challenges*, Commonwealth of Australia, Canberra, 2004.
107 Billy, above n 50.
108 Billy, above n 51, [241].
109 *Akiba*, above n 7, [283].
110 Ibid., [284]. See *R v Ben Ali Nona and anor* (District Court, 6 February 2001, unreported).
111 TSRA, above n 6, note preferred/authoritative spelling of Kod and Kastom.
112 Francis Nai, pers. comm., Badu Island, 3 April 2009.
113 Torres Strait Regional Authority (TSRA) and Chairs of Native Title Bodies, 'Shared histories and native title', unpublished document, TSRA, Badu Island, 2009.
114 Ned David, pers. comm., Canberra, March 2011.
115 See the Torres Strait Islander Timeline published at AIATSIS webpage, '*Ngalpan danalayg; keriba kerker* (Our life; our time)', 2009, http://www.aiatsis.gov.au/ntru/tsitimeline.html, accessed 12 June 2013.
116 TRAWQ, above n 62.
117 Torres Strait Regional Authority (TSRA), *Annual report 2009–10*, TSRA, 2010, http://www.tsra.gov.au/__data/assets/pdf_file/0013/1732/AR_2009-2010_Full.PDF, accessed 13 June 2013. Torres Strait Regional Authority (TSRA), 'Torres Strait, Caring for our Country', *TSRA News*, no. 99, February 2009, http://www.tsra.gov.au/__data/assets/pdf_file/0004/1759/feb2009_newsletter.pdf, accessed 4 July 2013.

118 Recommended at Masig PBC meeting, 2008. Torres Strait Regional Authority (TSRA), submission to the Commonwealth review of native title funding, unpublished, TSRA, 2008.
119 G Lui (Jnr), 'A Torres Strait perspective', in M Yunupingu, D West, I Anderson, J Bell, G Lui (Jnr), H Corbett & N Pearson, *Voices of the Land, 1993 Boyer Lectures*, the Australian Broadcasting Corporation, Sydney, 1993, pp. 62–75.
120 G Lui (Jnr), TSRA chairperson, *Canberra Times*, 16 July 1996; Terry Waia, *Greater autonomy and improved governance in the Torres Strait region*, paper presented at the Indigenous Governance Conference, Canberra, 3–5 April 2002; E McDonald, 'The Torres Strait Regional Authority: is it the answer to regional governance for Indigenous people?', *Australian Indigenous Law Review*, vol. 11, no. 3, 2007, p. 43.
121 For further reading see W Sanders & B Arthur, *A Torres Strait Islanders Commission? Possibilities and issues*, CAEPR Discussion Paper, no. 132, CAEPR, Australian National University, Canberra, 1997, <http://caepr.anu.edu.au/sites/default/files/Publications/DP/1997_DP132.pdf>, accessed 5 June 2013.
122 House of Representatives Standing Committee on Aboriginal and Torres Strait Islander Affairs (HRSCATSIA), *Torres Strait Islanders: a new deal, a report on greater autonomy for Torres Strait Islanders*, HRSCATSIA, Canberra, 1997, p. 1, http://www.aph.gov.au/parliamentary_business/committees/house_of_representatives_committees?url=atsia/tsi/tsi.pdf, accessed 5 June 2013. More generally see W Sanders & WS Arthur, *Autonomy rights in Torres Strait: from whom, for whom, for or over what?*, CAEPR Discussion Paper, no. 215, CAEPR, Australian National University, Canberra, 2001, http://caepr.anu.edu.au/sites/default/files/Publications/DP/2001_DP215.pdf, accessed 13 June 2013.
123 HRSCATSIA, above n 122, [6] and [15].
124 Ibid., [11] and [22]; Recommendation 7.
125 The Bamaga Accord was the result of consultations on regional autonomy conducted by the Greater Autonomy Taskforce (constituted by the chairs of the TSRA and the Indigenous Coordination Centre (ICC), the Torres Shire Council mayor and community representatives). Further, see M Nakata, 'Treaty and self-determination agendas of Torres Strait Islanders: a common struggle', in H McGlade (ed.), *Treaty: let's get it right*, Aboriginal Studies Press, Canberra, 2003, p. 166; G Nettheim, 'Toward regional government in the Torres Strait', *Indigenous Law Bulletin*, no. 20, 2002, p. 20.
126 Altman et al., above n 27, p. 3.
127 Compare A Shnukal, above n 14, who suggests that there is a recognition that economic independence and stable industry are preconditions of self-government in the region.
128 S Elks, 'For Mabo's sake, let my island home go: Torres Strait elder George Mye', *Australian*, October 15, 2011.
129 Day, above n 97, p. 40.
130 *Torres News*, 5–11 September 2003.
131 Eddie Mabo quoted in G Lui, 'A perspective from the Torres Strait', in J Griffin (ed.) *The Torres Strait border issue: consolidation, conflict and compromise*, College of Advanced Education, Townsville, 1976, p. 35.
132 E Mabo, 'Land rights in the Torres Strait', in E Obrei (ed.), *Black Australians: the prospects for change*, Students Union, James Cook University, Townsville, 1982, p. 147.
133 J Marszalek, 'Queensland Premier Anna Bligh takes up case for Torres Strait autonomy', news.com.au webpage, http://www.news.com.au/breaking-news/queensland-premier-anna-bligh-takes-up-case-for-torres-strait-autonomy/story-e6frfku0-1226124308993, accessed 15 August 2013.
134 G Bani, 'Torres Strait cultural worldview — values and ethics: Muruygawanal Muy kupal Patha Mukmik', in Rehoboth, above n 21, p. 20.

135 Mer Gedkem Le in particular has identified this challenge.
136 This has been a problem in relation to resolving internal disputes on Mer, for example, where community members refer to Haddon's maps to argue their inheritance.
137 Joint Working Group on Indigenous Land Settlements (JWGILS), *Guidelines for best practice, flexible and sustainable decision making*, JWGILS, Canberra, August 2009, p. 37, http://www.aiatsis.gov.au/ntru/docs/researchthemes/agreement/agreements/GuidelinesForBestPractice.pdf, accessed 5 June 2013.
138 Ibid.

Update: Torres Strait Native Title Bodies Corporate 2013

Lisa M Strelein

Since Chapter 3 was written there have been a number of developments relevant to priorities of the Torres Strait RNTBCs and their interactions with this region's complex governance arrangements.

While the transfer of the superseded statutory lands rights tenure (DOGIT) over Badu from the Torres Strait Regional Council to the RNTBC has not yet been finalised, the tenure issue on Murray Island was resolved in December 2012,[1] with the removal of the state government reserve referred to in the case study and granting of inalienable freehold title, now known as Torres Strait Islander Land, under the *Torres Strait Islander Land Act 1991* (Qld) to Mer Gedkem Le. This was a significant agreement, as the transfer included the township area, which has been a source of contention on other islands.

The ATSI Act was amended to incorporate election of all board members of the TSRA (div 5 of the Act), which replaces the previous direct appointment of councillors from the TSIRC and the Northern Peninsula Area Regional Council. Twenty TSRA electoral wards have been created and in September 2012 the first separate TSRA Board election was conducted by the Australian Electoral Commission. This clearly differentiates membership of the TSIRC and TSRA boards, addressing some of the issues of roles and responsibilities highlighted by Torres Strait RNTBCs. Amendments to the ATSI Act followed a review of governance undertaken in 2011.[2]

To address the gap in regional representation of Torres Strait RNTBCs, the long-awaited peak body was finally established with the ORIC registration of the Gur A Baradharaw Kod Torres Strait Sea and Land Council Torres Strait Islander Corporation in March 2012. Many of the aspirations of the native title holders and their RNTBCs discussed in the chapter have been incorporated as objectives for the corporation in their rule book.[3]

On 7 August 2013, the High Court of Australia handed down its decision in relation to commercial fishing in the Torres Strait.[4] The Court held that the successive statutory regimes which prohibited commercial fishing without a licence were not inconsistent with the continued existence of the native title right. The decision upheld the primary decision that native title holders have the right to take fish and other marine resources from within the determination area for any purpose, including commercial purposes.

Although an MOU referred to in the case study between RNBTCs and the TSRA has not eventuated, in December the TSRA Board agreed to support the transfer of the NTRB functions to the new Gur A Baradharaw Kod Torres Strait Sea and Land Council.[5] This issue is likely to be considered as part of the current review of native title organisations being undertaken by the Australian Government.

Endnotes

1 Minister for Aboriginal and Torres Strait Islander and Multicutural Affairs and Minister Assisting the Premier, 'Return of Mabo's land to traditional owners', media release at the Queensland Cabinet and Ministerial Directory website, http://statements.qld.gov.au/Statement/2012/12/14/return-of-mabos-land-to-traditional-owners, accessed 1 August 2013.

2 Effective Governance, *Torres Strait Regional Authority: review of the governance structure*, Effective Governance, Milton, Queensland, 2011, http://www.tsra.gov.au/__data/assets/pdf_file/0003/1776/tsra20governance20review20report20final.pdf, accessed 1 August 2013.

3 Gur A Baradharaw Kod Torres Strait Sea and Land Council Torres Strait Islander Corporation, *Rule book: Gur A Baradharaw Kod Torres Strait Sea and Land Council Torres Strait Islander Corporation*, Gur A Baradharaw Kod Torres Strait Sea and Land Council Torres Strait Islander Corporation, Thursday Island, 2012.

4 *Leo Akiba on behalf of the Torres Strait Regional Seas Claim Group v Commonwealth of Australia and Ors* [2013] HCA 33 (Akiba case).

5 Maluwap Nona, TSRA Board member and native title portfolio holder, pers. comm., 16 November 2012.

Chapter 4

The Djabugay native title story: getting back in town

Toni Bauman

We thought the PBC would look after us. But they only gave recognition not native title rights — these are two different things — it's different if you've got title [that is, exclusive possession]. We had a meeting with the government and asked them to explain what our native title means, but they couldn't explain. We see native title as the land, going hunting and gathering, the land providing for us. We have proof of the land, our arts and painting. Before the white man the land was ours anyway, it was there forever, written through our painting. We feel disappointed thinking about our PBC. We expected to use the land, not just recognition.

Barry Hunter[1]

Introduction

The Djabugay native title story begins with the ancient history of the Djabuganydji Bama rainforest people who speak the Djabugay language (the Bama) and of Djabugay country (*bulmba*) which is given voice through Storywaters.[2] These Storywaters speak of the activities of *Gurra-Gurra* ancestors such as *Bulurru* Rainbow Serpent, the Two Brothers *Damarri* and *Guyala* and *Budadji* Carpet Snake (associated with *Din Din* or Barron Falls) from whom all Djabugay are descended and who gave meaning to the Djabugay landscape.[3] This landscape, crisscrossed by a network of walking tracks from coast to inland, is located in the Cairns Rainforest region of Australia. It takes in the small town of Kuranda and runs north towards Port Douglas and west towards Mareeba in Far North Queensland. It encompasses a number of national parks and conservation and state forest reserves, including the 28 square kilometre Barron Gorge National Park (the Park), which is part of the Wet Tropics World Heritage Area. The Skyrail cableway (Skyrail) and Queensland Rail's (QRail's) Kuranda Scenic Railway operate daily in the Park, and it is the most visited national park in Australia with approximately 1.6 million visitors per year. The Park borders Cairns and is about two kilometres from Kuranda, which is about 20 kilometres north-west of Cairns.

Many of the 500–700 people with Djabugay affiliations live in Kuranda or in small community land trust areas nearby, at Mantaka, Koah, and Kowrowa or on the old Mona Mona Mission. Some live further afield across the Atherton Tablelands in small towns such as Mareeba, in Cairns and on Aboriginal communities such as Palm Island and beyond.

Djabugay Storywaters and their laws and customs provided the basis for a Djabugay native title application over the Park, which was lodged with the National Native Title Tribunal (NNTT) in 1994. With assistance from the North Queensland Land Council (NQLC), a connection report was prepared[4] and numerous mediation meetings were held with the Queensland Government and other parties. A consent determination was finally handed down by the Federal Court on 17 December 2004[5] (see Figure 4.1). Significantly, the determination was conditional upon the registration of the Barron Gorge Indigenous Land Use Agreement (ILUA) between the Djabugay applicants as representatives of Djabugay people, the State of Queensland and the Djabugay Native Title Aboriginal Corporation (Registered Native Title Body Corporate) (DNTAC).

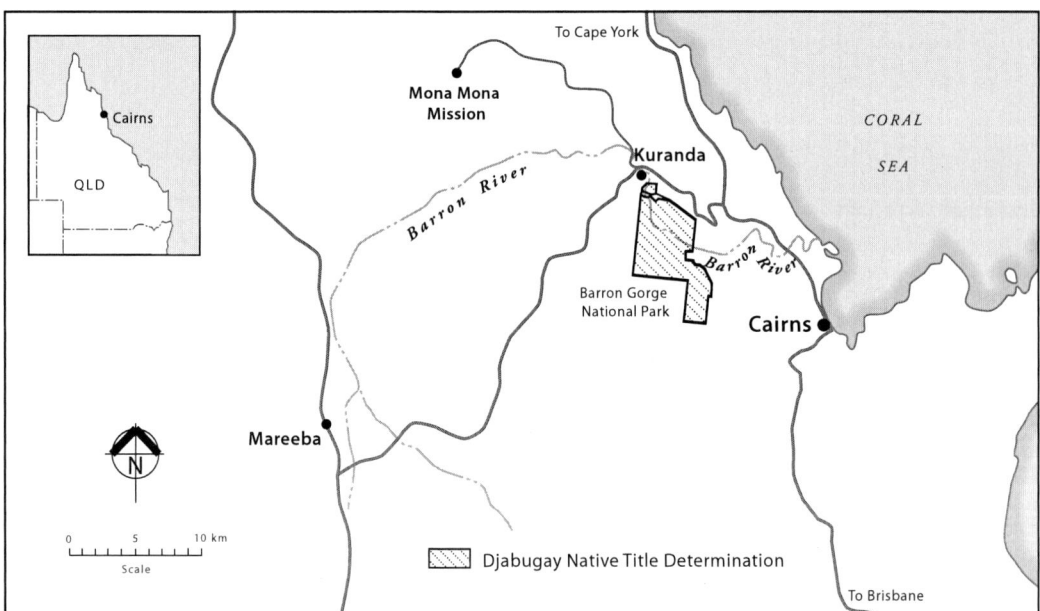

Figure 4.1 Djabugay native title determination. Map by Brenda Thornley for AIATSIS

DNTAC was incorporated in 2004 to hold and manage Djabugay native title rights and to hold and invest money held in trust. In 2009, it was part of a Djabugay governance network of four corporations including: the Djabugay Tribal Aboriginal Corporation (DTAC),[6] which was established in 1992 and was the umbrella corporation and the primary corporate vehicle for conducting Djabugay business; Buda:Dji Aboriginal Development Association Aboriginal Corporation (BADA), which was established in 1995; and the Djabugay Business Development Aboriginal Corporation (DBDAC) incorporated in 2005. Since the 2008 Djabugay annual general meeting (AGM), all corporations have the same Djabugay Governing Committee representing all Djabugay people.

The Djabugay native title determination was much lauded as the first consent determination over a national park, and in 2009 there was a public perception that Djabugay native title issues had been settled and that the Djabugay were 'okay'. Yet many Djabugay could see little benefit from native title, and were disappointed and ambivalent about it. The quote that begins this paper demonstrates this disappointment. Djabugay native title holders were confused about what native title actually delivers and what it really is: expecting to get their land back but receiving only a non-exclusive determination with a limited 'bundle of rights' in relation to the Park. From a position of relative optimism and confidence in the preparations and negotiations over the claim, they sometimes felt disheartened and regretful about the past, including the demise of a number of earlier Djabugay initiatives as a result of poor governance, lack of funding, financial mismanagement and conflict among themselves. Nevertheless, negotiations over the Park with the Queensland Government's Environmental Protection Agency (EPA; after 26 March 2009 a part of the Department of Environment and Resource Management or DERM)[7] had a new momentum, and Djabugay were hopeful of a new start. As Gerald Hobbler, then Chairman of DNTAC noted during his opening address to the planning workshop in September 2008 in Kuranda, sponsored by AIATSIS and the Minerals Council of Australia (MCA), there was a need for the Djabugay to become active again, as they were in the days of preparing the native title claim — to get 'back in town', as he described it, and to learn from past mistakes.[8]

'Getting back in town' will involve Djabugay confronting their own recent history, including issues relating to the Tjapukai Aboriginal Cultural Park (the Cultural Park),[9] Skyrail, the former Mona Mona Mission, the Djabugay Ranger Agency (DRA) and associated conflict. It will also require the development of partnerships and relationships, coordination, a range of expertise, effective governance and administration. Above all it will require participatory community development approaches which bring all Djabugay together and capitalise on existing skills. A major issue confronting the Djabugay concerns a number of RNTBCs across Australia; that is, how to maintain a paradigm of 'all Djabugay as one group' and simultaneously recognise and account for the interests of the specific 'clan-like' affiliations which subgroups have to local areas within the Djabugay estate.

This paper discusses some of these histories and issues confronting the governance of Djabugay corporations in doing native title business, including negotiations over a plan of management over the Park. It draws not only on field work conducted with the Djabugay between 2007 and 2009 and ongoing discussions since then, but also on the planning workshop conducted by Bushwork Consultants as part of an action research partnership between DNTAC and AIATSIS.[10] References to 'the Djabugay' throughout this chapter are to Djabugay people as they are represented by the Djabugay Governing Committee.

The Tjapukai Dance Theatre and Tjapukai Aboriginal Cultural Park

The opening of the Kuranda Range Road in the 1940s saw an influx of new settlers and, from the late 1960s, increasing numbers of 'hippies' who forged close relationships with the Bama, and who took a strong interest in Bama lifestyles and cultural practices. By the 1980s, tourism was thriving in Kuranda, as QRail's Kuranda Scenic Railway through Barron Gorge brought large numbers of visitors to the renowned weekly Kuranda art and craft markets where Djabugay sold their weaving and carvings.

The Australian community at this time was fast developing a fascination with the 'exotic' and 'primitive' qualities of Aboriginal dances, songs and art work, and 'Aboriginal culture' was experiencing something of a renaissance.[11] The Tjapukai Dance Theatre (the Theatre), established modestly in rented premises in Kuranda in 1986 as a partnership between Don and Judy Freemen and David Hudson, a Western Yalanji man, and his wife Cindy, quickly became a huge success. Within six years, aside from the Community Development Employment Program (CDEP), it was the largest regional employer of Aboriginal people with a staff of 37 local Aboriginal people and a turnover of over $1 million.[12] The dance troupe travelled widely, earning international recognition and acclaim, and won many awards including the Pacific Asia Travel Association's Gold Award for 'cultural development' in 1989.[13]

The Theatre's activities changed the local and international reputation of Kuranda and were an enormous morale booster for local Aboriginal people who provided a ready pool of dancers under flexible employment arrangements. The Theatre was a focus of Djabugay group cohesion, pride and wellbeing and became a regular gathering point for local Aboriginal people. As David Hudson commented in 1986: 'The Tjapukai Dance Theatre has changed all our lives. And it has also changed the attitudes of the white residents of Kuranda to the Aborigines who live here.'[14] As Djabugay gained confidence, they also began to insist upon a larger share of the takings, often couching their dissatisfaction in terms of issues around the need to maintain cultural authenticity and to protect Djabugay intellectual property.[15]

The closure of the Theatre in 1996 and its replacement by the massive Cultural Park based in Cairns at the foot of the Kuranda Range and ostensibly worth around $6.5 million, with theatres, a museum, a traditional Aboriginal camp, an art gallery, shop and restaurant, brought significant change for the Djabugay. Many Djabugay who were formerly employed at the Theatre in Kuranda found it difficult to make the travel arrangements to get to work and some missed out on the bonus for arriving at work early.[16] The location of the Cultural Park away from the Djabugay's home base in Kuranda and the scale of the enterprise also appear to have detracted from Djabugay's sense of ownership and to have given rise to internal conflict. This occurred as a subgroup of Djabugay, the Yirrganydji, asserted the primacy of their coastal native title rights and interests in the Cultural Park location over those of the Djabugay group as a whole.

Many Djabugay were ambivalent about the Cultural Park: while they were proud of it and it generated 'Djabugay' as a 'positive public identity',[17] they were also being swept along in a commercial venture and complicated business partnership over which they appeared to have little control and for which they were ill prepared. The make-up of shareholders, which comprised some of the original stakeholders of the Theatre, was complex. It included: Don and Judy Freeman; Hudson Investments (David Hudson and his wife); Triamid (Skyrail, see below); Martin Investment; Channer Investment; the Commercial Development Corporation (CDC), the commercial arm of what was the Aboriginal and Torres Strait Islander Commission (ATSIC) and has now been replaced by Indigenous Business Australia (IBA); BADA; the Irukandji Aboriginal Corporation, which was the name chosen by the Yirrganydji for its corporate entity; and Ngandjin Aboriginal Corporation representing the dancers.

CDC purchased a 23 per cent shareholding on the understanding that it would eventually be bought out by Aboriginal interests. Ngandjin was gifted 3.5 per cent, which now stands at seven per cent. BADA, which was set up as a community trust fund to receive dividends earned from its shareholding, was originally gifted four per cent, and its shareholding at the time of writing was 15.8 per cent, with additional shares purchased through a CDC loan. The Irukandji Aboriginal Corporation shareholding was originally 5.5 per cent, and in 2009 was 10 per cent. A commitment from the partners gave Djabugay, through BADA, the first option to buy when the partners decided to sell their shares.[18] BADA and Irukandji also received a grant from ATSIC to purchase the land where the Cultural Park is located, which was owned by one of the Skyrail proprietors.[19] The land was then leased to the partnership for a 50-year term for a nominal sum, with a further 50-year option.[20]

In partnership with the Djabugay Land and Natural Resources Management Agency, representing the Djabugay Rangers and the Djabugay Elders Group, BADA entered into a Djabugay Cultural Coordination Agreement which required the establishment of a Cultural Coordinating Committee to promote and protect the integrity of Djabugay and Yirrganydji cultural interests and to provide advice on cultural issues.[21] In the past, Djabugay bore the brunt of accusations of 'borrowing' from other cultural areas. The Heads of Agreement for the Cultural Park, signed on 12 April 1995, noted an annual $20,000 benefit to be reviewed after three years, and to be paid at the discretion of Djabugay elders to a trust fund for community social benefits, such as funerals. A recruitment and employment policy was to be one of its outcomes, since the wage awards for the dancers meant that they were employed only as casuals.[22]

Despite the accolades received by the Cultural Park, it being lauded as a major successful Aboriginal enterprise and a business expectation of 'breaking even' after five to six years, the Park did not attract expected numbers. It encountered management and outdated product development issues and made a loss for some years. Tourist numbers were also severely affected by a range of factors including concerns about terrorism following the bombing of the New York World Trade Centre in 2001, an outbreak of Severe Acute Respiratory Syndrome (SARS) in 2003 and a downturn in global finances.

While BADA expected to repay the CDC loan within two to three years, profits did not materialise and the loan grew. In 2009 IBA purchased all the shares to protect the status of the Cultural Park as an important cultural icon and because of its potential to influence commercial confidence in other Aboriginal tourism enterprises and tour operator networks across Australia. A new Cultural Coordination Agreement between IBA and BADA reflected Djabugay's ongoing cultural ownership over the display of 'Djabugay' cultural products.

In the meantime, apart from one non-Djabugay Aboriginal owned art and craft shopfront in Kuranda, there was little Djabugay content in Kuranda's tourism enterprises. There had also been significant changes in the town as outdoor market venues were integrated into shopfronts, and the town was inundated daily by visitors from buses, QRail and Skyrail. Once the visitors departed around 3.30 pm each afternoon, the town resumed a semblance of 'normality'.

Skyrail cableway

In the mid-1990s the announcement of the intention to move the Theatre from Kuranda to Cairns and to establish the Cultural Park in its place came amidst considerable political unrest for the Djabugay. Skyrail's project to build a cableway from Cairns to Kuranda through the Barron Gorge National Park and to establish the base adjacent to the Cultural Park at Caravonica was of particular concern. The Djabugay had registered their native title application in 1994 and the claim was subject to mediation before the NNTT. However, the lease Skyrail required over parts of the Park had been already granted by the Queensland Government in 1993 without consultation or Djabugay approval.

There were protests and blockades which saw a range of shifting alliances between environmentalists, Cairns residents and Aboriginal people, including some Djabugay, under the banner of PAKS (People against Kuranda Skyrail).[23] Submissions on behalf of Djabugay under the *Aboriginal and Torres Strait Islander Heritage Protection Act 1984* (Cth)[24] rejected Skyrail's proposal and noted that it would interfere with a number of significant Djabugay sites. The submissions were refused by the Commonwealth Minister for Aboriginal and Torres Strait Islander Affairs in 1995. Some Djabugay were concerned that the cultural heritage surveys carried out for the applications had concluded that there were no places of Djabugay cultural significance under threat by commencement of work on the tower sites. The absence of a respectful negotiation process was at the heart of their concerns.[25]

A deal was finally struck facilitating the building of the cableway, involving the approval of Skyrail leases by DTAC's Governing Committee and DTAC's agreement not to seek compensation in the future on the proviso that Skyrail invested in the Cultural Park and did not oppose the Djabugay native title claim.[26] DTAC and Yirrganydji purchased the Cultural Park land from Skyrail for around $1 million with a grant from ATSIC. The deal virtually balanced out Skyrail's investment of $1.4 million in the Park and provided Skyrail with interests in the adjacent premises and access to some of the Park's infrastructure.

A six-member coordinating committee with equal Djabugay and Skyrail representation was established and Skyrail was to develop a comprehensive Djabugay employment and training strategy. Funds for an enterprise development strategy were to be sought through the Queensland Department of Family Services and the Department of Aboriginal and Islander Affairs. Skyrail was to invest $200,000 in joint ventures with Djabugay over five years.[27]

The cableway was officially opened in September 1995 and the Djabugay continued to be embroiled in negotiations over their native title claim for years to come, finally arriving at their consent determination in 2004. In 2008, Skyrail and DTAC agreed to investigate common projects and in 2009 these investigations were underway.[28]

The Djabugay native title consent determination over the Barron Gorge National Park

The Djabugay native title consent determination over the Park was made in light of the High Court decision in *Western Australia v Ward* which was handed down on 8 August 2002.[29] The decision meant that native title determinations over national parks could only recognise a non-exclusive bundle of limited rights and interests, over which the interests of the Crown and other stakeholders prevail.

The rights and interests in the determination, all of which relate to 'traditional activities', are to:

(a) be physically present on the Determination Area;
(b) camp on the Determination Area;
(c) hunt, fish and gather on, and take the natural resources of, the Determination Area for the purpose of satisfying their personal, domestic, social, cultural, religious, spiritual, ceremonial, and communal needs for non-commercial purposes;
(d) maintain and protect by lawful means places within the Determination Area of importance to the Djabugay People;
(e) perform social, cultural, religious, spiritual or ceremonial activities on the Determination Area and invite others to participate in those activities;
(f) make decisions about the use and enjoyment of the Determination Area by Aboriginal people who are governed by the traditional laws acknowledged and traditional customs observed by the Djabugay People.[30]

The rights to make decisions about access and use, to use fire or to erect permanent structures were not included in the determination. It excludes a number of areas in the Park under provisions in the NTA, including those relating to public works and where native title has been extinguished: areas previously covered by a freehold grant or exclusive lease which extinguish native title; leases and cableway for Skyrail areas; the boardwalk linking the Barron Gorge train station with the car park off Barron Falls Road; the Cairns–Kuranda railway corridor; and other public works associated with Barron Gorge Hydro-Electric Power Station. A range of other interests are said to 'continue to have effect and prevail over' native title interests, including those of the Wet Tropics Management Authority, the Stanwell Corporation (power generation), the Cairns and Mareeba city councils (now Tablelands Regional Council and Cairns Regional Council), Queensland Electricity Transmission Corporation Ltd, Ergon Energy Corporation and Skyrail.[31]

The native title rights and interests recognised are further subject to and exercisable in accordance with Commonwealth and state laws and the common law, and with traditional laws and customs observed by the Djabugay People. They are also subject to the *Nature Conservation Act 1992* (Qld) (NCA)[32] and the *Native Title Act 1993* (Cth) (NTA),[33] such that some existing native title rights might be extinguished in the future.[34]

The determination was accompanied by an ILUA which seems to further constrain the realisation of native title rights and interests.

The Djabugay Indigenous Land Use Agreement

During the years of mediations and meetings leading up to the determination, Djabugay repeatedly expressed their interest in jointly managing the Park with the Queensland Parks and Wildlife Service (QPWS). A government Interdepartmental

Working Group was established to formulate the policy parameters of joint management arrangements. Organisations representing a range of traditional owner interests, including the Queensland Indigenous Working Group were also in discussions with the government.[35] The Djabugay agreed to proceed to seek a consent determination and to negotiate the detail of future Park management arrangements at a later date.

The Barron Gorge ILUA was registered on 25 July 2005 on the NNTT Register.[36] The emphasis of clause 3 of the ILUA is on cultural and natural resources and values. The ILUA contractually constrains the exercise of the native title right to hunt, fish, gather, camp and use firearms. Camping in the Park is subject to the agreement of QPWS, and restricted to a period of four weeks without further agreement, and firearms may not be used without permission from QPWS. Activities must be nature based and ecologically sustainable.

The ILUA affirms the management principles for national parks under the NCA in preserving, protecting and presenting the area's 'cultural resources and values',[37] ensuring that use of the area is 'nature based' and 'ecologically sustainable'[38] and ensuring that a joint management area is to be managed, as far as practicable, 'in a way that is consistent with any Aboriginal tradition applicable to the area, including any tradition relating to activities in the area'.[39] Under clause 4, the parties agree to 'continue with bona fide negotiations towards a long term agreement to address each Party's concerns about land management, employment, cultural heritage protection and other matters they agree on, as soon as reasonably practicable'.[40] Without legislative change, there can be no contractual obligation in the ILUA for the state to seek Djabugay approval of management processes in the Park, and Djabugay cannot compel the state to enter an agreement (of unknown terms). That is, the Djabugay may rely only on the limited application of the future act provisions of the NTA (see below).[41]

Most significantly, clause 2.4 of the ILUA states that the ILUA expires in the event of any of the following:

(a) a regulation giving effect to a Management Plan in accordance with s 69 of the NCA;
(b) 31 December 2010;
(c) a Determination by the Federal Court that Native Title does not exist in the ILUA area.[42]

By late 2008, negotiations had stalled between the Djabugay, QPWS and DERM over the Barron Gorge National Park 2008 Draft Management Plan (the 2008 draft plan).[43] At the time of writing, no comprehensive long-term agreement with the Queensland Government over management of the Park had been reached, nor had a regulation giving effect to a management plan in accordance with s 69 of the NCA been put in place, and the ILUA was due to expire on 31 December 2010.

Djabugay responses to the Barron Gorge National Park 2008 Draft Management Plan

The 2008 draft plan is a standard park plan subject to a range of other legislation and plans, the impacts of which were unclear to the Djabugay Governing Committee. These include the NCA,[44] which describes the management regime for protected areas including national parks, which are to be managed in accordance with their management principles and management plans; the *Wet Tropics World Heritage Protection and Management Act 1993* (Qld), the *Wet Tropics Management Plan 1998* (Qld) made under that Act and other Wet Tropics management strategies; the *Environment Protection and Biodiversity Conservation Act 1999* (Cth) and its regulations; a range of water plans; and the ILUA. Para 6, which hyperlinks to a range of relevant plans and legislation, lists the *Queensland Heritage Act 1992* (Qld) (but curiously not the *Aboriginal Cultural Heritage Act 2003* (Qld) (ACHA) nor the NTA).[45]

For many years Djabugay had high expectations of what might constitute their management agreements and plans over the Park, as well as over the full extent of their traditional estate. Over the years they had detailed their aspirations in a range of draft agreements, business and strategic plans, and natural resource management strategies.[46] These aspirations, which had not changed significantly since 1997 when Djabugay worked on their Land Use and Management Strategy in preparing for their native title claim, were reaffirmed at the 2008 planning workshop. They included their interest in managing the Park at every level; their requirement for a Djabugay majority board of management; and the need for resourcing of a Djabugay office within the Park with appropriately paid Djabugay staff and a realistic operational budget.[47]

But unfortunately the details of employment and economic aspirations and associated strategies fall outside the framework of a management plan, which tends to focus on natural and cultural resource and visitor management; and the Djabugay could see few, if any, realisations of their vision and aspirations in the 2008 draft plan.[48] It refers to the Park as home to Djabugay[49] and the Park is described in para 1.0 titled 'Management intent' as under cooperative management[50] by the Queensland Government's Environmental Protection Agency (EPA) and 'Traditional Owners', as well as Skyrail and QRail, to the surprise of the Djabugay who had not been consulted about these partners.[51] Under 'Partnerships' in para 1.0, the management approach is said to be adaptive, cooperative and collaborative with stakeholders and neighbouring property owners, including the Department of Natural Resources and Water, Cairns Regional Council, Tablelands Regional Council, QRail, Skyrail, Stanwell Corporation Limited and Powerlink, but there is no mention of the Djabugay native title holders. In s 4.3 'Indigenous cultural values' and under the heading 'Actions and guidelines', A19 refers to a Barron Gorge National Park Steering Committee comprising representatives from the EPA and DNTAC, with the committee terms of reference to be jointly developed; and A20 states that the

Djabugay will be 'advised' of management activities within the Park, such as work programs and permit applications.⁵²

At the 2008 planning workshop, Djabugay reluctantly accepted the reality that the limitations of their native title determination would not permit their 1997 demand for formal recognition of their native title rights and interests through ownership over the Park. However, they were concerned that the 2008 draft plan does not contain an accountability framework regarding 'advice' provided by Djabugay and does not adequately address QPWS obligations under the ACHA. They also were concerned that there are no financial or governance commitments in agreements or implementation strategies linked to the plan — such as there are in the Indigenous Management Agreements available under the national park (Cape York Peninsula Aboriginal land) arrangements. Such commitments might include recognition of Djabugay labour in the provision of fees for service for traditional owner participation in committee meetings and formal consultation processes about works and commercial activities to protect cultural and native title interests. They might also include giving first preference to Djabugay for capital works or maintenance contracts, as the Djabugay were seeking. Although Djabugay involvement in the Park is not necessarily contingent on funding, and while the management plan may be seen as an aspirational document rather than a forum for addressing funding issues, the question of whether or not Djabugay have the capacity to effectively coordinate and undertake the envisaged cooperative and collaborative arrangements remains.

At a number of governing committee meetings and at the planning workshop, the Djabugay expressed frustration over their negotiations with QPWS. Their requests for fees for service in attending meetings and providing advice usually elicited responses that only meals and transport to and from the meetings would be provided. They felt that their suggestions fell on deaf ears, were dismissed as impractical and illegitimate, or not within the purview of the government. They expressed concern that their unique position as native title holders was not appropriately recognised, and that the 2008 draft plan exacerbated power imbalances between Djabugay and the government. They also pointed out an issue that had arisen in the mediations leading up to their native title determination: that while QPWS and DERM staff they were talking to were sympathetic to their views, the staff did not have the authority to make decisions and were bound by forces and policies 'higher up'.⁵³

Ultimately, the Djabugay did not want to enter into an agreement which required significant commitment and investment on their part, but which did not seem to secure practical benefit. Two governing committee members, Rhonda Brim and Gerald Hobbler, summarise the overall reactions to the 2008 draft plan:

> The plan is not celebrating Djabugay in the Park; we're hidden in the plan. Djabugay come after the weeds, fire and feral — QPWS doesn't have to listen. We sound like we were silent; they're sweeping us under the carpet. We don't

want to entrench something that's third rate. We want full-time involvement on the ground.[54]

Millions of people through the Park, there's nothing for TOs [traditional owners], not even jobs. In the NT, they get royalties; we get nothing. We going to sit down here, we need an office space going forever, our coordinator is working for nothing, we have to represent Djabugay.[55]

For his part, the Director-General of the EPA wrote to DNTAC in 2008 in response to its letter which set out Djabugay concerns in relation to the management plan, including a lack of decision-making power in relation to the Park.[56] He noted that the EPA had a 'long history of working with Djabugay people to improve involvement in management of protected areas', setting out a number of activities with which they had been jointly involved.[57] These included activities relating to the Park, such as negotiating the ILUA, interpretative signage, a commercial activity agreement for Djabugay tourism enterprise and employment of a Djabugay casual in consultation processes for the management plan.

In July 2009, the Djabugay Governing Committee met with QPWS's General Regional Manager, its Manager Coastal Area and its Team Leader of the Indigenous Engagement Unit. During this meeting, Djabugay representatives informed them that:

- The Barron Gorge National Park management plan was a low priority for Djabugay given the impasses in negotiations thus far.
- Djabugay wanted a plan of management for all of Djabugay country.
- Djabugay wanted to set up and enter into a framework agreement before progressing the management plan.[58]

Subsequent discussions also considered the possibility of an agreed short-term, two- to three-year management plan for the Park, after which the framework agreement would set the direction for a subsequent plan. Djabugay indicated that they were prepared to work on building productive relationships regarding the Park in person with QPWS staff, but that these relationships could not compensate for what they perceived as their weak structural position in the 2008 draft plan.

At the same time, in the discussions between Djabugay and QPWS, which I observed, there appeared to be a number of complex historical 'elephants in the room'. These required frank exploration and reality checking. But these explorations were unlikely to materialise given the relatively entrenched positions which both Djabugay and QPWS and DERM staff, who were restrained by government policy, brought to the negotiating table. These included:

- conflicting views on the histories of relationships
- whether Aboriginal rangers work best away from their home countries, or whether, as the Djabugay insisted, Djabugay Rangers should work on Djabugay country

The Djabugay native title story: getting back in town

- whether many of the issues in QPWS employing Aboriginal rangers in the past might be addressed if the rangers were employed by the Djabugay themselves in a DRA
- reasons for the demise of the previous DRA
- how QPWS offers to Djabugay of short-term contracts could impact social security arrangements, including Djabugay being suspended from social security benefits for a considerable period of time
- how QPWS suggestions that Djabugay should send in their resumes to be considered for work along with everyone else recognised neither their unique status as native title holders, nor the capacity of many unemployed Djabugay to do so
- the general capacity of Djabugay to undertake work and be involved in the Park.

There also seemed to be a need to explore the complex reasons that Djabugay did not appear to frequent the Park: that Djabugay had been effectively excluded from the Park for many years, and that the Park is small with high visitation and commercial activities — leaving little space for Djabugay interests, including areas where they might camp or set up living areas. A number of complex dynamics are alluded to in the following quotations from Rhonda Brim and Gerald Hobbler:

> People don't always go in the park. Not that they don't want to go there; there's no ownership. They want to do things they want to do, not with people watching them — can't do this, can't do that. Sure as hell if I took a group of kids, rangers would be there: 'Can't go there', 'What you doing?' 'Can't do this, can't do that'. Sometimes they're okay, long as they know where we are and what we're doing.[59]
>
> We can go in the park, but we don't feel we're owners. We can go in if we want to, but someone will come along and say, 'What are you doing?' They are depriving people of something that are close to their heart. The rangers don't know who's Djabugay.[60]

Djabugay corporate governance and fulfilling statutory requirements

As noted above, in 2009 Djabugay native title business was located in a governance network of four corporations. The DTAC, which was incorporated in 1992 and is the oldest corporation, was the umbrella and primary corporate vehicle representing Djabugay interests. DTAC's objectives required it to look after land and cultural heritage, and Djabugay welfare, including employment, social welfare and housing. The second, BADA, with its acronym meaning 'head', was established in 1995 to earn money for Djabugay through shareholdings in the Cultural Park and to be the trustees of a community trust fund. The third, DBDAC trading as Djabugay Country Tours (DCT), was set up to be a tour guide agency in 2005, following an

ATSIC sponsored community survey which recommended a land-based, outdoors tourism-oriented business. The fourth, DNTAC, was incorporated in 2004, and was inserted into an already complex arrangement of corporate structures. All were originally incorporated under the *Aboriginal Councils and Associations Act 1972* (Cth) and are now incorporated under its successor, the *Corporations (Aboriginal and Torres Strait Islander) Act 2006* (CATSI Act).

These multiple incorporated entities allow Djabugay to expand their operations while reducing the impact of failed ventures on the assets and operations of related entities. However, this risk reduction, allocating commercial operations to separately incorporated bodies, is offset by the multiplication of administrative and reporting responsibilities required by the Office of the Register of Indigenous Corporations (ORIC) and the CATSI Act. There is also the potential for any or all of these corporations to be captured by factions, to compete with each other and to be played off against each other by non-Djabugay interests.

At the planning workshop in September 2008, the Djabugay considered these and other issues relating to public benevolent institution (PBI) status. They then made a number of resolutions at their 2008 AGM to rationalise Djabugay corporate governance and to address ORIC's transition requirements to the CATSI Act. The effect of these resolutions was to declare DTAC to be the single Djabugay entity (sDe), and thus to ensure that all Djabugay corporations have the same governing committee, manager, contact person/secretary/public officer, contact details, a single board of directors and ultimately the same membership register. Governing committee meetings and AGMs were to be held at the same time for all the corporations, and meetings closed and reopened to conduct the business of each entity.

While DTAC's membership was conducive to PBI status, in that it was open to all adults of Aboriginal descent (including of Torres Strait Islander descent) who normally live in the Kuranda region, its objectives were not. The 2008 AGM resolved to change DTAC's objectives to address: 'The direct relief of poverty, sickness, suffering, distress, misfortune, disability or helplessness of Indigenous People', and for DTAC to operate the Djabugay Gift Fund in accordance with requirements of the *Income Tax Assessment Act 1997* (Cth).[61] The objectives of DBDAC were also changed to: 'Develop and operate business activities that: provide employment for Djabugay People; Promote and manage Djabugay's Cultural Heritage; provide for the management of the Djabugay Traditional Estate'.[62]

The 2008 AGM ratified a set of protocols for governing committee meetings. It also acknowledged that the Djabugay Governing Committee needed to develop protocols for interacting with external stakeholders, including governments, as Djabugay experience had been that stakeholder representatives did not follow up on undertakings and took considerable time to respond to correspondence.

Legal uncertainty: future acts and cultural heritage clearances

In addition to managing the compliance requirements of the four corporations, Djabugay are also impacted by requirements in the NTA concerning future acts, and in the ACHA. Both regimes create a number of uncertainties which impact on their governance capability and on future planning.

The Australian Government's Attorney-General's website defines a 'future act' as an act which 'affects native title if it extinguishes or is otherwise wholly or partly inconsistent with the continued existence, enjoyment or exercise of native title'. The word 'act' is defined widely to include the making or amendment of legislation, the grant or renewal of licences and permits and can include executive actions in some circumstances. An act of government may 'affect' native title if, for example, it allows someone to do an activity on native title land that they otherwise have no right to do, or it prevents a native title holder from doing what their native title entitles them to do.[63]

Under the NTA, notification of a future act is required to registered native title claimants, registered native title bodies corporate and other affected parties about the proposed act. Special procedural rights called the right to negotiate apply to the granting of certain mining tenements and compulsory acquisitions of native title rights and interests, among other things (pt 2, div 3).[64] For non-mining matters, including public works and management plans in national parks which require notification under s 24JB, notification is a question of 'consultation' which can mean little more than the right to receive notification and that activities automatically proceed 28 days after the notice.

The governing committee did not have a clear understanding of what constitutes a future act and when notification should occur, and had not received a future act notice for some time. In the past, Djabugay future act notifications had mostly been for requests to carry out research in the Park and were processed on a case-by-case basis by the Djabugay Governing Committee. If the future act fell outside an area under a native title application, or on the native title determination area, a notice was usually sent to the NQLC, which passed it on to Djabugay, though the Department of Main Roads and QRail had a practice, as a matter of course, of contacting DTAC directly when they wanted to undertake works outside the exclusion zone in the Park.

Ideally, formal future act notices would be issued for public works in the Park, including for proposed buildings and developments, and commercial activities, though this did not always seem to be the case. An agreement was reached with DERM for a class application structure for clearances of low-impact activities, including guided tours into the Park, though the definition of 'impact' was inevitably a matter of interpretation. Such complexities and uncertainties are common across the native system where future act notification processes do not seem to be overseen systematically, and instead seem to be a matter of goodwill and risk assessments taken at various levels of government.

Similarly, Djabugay were also uncertain about when cultural heritage clearances were required under the ACHA. The ACHA sets out a cultural heritage regime to ensure that Aboriginal people are involved in managing the recognition, protection and conservation of Aboriginal cultural heritage, and in establishing processes for the efficient management of activities to avoid or minimise harm to Aboriginal cultural heritage.[65] Applications to become a registered cultural heritage body for a specific area, as DTAC made on behalf of the Djabugay RNTBC, also take place under the ACHA.[66]

Unlike the future act regime, the ACHA does not require registered native title interests in order to have effect.[67] Djabugay had received a number of requests for cultural heritage clearances or permissions to carry out work on land that was part of their broader traditional estate but not the subject of native title applications or within their determination area. For example, during the field work period, they received a request from a researcher to carry out a cultural heritage survey for Powerlink, which wanted to replace its towers at the Bare Hill (Bunda Bibandji) Conservation Park. Conversely, and also during this period, the Queensland Department of Public Works notified DTAC that the department was not officially required to carry out a cultural heritage survey in relation to proposed works on an area adjacent to the determination area, and that they intended to make their cultural heritage management agreements with individuals rather than with Djabugay corporations.[68]

In attempting to address these idiosyncrasies, Djabugay began to formalise their approaches to cultural heritage clearances and to develop a template cultural heritage management agreement with a fee-for-service schedule. Ultimately, they recognised the need to break the pattern of giving permissions for activities that they did not see as having benefits — for example, applications for research activities in the Park which do not plan to involve Djabugay but which require significant Djabugay resources to process.

Djabugay cohesion and disputes

As is the case throughout many areas of Australia, native title processes have often been characterised by disputes among Aboriginal people which are frequently focused on who the 'right people' for country are. Over time, a number of 'language groups' which have strongly asserted their single nationhood, like the Djabugay, have splintered, as subgroups have asserted the primacy and exclusivity of their rights and interests over particular areas of land within a traditional estate, often as the areas become the focus of development activity and are in competition for scarce resources including money.⁶⁹ As individuals and subgroups assert their autonomy over the group, and as personal animosities with deep histories are played out on a native title platform, claims are often based on less inclusive groupings, such as the 'clan' or subgroup distinctions found in sometimes unreliable early ethnographies, such as Tindale's genealogies.⁷⁰

Previous ethnographies, including Tindale's, suggest that five clan distinctions were made within the broader Djabugay estate, each clan apparently speaking its own dialect of the Djabugay language. The names Tindale gave these clans — Djabuganydji, Nyagali, Bulway or Buluwanydji, Yirrganydji and Guluy — have been picked up in subsequent accounts of the Djabugay, where the clans are described as being linked by commonly held beliefs in Storywaters, walking tracks, intermarriages and descent from common ancestral beings.⁷¹ The many commonalities, interdependencies and interconnections between the clans provide the basis for the representation of Djabugay as a 'one nation' cohesive group and for an ongoing commitment on the part of Djabugay Governing Committee members to think inclusively.

While a number of members of the governing committee were concerned to maintain this cohesion, at the time of field work their efforts were challenged by claims based on the kinds of subgroup or clan affiliations described above. The first of these claims arose when the Yirrganydji asserted their primary coastal interests in the Cultural Park, as the relocation of the Theatre from Kuranda opened the field for disputes over the legitimate representative group to carry out negotiations. While the governing committee was adamant that those identifying as Yirrganydji were 'part of Djabugay', in order to see the deal proceed they agreed — albeit reluctantly — for Yirrganydji to have its own shareholding, though through BADA the Djabugay group as a whole was always intended to have the larger share. Similarly, a Bulway-only 'clan-based' approach to managing Djabugay Country Tours, which replaced the DRA and which focuses on the Bare Hill (Bunda Bibandji) Conservation Park and Davies Creek National Park, continued to give rise to significant dissatisfaction and conflict.

Addressing these conflicts among Djabugay will be difficult, since there have been serious and ongoing historical and personal disputes between some Djabugay associated with the Djabugay corporations and a few influential Djabugay who do not usually interact with the corporations. There are also broader systemic issues to address. While these disputes appear to be about competition for funds, they are underpinned by issues relating to poor governance in the past, including an apparent lack of transparency around decision-making processes and the absence of clear and agreed implementation processes. A lack of transparency and collectively agreed principles for the distribution of elders' funds in relation to the Cultural Park, for example, gave rise to a number of unanswered questions relating to the payment and distribution of the $20,000 annual payment in the Cultural Coordination Agreement. This required monies to be paid to a trust fund (BADA), from which it would be distributed at the discretion of the Djabugay Elders Group for community benefit. Instead, funds were apparently directly paid to elders by way of decision-making processes which were seemingly not transparent, including an absence of general agreement about the definition of 'elder' and about the processes that should be put in place for replacing deceased elders.

A third example of conflict, which was accompanied by the assertion of Tindale-like clan affiliations, concerned claims to the Mona Mona Mission by the non-Djabugay Muluridji group claim. Mona Mona was a Seventh Day Adventist Mission, established near Kuranda in the early 1900s, to which many Aboriginal people from the Kuranda region and beyond were removed. The mission was closed in the 1960s and its residents dispersed, having been told that the mission would be flooded in the construction of a dam on Flaggy Creek. There have been a number of attempts over the years to re-establish Mona Mona as an Aboriginal community.[72]

A coherent and persistent Mona Mona identity was born out of the mission which crossed boundaries between so-called 'historical people' who lived on the mission but came from traditional countries elsewhere and 'traditional peoples' who might lay claim to the mission under the NTA, which requires proof of continuing traditional laws and customs and connection to country back to sovereignty. Both Djabugay and the neighbouring Muluridji assert ownership over the mission, and Djabugay said they that had held off lodging a native title claim, not only because of the traditional owner disputes, but also because they feared that such a claim would be divisive since not all those with Mona Mona associations were Djabugay.[73]

Various planning exercises were undertaken over Mona Mona including one by the Centre for Appropriate Technology (CAT) as early as 1993, which was funded by ATSIC through the Koah Mantaka Kowrara Mona Mona (KMKM) Corporation.[74] The plan attracted funding from the National Aboriginal Health Service of $3.2 million for power, waste transfer and the upgrade of houses, but the funding was never released. Apparently the government was not willing to take action while the dispute between Muluridji and Djabugay continued in the context of a national policy discussion which rejected the development of infrastructure on small outstation communities that were seen to be 'unviable'.[75]

In 2007, a Mona Mona working party was established and a government facilitator spent some time at Kuranda 'consulting' with locals amidst calls from Mona Mona residents for the funding to be released and the land to be handed back. In October 2008, the Queensland Government decided that Mona Mona land would be held in trust by the Department of Communities, with 100 hectares to be set aside as a cultural heritage reserve and the remaining 1510 hectares as a national park or conservation reserve. No formal cultural heritage notifications occurred. The newly established Mona Mona Action Group (Action Group), consisting of Djabugay, those identifying as Muluridji and a range of others with associations with the mission, was opposed to this decision. The group was hopeful of a change of government in Queensland, believing that in the 2009 election campaign the Liberal National Party member had agreed to overturn the decision if elected.

At the time of writing, there had been no action taken in relation to Mona Mona, and the re-elected Labor government called for additional broad community consultations, further meetings, development of options by the Action Group and ongoing mediations. While key Muluridji representatives agreed to be part of the Action Group, they had not attended meetings, signalling further disunity and providing the government with reasons for more delay. At the same time, the delay over a number of years allowed the dispute between 'Djabugay' and 'Muluridji' to compound and gather momentum.

These examples of Djabugay disputes, involving the assertion of clan-like affiliations, compounded by government delays and poor Djabugay governance in the past, signal the need for DTAC as representative of a network of Djabugay corporations to build relationships not only with those who identify as Djabugay, but also with other Aboriginal individuals and organisations and the broader Kuranda community.

Building relationships

As is the case with other native title corporations that manage native title interests in towns, such as the Lhere Artepe in Alice Springs, native title business pervades many areas of community life in Kuranda, though it should be noted that the Djabugay native title determination does not include the town. Djabugay have diverse relationships across the community through intermarriage and daily life experiences with Aboriginal people with a range of other 'traditional' affiliations and with non-Aboriginal people. DTAC and its related corporations also have 'corporate' relationships with other Kuranda Aboriginal and non-Aboriginal corporations and community groups. Town-based agencies and committees often call on the Djabugay Governing Committee, as representatives of the traditional owners of the town area, to address a range of issues, including alcohol management strategies.

Building relationships with other entities, organisations and individuals is thus a priority of the 'back in town' strategy. This includes relationships with the Kuranda Business community, local Aboriginal corporations such as the Ngoonbi Housing Co-operative Society (Ngoonbi), other native title corporations nearby, and organisations and agencies supporting Aboriginal development, such as NQLC, the Cairns Regional Council, FaHCSIA's Cairns-based Indigenous Coordination Centre, DERM and QPWS.

As a consequence, at the time of writing DTAC was undertaking a number of relationship-building initiatives, such as improving communication with its constituents through its website (Djabugay.org.au) and preparing brochures that informed residents about Djabugay roles and responsibilities and provided information about the Djabugay office as a central point of contact. There were also plans to develop newsletters, hold gatherings and social events, and go on camping trips including into the Park, possibly with QPWS rangers. Ultimately, DTAC saw a need for a Kuranda Aboriginal community relations plan, which would bring all relevant organisations together in a 'whole-of-community, whole-of-government' approach.

However, while DTAC was concerned to build relationships in the community, it also wanted to strategically target beneficial relationships. Above all, if Djabugay were to become cooperative managers of the Park, and advance their ideas for a framework agreement as outlined above, DTAC would need to build relationships with staff and decision-makers of QPWS and DERM. At the same time, Djabugay, DERM and QPWS needed to decide whether this was a priority given the failure of past discussions. In targeting strategically beneficial relationships, DTAC also had to consider its capacity and the resources required.

Djabugay capacity, funding and economic opportunities

Without office space to use as a base to work out of, everything breaks down — telephones, faxes. Without communication, everything falls down.

Gerald Hobbler[76]

As is the case for many RNTBCs across Australia, funding is a major issue for the Djabugay. A lack of ongoing resources gave rise to poor governance in the past, including non-compliance with regulatory requirements and difficulties in dealing with disputes, and was a major cause of the failure of a number of Djabugay initiatives. During the course of field work, funding for DTAC was uncertain and constantly under threat. As Andy Duffin commented:

> It's the story of our life — funding running out. We wait for cyclone money. If cyclones don't come in, there's no money. We pray for cyclones but we never got any lately.[77]

Governance issues including managing disputes and strategically working with available resources formed a large part of discussion at the two-day Bushwork Kuranda planning workshop in 2008, which was attended by around 40 Djabugay people. The workshop recommended a broad strategy:

- to put behind any past issues surrounding programs and projects which are no longer operating;
- to continue to rectify any outstanding financial matters from past projects;
- to seek an appropriate 'foundation project' to get Djabugay "back in town";
- to avoid becoming involved in a lot of small projects which involve high administrative outputs; and

- to take every opportunity to promote a positive image of Djabugay, including in dealing with government private enterprise and the public.[78]

Over a number of years, the Djabugay repeatedly sought assistance for a coordinating office, sometimes within the Park, sometimes elsewhere, with appropriately renumerated and qualified staff and a realistic operational budget. Limited relief came with funding of $50,000 from FaHCSIA in the 2007–08 financial year. It was received in the fourth quarter of the financial year and had to be accounted for in that quarter, in the rush to disperse unspent funds from FaHCSIA's native title budget prior to the end of the financial year. The funding provided for a Djabugay office in the Kuranda Neighbourhood Centre and for the employment of a part-time chief executive officer (CEO) with administrative and commercial skills, who quickly identified a wide range of outstanding Djabugay business. These activities provided the rationale for a funding application to FaHCSIA in the 2008–09 financial year for an increased amount, though only the same amount of $50,000 was received, this time a little earlier, in the second quarter.

The Djabugay Governing Committee thus remained uncertain about the future of its office and the employment of its CEO. It was also dealing with increasing business, much of which had the potential to generate income. Since the opening of the Djabugay office in Kuranda in January 2007, many stakeholders, including QPWS, have contacted Djabugay through the office, often expressing relief that there was finally a contact point for conducting business. Although since 1995 there had been Djabugay operational working groups which might have provided a point of contact, these groups appeared to have lapsed and contact by external stakeholders was often made through individuals. A lack of effective communication of issues to the group as a whole meant that members were often misinformed and conflict was exacerbated among Djabugay people. The standing of DTAC had also diminished, as it was perceived to have been ineffective and unable to carry out its statutory functions.

Without knowing whether FaHCSIA funds would again be available, or what the level of funding would be, the 2008 AGMs of the four corporations resolved to keep the Djabugay office, by then relocated underneath a real estate office, open until June 2010 through anticipated income generated from the sale of the Djabugay shares in the Cultural Park to IBA. The Djabugay Governing Committee was hopeful that, in three years, it would also receive income from the new Cultural Coordination Agreement with IBA mentioned earlier, and from leasing land to IBA for the Park. However, this was dependent on the commercial success of the Park in the context of a downturn in global finances.

Having to use scarce funds generated commercially to operate the Djabugay office and to meet ORIC's time-consuming and imposed corporate governance requirements meant that DTAC had little money or capacity to meet other Djabugay aspirations.

The activities that Djabugay aspired to required substantial expertise and significant resourcing beyond funding for administration and compliance.

DTAC needed funds to employ a consultant to assist in formulating Djabugay interests in the management plan of the Park, to broker effective partnerships with QPWS and DERM and with other stakeholders, and to pursue a range of initiatives aimed at ensuring benefit to Djabugay over the long term. These initiatives included streamlining future act processes; developing fee-for-service structures; establishing effective partnerships with a range of other funding bodies; establishing joint ventures with commercial partners and growing non-government income streams through commercial agreements; establishing Indigenous owned tourism ventures; locating, safeguarding and recording places of cultural significance on a web-based database; re-establishing the DRA to create jobs both in land management and tourism; and developing community awareness and education about native title rights and Djabugay activities, including regular community newsletters.

Central to DTAC's success and its economic viability was its capacity to generate income. Given the significant visitation to the Park, the extensive use of the Park by tour operators and growing pressure to further develop tourism infrastructure in the Park, Djabugay could have been benefiting from a range of economic opportunities and playing key roles in decision-making in the Park. Djabugay ideas to generate income included donation boxes or a small 'head tax' for visitors to the Park to be collected by Skyrail and QRail, which would take a percentage for administration, with the remainder being paid to Djabugay. There was potential in the four-way management partnership model apparent in the 2008 draft plan between Djabugay, EPA, Skyrail and QRail. While Djabugay were initially taken aback at the introduction of two new partners without prior consultation — seeing this as another example of a lack of recognition — they did not dismiss the idea. Opportunities could well emerge from the discussions that were beginning with Skyrail.

Other opportunities could emerge from negotiations taking place during the field work concerning Ngoonbi Farm, a freehold lease area on the outskirts of Kuranda, which was held at the time of writing by the Indigenous Land Corporation (ILC). It wanted to divest the lease to Djabugay as its agent, providing them with an overarching role in managing the property.[79] Progress was slow, with the Djabugay Governing Committee nervous about ILC's proposal to 'management test' them over a period of two to three years and about its own capacity to manage additional responsibilities — the details of which had not been clearly identified. At the time of writing, an agreement had been reached that ILC would provide a consultant to develop a property management plan to assist the Djabugay Governing Committee in identifying future aspirations for Ngoonbi Farm and associated implementation issues. However, the requirement of a business plan, which set out the implementation in detail and which would require resources to prepare, had not been addressed.

While new funding options had been considered as a result of the activities of the Djabugay office, nothing concrete had emerged. In any event, government funding and the generation of income were not the only factors impacting Djabugay capacity to achieve their aspirations. Human capability and capacity were also critical factors. Djabugay people were often living in dire circumstances, including poor social conditions, low life expectancy and low levels of education, raising questions about Djabugay general capabilities, the opportunities that are actually open to them and the conditions of possibility.[80] Having the skills to be members of governing committees with qualifications and experience to advise about economic development and manage complex governance arrangements is even more challenging for the Djabugay than it is for the broader community.

Djabugay with education and skills were often already employed, meaning that governing committee members were frequently drawn from the ranks of the unemployed or the retired. There was also a general shortage of qualified Djabugay people to employ in the corporations. While many Djabugay had received a wide range of training through unemployment programs, it had never been followed by the necessary employment in which the skills learned could be practised. Committed Djabugay who led the native title mediations and negotiations before the determination were meeting-weary. Others who had been involved in managing the DRA or dancing at the Theatre or the Cultural Park were no longer involved in Djabugay business; some were running their own cultural activities. The closure of the CDEP and the introduction of subsequent employment programs also had an unintended impact on the capacity of Djabugay to attend meetings. Government agencies had relied on CDEP to organise their consultations and for CDEP management to give CDEP workers leave to attend the numerous meetings involved. DTAC was also concerned that the demise of CDEP had resulted in a diminishing sense of community, the collapse of community organisations, growing individualism and difficulties in having meetings with government.

Overall, there were divergences between Djabugay aspirations, the individual capacities of the Djabugay, and funding for the technical expertise required to achieve these aspirations. This was further compounded by a history of controversy. As Djabugay began to recognise these capacity issues, DTAC began to insist on only taking on projects that it had the capacity to fulfil. 'Welfare' activities, such as those carried out by the Kuranda Justice Group, Sports and Recreation, youth groups and housing issues, were generally left to other organisations such as CDEP and Ngoonbi. DTAC also softened its stance in seeking a framework agreement for the Park, with staged milestones and reviews for Djabugay involvement in its management. It also began to identify an appropriate 'foundation project' for 'getting back in town', as was recommended by Bushwork Consultants in their report on the planning workshop in 2008.[81]

Conclusion

This paper demonstrates the attempts of the Djabugay RNTBC, as represented by DTAC between 2007 and 2009, to implement the broad strategy for Djabugay 'getting back in town' which arose out of the 2008 Kuranda planning workshop. Getting back in town will involve confronting the history of Djabugay relations, including issues relating to the Cultural Park, Skyrail, the former Mona Mona Mission, the DRA and the Park.

Djabugay will need to address issues of capacity, including their management of disputes as they occur systemically in maintaining a paradigm of 'all Djabugay as one group' and simultaneously recognising and accounting for specific clan-like interests in local areas within the Djabugay estate. Conflict is inevitably embedded in structures and processes, and addressing it appropriately can be time-consuming and resource intensive. There is also the broader issue of building the capacity of future members of the Djabugay Governing Committee, which might be partly addressed over the long term as Djabugay leaders nurture and mentor their successors. It is the next generation with education and skills in whose hands the fate of Djabugay lies; without involving this next generation in the machinations of Djabugay business now, Djabugay affairs will be relegated to a few and will be meaningless for the next generation.

Finding appropriate and timely assistance in the form of skilled third party independent process managers, facilitators or mediators who understand the issues and can assist in addressing conflict and brokering partnerships will be difficult and costly. While the prospect of the four-way partnership model between Djabugay, the Queensland Government, Skyrail and QRail shows promise, it also raises issues that require careful consideration. These include the need for the clear identification of the roles, responsibilities and expectations of each of the partners, as well as addressing the additional governance required in managing multiple partnerships.

Djabugay reluctance to agree to the 2008 draft plan for the Park may appear to some observers as foolhardy, stubborn or a matter of political rhetoric. But there are a number of critical learnings for other RNTBCs to be taken from their approach. In the first instance, the development of management plans that purport to involve and recognise native title holders is a hollow gesture and damaging to the establishment of effective partnerships without accompanying secured resources, timelines and implementation processes. Rectifying this will require major changes involving the securing of resources through forward planning and estimates, and established budgetary procedures submitted to Treasury with explicit policy directions regarding joint management (or whatever terminology might be employed in describing such partnerships). Whole-of-government implementation plans that are produced cooperatively, funded and reality checked against the capacities and objectives of

Djabugay are essential. Such plans could go beyond mere statements of support. They could provide Djabugay with assistance in accessing sources of funding for a Djabugay office; for capacity development, training and cross-cultural awareness programs; or to re-establish the now defunct DRA, whose involvement in day-to-day management activities was supported and endorsed in the 2008 draft plan.[82] That is, real and ongoing commitment and coordination of resources is necessary if native title holders are to benefit from determinations over protected areas. While QPWS and DERM staff appeared supportive of Djabugay's intention to create and enter into a framework agreement, they also notified Djabugay that they did not have funds to support the process.

Secondly, deferring the negotiation of practical issues of the Park management, including the form of co-management and how it might be funded, until after negotiations for ILUAs accompanying determinations has left Djabugay with little bargaining power and without the substantial support that was available at the time of the negotiations. Ideally, there would be a staged, resourced process of capacity building in the Park over an initial five-year period, for Djabugay people and government staff to build relationships by working together in person, and to then reassess progress based on realities rather than on a 'big' vision for the Park whose implementation issues are never explored.

Thirdly, Djabugay actions highlight the need for RNTBCs and associated corporations to be realistic about their aspirations and strategic about their involvement with the range of agencies who seek interaction with them, particularly given limited resources. Staged, flexible and scaled approaches such as the framework approach suggested by Djabugay in 2009 in relation to the Park, accompanied by facilitated sustained and non-threatening dialogue, will be important to ensure that activities are matched to the capacity of all involved. This dialogue should explore histories, issues and feelings, and challenge some of the Djabugay oppositional stances and entrenched 'business-as-usual' approaches of government participants. All levels of the EPA need to participate: staff on the ground through to managers and beyond to decision-makers at the 'top'. Making any proposed partnerships work will require significant imagination on the part of all, including Skyrail and QRail as this dialogue is extended.

Djabugay will inevitably need government support for a number of years to go forward independently and to get themselves 'back in town'. As Rhonda Brim commented, they need a new start under very different circumstances:

> Is government going to take us seriously? If they are, they would resource us to act professionally. It makes you wonder why we put that claim! It's not visible but we're trying as hard as we can! We need a new start: an opportunity to prove we can do the right thing.[83]

But there is no formalised and designated long-term funding for RNTBCs to manage native title in the post determination landscape.

Finally, Barron Gorge is only a small part of Djabugay country. The Djabugay Governing Committee wishes to discuss management of Djabugay country over the whole Djabugay estate. At the time of writing, it had also signalled to the NQLC that it wanted to lodge native title claims over other protected areas in Djabugay country in a 'whole-of-traditional-country' planning approach, including over Davies Creek National Park, Jumrum Creek Conservation Park, Bare Hill (Bunda Bibandji) Conservation Park, other parts of the Barron River outside national park land, and state forest reserves along the Macalister and Lamb ranges. This intention highlights the importance of effective and well-resourced partnership brokering between what were then known as EPA, DERM and QPWS and the Djabugay in a single agreement-making process, and partnership within the kind of framework agreement proposed by the Djabugay.

Failing this, the Djabugay and the Queensland Government are destined to carry out piecemeal and costly native title negotiations for many years to come. Unfortunately, native title processes cannot offer exclusive possession determinations over parks, such as the Barron Gorge National Park and other protected areas. But, resources aside, this does not preclude the Djabugay and the Queensland Government working in productive partnerships to achieve whatever they can within the formal limitations that constrain them, goodwill on the part of both permitting. As the quote at the beginning of this chapter suggests, recognition is not enough.

Endnotes

1 Barry Hunter, pers. comm., 5 May 2009.
2 This paper is based on a number of visits to Kuranda between 2007 and 2009 and ongoing intermittent discussions since then. An initial meeting with the Djabugay Native Title Aboriginal Corporation (DNTAC) Governing Committee took place in November 2007 to enter into a research action partnership between Djabugay and AIATSIS. Visits of two weeks each were made to Kuranda in 2008; AIATSIS sponsored a pilot planning workshop which was facilitated by Ross Johnston and Ian Kirkby of Bushwork Consultants in September 2008; and I returned to Kuranda in May 2009 to confirm aspects of this case study with the Djabugay Governing Committee. I attended a number of governing committee meetings and had a range of other individual discussions and meetings with, for example: Djabugay such as Gerald Hobbler, Rhonda Brim, Andy and Rhonda Duffin, Barry Hunter and Willy Brim; Hanz Spier, Djabugay Tribal Aboriginal Corporation (DTAC) Chief Executive Officer; Martin Dore, Principal Legal Adviser for the North Queensland Land Council (NQLC); Margaret Saunders, Project Officer NQLC; Michael Neal of P&E Law who was Djabugay's solicitor throughout their native title determination; barrister David Yarrow who provided some pro bono legal advice to Djabugay; and staff of the Department of Environment and Resource Management (DERM), now the Department of National Parks, Recreation, Sport and Racing. I attended meetings between the Djabugay Governing Committee and external stakeholders including representatives of

the Queensland Parks and Wildlife Service (QPWS) and provided a range of assistance to the Djabugay. I wish to thank all who contributed to this case study and especially the Djabugay. Some of the information in this paper has been derived from Bushwork Consultants', 'Building Djabugay foundations: a wiki-based roadmap', unpublished document, Bushwork Consultants and AIATSIS, 2008, prepared for the Djabugay following their planning workshop and sponsored by AIATSIS. See also Djabugay Native Title Corporation, 'Building Djabugay foundations: summary of a 3 day workshop 24–26 October 2008', PowerPoint presentation to Djabugay annual general meeting, December 2008 http://www.aiatsis.gov.au/ntru/pbcpartnerships.html, accessed 30 March 2013.

3 T Bottoms, *Djabugay country*, Allen & Unwin, St Leonards, NSW, 1992, pp. 1–17.
4 The connection report and earlier drafts are not generally publicly available without permission from the Djabugay via their representative corporations. F Claffey, 'Preliminary report to the Djabugay Tribal Aboriginal Corporation: Djabugay native title rights and interests in the Barron Falls National Park', confidential report to Djabugay Tribal Aboriginal Corporation, Cairns, 1995; S Pannell, *Anthropological evidence in support of a determination of Djabugay native title rights and interests: Djabugay – Barron Gorge National Park native title determination application QC 94/4*, report to North Queensland Council Aboriginal Corporation, 1998.
5 *Djabugay People v State of Queensland* (2004) FCA 1652.
6 The spelling of 'Djubaguy' in the name of the corporation was changed to 'Djabugay' at the 2008 AGM.
7 See *Public Service Departmental Arrangements Notice (No. 2) 2009* (Qld). DERM became the Department of National Parks, Recreation, Sport and Racing following the 2012 elections in Queensland.
8 G Hobbler in Bushwork Consultants, above n 2, p. 7.
9 Djabugay is spelt 'Tjapukai' in the names of the 'Tjapukai Aboriginal Cultural Park' and the 'Tjapukai Dance Theatre'. Other than in this context, the common and preferred spelling 'Djabugay' is used throughout this chapter.
10 Bushwork Consultants, above n 2.
11 T Bauman, 'Shifting sands', *Oceania*, vol. 71, no. 3, 2001, pp. 202–25.
12 J Finlayson, *Aboriginal employment, native title and regionalism*, CAEPR Discussion Paper, no. 87, CAEPR, Australian National University, Canberra, 1995, p. 5.
13 R Henry, 'Practising place, performing memory: identity politics in an Australian town, the "village in the rainforest"', unpublished PhD thesis, James Cook University, Townsville, 1999, p. 269.
14 D Hudson 1986 quoted in Finlayson, above n 12, p. 12. A number of local reggae bands also began to gain prominence, including The Rainbow Country House Band and Mantaka.
15 Finlayson, above n 12, p. 13.
16 Gerald Hobbler, pers. comm., 5 May 2009.
17 Henry, above n 13, p. 285.
18 A Holden & R Duffin, *Negotiating Aboriginal interests in tourism projects: the Djabugay People, the Tjapukai Dance Theatre and the SkyRail project*, Research Paper, no. 4, March 1998, Centre for Australian Public Sector Management, Griffith University, 1998, p. 12.
19 Ibid., p. 10.
20 Henry, above n 13, p. 279.
21 Some documents refer to a 'Cultural Heritage Cooperative Agreement', a 'Djabugay Cultural Co-ordinating Committee' and a 'Tjupakai Cultural Theme Park Cultural Committee'; see, for example, Holden & Duffin, above n 18, Attachments 2A and 2B.
22 Hanz Spier, pers. comm., 23 June 2009.

23 R Henry, 'Performing protest, articulating difference: environmentalists, Aborigines and the Kuranda Skyrail dispute', *Aboriginal History*, vol. 22, 1998, pp. 143–61.
24 *Aboriginal and Torres Strait Islander Heritage Protection Act 1984* (Cth), under s 9 and s 10.
25 Henry, above n 23.
26 Holden & Duffin, above n 18, p. 14.
27 Ibid., Attachment 4, p. 31, pp. 40–3.
28 Ibid., p. 13. At the time of the Skyrail controversy, at least some Djabugay were not only in conflict with the Yirrganydji and divided among themselves over the building of the cableway, but also with Skyrail. Skyrail for its part questioned how it could enter into a business partnership with the Djabugay who had been trying to close it down, and Queensland Parks and Wildlife Service (QPWS) was seen, whether correctly or not, and by at least some Djabugay, as having supported Skyrail. Hanz Spier and Gerald Hobbler, pers. comm., 9 May 2009.
29 *Western Australia v Ward* [2000] 191 ALR 1.
30 *Djabugay People v Queensland* [2004] FCA 1652, order 3.
31 Ibid., order 8.
32 *Nature Conservation Act 1992* (Qld) (NCA).
33 In particular *Native Title Act 1993* (Cth) (NTA), s 24JA.
34 *Djabugay People v Queensland*, above n 30, order 6.
35 Queensland Indigenous Working Group (QIWG), 'Indigenous people, national parks and protected areas in Queensland: draft position statement', unpublished draft, QIWG, Brisbane, 2001; Queensland Indigenous Working Group (QIWG), 'Submission for Indigenous interests and protected area management. A policy review. A proposal for an Indigenous conservation estate, unpublished working draft, QIWG, Brisbane, 1999.
36 National Native Title Tribunal, Barron Gorge National Park Indigenous Land Use Agreement (Barron Gorge ILUA), NNTT reference no. QI2004/051.
37 NCA, above n 32, s 17(a) and (b).
38 Ibid., s 17(c).
39 Ibid., s 17(3).
40 Barron Gorge ILUA, above n 36, clause 4.
41 Ibid. While the ILUA appears to anticipate negotiation of an additional ILUA, clause 4 is simply an agreement to negotiate in good faith towards a further agreement. As a general principle, an 'agreement to agree' is not an enforceable contract term in Australian contract law.
42 Ibid., clause 2.4.
43 Environmental Protection Agency, 'Draft Barron Gorge management plan, Wet Tropical Rainforest Bioregion', unpublished draft for discussion purposes only, EPA, September 2008, DNTAC archive.
44 NCA, above n 32, s 15.
45 EPA, above n 43, pp. 34–4.
46 One of the earliest of these was a document which detailed Djabugay plans and aspirations to inform the native title mediation process. See R Johnston & F Claffey, *Djabugay native title, land use and management strategy, Barron Falls National Park*, North Queensland Land Council, 1997.
47 Ibid. Djabugay aspirations were broadly reconfirmed at Bushwork's planning workshop. See Bushwork Consultants, above n 2.
48 Bushwork Consultants, above n 2. The Djabugay vision was reaffirmed at the AIATSIS sponsored planning workshop and included:
   - a living dynamic Djabugay culture
   - the protection of cultural and natural heritage

- recognition and respect for Djabugay traditional owner status
- employment and security for Djabugay youth
- culturally friendly sustainable economic development
- joint management of the Barron Gorge National Park and other conservation areas in Djabugay country.

49 EPA, above n 43, p. 3.
50 This reference to 'cooperative management' reflects the fact that the cooperative involvement of Indigenous peoples is an element of the objects of the NCA, above n 32, s 5(f). Much of Queensland Government policy with respect to the management of protected areas also includes managing collaboratively or cooperatively with traditional owners. For Queensland Government policy in relation to partnerships with traditional owners in protected area management and the promotion of stronger Aboriginal and Torres Strait Islander involvement in natural resource planning and policy development, including establishing businesses linked with park management and visitation, see Environmental Protection Authority (EPA) *Master Plan for National Parks*, EPA, Brisbane, 2001; and Department of Communities, Office for Aboriginal and Torres Strait Islander Partnerships, *Partnerships Queensland: Future Directions Framework for Aboriginal and Torres Strait Islander Policy in Queensland 2005–2010. Baseline Report 2006*, Department of Communities, Office for Aboriginal and Torres Strait Islander Partnerships, 2006, http://www.datsima.qld.gov.au/resources/atsis/government/programs-initiatives/partnerships/2006-partnerships-qld-baseline-report/baseline-report-2006.pdf, accessed 7 August 2013.
51 EPA, above n 43, p. 5.
52 Ibid., p. 14.
53 Compilation of general statements made by members of the Djabugay Governing Committee at a range of governing committee meetings and following meetings with QPWS and DERM in 2008 and 2009, at which the author was present.
54 Rhonda Brim, pers. comm., 5 May 2009.
55 Gerald Hobbler, pers. comm., 5 May 2009.
56 Letter from Gerald Hobbler, Chairperson, DNTAC to the Director-General, EPA, 29 September 2008.
57 Letter from Terry Wall, Director-General, EPA to Gerald Hobbler, Chairperson, DNTAC, 10 October 2008.
58 Hanz Spier, pers. comm., 17 August 2009.
59 Rhonda Brim, above n 54.
60 Gerald Hobbler, above n 55.
61 The revised DTAC Rule Book from 2 February 2009 states that:
   1.1. The corporation shall maintain for the main purpose of the corporation a gift fund:
      1.1.1. to be named 'The Djabugay Gift Fund'
      1.1.2. which can receive gifts of money or property for the purposes of the objectives of the corporation
      1.1.3. which can have credited to it any money received by the corporation because of those gifts.
   1.2. The gift fund cannot receive any money or property other than that stated at (21.1.2)
   1.3. The corporation shall use gifts made to the gift fund and any money received because of them only for the principal purpose of the corporation.
   1.4. Receipts issued for gifts to the gift fund must state:
      1.4.1. the full name of the corporation
      1.4.2. the Australian Business Number (if applicable) and the Indigenous Corporation Number (ICN) of the corporation

1.4.3. the fact that the receipt is for a gift.
1.5. As soon as:
   (a) the gift fund is wound up, or
   (b) the corporation's endorsement as a deductible gift recipient is revoked under section 426–55 of the Taxation Administration Act 1953 any surplus assets of the gift fund must be transferred to another fund, authority or institution, which has similar objectives to the corporation. This body must also be able to receive tax deductible gifts under division 30 of the Income Tax Assessment Act 1997.

See, Djabugay Tribal Aboriginal Corporation (DTAC), *The rule book of Djabugay Tribal Aboriginal Corporation*, DTAC, Kuranda, 2009, p. 35.

62 Ibid., p. 1.
63 Australian Government Attorney-General's Department website, 'The future acts regime', http://www.ag.gov.au/www/agd/agd.nsf/Page/Indigenouslawandnativetitle_Nativetitle_Thefutureactsregime#section1, accessed 23 June 2009.
64 For further details, see P Sullivan, *Exclusions under S26(3) and (4) of the Native title Act 1993 from the right to negotiate*, Land, Rights, Laws: Issues of Native Title, no. 5, Native Title Research Unit, AIATSIS, Canberra, 1994; and E Keith, *Neither rights nor workability: the proposed amendments to the right to negotiate*, Land, Rights, Laws: Issues of Native Title, no. 15, Native Title Research Unit, AIATSIS, Canberra, 1997.
65 *Aboriginal Cultural Heritage Act 2003* (Qld) (ACHA), s 6.
66 Ibid., Part 4, s 36.
67 Ibid., s 35(7).
68 Hanz Spier, pers. comm., 20 July 2009.
69 T Bauman, 'Nations and tribes "Within": emerging Aboriginal "nationalisms" in Katherine'. *The Australian Journal of Anthropology*, vol. 17, no. 3, 2006, pp. 322–36.
70 T Pilbrow, 'Embracing our hallmark latencies: on centring anthropological', in T Bauman (ed.), *Dilemmas in applied native title anthropology in Australia*, AIATSIS, Canberra, 2010, pp. 97–108; and K Palmer, 'Understanding another ethnography: the use of early texts in native title inquiries, practice', in T Bauman (ed.), *Dilemmas in applied native title anthropology in Australia*, AIATSIS, Canberra, 2010, pp. 72–96.
71 T Bottom, *Djabugay country*, Allen & Unwin, Sydney, 1999, p. 2.
72 See J Finlayson, *Report to the Lands Branch, Department of Family Services and Aboriginal and Islander Affairs on the Mona Mona reserve land*, Department of Family Services and Aboriginal and Islander Affairs, Brisbane, 1993; S Collins, 'Mona Mona: a culture in transition', unpublished grad dip thesis, James Cook University, Townsville, 1981.
73 Djabugay state that they had a native title application prepared in the late 1990s, thinking that a court could decide whether the competing claims to Mona Mona by the Mulurindji group were valid. However, for various reasons, the claim did not proceed. Opportunities to transfer the title to Mona Mona residents were also lost before the 2005 sunset clause of the *Aboriginal Land Act 1991* (Qld).
74 The Koah, Mantaka Kowrowa and Mona Mona (KMKM) Aboriginal Corporation, which had fallen into abeyance and around which there was confusion about ownership of assets, had a licence over the property of Ngoonbi Farm, permitting CDEP to undertake sawmilling, orchard maintenance and general property maintenance.
75 S Kerins, *The future of homelands/outstations*, CAEPR Topical Issues, no. 1, CAEPR, Australian National University, Canberra, 2010.
76 Gerald Hobbler, pers. comm., 5 May 2008.
77 Comment by Andy Duffin at the Djabugay planning workshop, Kuranda, 24–26 October 2008.

78 Bushwork Consultants, above n 2, p. 7.
79 Ngoonbi Farm contained two houses managed by the Ngoonbi Housing Cooperative Society, which was established in 1975, and a shed which was being used by the Home and Community Care (HACC) program.
80 See MC Nussbaum, *Creating capabilities: the human development approach*, Harvard University Press, Harvard, 2011.
81 Bushwork Consultants, above n 2, p. 7.
82 In the early 1990s, the Mona Mona Aboriginal Corporation produced a report into the feasibility of establishing and incorporating a Djabugay Ranger Agency (DRA). The Djabugay Ranger Agency, established in 1991, was a source of pride for the Djabugay. It undertook land management activities in a number of areas, but continuously struggled for resources, and there were issues with Djabugay meeting employment requirements. It had some financial assistance from various state and Commonwealth government departments, including the Commonwealth Department of Environment and Heritage as it was at the time, but was reliant upon 'CDEP top up' which, as of 30 June 2009, was no longer active. A number of the rangers undertook TAFE ranger training courses and had expertise in cultural heritage management, cultural tourism and archaeological site surveys. The central control point of CDEP also moved to Cairns, making the management of any local CDEP a difficult issue. EPA, above n 43, A21.
83 Comments by Rhonda Brim to the Djabugay planning workshop, Kuranda, 24–26 October 2008.

Update: Djabugay Native Title Corporation 2013

Hanz Spier

Since 2009, when the case study in Chapter 4 was written, much has changed and little has changed for the Djabugay Native Title Aboriginal Corporation (Registered Native Title Body Corporate) (DNTAC) and the network of corporations in which it is situated.

Annual funding from the Department of Families, Housing, Community Services and Indigenous Affairs (FaHCSIA) of around $50,000 continues to partially support the employment of a part-time chief executive officer (CEO), with his salary and administrative expenses supplemented by annual income from Indigenous Business Australia (IBA), the current owners of the Tjapukai Cultural Aboriginal Park (the Cultural Park), for the use of 'Djabugay culture' and lease of the property. Djabugay Tribal Aboriginal Corporation (DTAC) has purchased shop space in the main street of Kuranda with the proceeds of the sale of shares in the Cultural Park to IBA. The shop is divided into two spaces: the area with street frontage is designated a shop, while the area behind it has been converted to an office. For about a year, the shop space was provided mostly at reduced rent to support a young Djabugay woman in establishing an art and craft outlet. Unfortunately, the business proved unviable and the space is currently rented out on a commercial basis.

Djabugay's governance structure was simplified following advice from KPMG, and a separate Djabugay business arm was set up. Since it receives income from the Cultural Park, Buda:dji Aboriginal Development Association Aboriginal Corporation (BADA) has become the administrative centre for all Djabugay corporate entities. A new business development corporation, Djabugay Enterprises Aboriginal Corporation, has been registered with DTAC as its sole member. The new corporation has two subsidiaries: Nyawarri Estate Aboriginal Corporation (NEAC) and Djabugay Tour Guiding Aboriginal Corporation (DTGAC). NEAC is leasing Ngoonbi Farm, a property on the outskirts of Kuranda, which has been renamed by Djabugay to

Nyawarri Estate in honour of the late Maggie Donahue, 'Queen' of Djabugay. DTGAC operates the recently established Djabugay Aboriginal Guided Tours (see below).

The leasing of Nyawarri Estate followed the completion of the property management plan (PMP) referred to in the case study. The PMP was put together by Djabugay, Sean Constable Consulting and John Hamilton with financial assistance from the Indigenous Land Corporation (ILC). The recommendations of the PMP form the basis of a work plan which is an integral part of the lease. On successful completion of the lease (during which Djabugay will have demonstrated that they can run the property effectively, pay all landholding costs and use the property for the benefit of the wider Indigenous community in Kuranda), Djabugay will receive the title deed from the ILC. In order to keep the land management costs down the ILC purchased a 55-horsepower tractor with slasher for Djabugay. Currently a boxing group and a women's sporting group (both open to the wider community) are using areas on the property and Djabugay have entered into a joint venture (Nyawarri's Passion) with Eco-Logical Earth for the establishment of an ecological crop-growing enterprise. Job Find (the local Job Network Provider) and Djabugay have gone into partnership to develop and implement a series of projects to take place on the property. These projects will support the sports and horticultural activities, using both as an avenue for training and work experience.

In 2011, with financial support from both Skyrail and DTAC, Djabugay successfully secured a tourism grant (T-QUAL) from the Queensland Department of Resources, Energy and Tourism to develop and establish a Djabugay tour guiding business. Working with Skyrail, who provided free access and on-the-ground support, a rainforest walking track was established leading from the back of Skyrail's Barron Falls Station to Streets Creek, in an area adjacent to the Barron Gorge National Park (the Park). Permits for the construction and use of the track were obtained from the Wet Tropics Management Authority and from what was then known as the Department of Environment and Resource Management. A rendition of Djabugay history and culture (Wait-a-While Camp) was put together by Djabugay elders Barry and Brian Hunter with the help of Djabugay's linguist, Michael Quinn. Following a successful training program (Certificate 3 in Tourism), hosted by Job Find and ITEC Employment, three staff were employed and further trained by Michael Quinn. DTGAC entered into a commercial agreement with Skyrail to facilitate access, sales and promotion of the tour guiding.

During a festive gathering at Streets Creek the tour guiding business was announced to the public by Gavin King, Member for Cairns and Queensland's Assistant Minister for Tourism, together with the Member for Barron, Michael Trout, on 15 June 2012. The former Commonwealth Minister for Tourism, Martin Ferguson AM MP, visited in August 2012 and congratulated the Djabugay on creating a unique tourism experience with the combined assistance of Skyrail and the T-QUAL grant program. The business has experienced a slow start and struggled financially during its first year of operation. Lately visitor numbers have picked up significantly and the future for the business is looking promising, although not yet secured.

Conflict among Djabugay 'clans' and neighbouring groups over land ownership and resources continues to impact Djabugay corporations as the extent of Djabugay country is challenged. The Djabugay estate appears to be 'under siege' from all sides as the country available for activity is being reduced. Two Djabugay clan groups assert exclusive access to areas of Djabugay country: Bulway assert interests over areas around Davies Creek and Bare Hill extending to Kuranda, while Yirrganydji recently lodged a native title claim over many areas of the coastal strip north of Cairns. The neighbouring Muluridji group continues to assert interests in the Mona Mona Mission (Mona Mona), while the Gimuy Yidinji group have started claiming areas around Lake Placid. Nevertheless, the ILC accepted the logic of more inclusive Djabugay representation through the Djabugay corporations, and the three-year lease for Nyawarri Estate was signed by NEAC despite the Bulway group asserting exclusive ownership over the property.

These conflicts have severely limited Djabugay in their ability to revitalise the Djabugay Ranger Agency, which was once successfully looking after the lands in and around Mona Mona. Both Djabugay and Muluridji were requested by the Mona Mona Bulmba Aboriginal Corporation (established to represent both Djabugay and non-Djabugay descendants of 'Mona Mona People') to withdraw from native title assertions related to Mona Mona to avoid disputes entering into their negotiations with the Queensland Government over a lease arrangement for Mona Mona. In the midst of considerable conflict over the years, Mona Mona Bulmba Aboriginal Corporation has emerged with a two-stage strategy; a 30-year lease over Mona Mona was secured, while it is hoped that this lease can be converted into Aboriginal freehold within the first five years of the lease. However, most residents have left Mona Mona, taking up government offers of housing elsewhere, and there are only a few remaining permanent households.

As foreshadowed in the case study, the Barron Gorge National Park Indigenous Land Use Agreement (ILUA) expired in December 2010. The Djabugay, Queensland Parks and Wildlife Services (QPWS) and the Department of Environment and Resource Management (DERM) were unable to reach agreement over a management plan[1] and did not have a strategy to either extend or renegotiate a new ILUA, although plans are afoot for the release of a draft mangement plan for a second round of public consultations. In 2009, as noted in the case study, Djabugay met with representatives of DERM and the QPWS to re-establish working arrangements and protocols between Djabugay and QPWS and DERM. During this meeting Djabugay proposed a framework agreement leading to a partnership between Djabugay, DERM and QPWS. The proposed framework agreement would establish a management model whereby Djabugay law and the *Nature Conservation Act 1992* (Qld) would be acknowledged as the main guiding management principles for the Park. Although

DERM said it would be happy to establish such a framework, it acknowledged that it did not have the capacity to implement it. According to the minutes of the meeting drafted by QPWS, 'it would involve the recognition of Indigenous law as equal to Government law; [and] this would involve other parts of government'.[2]

Later attempts by DERM representatives to get Djabugay to see any proposed 10-year management plan as a 'broad stroke' painting on which the finer detail would be filled in annually did not convince Djabugay. They could not see the point in agreeing to a 10-year outline when there was no certainty about what would actually happen on the ground. They did not accept the government's methodology, believing that it could change its mind and direction along the way. They preferred to discuss the fine detail. They were also informed that budgets were based on operational priorities, such as weed control and catering for emergencies, and that this provided the basis for district budgeting across parks as opposed to budgeting funds for specific park management. The Djabugay are also concerned about the inequity they see in comparing the joint management arrangements that their neighbours in Cape York have negotiated under the *Cape York Peninsula Heritage Act 2007* (Qld) and what's being offered to them.[3] Other opportunities appear to exist, as the first multi-tenured co-managed Indigenous Protected Area (IPA) has been negotiated by the Madingalbay Yidinji near Cairns following their native title consent determination and the development of a 'whole-of-country' strategic plan. The arrangements show that IPAs can co-exist with national parks and other conservation areas across a range of tenures.[4] It may be time for Djabugay to re-engage with QPWS to discuss some of the approaches taken by others, to see what Djabugay can put on the negotiating table and truly explore the barriers and impediments to common goals.

Despite these challenges, the directors of the Djabugay Governing Committee continue to think inclusively and are committed to avoiding confrontation as much as possible. There are a number of projects afoot which will provide for a positive future. With the assistance of a grant from the Department of the Environment, Water, Heritage and the Arts (DEWHA), Djabugay published a new Djabugay dictionary and is only months away from releasing a Djabugay Languages DVD. Djabugay language is again being taught at the Kuranda District State College.

Faced with a world where Indigenous land rights have become legislative 'tick boxes' and continue to divide people, and where fragmentation in the community has been exacerbated as a consequence of the disappearance of unifying forces, such as the Aboriginal and Torres Strait Islander Commission (ATSIC) and the Community Development Employment Program (CDEP), Djabugay directors aim to protect and promote Djabugay heritage through a process of building and strengthening partnerships with local businesses, service providers and the Kuranda District State College. Without the assistance of Skyrail and FaHCSIA funding and many others who have helped Djabugay over the years with small grants or pro bono services, the Djabugay would not have reached their current position. Djabugay will continue to require financial support for some years to come; nevertheless, they will persist in using and promoting their heritage as a resource to create jobs and wealth for the community, and Djabugay corporations aim to become financially independent. As Djabugay leaders grow older, it is becoming imperative for Djabugay to attract a younger generation of spirited men and women to become involved and set directions for the promotion and protection of the Djabugay heritage into the future.

Endnotes

1 Environmental Protection Agency (EPA), 'Draft Barron Gorge management plan, Wet Tropical Rainforest Bioregion', EPA, unpublished draft for discussion purposes only, September 2008, Djabugay Native Title Corporation (DNTAC) archive.
2 Queensland Parks and Wildlife Services, 'Draft meeting minutes Djabugay and Queensland Parks and Wildlife Service (QPWS)', unpublished document, Operational Working Group and Protocols Sport and Recreation Centre, Kuranda, 7 July 2009, p. 3.
3 T Bauman, C Haynes & G Lauder, *Pathways to the co-management of protected areas and native title in Australia*, AIATSIS Research Discussion Paper, no. 32, AIATSIS Research Publications, Canberra, 2013, pp. 29–30.
4 Ibid., p. 19.

Chapter 5

Karajarri: native title and governance in the West Kimberley

Jessica K Weir

Introduction

In 2002 and 2004, Karajarri had their native title rights and interests recognised to over 31,000 square kilometres of land in the West Kimberley, south of Broome.[1] This is an area about half the size of Tasmania, with pastoral stations, mining interests, coastal and desert lands, and the large Aboriginal community of Bidyadanga.[2] Bidyadanga has a young and growing population of around 800 people, with pressing infrastructure needs, including housing. Karajarri live as a minority within the diverse Bidyadanga population.

Karajarri had one of the first native title determinations to be recognised in the Kimberley and had the first native title application in which applicants were represented exclusively by the Kimberley Land Council (KLC).[3] Karajarri were thereby forging new ground in the Kimberley, as the Chair of the Karajarri Traditional Lands Association (KTLA) Registered Native Title Body Corporate (RNTBC), Mervyn Mulardy Jnr, said:

> No one in their wildest dreams could imagine getting beyond winning native title. Even KLC wasn't prepared. All was focused on winning native title and getting the land, there was never a plan for after native title... So there was no structure for us. No way for us to go to the next level.[4]

This chapter considers this 'next level'.

With native title recognition, native title holders are formally included in a range of land and water decision-making processes, including community development issues. To manage these relationships, as well as to protect and hold their native title, the *Native Title Act 1993* (Cth) (NTA) prescribes that native title holders establish an RNTBC.⁵ This very contemporary intercultural governance context involves the interplay of two distinct cultural traditions, and the innovation of new practices that draw on and combine different sources of cultural and legal authority.

Further, every RNTBC will face unique governance issues. Each native title holding group has its own traditional laws and customs; local land tenure history will determine the recognition of native title as exclusive or non-exclusive possession, or not at all; and governance is also influenced by the social–political context, settlement patterns, industry, ecological and geographic issues and so on. Often the work of RNTBCs takes place within the context of addressing the socio-economic disadvantage experienced by many Indigenous people.

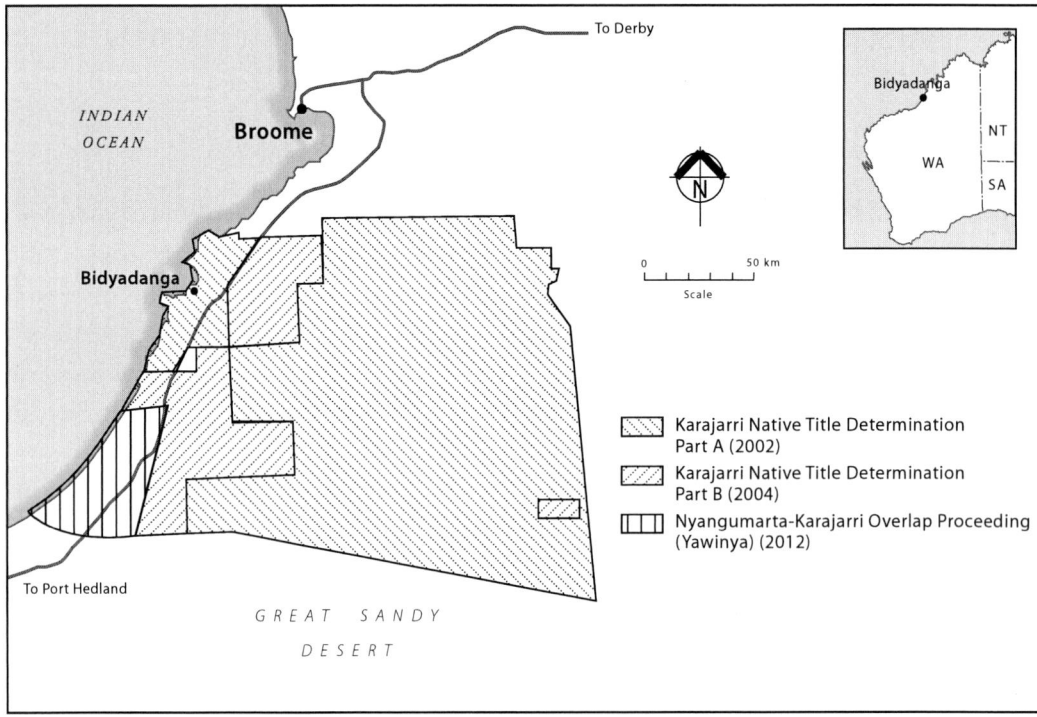

Figure 5.1 Karajarri native title determinations. Map by Brenda Thornley for AIATSIS

Where native title is recognised over the land tenures of Aboriginal communities, there is clearly a need to ensure that the new RNTBCs can work effectively with the pre-existing Aboriginal community councils.⁶ These councils were established to govern diverse Aboriginal communities in the 1970s under self-determination legislation.⁷ Subsequently, community councils in many parts of 'remote Australia' effectively became local governments.⁸ With native title, the specific legal rights of traditional owners are being identified within communities that were formerly treated, in policy and program terms, as having single and homogenous Indigenous identities.

This change obliges community councils and RNTBCs to identify and preferably agree on their governance roles in relation to each other, and then articulate such distinctions to other parties.

Because RNTBCs hold a key administrative role in the native title system, they necessarily work with the three levels of local, state/territory and federal government. Three aspects of these relationships are highlighted in this paper: the relationship between the RNTBC and local Aboriginal community councils; the influence of the NTA; and, the failure of state, territory and federal governments to invest in RNTBCs. Almost 20 years after they were created, there is still no explicit state or federal policy on RNTBCs.[9] Accompanying this policy issue is the absence of funding for native title corporations. Despite recent initiatives,[10] the prescribed management of native title is without a parallel prescribed funding mechanism. In addition to these challenges, native title holders also carry the expectations that the arduous native title application process, and the achievement of native title recognition, will deliver real benefits for their people.

In this chapter I begin with an overview of Karajarri country and Karajarri native title rights and interests. This provides the background for describing the Karajarri experience of holding and managing native title, including the key issues Karajarri face at their native title meetings; the challenges of running a native title corporation; and the effect of native title on social relations in Bidyadanga. I conclude by identifying some challenging issues faced by both Karajarri and governments, which affect the role of these RNTBCs.

I use the term 'Karajarri' to describe the Karajarri native title holders, a group of 700 people or more. However, the work of the RNTBC comes down to a few individuals who are motivated, skilled, and committed to find the time to do this work.[11]

Karajarri

Native title is a good thing. But I could not understand what was the meaning of it? 'Win the country'? It's already Karajarri country. We've been here all the time.

Wittidong Mulardy[12]

Karajarri country includes the West Kimberley coast, south of Broome, and stretches almost 200 kilometres east into the Great Sandy Desert. Karajarri have close cultural and social connections to the Yawuru, traditional owners of the Broome region to the north, Nyikina and Mangala to the east and Nyungamarta to the south.

Karajarri speak about their country being passed down to them by their ancestral beings. Anthropologist Geoffrey Bagshaw has described how Karajarri language (*muwarr*), territory (*ngurrarra*), social institutions and customary law (*wampurrkujarra*) were created in the distant past by supernatural beings (*pukarrikarra*).[13] Country provides them with the resources for life by 'lying belly-up' with respect to the people. The desert country is sustained by a diversity of groundwater springs. At the coast, old shell middens, fish traps and the continued popularity of going fishing all speak of the sea's fertility. The importance of relationships held between the inland and the coast is embedded in the word 'Karajarri' which means west facing/being; that is, west oriented (Kara = west, jarri = moving).[14]

Karajarri people were some of the first traditional owners in the Kimberley to experience the extension of the British Empire. A violent confrontation in the mid-1860s led to the deaths of three European explorers who were mapping country for sheep grazing; the Western Australian colonial government response resulted in widespread Karajarri loss of life. In the 1860s and 1870s Chinese and Malay pearlers traded and lived with Karajarri, and exploited their labour while diving for pearls along the coast. In 1899, the colonial authorities founded a telegraph station and more recently, in the 1930s, the La Grange ration depot was created and reserved lands were set aside for Aboriginal people.[15] The flat coastal land appealed to pastoralists, and the stations of Shamrock, Frazier Downs, Nita Downs and Anna Plains were established. Many Karajarri people lived and worked on these stations.

In the 1920s, desert tribes moved into Karajarri coastal country in response to a harsh drought, the destruction of their hunting grounds by stock, and the murders and massacres of their people by pastoralists.[16] In the 1950s, Catholic Pallottine missionaries established a mission at La Grange. With another drought in the 1960s, desert tribes were again persuaded to move west and take advantage of the amenities being developed, including a medical centre, a school, an airstrip and an improved road link with the highway to Broome.

Karajarri law includes customary requirements for strangers (*walanyu*) to seek and obtain permission to enter and move about in Karajarri country.[17] As the new tribes moved in — the Nyangumarta, Mangala, Juwaliny and Yulparija — they would camp nearby and wait to be welcomed to country. KLC native title officer Anna Mardling, who was a volunteer at the mission in the 1970s, remembers the incredible singing and dancing that accompanied the ceremonies.[18] As part of this welcome, Karajarri accorded *walanyu* permission to hunt and fish, as well as designated law grounds for their own ceremonial purposes.[19] These practical gestures were critical for the political and social arrangements of living together. The new tribes have made their home on Karajarri land, bringing up their kids far from their traditional country, while their prolific dot paintings illustrate the importance of places left far inland.[20] They have also applied for or have had their native title recognised to their traditional country.

In 1979, the Catholic lease was transferred to the Bidyadanga Aboriginal Community La Grange Inc ('the Community Council') — the new representative body for the diverse community that had been created.[21] This was enabled by state legislation designed to support Aboriginal people to formally manage communities mostly comprised of Aboriginal people.[22] At that time, Karajarri renamed La Grange as Bidyadanga, a new word based on the Karajarri word for 'emu', to represent the new, inclusive community. As Karajarri woman Shirley Spratt said, 'The community was built by the five tribes. Everybody was family.'[23]

Bidyadanga is the largest Aboriginal community in Western Australia. According to 2006 Census data 57 per cent of the community were under the age of 24, 34 per cent were between 24 and 54, and people 55 years and older made up nine per cent of the community.[24] This socio-demographic profile is typical of regional communities in north-west Australia. Many people were employed in positions centred on the Community Development Employment Projects (CDEP) scheme; however, in 2003 these positions were drastically cut from 260 to just 30.[25]

In addition to Bidyadanga, there are various outstations on Karajarri country where Karajarri people live, including Wanamalnyanung (also called Mijimilmaya), Najanaja, Kuwiyimpirna (Frazier Downs), Malupirti (Munro Springs), Purrpurrnganyjal (Kitty Well) and Karlatanyan. Many Karajarri also live in Broome, Derby and elsewhere.[26] Karajarri activities extend over the breadth of their country, whereas the other tribes tend to hunt and fish close to Bidyadanga.[27]

The authority and connection Karajarri hold with country stem from their beliefs about intimate relationships between creator beings, language, law and people. As one elder described this intimate relationship:

'Pukarrikarra' put everything in the country, everything in totality that is alive; this is true...In the hinterland, in the sea, the [game] food belonging to human beings was put in place by 'Pukarrikarra' — this is the truth, beyond which nothing more can be said — from long ago, these living things, to end the story, belong to us [so that] we may keep strong.[28]

Karajarri sense of identity, purpose and place is passed on to each new generation. With the recent history of rapid social change, Karajarri ceremonies, laws, relationships and responsibilities with country have continued to be performed, respected and adapted. The observance of cultural protocols in accordance with Karajarri skin section relationships has endured to ensure that cultural authority, access to country, decision-making, social behaviour and familial links continue to be reflected in contemporary living arrangements at Bidyadanga.[29]

The distinct authority held by Karajarri as traditional owners was apparent to anthropologist Geoffrey Bagshaw, who collected native title evidence in the mid to late 1990s. He noted the continued deference in Bidyadanga to the authority of Karajarri in matters that concerned Karajarri country.[30] The political importance of Karajarri authority was also part of the creation of the Bidyadanga Community Council. When it was established, governance was organised to include equal representation from all five tribes, with an informal understanding that the Karajarri held the position of chair. The recognition of Karajarri native title rights and interests has introduced another set of framings for social relations within the Bidyadanga community (discussed later in this chapter).

Karajarri native title rights and interests

In 2002 and 2004, Karajarri native title rights and interests were determined by consent; that is, by agreement.[31] These native title rights and interests are to be enjoyed and exercised in accordance with Karajarri law and the laws of the state and the Commonwealth, including the NTA[32] and Federal and High Court legal judgments.

In the 2002 consent determination,[33] Karajarri were recognised as holding exclusive native title rights and interests to 'possess, occupy, use and enjoy' their country 'to the exclusion of all others'.[34] This determination is largely over Crown radical title (or 'unallocated' Crown land).[35] The Federal Court listed Karajarri rights and interests as including:

(i) the right to live on the land;
(ii) the right to make decisions about the use and enjoyment of the land and waters;
(iii) the right to hunt, gather and fish on the land and waters in accordance with their traditional laws and customs for personal, domestic, social, cultural, religious, spiritual, ceremonial and communal needs;
(iv) the right to take and use the waters and other resources accessed in accordance with their traditional laws and customs for personal, domestic, social, cultural, religious, spiritual, ceremonial and communal needs;
(v) the right to maintain and protect important places and areas of significance to the Karajarri people under their traditional laws and customs on the land and waters; and
(vi) the right to control access to, and activities conducted by others on, the land and waters, including the right to give permission to others to enter and conduct activities on the land and waters on such conditions as the Karajarri people see fit;[36]

Karajarri can therefore continue to live on the land, make decisions about the use and enjoyment of the land, hunt, fish and gather, conduct ceremonies, protect important places, control others' access to the land and control activities conducted by others on the land. Karajarri have exercised the right to live on their land through the allocation of outstations, also called 'blocks'. The allocation of blocks allows people to spend more time living on country, teaching their kids, and keeping their own knowledge alive: enjoying native title and passing it on.

The right to control access and the activities of other people is important for Karajarri responsibilities to their country, including looking after law grounds, the graves of their ancestors and other sites. Local people and people from Broome are used to accessing this land for fishing, hunting and camping and tourists who pass through have enjoyed what was previously largely unregulated Crown land. One tourist drove over and destroyed an important site, where human footsteps thousands of years old had been recorded in the hardened silt. Karajarri hold stories about these footsteps from their ancestors. Karajarri are also concerned about the impact of tourists on the coastal and marine creatures. Shirley Spratt thinks the tourists are 'taking too many fish and crabs'.[37] Karajarri are particularly concerned about tourists coming onto their country from the popular caravan park at Port Smith, a beautiful place with mangroves, a lagoon and beaches. Surrounded by exclusive possession native title land, Port Smith Caravan Park is on a special lease that was determined to be an exclusive possession act that extinguishes Karajarri native title.[38]

In contrast to the 2002 determination, the 2004 consent determination was largely over pastoral leases and nature reserves, as these land tenures were excluded from the 2002 determination to await the much-anticipated outcome of the High Court decision in Miriuwung and Gajerrong.[39] In line with the High Court judgment (in August 2002), the parties agreed that non-exclusive native title interests exist on the same land as pastoral leases, while nature reserves extinguish native title. With respect to Crown land leased for pastoral activities, Karajarri had their non-exclusive rights recognised to Shamrock, Nita Downs and Anna Plains stations.[40] Under Western Australian legislation, Aboriginal people already have access to pastoral leases to seek 'sustenance in their traditional manner',[41] but this native title recognition explicitly identifies specific people and specific pastoral leases. Non-exclusive native title rights were also recognised between the mean high water mark and the lowest astronomical tide. The non-exclusive native title interests were listed by the court as:

(i) the right to enter and remain on the land and waters;
(ii) the right to camp and erect temporary shelters;
(iii) the right to take fauna and flora from the land and waters;
(iv) the right to take other natural resources of the land such as ochre, stones, soils, wood and resin;
(v) the right to take the waters including flowing and subterranean waters;
(vi) the right to engage in ritual and ceremony; and
(vii) the right to care for, maintain and protect from physical harm, particular sites and areas of significance to the Karajarri people.[42]

Karajarri hold many shared interests with pastoralists. Taking care of the country, the soils, trees, plants and waterholes is important both for pastoralists and native title holders. Pastoralists have particular responsibilities for the grazing pastures and native vegetation.[43] With these shared interests, negotiations are now a necessary part of land management. An example is the role of fire in land management. In the

Miriuwung and Gajerrong decision, the majority found that the burning of land by traditional owners was probably inconsistent with the rights of pastoral leaseholders;[44] however, this conclusion runs against evolving pastoral practice. Pastoralists burn land to improve pasture quality, suppress weeds and manage wildfires. Smaller, more regular fires also offset carbon emissions and this fire management could be part of the new carbon economy. There is therefore an opportunity for pastoralists and traditional owners to work together. Karajarri speak about how burning the land used to be done by the old people when they were walking through country, and are keen to see this practice continue.

Conflicts may arise where priorities differ. Indeed, different priorities led to the first Karajarri native title application. Karajarri became mobilised around native title when Karajarri elder Wittidong Mulardy became concerned about a fence built on Shamrock station that threatened access to the culturally significant Parturr hills.[45] Where there is a conflict, the rights under the pastoral lease prevail over the native title interests to the extent of any inconsistency and without extinguishing native title.[46]

Mervyn Mulardy Jnr talked to me about the importance of building good relationships with pastoralists to work out their own arrangements about how to manage country, rather than relying on what is prescribed by the law. Karajarri hold the lease to Frazier Downs (as discussed in the next section) and have a very good relationship with the manager whom they employ. This relationship includes the pastoralist's support for the Karajarri dancers and basketball team. Relationships based on shared interests and shared lives form a good basis for working through different land management activities, as Mervyn said:

> If we can do that kind of relationship building with station owners, we can build co-existence with them. We want to go hunting, and sometimes they ask us not to go hunting when they are on muster. It is a safety thing. They don't want bullets flying around. [47]

Another complex part of living with native title is interpreting how the Federal Court recognition relates to Karajarri activities, as some of their traditional activities are recognised as native title rights and interests and other activities are excluded. Karajarri native title recognises their rights to continue to go fishing and crabbing at their favourite places and take advantage of the seasonal schools of salmon that migrate up the coast. However, they cannot sell the fish because trade and commercial activities are not recognised among their native title rights or interests.[48] Fish and other natural resources within the native title determination area, such as timber, pearls and water, can be licensed by the state to commercial operators, in line with the entitlements under freehold title.[49] The ownership of minerals is also excluded from native title rights, with the exception of ochre.[50] However, Karajarri can negotiate and charge companies for access to land where the minerals are located.[51]

While similar to freehold title, exclusive possession native title land is different in many ways. Native title is inalienable, it cannot be sold, and to many people this is recognition of sovereign title. However, native title has also been construed by the authors of common and statutory law as a vulnerable title.[52] Native title can be impaired or extinguished by the rights of others and it can be lost if traditional laws and customs are not practised. While extinguishment is not possible under their law, Karajarri have to consider this in the decisions they make.[53]

Native title rights are also different from freehold property rights because they include procedural rights about certain activities on native title land, both exclusive and non-exclusive, designed to protect native title into the future. In native title terminology, these activities are called 'future acts'; they are developments that could affect native title rights and interests.[54] With some future acts, Karajarri have the right to be consulted or notified about the activities, including water allocations and/or water infrastructure and the renewal of pastoral leases.[55] With respect to larger developments, Karajarri have the 'right to negotiate', which is a procedural right to be involved in the development process, not to veto the development.[56] Many of the future acts for Karajarri concern mining and petroleum exploration licences with companies interested in exploring for lead, zinc, silver and kaolin.

There is a specific process for advising native title holders and applicants about future acts. Karajarri (or the relevant native title holder) are notified about future acts by mail, and they have three months to respond if they wish to exercise the right to negotiate. If the relevant state government (here, Western Australia) considers that the future act will not have a significant effect on native title, then the expedited procedure applies — and native title holders are not required to be notified. Where there are disagreements about future acts, the National Native Title Tribunal (NNTT) arbitrates and makes a 'future act determination'. Every year Karajarri, supported by the KLC, will lodge at least one future act objection application. Several times Karajarri have successfully contested the application of the expedited procedure to the granting of mining tenements and exploration licences.

The Karajarri Traditional Lands Association

> *'Native'? Is it Aboriginal people? It could be trees? Our God what we believed in the Dreamtime? Our land? The sea? Everything our old people walked on?*
>
> Devina Shoveller[57]

Realising the potential of their native title rights has a lot to do with how the Karajarri meet and make decisions as a native title corporation. In 1998, Karajarri established the KTLA as the legal entity for their Prescribed Body Corporate (PBC). Once their native title was determined to exist, and registered on the National Native Title Register, the KTLA became an RNTBC, although Karajarri and others continue to refer to the KTLA as their 'PBC'. As with many other RNTBCs, the KTLA was established without funding and committee members volunteer their time.

The federal government has identified two key roles for RNTBCs: to protect and hold native title, and to provide a legal entity for other parties with business on native title lands.[58] In their 2006 review of the structures and processes of RNTBCs, the federal government noted the different expectations surrounding the roles of RNTBCs.[59] The report identified that community expectations may be placed on RNTBCs to engage in issues that reflect their status as traditional owners, such as town planning, social harmony projects, cultural protocols, welcomes to country and interpretative and cultural signage.[60] The report says that these expectations place additional responsibilities and pressures on RNTBCs; however, this work is secondary to the native title responsibilities of RNTBCs.[61] This position reflects the split around different understandings of native title and, as policy analysts Michael Dillon and Neil Westbury argue, the tendency of governments to restrict their understandings of native title to a narrow legal regime.[62]

Karajarri have expressed a broad understanding of the KTLA's work, being responsible for five key activities:

- the PBC
- the rangers program
- Yiriman [youth] Project
- outstations
- the Karajarri Cattle Company.[63]

This reflects the integrated business of the five Karajarri activities, with the RNTBC viewed by KTLA members as just one of their responsibilities. For example, the rangers and Yiriman projects work to support Karajarri country and Karajarri youth, which are both essential to the intergenerational sustainability of native title. The rangers undertake land and water project work for government and business, including a contract with the Australian Customs and Border Protection Service to check driftwood for insects and weeds.[64] The Yiriman Project is a grassroots community initiative to look after young people and pass on traditional laws and customs. Yiriman was conceived by Niyikina, Mangala, Walmajarri and Karajarri elders who 'saw the need for a place where youth could separate themselves from negative influences, and reconnect with their culture in a remote and culturally significant place'.[65] Karajarri are working with the KLC Land and Sea Unit to build a Yiriman land management project around the beautiful Gourdon Bay and Port Smith areas. These activities extend across the work of Yiriman, the rangers and the RNTBC, with some individuals involved in all three groups.

The relationship between the Karajarri pastoral enterprise and the KTLA is an example of community expectations of the KTLA combined with the operation of a commercial enterprise. Frazier Downs station is exclusive possession native title land. The pastoral lease had been run by the Catholic mission on Aboriginal Lands Trust (ALT) lands, over which the historical extinguishment of native title is disregarded because it is a form of land tenure with a dedicated purpose for the use and benefit of Aboriginal people.[66] In 1976, the Frazier Downs pastoral lease was purchased by the Aboriginal Land Fund Commission under the direction of the former Commonwealth Department of Aboriginal Affairs. The Land Fund Commission vested ownership of the pastoral lease in the Bidyadanga Community Council, and a pastoral company known as 'Quimbeena Pastoral Company' (Quimbeena) was established by the Community Council.[67] In 1998, the Bidyadanga Community Council agreed to transfer ownership of the Frazier Downs pastoral lease to a Karajarri legal entity, prompting the formation of the KTLA to hold this title.[68] In December 2006, Quimbeena was amicably dissolved, with the sale proceeds (after costs) split between the Bidyadanga Community Council and the KTLA.

Karajarri do not run their own cattle on Frazier Downs but receive income from agisting cattle from neighbouring pastoral stations. Karajarri man Thomas King Jnr is the driving force behind a Karajarri pastoral business on Frazier Downs and, in 2008, the corporation 'Karajarri Cattle' was registered. Karajarri is good country for cattle and is close to the major highway in Western Australia and the port at Broome, but pastoral businesses need a lot of investment in infrastructure. The capital from the sale of the cattle and the income from the agistment are used to fund the maintenance of fences and bores, and for paying bills such as land taxes. However, some of this money is also used for KTLA costs, including meetings. The income stream from the cattle is not seen as separate to the KTLA native title work. Instead, many people make a strong connection between that income and the recognition of their native title rights. This is complicated by confusion when some people equate the cattle money with the type of 'royalty' money received under the Northern Territory land rights system. In the territory, the administration of land rights is funded via a royalty equivalent scheme, which provides for monies from consolidated revenue to be paid into a trust account — the Aboriginals Benefit Account. This in turn provides for the operation of Northern Territory land councils, for regular payments to traditional owners and payments for the benefit of Aboriginal people living in the Northern Territory. As stated earlier, there is no prescribed funding scheme for native title holders in the native title sector. There is conflict because some Karajarri expect native title to result in a royalty stream to fund Karajarri individual and collective priorities, and they look to the cattle money. How the relationship between Karajarri Cattle and the KTLA will work into the future is key native title business for Karajarri. More than just a business model, there are complex issues of communal lands and group and individual rights that require innovation beyond the categories of public and private.[69]

The allocation of outstations or 'blocks' is also listed as key KTLA business. This is a long-term land use challenge as well as a political negotiation within the

Karajarri community. If KTLA committee members respond positively every time there is a request for an outstation, the incremental effect of this settlement has implications for access to hunting and fishing grounds, the maintenance of roads, pastoral operations and more. The development of an outstation policy has been discussed at Karajarri meetings. A policy would relieve the political and personal pressure of the allocation of blocks between families and individuals. Perhaps an easier route is to continue on an ad hoc basis but within a long-term planning perspective; this approach will narrow future options. Because of their popularity, an outstation policy and planning framework will have to be addressed one day. As Karajarri man Andrew Bin Rashid said, 'otherwise in the future everyone will want a block... It's a real problem and it is not going to go away. It is going to happen, somewhere down the track.'[70]

In addition to the rangers, the outstations, Yiriman and the cattle, the KTLA members have to undertake native title related work to ensure certainty for governments and other parties with an interest in accessing or regulating their native title lands and waters. This certainty is provided by having a functioning legal entity (the RNTBC) through which these parties can conduct business with native title holders. This work with governments and third parties can be an opportunity for the KTLA to negotiate benefits. These could include forming partnerships to reach shared goals, negotiating an income stream to support KTLA business or gaining individual employment in work such as heritage clearances.

By far the largest industrial project with interests in Karajarri land is known locally as 'the gas'. Karajarri are one of many traditional owner groups across the Kimberley consulted on the location of an enormous liquefied natural gas plant to process gas from the Browse gas reserve 200 kilometres off the Kimberley coast. Many KTLA meetings and Karajarri activities were scuttled by the frenetic activity around the gas project timetable, as Gourdan Bay, next to Port Smith, was on the shortlist of locations.[71] For Karajarri, the gas would have meant dramatic change, but it might also have brought economic opportunities. In the governance context, where native title funding is virtually absent and socio-economic disadvantage is common, the opportunities provided by a large development were taken very seriously. After much consideration, in December 2008, Karajarri decided to withdraw their support for a gas processing plant on their country.[72]

The Bidyadanga Community Council (discussed later in this chapter) is a key local external source of requests for KTLA meeting time. Bidyadanga was established on ALT land, which has been recognised as exclusive possession native title land. The ALT leased the land to the Community Council for 99 years, commencing from 22 October 1998.[73] This situation is complicated by parts of the community not being physically located within the community lease area.[74] Karajarri will be negotiating these inconsistencies in tenure and development and other related matters as part of a planned future 'global' Indigenous Land Use Agreement (ILUA) (discussed later in this paper).[75] The Community Council also request Karajarri to undertake heritage clearances for community development purposes.

Karajarri native title business does not fit neatly within the legally prescribed native title system. The KTLA committee manages several expectations: their integrated land and governance activities and their functions as an RNTBC. The KTLA committee members find that KTLA business ends up competing with the business of resourced parties with interests in Karajarri land. Indeed, responding to the priorities and timetables of persistent others is often the trigger for holding a KTLA meeting.

Corporate governance

It's about time that the government trust us. They gave us the land back, now they need to trust us to manage it.

Thomas King Jnr[76]

Corporate forms have been central to the exercising of Indigenous peoples' land rights and native title because of the communal profile of these rights and interests, and the practical necessity of forming a legal entity to participate in transactions with governments and others.[77] As an incorporated body, the KTLA is required to conduct business in a particular way to ensure compliance with corporations' legislation.[78] This includes formal rules about who can be members of the KTLA, how and when meetings are held, quorum numbers, annual general meetings (AGMs), taking minutes and an executive committee which meets and holds roles, such as chair, deputy chair, treasurer and public officer.

However, since these corporations proliferated when self-determination policy was introduced in the 1970s, there have been problems with the governance requirements and other rules for Aboriginal and Torres Strait Islander corporations. Aboriginal corporations negotiate two quite different cultural traditions. Research into Indigenous governance has found an interplay of the influences of western corporate notions, which place a priority on accountability, representation, compliance, equity and capacity, and Indigenous people's understandings of culture as fundamental in organisational processes.[79] RNTBC members have significant work adapting mainstream governance structures to facilitate their own laws and customs. This is part of the challenge of legitimacy or 'cultural match' — in which corporate institutions must meet local expectations if they are to be considered legitimate by their membership.[80]

The *Corporations (Aboriginal and Torres Strait Islander) Act 2006* (Cth) (CATSI Act) provides more flexibility for Aboriginal corporations to negotiate issues of legitimacy and cultural match.[81] It is possible to include traditional laws and customs in corporation constitutions or rule books. For example, in their rules Karajarri can include that decisions are to be made by consensus or that such decisions can be referred to the authority of the elders. The CATSI Act also has special provisions making it clear that a director acting in good faith with the belief that they are complying with native title legislation obligations cannot breach their obligations under the Act.[82] Further, the CATSI Act reduces the reporting requirements for 'small' corporations (defined according to income and staff numbers), which benefits the vast majority of RNTBCs in this category — including the KTLA. Previously, all Aboriginal corporations (approximately 2600) had the same reporting requirements.

The capacity of the KTLA to manage their native title rights and interests was an issue for the Federal Court when making the 2004 consent determination. As Justice North wrote at the time:

> It would be an absurd outcome if, after the expenditure of such large sums to reach a determination of native title, the proper utilisation of the land was hampered because of lack of a relatively small expenditure for the administration of a PBC.[83]

The establishment and operation of the KTLA was not funded after the native title determination. Members of the Karajarri RNTBC have contributed their work voluntarily, without an office, and the committee meet without administrative support. In managing this situation, KTLA have had a temporary arrangement with the KLC in Broome, including a desk, computer and filing cabinet. Very rarely, grant monies or a volunteer have enabled the desk to be staffed. Without staff, there is no one to be a point of contact or to answer the phone, the email or other correspondence.

Lack of an office in Bidyadanga has put pressure on the homes and workplaces of local KTLA committee members. During the field work period, Karajarri woman Fay Dean worked at the Kimberley Regional CDEP office, which is centrally located across the road from the Bidyadanga Telecentre where KTLA meetings are usually held. With a telephone and internet connection, it often fell to Fay to be a point of contact for the KTLA. She also held the position of KTLA Secretary in 2008. She spoke about how unsatisfactory the KTLA administration situation was for her:

> We need decent pay to get somebody in there. It needs to be done. It's all a jumble, with paperwork everywhere. I can't do up any minutes [at my work] because it isn't private. We need our own office. I get abused if I don't put out flyers, but I'm not paid to do it. It is frustrating.[84]

Looking after the paper stream associated with being a native title corporation requires office management skills to ensure valuable information is not mislaid, disregarded or forgotten. For example, where matters have been formally worked out between Karajarri and the Bidyadanga Community Council, there can still be confusion about the particularities of agreements in meetings. This situation is not easily resolved at Bidyadanga meetings when most of the KTLA paperwork is in a filing cabinet in Broome. The uncertainty can either stall or railroad the meeting's agenda.

At a KTLA meeting in April 2008,[85] the committee were considering the specifics of an outstation request. Nyaparu Hopiga wondered about the size of the block and what it looked like on site, and whether it conflicted with a stock route, while Karajarri man Joe Edgar expressed his frustration about meeting to discuss matters without the necessary maps and computers. Lack of administrative support regularly places KTLA committee members in the uncomfortable position of making decisions without the relevant information. Without support staff, the board is responsible for both making decisions and implementing them. Joe Edgar described this arrangement as problematic:

> When it comes to making decisions the whole process falls away. The follow-up is all over the place. We need to bring it all together to get direction. Otherwise things don't happen.[86]

The capacity to organise and respond to various paperwork, or *mili mili* as Karajarri call it, is central to Karajarri engagement with the mainstream community. Without the paperwork in order, it can be very difficult to access government grants, services and other opportunities, including employment. Compliance with the rules of being an incorporated body, including having financial records in order, is important when applying to potential funding bodies. If the committee members do not do the paperwork, the KTLA is listed as 'non-compliant' by the Office of the Registrar of Indigenous Corporations (ORIC).

Joe Edgar worries about how their governance context affects the ongoing commitment of the KTLA committee. Committee members regularly speak about their frustration. They absent themselves from other responsibilities to fulfil committee roles on a voluntary basis, while also having to bridge the gap created by lack of basic administrative support. A lot of energy is expended just in organising the meetings and ensuring there is a quorum, before even getting to the meeting's agenda.

For Karajarri, the paperwork and their compliance status is just a small part of whether the KTLA is being properly governed. Karajarri are working through how to manage their recognised native title rights and interests with respect to Karajarri laws and customs. Early on, the KTLA committee ruled that anything to do with land had to go through the elders. Joe Edgar, Deputy Chair of the KTLA, sees a need for KTLA policies about 'how we spend our money — personal loans, looking after our elders, cultural business and the land'.[87] Without resources, a coordinated, planned approach to land does not take place, and things get done wherever and however they can. Reliance on ad hoc income from small projects has become a management issue in itself.[88]

Making decisions without a broad framework to guide those decisions is a complex and uncomfortable task. There is some discussion at KTLA meetings about developing a comprehensive land management policy and plan so that decision-making can occur within a framework developed around long-term considerations. Planning would also reduce the burden of responding to issues one by one.

Business mentor Edgar Price sees the role of the KTLA as fundamental to allowing a range of other activities to progress.[89] The cattle station, business ideas and land and sea management all share the same problem of under-resourced decision-making around native title. The under-resourcing of the KTLA has an impact beyond frustrating the responsibilities of the RNTBC; Karajarri capacity to address a host of other Karajarri business is frustrated by the lack of support for KTLA governance and administration. While income does not lead to good governance, a lack of income certainly undermines it.[90]

In Bidyadanga, uncertainty and inefficiencies around native title have aggravated local politics and social relations, and this tension is generating additional obstacles to good governance. This was acute in 2007, when Karajarri were deeply dissatisfied with their relations with the Bidyadanga Community Council.[91]

Bidyadanga: the new social relations of native title

In Bidyadanga, prior to the recognition of Karajarri native title, established political and cultural processes respected Karajarri as the law people of country, which facilitated their relationship with the broader community. With the recognition of their native title, Karajarri found that their relationship with the Bidyadanga Community Council was challenged by the formal distinction of Karajarri rights and community disquiet about what those rights may be.

Karajarri have exclusive possession of ALT land where Bidyadanga is sited and many community people are worried that the Karajarri will move them out of the town, or not let them go hunting and gathering on the other native title land tenures, despite a 99-year lease between the ALT and the Bidyadanga Community Council, and Karajarri assurances to the contrary.

To add to this tension, the Community Council governance arrangements changed around the same time as the native title determinations; the outcome was that the chair was no longer a Karajarri representative.

The position of Karajarri in relation to the rest of the Community Council was further muddied when the council voted for a change in membership rules, whereby outstation residents were ineligible for voting on the council, partly because they did not reside in Bidyadanga or pay rates. The effect was to remove the voting rights of Karajarri who live on outstations. Meanwhile, the Aboriginal and Torres Strait Islander Commission (ATSIC) was abolished and the resources to maintain outstation infrastructure became scarce.

Fay Dean spoke about how their native title recognition related to their relationship with the broader Bidyadanga community:

> It didn't seem like a win for anything, because we lost all our rights in the community... It wasn't a win-win situation, it was a win-lose. We lost entitlements here: memberships, voting rights... It was all in together before, with the elders holding everything in place. The chairman was always a Karajarri person. As soon as we won native title we lost that.[92]

A report about the future of Bidyadanga is revealing, showing how the different aspirations between Karajarri and the rest of the Bidyadanga community for Bidyadanga are expressed in town planning priorities. In it, the Bidyadanga Aboriginal Community La Grange Inc identifies the priorities:

- maintain land for intensive orchard activities
- develop a cyclone shelter
- find a new tip site
- find land for sewage pond extensions
- develop a new arts and cultural centre
- find land for new community housing
- resolve disputed no-go areas
- resolve community boundary
- include airport within community boundary
- allocate land for pool manager's house
- correct and proper process for all future development and land use within Bidyadanga.[93]

Whereas, the KTLA identifies the priorities:

- resolve compensation for development at Bidyadanga
- be consulted in future development of Bidyadanga
- identify a Karajarri Office site
- make sure land is given back to the KTLA
- allocate land to Karajarri for future commercial development
- more houses for Karajarri people.[94]

When Karajarri centres were consulted on the future development of Bidyadanga and on ensuring specific outcomes for Karajarri, their list of community aspirations reflected their concerns about being marginalised in Bidyadanga, and that their native title rights and interests should be accorded due process.

Issues of difference and equity within a heterogenous Aboriginal community are at the heart of the native title tensions in Bidyadanga.[95] As one of the five tribes Karajarri are part of the Bidyadanga community. However, as traditional owners, they have always had authority over matters to do with land. These issues of difference and equity have been highlighted by native title. For example, Karajarri are now formally consulted about the gas and other mineral and petroleum exploration projects on their native title lands. Future acts may also have consequences for the community of Bidyadanga, but the Community Council may find that they are not as involved in the consultations as they would expect. It is important that Karajarri manage relationships with the Community Council and other land use interests sensitively. However, as I have pointed out, the KTLA is not sufficiently funded to undertake its many responsibilities, which is likely to undermine its relationship to all the organisations it has dealings with — including the Bidyadanga Community Council. The Community Council receives funding from the state government to maintain an office, employ staff and deliver services to the community, while the KTLA is starved of funds by both federal and state governments.

During the case study research period, the state government was required to take the interests of the native title holders seriously in the building of community infrastructure, no matter what administrative challenges faced the KTLA. The rights of native title holders vis-a-vis state and local governments were confirmed in a 2003 case, *Erubam Le (Darnley Islanders) No. 1 v Queensland* ('Darnley'), which clarified the provisions of subdiv J of the NTA.[96] Until that judgment, the Western Australian Government had interpreted subdiv J as permitting it to construct public works (mainly housing) on Aboriginal reserves, without seeking traditional owner consent and without agreeing that their actions did not extinguish native title. The Darnley case, by clarifying the obligations of governments to native title holders, caused changes in government practice, whereby the construction of such public works now involves an investment in land use negotiations with the native title holders.[97]

In 2007, when the state government wanted to build several developments in Bidyadanga — 16 houses, a basketball court, a cyclone shelter, a rubbish tip, an arts and culture centre and additional sewerage infrastructure — it initiated an agreement-making process, whereby all parties could sit down and agree on the community development priorities. Until this time, KTLA committee members had been expected to respond to future act requests from the Community Council on an ad hoc basis and without funding. The new process has resulted in the KTLA, the Bidyadanga Community Council and the state government agreeing to arrange the relevant matters into two sequential ILUAs. The housing, sewerage facilities, tip, cyclone shelter and other pressing infrastructure needs were allocated to an initial, smaller ILUA process, which has been substantively negotiated and is awaiting registration to become a legal agreement.[98]

Significantly, the smaller ILUA provides for an office and administrative support for the KTLA by the state government. It is a one-off arrangement for the Karajarri RNTBC, specific to the ILUA negotiation.

A bigger, 'global' ILUA is scheduled to follow, to address issues more comprehensively, including inconsistencies in tenure and development, as the rubbish tip, nurses' houses and part of the oval are located on both Frazier Downs and the De Grey Stock Route.[99] This global ILUA will include the resolution of current development beyond the extent of the leased land, the identification of the future land requirements of the Bidyadanga community, the transfer of the Management Order from the ALT in accordance with the findings of the Bonner Report in 1996 and state government policy, and the issuing of a new lease from the KTLA to the Community Council for the extent of the community area.[100] This ILUA will require all parties to make much more investment in time and decision-making.

The motivation for each party to enter into this agreement-making process reflects how good governance processes and achieving outcomes are intertwined. The two ILUA processes in Bidyadanga are opportunities to clear the air, to improve local politics and to get moving on the development of key infrastructure for the community.

Joe Edgar has written about the importance of this agreement and agreement-making process:

> To be successful and to form a best practice precedent, the ILUA must be open, friendly and transparent to the 'historical' people of Bidyadanga and the Karajarri traditional owners, with all parties provided ample time for reflection and to seek independent advice. Adequate resources must also be provided to the KTLA for the conduct of negotiations over the ILUA and for future management of Karajarri traditional lands. Evidence of good faith is clear from the offer by Bidyadanga Council to the traditional owners of a meeting space at its Telecentre throughout 2009, and a building to establish an office, and the commitment by DIA WA [the Department of Indigenous Affairs Western Australia] to fund office refurbishment and possible administrative positions in light of the lack of national funding for Registered Native Title Bodies Corporate (such as the KTLA). These are steps in the right direction which, it is hoped, will build a better social, political and economic environment for all at Bidyadanga.[101]

The willingness of parties to sit down together to agree on an ILUA in Bidyadanga reflects a pragmatic shift towards native title being accepted as part of land use planning in Australia.[102] ILUAs bring parties together to negotiate issues directly and find common ground, rather than relying on what is or is not possible under legislative regimes. In Bidyadanga, this process has brought the state government, the Bidyadanga Community Council and Karajarri to the same meeting room to work through the disagreements between Karajarri and the broader Bidyadanga community, and the concerns the KTLA members have about governing and administering their RNTBC work.

While agreement-making has become a trend in doing native title business, in 2010 there was a setback in the impetus for governments and others to enter into ILUAs with native title holders to build public housing and other community infrastructure. The NTA was amended to reduce the future act rights of native title holders.[103] These amendments again raise the parliamentary preference of addressing native title issues through technical legal frameworks, as argued by Dillon and Westbury, rather than addressing the bureaucratic and policy issues, and other blockages that persist around community development, such as the failure to include native title considerations at the outset of a project.[104]

Entitled futures

It's been a mixture of feelings and emotions getting native title. You are happy in one sense that you have achieved this milestone and recognition, basically from the white law; a battle since colonisation. But to the other extreme it's been a bit sad, frustrating and disappointing because of a lack of support from the government for PBCs. At the same time, I want to remain optimistic so that we can move forward and not let obstacles stop us or be a cause and/or an excuse for our failure.

Thomas King Jnr[105]

The 2002 Karajarri native title consent determination marked the beginning of a complex and formalised relationship between Karajarri and all the other people who live or hold interests in Karajarri country. Despite all the problems that have come with native title, Karajarri woman Devina Shoveller talked to me about how much she enjoys working with the KTLA. For her it has been a joyful experience, where she has learnt a lot and been inspired:

First of all I didn't understand what they were arguing for, about the land. But now I've been going to the meetings, learning everything and getting brave. Then I started talking up, and now I can't stop... It's been really good having KTLA. There's a lot of respect in the family group. The things they come up with are inspiring. When they come up with an idea I think, 'I can do that' but then I think I can't have everything. My family inspires me.[106]

The enthusiasm and commitment of these Karajarri people for the KTLA to be a vehicle for doing Karajarri business, their way, is also an opportunity for governments who make the connection between recognising native title, supporting Indigenous leadership and building a more equitable society.

Native title holders have worked hard to achieve native title, with the anticipation that their position in Australian society will be transformed through this recognition.[107] For this to occur, the attention of the major native title institutions needs to expand out from the focus on achieving native title determinations in court. Native title is also a governance responsibility. The expectations of native title holders, governments and others for outcomes on native title land rely on the workings of these native title corporations and the key individuals who manage them.

There are three key concerns among the multiple impacts of the Karajarri experience of living with native title that require immediate attention from governments. They relate to policy, understandings of native title and resourcing.

First, because native title is a 'notoriously complex' legal system,[108] it is critical that state, territory and federal governments develop policy responses that support all native title parties to manage their interests in native title lands. Native title issues are open to interpretation and can be settled through policy and agreement-making, not just through amending the NTA. A suite of useful policy responses that address governance, agreement-making, and decision-making over land, water and town planning is needed.[109] The complexity of communal and individual interests held in perpetuity necessitates such policy innovation.

Second, the notion that the work of the KTLA is limited to a narrow legal interpretation of native title belies the lived experience of Karajarri who identify and articulate logical, meaningful and practical connections between country, their elders and their future generations. This approach includes referencing Karajarri people's own laws, customs and cosmologies of being. Indeed, Karajarri laws and customs were presented and recognised as evidence of their native title, and thus it is the work of native title holders to respect and maintain them.

The work of governments with Indigenous people needs to extend to understanding the importance of Indigenous peoples' laws, customs and cosmologies and the implications of doing business with RNTBCs. Ignoring this governance context results in governments and the members of RNTBCs being placed at cross-purposes, wasting valuable meeting time and providing additional challenges to the negotiation and implementation of land use agreements. There are clear synergies between the work of the KTLA and programs such as Yiriman, which could be productively developed rather than disregarded.

Third, federal, state and territory governments have failed to provide policy and funding support for these corporations which are legally obliged to undertake numerous native title responsibilities, including responding to the agendas of other parties who are generally better funded. This absence of support from government destabilises the governance of RNTBCs from the very start.[110] For Karajarri, the flow-on effects of an inadequately administered RNTBC have included: placing undue pressure on the personal capacity and commitment of KTLA members; draining resources and energy from other projects and activities which have governance capacity within the native title group; and causing tension in the local community. The same individuals who are under pressure to meet the legal obligations and community expectations of the KTLA are also active in coordinating Karajarri activities, such as Yiriman, the rangers and the pastoral enterprise. The failure of governments to invest in the KTLA frustrates these key people and affects their leadership capacity.

Further, the KTLA experience shows that there is clearly a case for funds to be allocated on establishment of an RNTBC, rather than being dependent on an ILUA process which needs to address many issues and may be lengthy. Indeed, in terms of supporting good governance, an operational RNTBC is an investment for the ILUA process not an outcome of one.

As Karajarri start to leverage some outcomes from the ILUA process,[111] they still face the many other problems besetting the KTLA. They have a pressing need to undertake a lengthy planning exercise to establish processes and policies to hold and manage their native title, including the complex issues surrounding individual and group interests in communal land. This planning exercise requires negotiating the Indigenous and non-Indigenous laws, customs and cultures which coalesce around native title business. This work must maintain legitimacy and engagement with the broader Karajarri community, or cultural match, to ensure that any agreements and decisions are sustainable.

There is also much for Karajarri to undertake with the Bidyadanga Community Council on the many issues where their interests intersect. As the Bidyadanga desert tribes go through their own process of gaining native title recognition for their traditional country, there is an opportunity for improved dialogue between RNTBCs about the role of native title holders within diverse Aboriginal communities. Significantly, what happens in Bidyadanga will establish a critical point of reference, as there are many more Aboriginal communities in Western Australia which are on ALT lands subject to native title applications.

RNTBCs are at the forefront of the legal changes since *Mabo*.[112] Native title is changing both how Indigenous peoples' interests are represented and how business is done on native title land. This paper demonstrates how these changes extend beyond RNTBCs to include myriad interactions with local, state and territory, and federal governments. Significantly, the people innovating and interpreting around native title today, in places such as Bidyadanga, are creating models for what will be considered normal into the future when native title is known and accepted as a familiar part of our governance landscape.

Innovations in governance are occurring as Karajarri and governments find ways to work together. Late in 2008, the Karajarri Rangers received a boost in government support, with five years of funding from the Department of Sustainability, Environment, Water, Population and Communities (SEWPaC) Working on Country program. Prior to this, the rangers operated from the back of Nyaparu Hopiga's veranda, with 'top-up' wages from CDEP. Karajarri are also in the consultation phase of establishing an Indigenous Protected Area (IPA) under a federal government program which provides funding for conservation work on Indigenous and public lands. Logistically, this environmental money is an investment in Karajarri staff, office facilities, transport and more.

Karajarri are enthusiastic about how the Karajarri Rangers could work on many native title matters, such as regulating tourists, taking care of important sites, monitoring changes to water management and undertaking conservation work on the pastoral leases. It is an integrated perspective which understands and seeks to consolidate the links between native title, country, land and water management, local employment and Karajarri futures.

Endnotes

1 The chapter is an edited version of a paper published as JK Weir, *Karajarri: a West Kimberley experience in managing native title*, AIATSIS Research Discussion Paper, no. 30, AIATSIS, Canberra, 2011, http://www.aiatsis.gov.au/research/documents/DP30NTRU.pdf, accessed 27 June 2013. This chapter has been facilitated by the relationships I built with Karajarri, KLC staff and other people who have worked with Karajarri. Their willingness to share information and support this work made this case study possible in three trips to the Kimberley in 2007 and 2008. I am deeply grateful for their support. For comments on earlier drafts of this chapter, I would like to thank Jess De Campo, Joe Edgar, Bruce Gorring, Krysti Guest, Anna Mardling, Howard Pedersen, Lisa Strelein and Sarah Yu. For their assistance I also thank Jane Blackwood, Jess Clements, Maree Gaffney, Kate Golson, Nyaparu Hopiga, Tiffany Labuc, Mervyn Mulardy Jnr, Edgar Price, Shirley Spratt, Claire Stacey and the anonymous peer reviewers. I thank Cynthia Ganesharajah, Bruce Gorring and Sayuri Piper for clarification with specific technical questions. I thank Toni Bauman, Cynthia Ganesharajah, Zoe Scanlon and Christiane Keller for their editorial work to prepare this chapter for publication. Any errors or omissions are my responsibility. The research for this paper was supported by a research agreement between the KTLA and AIATSIS. This case study is part of a larger AIATSIS PBC project, focused on planning and governance issues facing RNTBCs across Australia.

2 An 'Aboriginal community' is a community or association wholly or principally composed of persons who are of Aboriginal descent, as defined by the *Aboriginal Communities Act 1979* (WA) (ACA Act), s 3.

3 The applicants in the Tjurabalan native title application (*Ngalpil v State of Western Australia* [2001] FCA 1140 were represented by the KLC, but the matter was settled by consent prior to the Karajarri application. The KLC also represented individual applicants in the Miriuwung Gajerrong application (*Western Australia v Ward* (2002) 213 CLR 1), but the majority were represented by the Aboriginal Legal Service (Western Australia) and the Northern Land Council; Krysti Guest, pers. comm., 12 May 2009.

4 Mervyn Mulardy Jnr, interview with the author, Jarlmadangah, 14 October 2008. See also M Mulardy, 'Traditional owner comment', *Native Title Newsletter*, no. 5, Native Title Research Unit, AIATSIS, Canberra, 2008, http://www.aiatsis.gov.au/ntru/docs/publications/newsletter/septoct08.pdf, accessed 27 June 2013.

5 *Native Title Act 1993* (Cth) (NTA), div 6; Attorney-General's Department Steering Committee (AGDSC), *Structures and processes of Prescribed Bodies Corporate*, AGDSC, Canberra, 2006, p. 6. See also JK Weir, *Native title and governance: the emerging corporate sector prescribed for native title holders*, Land, Rights, Laws: Issues of Native Title, vol. 3, no. 9, AIATSIS, Canberra, 2007, http://www.aiatsis.gov.au/ntru/docs/publications/issues/ip07v3n9.pdf, accessed 27 June 2013.

6   See J Edgar, 'Indigenous Land Use Agreement — a road map to building relationships between Karajarri traditional owners, Bidyadanga Aboriginal Community La Grange Inc and the Government of Western Australia', *Australian Aboriginal Studies*, AIATSIS, Canberra, 2011.
7   For example, ACA Act, above n 2.
8   T Rowse, *Indigenous futures: choice and development for Aboriginal and Islander Australia*, University of New South Wales Press, Sydney, 2002, p. 226.
9   Christos Mantziaris and David Martin noted that much of the RNTBC regime was a hasty legislative response to a Senate debate on group rights, C Mantziaris & D Martin, *Native title corporations: a legal and anthropological analysis*, The Federation Press, Sydney, 2000, p. 94. See also p. 98.
10 In 2007, the funding situation began to be partly addressed, with nominal 'crisis' funds provided on application to a handful of native title corporations by the Commonwealth Government. It is not common for Indigenous Land Use Agreements (ILUAs) to include long-term funding and institutional support for RNTBCs, although Victoria is a notable exception. The Commonwealth Government has also changed native title funding policies to provide native title holders with more support from their representative bodies. For a discussion of these funding changes see: AGDSC, above n 5, pp. 8–9; LM Strelein & T Tran, *Native Title Representative Bodies and Prescribed Bodies Corporate: native title in a post determination environment*, Native Title Research Report, no. 2, Native Title Research Unit, AIATSIS, Canberra, 2007, http://www.aiatsis.gov.au/ntru/documents/PBCReport.pdf, accessed 27 June 2013; T Bauman & T Tran, *First National Prescribed Bodies Corporate meeting: issues and outcomes, Canberra 11–13 April 2007*, Native Title Research Report, no. 3, Native Title Research Unit, AIATSIS, Canberra, 2007, http://www.aiatsis.gov.au/ntru/docs/researchthemes/pbc/PBCMeeting2007.pdf, accessed 27 June 2013; Weir, above n 5. Also, the *Native Title Amendment (Technical Amendments) Act 2007* (Cth) permits native title corporations to establish a 'fee for service' regime to meet and recover costs associated with various native title related activities. As at October 2010, the native title regulations to implement this amendment were still in draft form.
11 I would like to thank the Karajarri men and women who shared their experiences of native title with me, some of whom I have quoted in this document: Sylvia Shoveller, her daughters Shirley Spratt, Madeline Shoveller and Devina Shoveller, her nieces Jaqueline Shoveller and Pamela Shoveller, as well as Fay Dean, Joe Edgar, Nyaparu Hopiga, Thomas King Jnr, Elaine McMahon, Mervyn Mulardy Jnr, Andrew Bin Rashid and Frank Shoveller. I would particularly like to thank Karajarri elder Wittidong Mulardy and acknowledge the leadership of Karajarri elders Donald Grey, Nita Marshall, and Nyaparu Possum. I also thank Jessica Bangu.
12 Wittidong Mulardy, interview with the author, Bidyadanga, 6 May 2008.
13 G Bagshaw, *The Karajarri claim: a case-study in native title anthropology*, Oceania Monograph, no. 53, University of Sydney, 2003.
14 Ibid., pp. 29, 53.
15 F Skyring & S Yu, with the Karajarri native title holders, '"Out-of-country": too many cooks spoilt the broth', in P Veth, P Sutton & M Neale (eds), *Strangers on the shore: early coastal contacts in Australia*, National Museum of Australia Press, Canberra, 2008.
16 K McKelson & T Dodd, *Nganarna Nyangumarta Karajarrimili Ngurranga: we Nyangumarta in the country of the Karajarri*, Wangka Maya Pilbara Aboriginal Language Centre, South Hedland, 2007, p. 182.
17 Bagshaw, above n 13, pp. 86–7.
18 Anna Mardling, pers. comm., 28 April 2008.
19 Edgar, above n 6.
20 D Batty & J McMahon, *Desert heart*, film, screened on ABC TV, 18 March 2008.

21 The Community Council is a representative forum comprising and elected on behalf of community members.
22 ACA Act, above n 2.
23 Shirley Spratt, interview with the author, Bidyadanga, 28 April 2008.
24 Australian Bureau of Statistics (ABS), *2006 Census community profile series, Bidyadanga*, ABS, Canberra, 2007.
25 See Edgar, above n 6. See also J Taylor, *Indigenous people in the West Kimberley labour market*, CAEPR Working Paper Series, no. 35, Centre for Aboriginal Economic Policy Research, Australian National University, Canberra, 2006.
26 Bagshaw, above n 13, p. 35.
27 Ibid., p. 87. See also Edgar, above n 6.
28 Translated quote in Bagshaw, above n 13, p. 52. The speaker is identified as DW.
29 Bruce Gorring, pers. comm., 2 June 2009. See also Edgar, above n 6.
30 Bagshaw, above n 13, pp. 62, 86–7.
31 *Nangkiriny v Western Australia* (2002) 117 FCR 6 and *Nangkiriny v Western Australia* [2004] FCA 1156.
32 NTA, above n 5.
33 *Nangkiriny* (2002), above n 31.
34 Ibid.
35 Prior to the *Mabo* decision (*Mabo v Queensland [No. 2]* (1992) 175 CLR 1) (*Mabo (No. 2)*), Crown radical title was called unallocated Crown land within the Australian property law system; see *Mabo (No. 2)*, at [30]. Such lands continue to be commonly described as unallocated Crown land even though the High Court determined otherwise in *Mabo (No. 2)*.
36 *Nangkiriny* (2002), above n 31.
37 Spratt, above n 23.
38 Special lease 3116/9944 under s 116 of the now repealed *Land Act 1933* (WA), *Nangkiriny* (2002), above n 31, first sch. This lease is an exclusive possession act under s 23B of the NTA, above n 5, which extinguishes native title under s 23G.
39 *Western Australia v Ward*, above n 3.
40 *Nangkiriny* (2004), above n 31, at [2], [6].
41 These reservations are provided for in the *Lands Administration Act 1994* (WA) s 104, and have existed in state pastoral lease statutes since the early years of colonisation in Western Australia; Western Australian Government, *Aboriginal access and living areas final report*, Pastoral Industry Working Group, Western Australian Government, Perth, 2003, p. 11.
42 Nangkiriny (2004), above n 31, at [5].
43 Relevant Western Australian legislation includes: *Land Administration Act 1997* (WA) pt 7; *Dividing Fences Act 1961* (WA); *Agriculture and Related Resources Protection Act 1976* (WA); *Soil and Land Conservation Act 1945* (WA); *Environmental Protection Act 1986* (WA); *Rights in Water & Irrigation Act 1914* (WA); *Wildlife Conservation Act 1950* (WA); and *Conservation and Land Management Act 1984* (WA).
44 Western Australia, above n 3, at [194].
45 S Yu, 'Land interests of Karajarri in the area around Port Smith Caravan Park, report to support application to the Indigenous Land Corporation to purchase special lease 3116/9994: Port Smith Caravan Park', unpublished report, 1998, p. 1.
46 NTA, above n 5, s 44H(c).
47 Mervyn Mulardy Jnr, interview with the author, Jarlmadangah, 14 October 2008.
48 For a general discussion about the 'un-economic' casting of native title, see LM Strelein & JK Weir, 'Conservation and human rights in the context of native title in Australia', in J Campese,

T Sunderland, T Greiber & G Oviedo (eds), *Exploring issues and opportunities in rights based approaches to conservation*, CIFOR, IUCN and CEESP, Bogor, Indonesia, 2009.
49 NTA, above n 5, s 47A(4) and s 212.
50 To the extent that ochre is not a mineral pursuant to the *Mining Act 1904* (WA).
51 See also D Ritter, *The native title market*, University of Western Australia Press, Crawley, 2009, p. 7.
52 See Justice Kirby's judgment in *Fejo v Northern Territory* (1998) 195 CLR 96.
53 See also the discussion on de-facto extinguishment in K Magarey, 'Native Title Amendment Bill (No 2) 2009', Bills Digest, Parliamentary Library, Canberra, 2010, pp. 12–13.
54 NTA, above n 5, s 233.
55 See, for example, ibid., s 24HA(7).
56 See ibid., div 3, subdiv P.
57 Devina Shoveller, interview with the author, Bidyadanga, 8 May 2008.
58 AGDSC, above n 5, p. 6.
59 AGDSC, above n 5.
60 Ibid., p. 10.
61 Ibid.
62 MC Dillon & ND Westbury, *Beyond humbug: transforming government engagement with Indigenous Australia*, Seaview Press, West Lakes, South Australia, 2007, pp. 111–12.
63 This was identified in a KTLA office workshop, 11 November 2008, facilitated by Sarah Yu and Edgar Price, funded by AIATSIS.
64 J Blackwood & J Hopiga, 'The survival of land and sea units', *Native Title Newsletter*, no. 6, Native Title Research Unit, AIATSIS, Canberra, 2008, pp. 2–5, http://www.aiatsis.gov.au/ntru/docs/publications/newsletter/novdec08.pdf, accessed 27 June 2013.
65 Yiriman Project, *Yiriman Project building histories in our young people: history*, Yiriman Project, Derby, http://www.yiriman.org.au/history.htm, accessed 22 December 2008.
66 NTA, above n 5, s 47A.
67 Quimbeena had two shareholders: the Community Council and Nigel Gill (former community administrator) who held a share on behalf of Karajarri traditional owners because they had no legal entity to hold and preserve their interests at the time. Quimbeena operated well before the native title determination on this shareholder basis. However, due to responsibilities arising out of the Community Development Employment Projects (CDEP) scheme and other subsidised activities managed through the Bidyadanga Commmunity Council office, Quimbeena management decisions and funding administration became subsumed into the Community Council administration. This led to poor record-keeping, difficulties in tracking expenditure, potential redirection of funds prescribed for Quimbeena activities being used for other purposes, limited transparency in decision-making and, hence, a deteriorating pastoral station. Gorring, above n 29. See also T King & K Carter, 'Moving forwards', Quimbeena Pastoral Company Development Plan (second draft) for Frazier Downs, unpublished document, May 2002.
68 Gorring, above n 29.
69 See Rowse's discussion, above n 8, pp. 231–3.
70 Andrew Bin Rashid, interview with author, Bidyadanga, 30 April 2008.
71 Department of Industry and Resources, *Northern development taskforce interim report June 2008*, Western Australian Government, Perth, 2008, p. 4.
72 A site in the country of the Goolarabooloo and Jabirr Jabirr people, north of Broome, has been negotiated between the gas proponents, the KLC and some of the traditional owners.
73 The Bidyadanda community is built on Reserve 38399 for which the Management Order is vested in the Aboriginal Lands Trust (ALT) (with the power to lease) in accordance with the

Land Administration Act 1997 (WA) for the dedicated purpose of 'use and benefit of Aboriginal inhabitants'. See Gorring, above n 29.

74 Department for Planning and Infrastructure (DPI), *Bidyadanga community layout plan no. 2, draft for comment and review*, Western Australian Government, July 2007, p. 7. It is worth noting that the full extent of the community development exceeds the area of Reserve 38399. The community bylaws area is not proclaimed and therefore irrelevant.

75 Gorring, above n 29.

76 Thomas King Jnr, interview with author, Port Smith, 7 May 2008.

77 Rowse, above n 8, p. 179; Mantziaris & Martin, above n 9, pp. 100–1.

78 *Corporations (Aboriginal and Torres Strait Islander) Act 2006* (Cth) (CATSI Act).

79 J Hunt, DE Smith, S Garling & W Sanders (eds), *Contested governance: culture, power and institutions in Indigenous Australia*, CAEPR Research Monograph, no. 29, Centre for Aboriginal Economic Policy Research, Australian National University, Canberra, 2008; and, P Sullivan, *A sacred land, a sovereign people, an Aboriginal corporation – prescribed bodies and the Native Title Act*, North Australia Research Unit, Australian National University, Darwin, 1997.

80 For a discussion on cultural match see S Cornell & JP Kalt, 'Reloading the dice: improving the chances for economic development on American Indian reservations', in S Cornell & JP Kalt (eds), *What can tribes do? Strategies and institutions in American Indian economic development*, American Indian Manual and Handbook Series no. 4, University of California, Los Angeles, 1993; D Martin, 'Governance, cultural appropriateness and accountability', in D Austin-Broos & G Macdonald (eds), *Culture, economy and governance in Aboriginal Australia, workshop proceedings*, Sydney University Press, Sydney, 2005.

81 The CATSI Act repealed and replaced the *Aboriginal Councils and Associations Act 1976* (Cth).

82 CATSI Act, above n 78, s 265-20.

83 *Nangkiriny* (2004), above n 31, at [11]. As KTLA chair Mervyn Mulardy said at the time, 'I may be the Chairman, but we can't afford a chair.' Quoted in D Ritter, 'Casenote: *Nangkiriny v State of Western Australia* [2004] FCA 1156', *Indigenous Law Bulletin*, v. 65, 2004, p. 21.

84 Fay Dean, interview with the author, Bidyadanga, 7 May 2008.

85 Karajarri Traditional Lands Association RNTBC meeting, Bidyadanga Telecentre, 30 April 2008.

86 Joe Edgar, interview with the author, Broome, 9 May 2008.

87 Ibid.

88 Blackwood & Hopiga, above n 64.

89 Edgar Price was funded by AIATSIS to begin a KTLA business plan as part of the PBC project.

90 For a discussion on the optimal factors for good governance, see Cornell & Kalt, above n 80, pp. 187–214; Hunt et al., above n 79; and Weir, above n 5.

91 See also Edgar, above n 6.

92 Fay Dean, above n 84.

93 DPI, above n 74, p. 17.

94 *Nangkiriny* (2004), above n 31.

95 For a discussion on the residency vis-a-vis traditional ownership rights of Indigenous peoples in remote Indigenous communities see Rowse, above n 8, pp. 111–23.

96 *Erubam Le (Darnley Islanders) No. 1 v State of Queensland* (2003) 134 FCR 155.

97 As ALT lands do not extinguish native title rights and interests, it is expected that compensation cases will be lodged by RNTBCs and Native Title Representative Bodies in response to *Darnley*. Gorring, above n 29.

98 See further Edgar, above n 6.

99 DPI, above n 74, p. 7.

100 Gorring, above n 29. The Bonner Report recommended that all ALT land be transferred back to Aboriginal corporations to be held on trust for Aboriginal people. See Aboriginal Lands Trust Review Team & N Bonner, *Aboriginal Lands Trust*, Aboriginal Affairs Department, Perth, 1996.
101 Edgar, above n 6.
102 See further, D Ritter, *Contesting native title*, Allen & Unwin, Sydney, 2009, pp. 174–5.
103 The amendments include the granting of a 'right to comment', which seems an unnecessary legislative provision in a democracy. Magarey, above n 53, pp. 16–17. See also text box 3 in Weir, above n 1.
104 Dillon & Westbury, above n 62; see also Magarey, above n 53, pp. 19–20.
105 King Jnr, above n 76.
106 Shoveller, above n 57.
107 See, for example, K Guest, *The promise of comprehensive native title settlements: the Burrup, MG-Ord and Wimmera agreements*, Research Discussion Paper no. 27, Native Title Research Unit, AIATSIS, Canberra, 2009.
108 Magarey, above n 53.
109 As also argued by Dillon & Westbury in their discussion of the agreement-making which led to joint-management arrangements for the majority of national parks in the Northern Territory, above n 62, p. 113.
110 See Rowse, above n 8, p. 222 for a discussion on state/territory relations with the Commonwealth on Indigenous issues.
111 The first ILUA was signed in late 2010; the global ILUA is being negotiated.
112 *Mabo (No. 2)*, above n 35.

Update: Karajarri Traditional Lands Association 2013

Claire Stacey

The Karajarri Traditional Lands Association (Aboriginal Corporation) (RNTBC) (KTLA) has been the legally determined native title holder of Karajarri country for 11 years; however, recognition has been slow both for Karajarri people as the cultural custodians of country and the KTLA as a self-governing body with authority for country.[1] In recent years, KTLA directors have recognised a positive shift whereby the Western Australian Government and other stakeholders are more likely to consult the KTLA earlier in their projects or activities planned for Karajarri country.[2] There are also emerging opportunities for the KTLA through the declaration of an Indigenous Protected Area (IPA)[3] and the creation of a marine park over the Eighty Mile Beach area.[4]

Yet there remain significant barriers for Karajarri to realise benefits from their native title. These include the ongoing chronic lack of funding and resourcing for Registered Native Title Bodies Corporate (RNTBCs), a continuation of the historic socio-political marginalisation of Indigenous people,[5] as well as the challenges for KTLA in building an effective relationship with Bidyadanga Aboriginal Community La Grange Inc (the Bidyadanga Community Council).

In 2012, Karajarri and their southern neighbours Nyangumarta, agreed on 2000 square kilometres of exclusive and non-exclusive possession native title as shared country, also known as Yawinya.[6] While not the preference of the traditional owners, who each already have an RNTBC (the KTLA and the Nyangumarta Warrarn Aboriginal Corporation RNTBC), an additional RNTBC was established: the Nyangumarta Karajarri Aboriginal Corporation RNTBC (NKAC). Some KTLA directors now also act as directors on NKAC. Its intention is to jointly manage the shared country between Karajarri and Nyangumarta; however, both groups have little capacity within their existing corporations, and are now responsible for another set of meetings and compliance obligations. With the Yawinya determination, Karajarri have native title responsibilities for more than 33,000 square kilometres.

Two Indigenous Land Use Agreements (ILUAs) were registered alongside the Yawinya determination. The Nyangumarta Karajarri and Mandora Station ILUA and the Nyangumarta Karajarri and Anna Plains Station ILUA set out the terms of the relationships between all three RNTBCs and the respective pastoral stations.

Karajarri are also part of negotiations for an ILUA with the Western Australian Government relating to the community of Bidyadanga, referred to as a 'global ILUA', to address long-standing community development issues and address most future act agreements with the Western Australian Government simultaneously. However, this global ILUA was conflated with the Western Australian Government's introduction of the Government Indigenous Land Use Agreement (Government ILUA) policy in 2011. Under a Government ILUA the KTLA is required to provide comprehensive agreement to all 'low impact' future acts in exchange for revenue arising out of exploration and prospecting licences to which they currently do not have access.[7] From the state's perspective the Government ILUA is mutually beneficial; however, critics have described the process as an ultimatum from the state government. At the time of writing, no RNTBCs in Western Australia had signed the Government ILUA.[8]

The KTLA was finally able to open an office in Bidyadanga in 2013, a significant outcome reached through the Bidyadanga Initial Works ILUA, an agreement between the KTLA, the Community Council and the Western Australian Government in 2011.[9] There is still no funding to employ full-time staff and the KTLA still relies on the volunteered time of directors, and coordination, travel and other support from the Kimberley Land Council (KLC). The directors continue to struggle with the many expectations of their members and other stakeholders and the responsibilities involved in their executive roles. The KTLA is not yet charging fees for service, a potential source of income for RNTBCs that emerged from the 2011 amendments to the PBC Regulations,[10] as this requires functional administrative systems.

Karajarri people suffered the loss of a senior elder in 2012 and due to 'sorry business' the KTLA was not able to hold a directors meeting for many months. When the KTLA Board finally met, directors were overwhelmed with the workload and decisions required by external stakeholders, and had little to no time to make informed decisions. Presentations, consultations or requests for decisions came from the Western Australian Department of Housing, the Department of Agriculture and Food, the Department of Environment and Conservation, the Department of Indigenous Affairs, the Department of Planning, the Department of Premier and Cabinet, Nita Downs pastoral station, Kimberley Regional Economic Development (KRED) Enterprises Charitable Trust, AIATSIS, KLC Land and Sea Management Unit and Pangea Minerals and Energy (Pty) Ltd. Also at this February 2013 meeting, a new board of directors, a new chairperson and cultural advisers were elected.[11] To assist with the extensive requests from state government the KTLA has signed the State Activities Funding Agreement with the KLC which enables the KLC to act on the KTLA's behalf in negotiations with the state government.

The Karajarri Rangers are a key KTLA activity, and are responsible to the RNTBC and the elders. The ranger office in Bidyadanga provided informal administrative support to the KTLA until its own office opened. The rangers are funded through Working on Country (WoC), a program run by the Department of Sustainability, Environment, Water, Population and Communities. The KLC administers the WoC funding for several ranger groups, which enables it to provide intensive support to the rangers and draw on its administrative capacity to pay staff and deploy funds. However, this limits KTLA opportunities, such as obtaining administrative income and developing capacity to manage grant funding and employ staff, and there have been ongoing requests from RNTBCs that they receive WoC and IPA funding directly. In addition to WoC, an IPA is scheduled to be declared over Karajarri country in 2013, bringing funding and other opportunities for KTLA. Also in 2013, the Eighty Mile Beach Marine Park became part of the Kimberley Science and Conservation Strategy.[12] The marine park is in the southern part of Karajarri country continuing south to Nyangumarta country, and is proposed to extend inland to meet the border of pastoral leases. It is likely to provide another collaboration opportunity for the KTLA and the Karajarri Rangers with government environmental interests. KTLA directors link in this work with their other related priorities, including the Yiriman Project and the Karajarri Cattle Company.

Relationships between KTLA and the Bidyadanga Community Council remain strained. Implementation of the Bidyadanga Initial Works ILUA has taken time, including delays building a cyclone shelter, and there has been local tension about the distribution of public housing. In 2012, Karajarri did not hold any of the senior positions on the Community Council.[13] Of the two Karajarri representatives on the council board, neither are KTLA directors and one is not a KTLA member.[14] There are also no formal reporting mechanisms between the Community Council and the KTLA.

The challenge of negotiating an effective working relationship between an RNTBC and a community council is not specific to Bidyadanga.[15] This was the focus of an intensive governance project north of Broome looking at the roles, responsibilities and communication pathways between an RNTBC and the three community councils in its native title determination area.[16] This process has been recognised by the Broome Regional Operations Centre (a partnership between the Western Australian Department of Indigenous Affairs and the Commonwealth Department of Families, Housing, Community Services and Indigenous Affairs (FaHCSIA)) as necessary for many RNTBCs in the Kimberley. However, the time, funding and expertise required means that it is very unlikely that the KTLA and the Community Council will participate in such a governance program.[17]

The KTLA continues to seek further recognition of its status through the divestment of Aboriginal Lands Trust (ALT) land held by the Western Australian Government to the KTLA. In Western Australia the divestment of ALT land to traditional owners has been in process since 1996.[18] The growing number of RNTBCs in Western Australia makes recognition of the appropriate bodies to hold this land a much simpler process. However, a key obstacle to transferring ALT land to RNTBCs is the requirement of creating a new form of Aboriginal title, or transferring ALT land into an existing but more 'vulnerable' tenure.[19] Also, the ALT has acknowledged that, while the KTLA are the traditional owners for Bidyadanga community, ALT land is held 'for the benefit of persons of Aboriginal descent'.[20] Therefore, any divestment of ALT land in Bidyadanga community is required to recognise the interests of all Aboriginal people in the community.[21] Under current Western Australian Government policy, it is unlikely that Bidyadanga community land that is currently ALT land would be solely divested to the KTLA.

There is continued economic development interest in the La Grange Basin and protecting groundwater is an ongoing struggle for KTLA. The KTLA has serious concerns about the management of water licences, as water resources for mining developments are determined and approved through agreements outside the water planning process.[22] The growing interest in coal seam gas mining in the region is also of great concern to Karajarri, as it is unclear how this could impact groundwater, and therefore Karajarri culture.[23] There is increasing interest in onshore mining of natural gas reserves of the Canning Basin, a significant area extending into Karajarri country, and exploration of the area has been facilitated by the *Natural Gas (Canning Basin Joint Venture) Agreement Act 2013* (WA) which authorises four mining companies to pursue exploration and mining and to construct a liquefied natural gas pipeline.[24] Inadequate consultation with native title holders in favour of mining interests in passing this legislation has raised serious concerns for traditional owners in the Kimberley.[25]

The KTLA continues to explore its diverse interests in business developments, including the expiration of all pastoral leases in Western Australia in 2015.[26] Recently the advertised sale of the Port Smith Caravan Park sparked great interest from the KTLA, as its ownership and management align with KTLA business development priorities. Owning the caravan park would also solve the ongoing dispute with current owners about erecting signs on Karajarri exclusive native title land which incorrectly indicate that the areas are the private property of the caravan park.[27]

Navigating the many functions of an RNTBC while pursuing opportunities for people and country is a constant challenge for the KTLA directors. As the new Chair of the KTLA, Joe Edgar, said:

We have everything to lose if we don't react and try to look after our country. That's a responsibility that our elders left for us, to do the best we can to look after that country, and to make proper decisions about it.[28]

Endnotes

1 This update is based on field work conducted as part of an AIATSIS research project investigating native title and climate change. See T Tran, L Strelein, J Weir, C Stacey & A Dwyer, *Native title and climate change: changes to country and culture, changes to climate: strengthening institutions*

    for Indigenous resilience and adaptation, National Climate Change Adaptation Research Facility, Gold Coast, 2013.
2. KTLA Director Fay Dean, pers. comm., Bidyadanga, August 2012.
3. Department for Sustainability, Environment, Water, Population and Communities (SEWPaC), 'Indigenous protected areas July 2012' (map), http://www.environment.gov.au/indigenous/ipa/pubs/map.pdf, accessed 16 July 2013.
4. Department of Environment and Conservation, 'Eighty Mile Beach marine park created', http://www.dec.wa.gov.au/management-and-protection/marine-environment/marine-parks-and-reserves/6717-proposed-eighty-mile-beach-marine-park.html, accessed 16 July 2013.
5. T Rowse, *Rethinking social justice: from 'peoples' to 'populations'*, Aboriginal Studies Press, Canberra, 2012.
6. *Hunter v State of Western Australia* [2012] FCA 690.
7. Tran et al., above n 1, p. 78; Land Approvals and Native Title Unit, 'Whole of Government', http://www.dpc.wa.gov.au/lantu/Pages/WholeofGovernment.aspx, accessed 16 July 2013.
8. See AIATSIS, 'Indigenous land use agreements summary', http://aiatsis.gov.au/ntru/documents/IluaSummary.pdf, accessed 16 July 2013.
9. National Native Title Tribunal (NNTT), 'WA – Registered ILUA – Bidyadanga Initial Works ILUA WI2011/004', http://www.nntt.gov.au/Indigenous-Land-Use-Agreements/Search-Registered-ILUAs/Pages/WA_-_Registered_ILUA_-_Bidyadanga_Initial_Works_ILUA_WI2011_004.aspx, accessed 16 July 2013.
10. Native Title (Prescribed Bodies Corporate) Amendment Regulations 2011.
11. Tran et al., above n 1, p. 71.
12. Department of Environment and Conservation, above n 4.
13. Peter Yip, email to author, 24 September 2012.
14. Ibid.
15. See, for example, the experiences of the Abm Elgoring Ambung Aboriginal Corporation RNTBC in Kowanyama, in Tran et al., above n 1, pp. 80–106.
16. Kimberley Land Council, *Bardi Jawi Governance Project newsletter*, Kimberley Land Council, Broome, 2011, http://www.aiatsis.gov.au/ntru/documents/BJGOVNEWSLETTER1sm.pdf, accessed 16 July 2013.
17. Ian Thomas, pers. comm., 15 August 2012.
18. Aboriginal Lands Trust Review Team & N Bonner, *Aboriginal Lands Trust*, Aboriginal Affairs Department, Perth, 1996.
19. Tran et al., above n 1, p. 66.
20. *Aboriginal Affairs Planning Authority Act 1972* (WA), s 2.
21. Rob Baker, pers. comm., 17 August 2012.
22. Tran et al., above n 1, p. 68.
23. Ibid.
24. Department of the Premier and Cabinet, 'Western Australian legislation', http://www.slp.wa.gov.au/legislation/statutes.nsf/main_mrtitle_13065_homepage.html, accessed 16 July 2013.
25. Australian Associated Press, 'Native title challenge to Canning gas bill' (20 June 2013), Perth Now website, <http://www.perthnow.com.au/business/wa-premier-colin-barnett-digs-in-with-browse-gas-vision/story-fnhocr4x-1226666889343>, accessed 16 July 2013.
26. Tran et al., above n 1, p. 53.
27. Ibid., p. 55.
28. Ibid., p. 68.

Chapter 6

The Ord River Stage 2 Agreement and Miriuwung Gajerrong native title corporations

Patrick Sullivan

Introduction

This chapter concerns the land management corporation of the Miriuwung and Gajerrong people (MG people), and their agreement with the Western Australian Government over the development of an area of irrigated agriculture — the Ord Final Agreement (OFA or the Agreement).[1] Miriuwung and Gajerrong are two related languages of the Aboriginal people of the far north-west of Australia who live on the boundary between the State of Western Australia and the Northern Territory. Some eastern Gija people were also recognised in the determination of the native title claim that gave rise to the OFA. They are neighbours of the Miriuwung and Gajerrong, to the south-west. The OFA is an Indigenous Land Use Agreement (ILUA) under the *Native Title Act 1993* (Cth) (NTA).[2]

The land management corporation is called the Yawooroong Miriuwung Gajerrong Yirrgeb Noong Dawang Aboriginal Corporation — more commonly referred to as the 'MG Corporation'. Yawooroong Miriuwung Gajerrong Yirrgeb Noong Dawang means 'Big Mob Miriuwung Gajerrong People Talking Place for Country'. The corporation holds, through three distinct trusts, the benefits derived from the native title rights of the people. It manages the business of two Registered Native Title Bodies Corporate (RNTBCs), following Miriuwung and Gajerrong native title consent determinations in 2003 and 2006 (*MG (No. 1)*[3] and *MG (No. 4)*[4]) (Figure 6.1). Establishment of these RNTBCs is a requirement of the NTA.

MG Corporation is intended to reflect different aspects of traditional social organisation in its structure, and is required to use traditional processes for many of its crucial functions. It is also a modern organisation. An important part of its function is to encourage economic development among the Miriuwung and Gajerrong people. Economic development is made possible by funds provided by the Western

Australian Government under the OFA, as compensation for taking away land through the extinguishment of native title under the NTA.

MG Corporation and the OFA are enmeshed — the Agreement requires the corporation to be established in a particular way and to carry out functions laid down in the OFA. The 2006 MG Corporation rules[5] also require it to carry out and implement the OFA,[6] which is seen by the Miriuwung and Gajerrong people as redress for social, cultural and economic hardship due to colonisation.

The chapter begins with a description of Miriuwung and Gajerrong people and their traditional country, and then discusses the people's successful claim of native title to their lands. A discussion of the OFA in the first year of MG Corporation's operations in 2006 follows.[7] The stage is set for an analysis of the MG Corporation and its governance issues as well as the difficulties it was having, at the time of writing, to materialise these benefits.[8]

The chapter is based on a report written for the Australian Government Overseas Aid Program (AusAID) in 2007 as part of its Pacific Land Program Case Studies project.[9] It was originally written for an audience with no knowledge of Australian customary land tenure issues and whose first language is often not English. The AusAID paper has been amended for this volume, though the language has not been substantially changed.

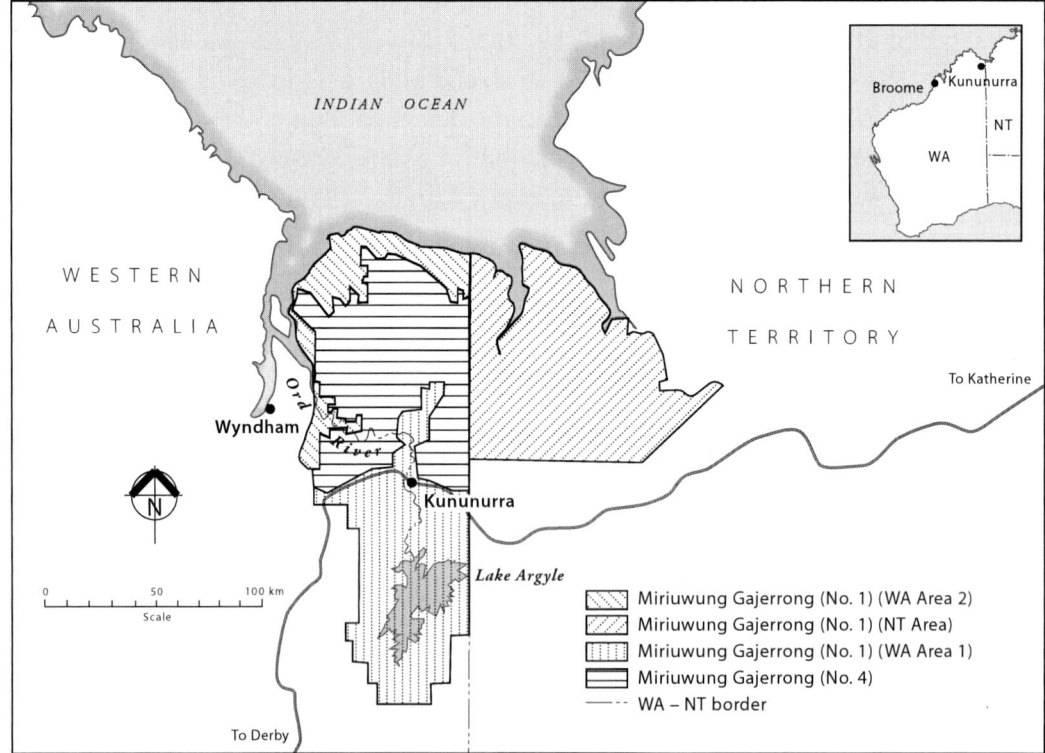

Figure 6.1 Miriuwung Gajerrong native title determinations. Map by Brenda Thornley for AIATSIS

The historical and contemporary setting

To understand the MG Corporation and the OFA it is important to know something about the people, their place, the history of their relations with the white settlers, and the governance setting into which MG Corporation was introduced. This section outlines the affiliations of MG people to their traditional lands, the settlement of Miriuwung and Gajerrong lands, including the involvement of MG people in the pastoral industry, and the impact of the Ord River scheme.

The people and their country

The Miriuwung and Gajerrong are people of the Ord River plains, its tributaries and its delta. Their traditional territory spans the contemporary boundaries of the State of Western Australia and the Northern Territory. They have owned the land since time immemorial, in all probability some 60,000 years. Until white settlement they were mobile hunter-gatherers. Since settlement their mobility has been reduced, though they still hunt, fish and collect bush foods and medicines.

Each individual has primary rights over a relatively well-defined area of land, their *dawang*, which is usually the land of their father. They may also claim rights in the lands of their mother and their grandmother. They can claim rights by birth in a particular place by having their spirit 'found' in a place (not always the place of their birth) or by becoming the 'namesake' of a senior person of a place. People with deep knowledge of the myths and ritual of the land may also exercise some ownership rights, even if they are not related by descent to Miriuwung or Gajerrong people. In this way, each individual is the centre of a constellation of rights to lands beyond the *dawang* of their primary attachment. In other words, any area of land, and the whole of a group's territory, has Miriuwung or Gajerrong people who express their rights to it in various ways. These overlapping attachments, a complex kinship system, intermarriage and shared languages bring Miriuwung and Gajerrong people together as a group.[10]

Miriuwung and Gajerrong people do not live in isolated groups, and theirs is not simply an economic right in land. The older people in particular always firstly talk of their rights to land by emphasising their responsibility for its sacred places and their knowledge of its sacred stories, songs, paintings and designs, and the rituals that go with them. Primary rights to these symbols of the land are fiercely defended by their owners, but they are also shared. Miriuwung and Gajerrong people celebrate the creation of features of the land by conducting ceremonies with large groups, including their neighbours who do not speak the same languages. During the native title hearings they demonstrated the continuity of their cultural practices and their enduring use of the land, even though use of the land has been disrupted by white settlement, as the following section describes.

Settlement of Miriuwung and Gajerrong land

It is important to understand the relatively recent colonial period because it continues to have an effect on the vigour with which the Miriuwung and Gajerrong people pursue their native title rights, and the context in which they see restitution due to them in the OFA. In the early 1880s, two almost simultaneous events disrupted the traditional way of life of the Aboriginal people in the area. Cattlemen in search of cheap grazing land drove their herds from eastern Australia through the Northern Territory, arriving at the first major river system in Western Australia, the Ord.[11] At the same time a gold discovery to the south west at Halls Creek attracted a large number of miners. Pat Durack, one of the founding cattlemen, heard of the goldfields on arriving at the Ord and immediately doubled back to Darwin, where he chartered a boat with provisions and landed it at the river mouth. This supply depot later became the town of Wyndham[12] which is located just outside the traditional country of the Miriuwung and Gajerrong people. From this time, the lands of the Miriuwung, Gajerrong and their neighbours to the south and the west became a thoroughfare for miners and pastoralists.

Settlement was not peaceful on either side. As Pat Durack put it:

> The blacks in the North have been notoriously more troublesome than the tribes found further south. In the days I speak of the overlander always carried firearms for his own protection; and of course we were armed. It should be added that the blackfellow on the whole was never given a chance, and the coming of the whites meant the going of the blacks. On the big stations throughout the country the black has proved a valuable 'hand' among stock, and he is usually a fine rider. It was the uncivilised or semi-civilised blacks who were a menace to the first whites in the outback districts.[13]

The introduced cattle were easy prey for the local people, and competition with the stock for water sources, particularly in the long dry season, caused conflict. There are consistent reports of settler raiding parties massacring entire camps of Aboriginal people. Many were captured, chained and taken to work on prison gangs reclaiming the mud flats of Wyndham for the expansion of the town.[14] Settlers were speared or shot with captured rifles; the Durack family lost two of its members in separate incidents.[15] Conflict continued into the 1930s and while most who witnessed it have passed on in the last two decades, they have handed down their recollections to the present generations.[16]

A form of accommodation was eventually reached in the context of violent and unequal conflict. The first settlers began to provide beef for local people if they would settle near the homestead.[17] Their children learned stock work. They developed attachment to their cattle station communities at Carlton Hill, Ivanhoe, Argyle Downs, Lissadell, Rosewood and Newry. Missions were established on neighbouring land at

Port Keats, Forrest River and Violet Valley. Importantly, the Miriuwung and Gajerrong people came under the laws of the State of Western Australia. They were controlled by the *Aborigines Act 1905* (WA) and its successors. Bolton describes their status:

> The chief protector could exercise the right of control over any property belonging to an Aboriginal or part-Aboriginal; he could order the removal of any unemployed Aboriginal to a reserve; he could declare specific areas out of bounds to Aborigines; and he alone could regulate the employment of Aborigines, fix conditions and issue permits. The police were given the right to arrest Aborigines without warrant. The chief protector became the legal guardian of every Aboriginal or part-Aboriginal child up to the age of sixteen. It became an offence to supply an Aboriginal with liquor, to marry one without the consent of the protector, or to cohabit with one without marriage. [18]

The last discriminatory provisions in Western Australian legislation that related explicitly to Aboriginal people, restrictions on serving alcohol in the Kimberley district, were abolished under the *Liquor Act Amendment Act 1972* (WA),[19] well within the memory of senior Miriuwung and Gajerrong people.

Dispossession and the Ord River scheme

The period of segregation on missions and pastoral stations, which lasted into the late 1970s, has had a profound effect on the people of the Ord River. Though Miriuwung and Gajerrong people were not formally equal in rights to the settlers, their relative numbers and their importance to the pastoral industry gave them a certain dignity and confidence among the pastoralists. Their work on the cattle stations was compatible with the continuation of cultural practices, particularly during the lay-off period of the wet season when they often left the stations to visit their traditional countries, hunting and gathering, holding ceremonies and meeting up with other relatives.[20] Traditional languages and knowledge were also largely preserved. In their relatively gainful employment on the cattle stations the people found a substitute for their traditional economy, allowing for the vigorous social health of the community. This form of accommodation and adaptation lasted for roughly 100 years, until the exodus from pastoral stations and missions in the late 1970s and early 1980s.

The removal of Aboriginal people from the pastoral stations is usually blamed on the introduction of equal wages and the unwillingness of pastoralists to pay increased wages to Aboriginal workers. This is not strictly true; it was also due to changes in the pastoral industry itself. The industry had become more capital intensive and required less labour.[21] The early pastoralists were replaced by absentee landlords or newcomers who had no understanding of the social contract worked out between pastoralists and Aboriginal people in the early years of conflict. The equal wage decision in the 1960s was itself a reflection of broader changes in federal policy following the Second World

War, which encouraged assimilation and equality of formal rights. The missions were closed or declined in prominence, later to reopen under Aboriginal management. As the region developed and legal constraints were lifted Aboriginal people began to travel away from the stations for work more frequently.[22] Increasingly they found that they could not go back to the stations in their traditional country and they camped on reserves on the edges of the towns. By now there were two towns in the region, as Kununurra began to replace Wyndham as the supply centre.

Kununurra was established in 1963 to service the Ord River Irrigation Scheme. The Ord was dammed, creating an artificial lake of 10,760 million cubic metres capacity, which is commonly described as nine times the size of Sydney harbour.[23] The water in controlled release is diverted into irrigation channels that service the new farms surrounding Kununurra. The Miriuwung people, whose country was flooded on Argyle Downs station, were entirely dispossessed without compensation. Initially they and their countrymen from surrounding stations found work on the Kununurra farms. Increasingly, mechanisation and a new wave of settlers from the southern parts of Australia took over the work. The Miriuwung and Gajerrong and their neighbours retreated to the town reserves where they survived on welfare payments,[24] and where social conditions today are similar to settlements of the dispossessed elsewhere in the world: poverty, ill-health, alcoholism, family violence and for many, particularly the youth, despair.

It was in this milieu of cultural dislocation, discrimination and great need that several local organisations were born, and which the MG Corporation joins. Mirima Council, as it was then known, was among the earliest, established to represent the people of the town reserve.[25] Warringarri Aboriginal Corporation also was initially set up as a town-based progress association, but then turned to establishing and servicing small living areas on traditional lands in the region. In the mid-1980s it became a multi-service organisation, with a mechanical workshop, building company, radio station and art centre.[26] The Miriuwung and Gajerrong Families Heritage and Land Council was established to further the interests of a group of Miriuwung and Gajerrong families around this time. In the 1990s, the Wunan Foundation invested development funds in local commercial enterprises.[27]

MG Corporation, therefore, has been established in a landscape already populated with Aboriginal community organisations with a 30-year history of self-management. This experience and social infrastructure were important in providing the necessary fortitude for a long battle for the recognition of native title rights.

The Miriuwung Gajerrong native title corporations

The Federal Court handed down its first determination that native title existed in the Miriuwung and Gajerrong area in late 1998.[28] The determination was appealed to the Full Bench of the Federal Court which set aside the judgment in 2000.[29] The

Full Bench decision in turn was appealed in the High Court. In 2002 the High Court sent the case back to the Federal Court for reconsideration.[30] The High Court had decided that native title rights could coexist with the rights of others where they were not incompatible.[31] The Federal Court mediated between the parties and achieved a determination by consent referred to as *MG (No. 1)* in late 2003.[32] After nearly 10 years and protracted negotiations at great expense, the State of Western Australia had to concede that the area was held under native title. A subsequent claim over areas not covered in the original claim, but subject to the same case for rights, was settled by a consent determination of the parties in November 2006. This determination is referred to as *MG (No. 4)*.[33] In the meantime, following the success of the first appeal, the Western Australian Government had begun to negotiate a comprehensive settlement.

RNTBCs are often located in a complex of incorporated organisations (see Figure 6.2). Since the MG claims were lodged separately, and determined at different

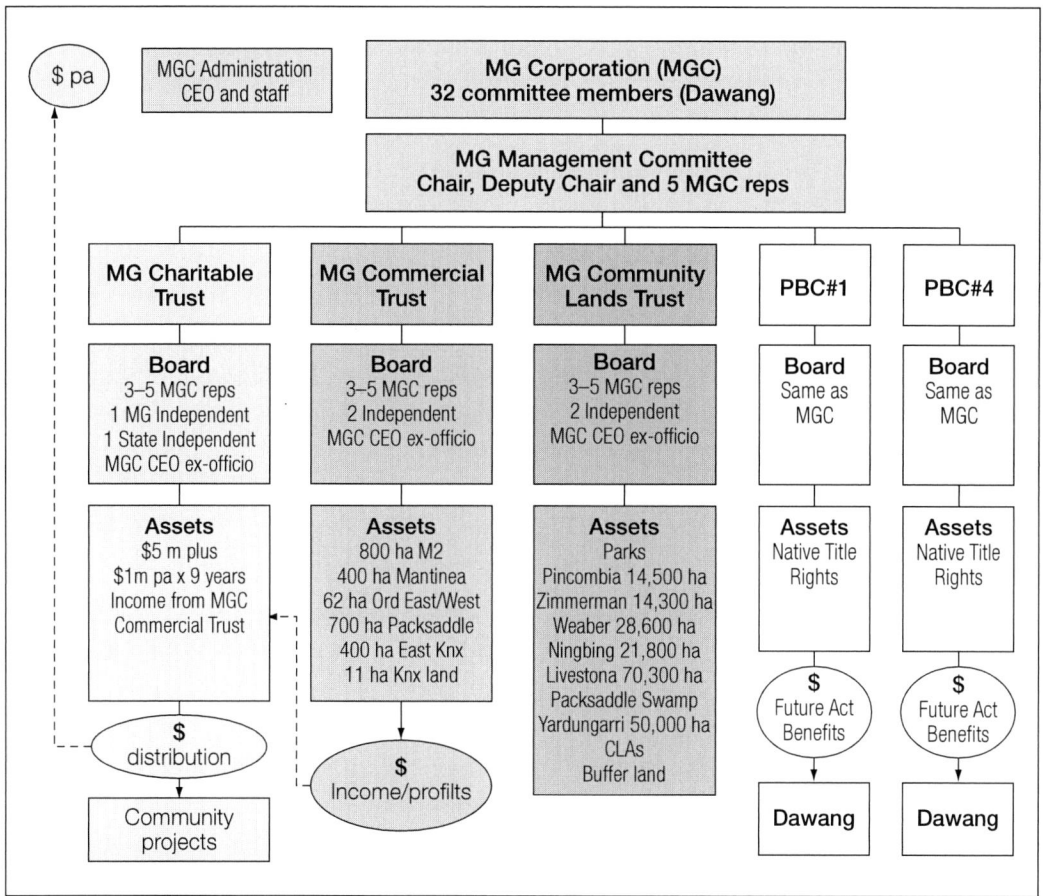

Figure 6.2 Corporate structure of MG Corporation, 2006, including MG#1 and MG#4 RNTBCs (shown here as 'PBC#1' and 'PBC#4'). Diagram courtesy of MG Corporation

times, they have produced two RNTBCs, though the native title holders are the same. These are called the Miriuwung and Gajerrong #1 (Registered Native Title Body Corporate) Aboriginal Corporation (referred to as MG#1 RNTBC below) and the Miriuwung and Gajerrong #4 (Registered Native Title Body Corporate) Aboriginal Corporation (referred to as MG#4 RNTBC below). They have identical constitutions and identical membership. They were both registered under the *Aboriginal Councils and Associations Act 1976* (Cth) (ACA Act), which has since been superseded by the *Corporations (Aboriginal and Torres Strait Islander) Act 2006* (Cth) (CATSI Act). In the preamble to their rules, both constitutions refer to the OFA and their intention that MG Corporation will hold its benefits on their behalf.

The members of both RNTBCs and of MG Corporation belong to 16 sub-areas, *dawang*, or 'countries'.[34] In its 2006 rules, the *dawang* elect two members each to the MG Corporation Governing Committee. Ideally this would be the same two members for each of the corporations, though on registration of the two RNTBCs there were some anomalies. The chairs of the two RNTBCs differed from each other and from the MG Corporation. In practice, though, at the time of writing, all corporations met as a single governing committee, from time to time distinguishing their roles in the RNTBCs or in the MG Corporation depending on the business before them. The major activity of the RNTBCs is to receive notice of proposed developments or future acts under the NTA on native title land. As it did in the past, the Kimberley Land Council (KLC) deals with these notices and the MG Corporation provides logistical support and management services. The potential for independent action by the RNTBCs is limited by lack of resources, which are concentrated in the MG Corporation as a result of the OFA.

The Ord Final Agreement

The Western Australian Government's plans to extend the Ord River Irrigation Scheme downstream in Stage Two were disrupted by the success of the first MG native title claim (*MG (No. 1)*). The claimants benefited from some of the uncertainty surrounding the new native title regime in Australia. If the government had moved unilaterally to Stage Two development, legal challenges by the Miriuwung and Gajerrong would have tied up progress for a considerable time. This course of action would also have compounded the ill will still felt by Miriuwung and Gajerrong as a result of the imposition of the first Ord scheme and by the Western Australian Government's opposition to the native title claims. The government decided instead to negotiate a determination of native title by consent of all parties, to go hand in hand with voluntary acceptance of extinguishment of native title or surrender of some areas under claim, the compulsory acquisition by the Western Australian Government of others, and a comprehensive package for compensation.[35]

Negotiations were complex on both sides. On the Aboriginal side the relations between all the claimants were by no means smooth. Agreeing to extinguishment of rights in land was not an easy decision. For some it caused emotional turmoil of a deep religious nature. Native title claimants also demanded recognition of past wrongs. On the government side, precise planning for a variety of land uses over a large area was as much of a challenge as finding the right legal instruments to implement it in the context of the existence of native title. Negotiations began in September 2003 and the OFA was signed in October 2005. This case study does not dwell on the process of negotiation, which deserves a study in itself;[36] rather the chapter focuses on the results of the negotiations, as these brought the MG Corporation into existence.

The OFA provides for a range of benefits to be held and administered by the MG Corporation, which are said to be worth $57 million.[37] They are outlined here before a brief consideration of the justice of the arrangements and some of the issues in implementing the Agreement.

Establishment funds

In the OFA, the Western Australian Government agrees to provide an initial $350,000 to cover costs in setting up the MG Corporation,[38] a charitable trust, and another corporation to hold the trust. In this part of the OFA, some of the provisions of the MG Corporation constitution, which are examined below, are also mandated. Remembering that all provisions arose out of reasonably friendly negotiations, it cannot be assumed that the provisions for the structure of the corporation were imposed by the government.

Financial contribution to MG Corporation

In the OFA, the Western Australian Government agrees to pay to MG Corporation $10 million over 10 years, commencing in 2006. Each year $750,000 is for administration of the corporation and the remaining $250,000 for an Economic Development Unit (EDU) administered within the corporation.[39] The EDU is not intended to engage directly in economic activity. Its functions, as set out in the OFA, are to encourage employment by:

(a) researching, identifying and facilitating employment, economic development, investment and business opportunities for the MG People;
(b) facilitating and assisting in improving the capacity and capabilities of the MG People in relation to employment and enterprise development;
(c) liaising with, and making applications to, the state and the Commonwealth to facilitate and obtain public funding for programs that provide for improving the capacity and capabilities of the MG People in relation to employment and enterprise development;

(d) procuring support and commitments from the state, the Commonwealth, the Shire of Wyndham-East Kimberley and non-government enterprises in relation to employment and enterprise development for the MG People; and

(e) providing information and assistance to the MG Entities.[40]

Financial contribution to an investment trust

Under the OFA, the Western Australian Government gives an initial payment of $5 million, then $1 million per year over the next nine years, to the charitable trust administered by the MG Corporation through a subsidiary. The trust also holds the funds and other benefits, such as land provided under the OFA. The cash contribution direct to the trust must be invested in low or medium risk investments, and at least 50 per cent of the income from them must also be invested in low to medium risk investments.[41] Clearly, the intention is to provide a modest but secure income stream. The trust must hold and manage its assets for charitable purposes for the benefit of all the Miriuwung and Gajerrong people. It is governed by a board of directors of the trustee company of three to five people. Two must be independent directors, one of these nominated by the Western Australian Government and the other by MG Corporation.

Establishing and funding the Ord Enhancement Scheme

In the OFA, the Western Australian Government pays $11,195,000 in diminishing portions over four years to the Kimberley Development Commission (KDC) to operate the Ord Enhancement Scheme. The KDC is a regional statutory body of the Western Australian Government with broad community representation on its governing body. It has set up the Ord Enhancement Scheme Management Committee to run the scheme. The committee has seven representatives appointed by MG Corporation and one appointed by the KDC.[42]

The intention of this part of the Agreement is to address the Miriuwung and Gajerrong peoples' concerns about the impact of the first Ord River Irrigation Scheme on their lives and their culture. In local Aboriginal conceptions, the health of the land and the health of the people are part and parcel of each other. The first stage of the Ord River scheme dispossessed some of the native title holders of their lands through the creation of Lake Argyle, the town of Kununurra and the surrounding irrigated farmland. The irrigation itself has caused environmental damage and loss of natural waterways. In 2004 the regional Native Title Representative Body, the KLC, conducted a study of these impacts, called the Aboriginal Social and Economic Impact Assessment (ASEIA).[43] Many of its recommendations were implemented through the benefits of the OFA discussed in this chapter.

Other recommendations, such as those relating to the establishment of cultural and language maintenance programs, were more difficult to mandate in an agreement.

They required the cooperation of many state and Commonwealth government departments in areas identified as employment and training; health, family and children's services; housing; aged care; education; youth; and local planning (among others).[44] The Management Committee of the Ord Enhancement Scheme was to use the Western Australian Government funding to coordinate projects and programs in these areas with government and non-government partners.

Transfer and funding management of new conservation areas

In the OFA, the Western Australian Government agrees to create freehold title over six new areas for conservation. Five of these have been surrendered from surrounding cattle station leases under compensation arrangements with the owners. The freehold titles are to be transferred to the MG Corporation on condition that they are immediately leased back to the Western Australian Government. This is a common, though not exclusive, arrangement for conservation areas in Australia. The government will provide $1 million to its own department — the Department of Conservation and Land Management (now the Department of Environment and Conservation (DEC)) — for development of plans of management and joint management structures between DEC and MG Corporation. The government will then provide $1 million for infrastructure and $1 million[45] per year for four years for management of the conservation areas.[46] In the OFA there is a similar arrangement with the Waters and Rivers Commission of Western Australia for joint management of conservation reserve for waters and wetlands, with less funding of $119,700 over four years for management and planning.[47]

Land and water benefits

Under the OFA, the Western Australian Government agrees to create freehold title over three areas of land at Packsaddle, East Kununurra and Yardungarrl, which are currently Crown land, reserve or pastoral lease. It will transfer these titles to the MG Corporation. The state also agrees to create titles over 11 smaller living areas and transfer the titles to MG Corporation.

From the date of the OFA in 2005, the MG Corporation has two years to nominate to the government an area of Lake Argyle suitable for aquaculture. The aquaculture reserve is to be managed by the state minister for fisheries. The reserve is to be leased to the MG Corporation and a licence to carry out an aquaculture industry issued, though this may be in joint venture with an unrelated commercial enterprise. The corporation does not receive any Western Australian Government funding to develop the aquaculture venture.

Under the Agreement, the MG Corporation has priority in picking irrigated farm lots in the new farm area. It can choose up to 7.5 per cent of the area, assessed by land value not the size of the lots. Five per cent will be transferred to the corporation without payment and it must pay market rates for the remaining 2.5 per cent. This potentially gives the corporation the option to pick the best farm lots prior to release. In keeping with usual practice in Australia, the new farm area is to be serviced and marketed by a commercial development company, and this company must, under the OFA, produce an Aboriginal Development Package which must be negotiated with the MG Corporation.

The OFA also has provisions for the protection of Aboriginal cultural and archaeological heritage in some nominated areas.

Is the Ord Final Agreement a good agreement?

At least three issues should be taken into account when assessing whether the OFA is a good agreement:

1. What is its value in relation to the current circumstances of the MG people — how much better off will they be?
2. What is its value in relation to the rights relinquished?
3. Is implementation sufficiently resourced so that benefit can be realised and sustainable?

On the face of it, this agreement represents a significant advance for the MG people. Currently living in extreme poverty, by state government estimates they will receive some $57 million worth of benefit from the package. The package is balanced in its regard to:

- protection of cultural heritage, both in areas of land and in the management structure of the MG Corporation
- economic opportunities in irrigated agriculture, aquaculture and employment creating strategies
- living areas
- income streams from investment
- initial funding of MG Corporation.

It is not reasonable, however, to judge the amount of the benefit against the current circumstances of the MG people. Coming from nothing, almost any benefit package would represent a substantial advance. It is more realistic to assess the package against what has been given up or lost on each side, and the potential for what remains. Assessing the package in this way means that only approximate estimates are achievable.

The loss of land by MG people, both in the past and in the proposed development, is a cultural as well as an economic loss. The cultural impact results in dysfunction which has community, personal and economic dimensions, and this dysfunction has been severe in the past. It remains to be seen whether the administrative arrangements for these benefits, which give substantial control to MG people and acknowledge their distinct cultural processes for decision-making, provide a significant mechanism of recovery and for re-establishing the MG native title holders as a major presence in the region, countering the shock to their culture and wellbeing through the loss of land and loss of control over their lives.

In monetary terms, it is also difficult to assess the benefits against the native title rights taken from the MG people by the Western Australian Government. Whether the rights themselves may lead to monetary reward is contingent on the capacity and resources of MG Corporation to use their members' rights as a springboard to economic development. Nevertheless, a broad monetary assessment can be made by estimating the value remaining to non-Indigenous interests after the agreement against the value that has been transferred. From this perspective, $57 million over 10 years appears a small price for non-Indigenous interests to pay.

With respect to implementation of the OFA, the establishment funds have fallen far short of the organisation's needs. At the time of writing, it operated from a demountable building on Aboriginal reserved land at the back of the KLC office in Kununurra. Constructing houses and offices in Kununurra is very expensive because of its remote location. It would take the equivalent of several years' operating budget to build offices alone, let alone to staff them adequately. In 2007, the MG Corporation employed three staff members, one of whom was dedicated to the EDU. However, administration of the benefits set out in the Agreement, and servicing the RNTBCs, is a vast task that will require more staff. With on-costs it would not be unusual if those three positions alone consumed about one-quarter to one-third of the operating budget of $1 million per annum. Attracting good staff to the region also requires provision of housing, which is in short supply and is expensive.

While the benefits under the OFA appear considerable, they provide little in the way of direct sustainable income for the membership. The staff and the governing committee drew up a strategic plan for the first five years of operation.[48] There they identified the need for an income stream as a priority. The OFA has three provisions that could provide this: the investment fund, the aquaculture lease and the farming land. Income from the investment fund is limited because 50 per cent of it must be reinvested and the investment policy must be low risk. While this provision may have limited the damage from the financial turmoil that devastated stock markets in late 2008, low-risk investments inevitably lead to low returns. Development of aquaculture requires planning and expertise, which rules it out as an immediate source of funding. During the early years of the Agreement, the Western Australian Government limited the third option by placing the development of the second stage of the Ord irrigation scheme temporarily on hold. The corporation had been pinning its hopes on it, and the announcement disrupted its plans.

Lack of infrastructure, lack of staff, and the root cause of this — lack of cash flow — make it difficult for the organisation to leverage partnerships with other interests in the region. The local Aboriginal-controlled Wunan Foundation, for instance, is party to a Regional Partnership Agreement with both the Commonwealth and Western Australian governments. This agreement concerns the cooperation of government agencies and commercial interests to increase the employment and business opportunities of the Aboriginal people of the Kununurra region. The MG Corporation is not a partner, though its landholdings and the purpose of its EDU could both usefully work to fulfil the agreement's aims. In its initial phase, the management group was concentrating on consolidating the MG Corporation's own operations and did not feel it had the capacity to engage with other organisations, nor was it approached to become engaged by other more consolidated players in the region.

Establishing the 11 living areas provided for in the OFA was also an initial priority. These will improve the social health of the membership by allowing them to leave the overcrowded living conditions of the town. They will also provide some economic opportunities via income substitution through hunting, tourist ventures and planned commercial tree-planting operations. Providing housing and sanitation in these areas has proved a challenge. The Commonwealth Government has in the past met this need but in recent years has changed its policy to concentrate resources on large settlements. So far there is no indication that the Western Australian Government will move to fill this gap. It is a failing of the OFA that it did not address in sufficient detail how the MG people would be able to take advantage of this aspect of the Agreement.

In addition to the financial benefits set out in the OFA, an unusual aspect of the Agreement is that it prescribes much of the structure of MG Corporation, including its governance arrangements, as a prerequisite for the benefits of the OFA. This structure is discussed in the following section.

The governance of Yawoorroong Miriuwung Gajerrong Yirrgeb Noong Dawang Corporation or MG Corporation

MG Corporation is the umbrella corporation for a number of organisations (see Figure 6.2) and is subject to complex regulatory regimes. One of the requirements in the OFA was that the MG Corporation incorporate under the then ACA Act, now the CATSI Act. The two RNTBCs administered by MG Corporation are also incorporated under the CATSI Act, as is a requirement of all native title holding bodies under the Native Title (Prescribed Bodies Corporate) Regulations 1999.

The CATSI Act establishes an Office of the Registrar of Indigenous Corporations (ORIC), provides model rules for Aboriginal and Torres Strait Islander corporations and determines which variations of the rules are acceptable. ORIC polices the rules and requires annual reports, and it may dismiss the governing committee and appoint an administrator if not satisfied with the operation of the corporation. This brings the MG Corporation into a three-way regime of regulation — that of the OFA,

ORIC and its own governing committee and membership. Among these, only the governing committee is bound by traditional law and custom.

The MG Corporation is intercultural, reflecting non-Indigenous norms in its structure and regulatory environment, and Aboriginal norms in its relationships with its members. In engaging with the native title processes it is inevitable that compromises have to be made between the relatively informal processes of traditional authority and the requirements of a modern corporation for the economic and social benefit of its members. For our purposes in this chapter, we can distinguish between those elements of the rules of the corporation that are standard and derive from non-Aboriginal concepts, and those that attempt to reflect traditional practice.[49]

The first of these elements that derive from non-Aboriginal concepts are about good management and fiscal practice. There are requirements in the 2006 rules that MG Corporation holds an annual general meeting (AGM) at which the membership can examine audited accounts, for a public officer who keeps a register of members, and for a number of other similar standard-setting provisions. The second type of rules or provisions, which are particularly important for an organisation that is intended to reflect traditional practice and which have a major bearing on the difficult task of running an efficient organisation, are discussed below. These include the objects of the corporation, criteria for membership, means of electing and recalling the governing committee, the decision-making process (including quorums) and the dispute resolution process.

Objects of the MG Corporation

The 2006 Objects of the MG Corporation are divided into two parts. The first are quite standard benevolent objects which mark the corporation as charitable and therefore able to attract tax concessions. The MG Corporation is a not-for-profit corporation and its dominant object is '…to provide direct relief from poverty, sickness, suffering, misfortune, disability, destitution, helplessness and disadvantage and undertake community development for the benefit of the MG people…'[50] There are several subclauses describing the kinds of services the corporation can provide to meet the broad aims of this dominant object in the 2006 rules. This is standard for CATSI Act corporations.

The second part of the objects, the ancillary objects, relates more specifically to the MG Corporation's obligations under the OFA. In this way the activities and structure of the corporation are tied very tightly to the OFA. The OFA sets out minimum requirements for the corporation's constitution,[51] and the 2006 rules of the MG Corporation confirm its major obligations under the OFA.[52]

These obligations, set out in the 2006 MG Corporation rules and in the OFA, largely relate to holding and administering land with substantial economic value, and to establishing an EDU. So from its commencement, the MG Corporation treads a fine line between its charitable status and its economic activities. This tension must be resolved by applying any gains it makes from investment or economic activity to its primary charitable objects.

Membership of the MG Corporation

It is no easy matter to find out, as a matter of fact, who is eligible to be a member of the MG Corporation. The 2006 rules say that only 'MG People' over 18 may be ordinary members.[53] 'MG People' are defined elsewhere in the rules[54] as the native title holders in the first *MG (No. 1)* claim and as the claim group and other native title holders in the *MG (No. 4)* claim. During the course of the claim and various appeals, the Federal Court made several determinations identifying native title holders. In *MG (No. 1)*, in regard to the land that lies within the Northern Territory, it referred to limited 'estate' groups, but allowed for the possibility of attachment to estates through several forms of descent, and on grounds other than descent.[55] In regard to land that lies within Western Australia, the Court did not refer to estates but rather to language and dialect groups, and reiterated that rights could be established by means other than descent. The Court followed this approach in *MG (No. 4)* where it was found that native title holders could belong to several language groups in the region, not just to the Miriuwung and Gajerrong groups. It said:

> Native title rights and interests in the Determination Area are held by:
>
> a) the members of the Miriuwung, Gajerrong, Doolboong, Wardenybeng and Gija groups in respect of Miriuwung, Gajerrong, Doolboong, Wardenybeng and Gija[56] country respectively in accordance with traditional law and custom
>
> b) other Aboriginal persons who are acknowledged by the respective Miriuwung, Gajerrong, Doolboong, Wardenybeng or Gija groups as having rights in the Native Title Area through descent, marriage, spiritual conception, birth or responsibility for sites of significance.[57]

While the Court also listed the ancestors of many of the native title holders,[58] it did not limit the potential range of native title holders only to their descendants.[59] In effect, then, the people of the language groups named are to decide for themselves who is a native title holder, and they can do so by referring to a range of forms of relatedness. This is fairly open-ended and could lead to conflicting claims being assessed by a court in the future. It does not provide the kind of certainty usually demanded by governments and developers, but it is fair and pragmatic and reflects cultural practice in the region.

As noted, the 2006 MG Corporation rules limit membership to those who are 18 years old or over. Younger people may be native title holders in law, but they cannot directly control the benefits from native title rights through the corporation. Anyone who is eligible for membership under the rules can apply to the governing committee for membership. This is the gateway, then, through which MG people pass from having rights in land under traditional law and custom to being able to control the benefit from these rights under a non-Aboriginal statute for a voluntary association. However, passing through the gateway requires some other compromises.

When applying for membership the applicant must say which *dawang* they belong to. Although there is no mention of *dawang* in the Court's determinations, this rule is one of the stipulations of the OFA. The 2006 rules define a *dawang* as 'the country of a local (or estate) group'.[60] Both these terms, 'local group' and 'estate group', are unique to the description of Aboriginal social organisation in the anthropological literature[61] and are contested. There is still debate among anthropologists about how useful they are for describing Aboriginal land relationships, with some insisting that they represent European rather than Aboriginal constructs.[62] It is true, though, that in a number of instances the terms have passed into the language of Aboriginal administration and from there into, or back into, Aboriginal ways of describing their relationships to country and to each other in formal administrative contexts.

Under the 2006 rules, a person can nominate only one *dawang*, despite the fact that most people have interests in several given intermarriages between neighbouring *dawang* and the dense kinship relationships arising from them. The governing committee can ask other members of the *dawang* for advice on a membership application before confirming the applicant as a member. If the governing committee asks for and receives confirmation of the membership status of an applicant, it must enrol the applicant as a member and record him or her as belonging to that *dawang*. Members cease to be members on death, if they resign or if they are expelled by the governing committee for serious or repeated breaches of law and custom. Expulsion of members means that they cannot qualify for the benefits of the OFA, so this is a severe sanction which could lead to litigation over the practice of law and custom.

The codification of belonging and traditional practice in the MG Corporation's rules in the form of *dawang* and expulsion for breaches of traditional law and custom is accepted by the membership, even though the rules do not reflect the decision of the Court in either native title determination. At present, the concept of *dawang* is used simply as the skeleton of traditional social organisation which is clothed in the flesh and blood of the actual practice of relations between the members. Here, respect for the knowledge of elders, understanding of protocols, kinship ties and daily interactions lessen the impact of the highly formal structure. An outside observer can be concerned, however; such codification holds potential problems for the future, which are discussed in a subsequent section.

The MG Corporation Governing Committee

The governing committee is the board of the MG Corporation. It is elected not by the members at large but by members of the subgroups — the *dawang*. There are 16 *dawang* listed in the 2006 rules of the MG Corporation.[63] Two members are elected from each, making a governing committee of 32. Half plus one of these (17 members) make up a quorum, as long as they represent half plus one (or nine) of the listed *dawang*. The rules encourage, where possible, the election of a senior and a junior person from each *dawang* to be the two delegates. In comparison to modern corporate practice this is a very complex and restrictive board structure, and is too large to be practical. The rules also require, if possible, that the elected delegates are the same as for the RNTBCs, though this is not required in the rules of these MG#1 and MG#4 RNTBCs.[64] Failure to align the corporations in this way could mean that *dawang* are represented by members with competing interests, some of whom have influence on the RNTBC and others on the MG Corporation.

The 2006 rules stipulate that alternative delegates must also be nominated to substitute when a delegate is not available. It is a slight weakness in the rules, though, that only the nominated delegate can actually appoint his or her substitute to a meeting in any instance. If the delegate is unavailable, it is likely that he or she is incapacitated in some way and so will not be able to make a substitution for the same reason that they are unavailable. Both the *dawang* and the governing committee can remove the delegate for a variety of reasons, and if the delegate misses four consecutive governing committee meetings their position is deemed to be vacant.

There are two important differences between the rules that govern *dawang* in controlling the RNTBCs and those that govern them in controlling the MG Corporation. In the first there is a requirement for consultation before making a decision that could affect native title rights. This requirement is stipulated in the NTA. There is no similar provision for consultation in MG Corporation. There is, though, a provision for delegates to be controlled by the *dawang*'[65] which is not present in the rules of the MG#1 and MG#4 RNTBCs.[66]

An important aspect of the 2006 MG Corporation constitution is that committee members are delegates rather than representatives. The members of each *dawang* can vote in a *dawang* meeting on the way that they require their delegate to vote in a governing committee meeting. This ensures some local control, but could provide problems for the governance of the MG Corporation. The members of the *dawang* are not likely to have the detailed knowledge of issues that the delegate has from participating in the governing committee. The delegate could be placed in a difficult position if the instructions from the *dawang* were different from his or her own views, or from the consensus view of the committee to which the delegate is a party.

Provisions for the governing committee to consult actively with the membership should be strengthened. This could be done when the corporation convenes *dawang* meetings, which at present it only does to assist in the election of delegates. The

AGM is not sufficient for wide consultation. Under cl 17 of the 2006 rules of the MG Corporation, the governing committee (as well as the members of MG Corporation at large and the management group (see below)) are required to:

(a) consider, be guided by, and where possible comply with the traditional laws and customs of the MG people, including traditional decision-making processes;
(b) act honestly, diligently and with reasonable care;
(c) act respectfully towards other members and employees and not engage in personal attacks;
(d) not make improper use of information or opportunities received through that position; and
(e) manage and control the affairs of the corporation in the interests of all the MG people and in accordance with these rules of the Act.[67]

These requirements are now standard for Aboriginal corporations under the CATSI Act and many native title holders now receive training from ORIC or the Institute of Company Directors about them. The MG Corporation committee members take them seriously, so at present there is a balance between the elements of the rules that would tend towards fragmentation and dispute and those elements of the rules and of current practice that tend toward unity. These are discussed below.

The MG Corporation Management Group

The MG Corporation Governing Committee is unwieldy at 32 members. It is only likely to be able to make broad decisions of principle. The 2006 rules require the appointment of a management group.[68] It has powers delegated to it by the governing committee, which can put restrictions or conditions on the exercise of those powers. The management group is made up of at least three and no more than five governing committee members. The governing committee chooses two of these as its chair and deputy chair. The general manager is also a member of the management group but cannot vote. The management group can invite other non-voting parties to sit with it. The governing committee can appoint, remove or replace members of the management group as it sees fit.[69]

The operation of the corporation is not clear in the wording of the rules. The management responsibilities of the governing committee and the management group overlap; both are charged with managing the organisation.[70] It appears from the wording that the power of the management group is not a delegated power but a function conferred by the rules.

The relationship between a general manager, with his/her executive team, and a board is a crucial one in any organisation. In the MG Corporation the general manager is a member of the management group, but the management group is responsible for supervision of his/her position, though he or she cannot vote. In most corporations the general manager is responsible to the board of directors or governing committee.

As well as dealing with the composition of the management group and the selection of the chair and deputy chair of the governing committee, the rules also outline the duties of the general manager. Again the purpose of this section, which is headed 'Management Group', is not clear.[71] The duties of the general manager are outlined along with the principles for recruitment to the position. The general manager must have expertise in two of the areas of: financial management, Aboriginal culture, legal practice, accounting, business development or 'any other area of expertise or experience desirable for the advancement of the MG people'.[72]

Dispute resolution procedures

The members of the governing committee are required to 'consider, be guided by, and where possible comply with the Traditional Laws and Customs of the MG People'.[73] Disputes are to be decided by reference to traditional laws and customs,[74] and if unresolved, then by an independent arbiter. Some implications of this are discussed below.

The codification of traditional practices in the MG Corporation rules

As the discussion above suggests, a number of the MG Corporation 2006 rules are a formal codification of traditional practices, elevating some aspects of them while reducing others. This is particularly evident in the elevation of *dawang* to a formal, institutionalised status.

In most areas of Aboriginal Australia, including among the Miriuwung and Gajerrong, there is a word to denote camp, home, homeland, heartland or country. These words do not usually have a single and precise referent; their meaning varies according to context, and the forms of attachment to an area under discussion can be many. It is also common in some areas of Australia for the size of a group's 'country' to wax and wane, and some distinctly named areas drop out altogether if the group with attachment to it doesn't thrive. When the group is large, a single named area can be split into two separately named areas. In some parts of Australia the territory of a group may be split up into different tracts of land that are not adjacent to each other. And, it is also common throughout Australia, that 'estate' boundaries are often indistinct.

None of these complexities and transformations is envisaged in MG Corporation's 2006 rules. In the MG case, the word *dawang* is not only a social descriptor as used in the rules; it is also a geographical descriptor broadly meaning 'country' which can be further qualified by geographical descriptors such as 'sandy *dawang*' or 'wetland *dawang*'.[75] As is the case elsewhere, *dawang* does not indicate a strictly bounded area. However, the reflection in the rules of the meaning of '*dawang*' as similar to 'counties' or 'cantons' within a linguistic nation is stark, despite the fact that there are no maps of *dawang* associated either with the rules or the native title determinations, or the OFA. Each of these is more concerned with identifying a group of people rather than an area of land.

The term *dawang*, as described in the 2006 rules, means the country of a local descent group or an estate group.[76] Anthropologists using these terms in referring to landowning groups have often meant a patrilineal descent group, or a clan to which people belong through an ancestral line from their fathers and paternal grandfathers.

Yet both *MG (No. 1)* and *MG (No. 4)* native title determinations explicitly allowed for other forms of membership of a group and attachment to several *dawang* by different means. In the first instance of *MG (No. 1)* the primary judge, Justice Lee, said:

> The evidence established that whilst there may remain a patrilineal bias or expectation in the organization of such sub-groups, young Aboriginal people may have several choices presented by lines of descent as to which sub-group they will identify themselves. Other grounds of choice may be provided by the locus of conception, birth and by adoption. According to the general tenor of the evidence in this case, any right to claim membership of a sub-group, and thus of the community as a whole, may depend upon the course of life of the child concerned.[77]

MG (No. 4) also allowed for other forms of membership of landowning groups, such as birth in the location, marriage into a group or deep knowledge of the myth and ritual of the terrain.[78]

The 2006 MG Corporation rules reflect the possibilities neither of moves away from a patrilineal bias nor of multiple memberships of *dawang* via a range of means. Neither do the rules seem to anticipate that the patrilineal line of a *dawang* might become extinct and descendants with other affiliations to the group could succeed to a *dawang*.

It is possible that MG Corporation's constitution will freeze in time not only the division of the land into homeland areas but also the people attached to these as specific families defined in a particular way, or at best a limited number of such families belonging to the same area. There is also a danger that, by emphasising the patrilineal descent group, male rights will become entrenched and privileged over the rights of the group's women.

Perhaps one kind of codification or another is inevitable when non-modern cultures adopt distinctively modern structures to activate their rights. The structure of MG Corporation, though, has some inherent dangers. Tensions over the distribution of benefits that derive from the country of a particular *dawang* to the broader MG group comprising members of other *dawang* are possible. Delegates may come under pressure to stress the narrow interests of *dawang* members against the interests of the group as a whole. Tension over the distribution of benefits among the *dawang* members themselves may also occur, and disputes over the accuracy of genealogies are likely. The members of one *dawang* can easily be played off against another by outside commercial and political interests. But policing the votes of *dawang* delegates will be difficult, as many MG Corporation decisions will be made by the management on a day-to-day basis and decisions of the governing committee will not always be put to a vote.

These tendencies may lead to conflict within the *dawang* group. *Dawang* delegates can be recalled by the *dawang* even if the governing committee feels the delegate is making a useful contribution. Conversely, where the governing committee decides to get rid of a delegate it is open to the *dawang* to immediately reappoint them. These provisions are potentially disruptive. The quorum for a *dawang* meeting is quite small. At four, it could comprise only the delegates and their alternative delegates. This raises the potential for convening rolling meetings only to overturn the decision of the previous one.

The very prescriptive rules for membership of the governing committee ensure that smaller *dawang* have proportionally more control over the organisation than larger *dawang* in terms of the enfranchisement of each individual member. In addition, choice of delegates from a small *dawang* may be limited, so individuals who are not particularly capable or apt may be chosen. Conversely, other *dawang* may have a large number of suitable people but can only appoint two, meaning expertise is lost to the corporation. Those native title holders with attachment to the land through deep knowledge and ritual responsibilities, recognised as potential native title holders by the Court's determinations, cannot be members if they do not also belong to a particular *dawang* by descent. Yet their expertise may be called on to determine the particular traditional law or customs that should guide the decision-making of the corporation under the dispute resolution procedures referred to above.

The potential problems outlined here have arisen in other Aboriginal corporations. Appeal to the traditional law and custom of the group is usually not enough to deal with these complexities, which may require the intervention of ORIC or the courts. The intention of the MG Corporation's dominant objects in the 2006 rules, to benefit the whole group equally, could be undermined by the fragmenting of interests in its governing structure. Any attempt to build traditional cultural practices and concepts into title holding bodies or an umbrella organisation is fraught with at least two difficulties. It risks codifying and freezing in time some aspects of traditional culture at the expense of others, and it risks building unwieldy governance systems into these organisations.

Conclusion

None of the governance problems above appeared to have arisen in the MG Corporation in its early stages. The large number of delegates on the governing committee gave their meetings the quality of a community meeting where significant members of the community get the opportunity to hear how the organisation is progressing. After its first year of operation, the MG Corporation Governing Committee members were enthusiastic and optimistic, but not reticent about describing the problems they had and those that lay ahead.

Nevertheless, this chapter has foreshadowed a number of potential problems that should be addressed before they lead to contention and disputes. These include clarifying the relationship between the general manager and the management group, whereby, as noted, the general manager is a member of the management group, but the management group is responsible for supervision of his/her position (though he or she cannot vote). This can be done by being precise about the formal matters for delegation and the limits or restrictions on the operation of delegated powers. Further consideration could also be given to: ensuring that the rules of the RNTBCs and MG Corporation are consistent, including that the elected delegates are the same as for the RNTBCs, which is not required in the rules of MG#1 and MG#4 RNTBCs;[79] how substitutes are appointed; how delegates are required to vote in governing committee meetings; methods of informing and consulting the wider community of members beyond the governing committee to involve them in effective dispute resolution procedures; and the long-term implications of the use of the term *dawang*.

In implementing the OFA, it is not surprising that the governing committee identified inadequate establishment funds as its first major hurdle and approached the Western Australian Government to augment them. Much will depend on the quality of the MG Corporation strategic plan in the early years, and the corporation's ability to implement it. After the first year of operation the management group was seriously concerned that the corporation had neither sufficient support nor resources from government to leverage benefits from the OFA. Long-term interests of the corporation to purchase or build adequate office space and staff housing, which is a prerequisite for supporting the staff needed to manage the organisation, are pressing.

In the OFA and the 2006 rules of the constitution there is also a tendency to position the MG people as the subjects or receivers of charitable aid, rather than as the motivators of their own development. To be successful, the corporation will need to resist this tendency. In the long run, the corporation's ability to leverage OFA benefits into sustainable economic development, in which all MG people participate, will be crucial. This will require, above all, attention to education and training in a range of skills, from business administration and management to trades and professions. Here the activities of the EDU, which concentrates on employment and business opportunities, and the Ord Enhancement Scheme, which encourages government entities to take up their responsibilities, are vital. Yet these are the most underdeveloped elements of the agreement package, and Western Australian Government assistance may be required for some time.

During the early years of the Agreement, as noted, the Western Australian Government placed the development of the second stage of the Ord irrigation scheme on hold. The corporation had been pinning its hopes on it and the announcement disrupted their plans. While Ord Stage Two again became a national development priority, uncertainty continued in the organisation, and the time of the Agreement was running out. The governing committee members felt that the way that the announcement to suspend Ord Stage Two was made, without any prior consultation with the organisation as the priority holder of new land releases, was a symptom of the Western Australian Government's inability to come to terms with the new status of native title holders in the region. There was apparently no consideration of the impact that the decision would have on the ability of native title holders to benefit from the OFA. They felt that after signing the Agreement, the Western Australian Government simply walked away.

Despite these problems the governing committee was optimistic that it would eventually be the 'mother ship' for numerous smaller development enterprises run by its community members. More immediately, however, it was facing the end of the 10-year establishment period without the ability to consolidate a sound footing for sustainable development. At the time of writing, the MG Corporation's potential to turn native title rights into self-regenerating benefits was hanging in the balance. It was hampered by a complex governance structure and without the liquid assets of its compensation agreement with the state government. If the annual operating funding ran out without substantial progress in economic and social ventures the corporation risked becoming, as other Aboriginal title holders have been described, 'land rich and dirt poor'.

The governing committee was well aware that to avoid this it needed to rapidly establish an economic base and commercial partnerships. To do so, the MG Corporation required substantially more financial liquidity than it had when this chapter was prepared. With these practical challenges in front of the corporation, it is important that the governance arrangements discussed here are reviewed and, where necessary, streamlined to provide commercially effective management as well as a culturally appropriate corporate structure.

Endnotes

1 Throughout this chapter the amended and restated version of the Ord Final Agreement is used for referencing. See Western Australia, *Ord Final Agreement Variation #2* (OFA), State Solicitor's Office, State of Western Australia, Perth, 2006.
2 See ibid., p W of Recitals.
3 *Attorney-General of the Northern Territory v Ward* [2003] FCAFC 283 (*MG (No. 1)*).
4 *Ward v Western Australia* [2006] FCA 1848 (*MG (No. 4)*).
5 MG Corporation, *Rules of the Yawoorroong Miriuwung Gajerrong Yirrgeb Noong Dawang Aboriginal Corporation*, Yawoorroong Miriuwung Gajerrong Yirrgeb Noong Dawang Aboriginal Corporation (MG Corporation), Kununurra, 2006.

6 Ibid., r 6.2(a).
7 MG Corporation, 'Historical overview', http://www.mgcorp.com.au/index.php/about-us/overview, accessed 22 May 2013.
8 Specific research for this chapter was carried out in 2007, drawing on the author's prior knowledge of the case and ongoing research with the people in the East Kimberley since 1983. The paper also relies on discussions with Julie Melbourne, the solicitor for the respondents to the claim and later adviser to the MG Corporation, and on a telephone interview with the MG Board of Directors in 2007. No on-site field work was conducted specifically for this chapter. Unless otherwise stated, the opinions expressed are the author's own and not those of the board or members of MG Corporation.
9 The chapter was written under the auspices of the National Centre for Indigenous Studies at the Australian National University.
10 I investigated Gija cultural attachment to land from 1997 to 1999. This work was initially carried out for the purchase of six pastoral stations on Gija traditional land and then for a connection report as part of the Gija native title claim. Barbara Glowczewski also contributed detailed ethnographic information for the claim. Gija, Miriuwung and Gajerrong people share cultural characteristics. Eastern Gija people were included in the native title determinations.
11 PM Durack, 'Pioneering the East Kimberley', *Early Days: Journal of the Historical Society of Western Australia*, vol. 2, 1933, pp. 2–28.
12 Ibid., pp. 29–30.
13 Ibid., p. 19.
14 See G Buchanan, '*Packhorse and waterhole — with the first overlanders to the Kimberleys*', Angus & Robertson, Sydney, 1933, pp. 157–63; GT Wood, *Report of Royal Commission of Inquiry into alleged killing and burning of bodies of Aborigines in East Kimberley and into police methods when effecting arrests*, Government Printer, Perth, 1927, http://archive.aiatsis.gov.au/removeprotect/93281.pdf, accessed 22 May 2013; K Willey, *Boss drover (reminiscences of Matt Savage)*, Rigby, Sydney, 1971, p. 13.
15 M Durack, *Kings in grass castles*, Corgi, Moorebank, NSW, 1983, pp. 299–300, 397.
16 B Shaw, *My country of the pelican dreaming — the life of an Australian Aborigine of the Gadjerong, Grant Ngabidj, 1904–1977*, Australian Institute of Aboriginal Studies, Canberra, 1981.
17 Buchanan, above n 14, p. 165; Durack, above n 15, pp. 372–3.
18 GC Bolton, 'Black and white after 1897', in CT Stannage (ed.), *A new history of Western Australia*, University of Western Australia Press, Nedlands, 1981, p. 131.
19 The *Liquor Act Amendment Act 1972* (WA), s 32, repeals s 130 of the *Liquor Act 1970* (WA).
20 A McGrath, *Born in the cattle: Aborigines in cattle country*, Allen & Unwin, Sydney, 1987.
21 JC Altman & J Nieuwenhuysen, *The economic status of Australian Aborigines*, Cambridge University Press, Cambridge, 1979, p. 67.
22 P Willis, 'Patrons and riders: conflicting roles and hidden objectives in an Aboriginal development programme', unpublished MA thesis, Australian National University, Canberra, 1980, p. 31.
23 See Travelling Australia, 'Ord River Irrigation Scheme', http://www.travelling-australia.info/InfsheetsO/Ordriverscheme.html, accessed 21 May 2013.
24 Willis, above n 22.
25 Ibid.
26 P Sullivan, *All free man now: culture, community and politics in the Kimberley region*, Aboriginal Studies Press, Canberra, 1996, pp. 71–104.
27 See Wunan Foundation, 'Building a nation for the future', http://wunan.org.au/about, accessed 28 May 2013.

28 *Ward on behalf of the Miriuwung and Gajerrong Peoples v State of Western Australia* (1998) 159 ALR 483; for a full analysis of the MG native title determination history refer to LM Strelein, *Western Australia v Ward on behalf of Miriuwung Gajerrong High Court of Australia, 8 August 2002 Summary of Judgement*, Land, Rights, Laws: Issues of Native Title, vol. 2, no. 17, AIATSIS, Canberra, 2002, http://www.aiatsis.gov.au/ntru/docs/publications/issues/ip02v2n17.pdf, accessed 21 May 2013.
29 *Western Australia and Ors v Ward and Ors* [2000] FCA 611 (form of determination) and *Western Australia and Ors v Ward and Ors* [2000] FCA 191 (reasons for determination).
30 *Western Australia v Ward* (2002) 191 ALR 1.
31 Strelein, above n 28, p. 2.
32 *MG (No. 1)*, above n 3.
33 *MG (No. 4)*, above n 4.
34 For names of *dawang* see MG Corporation, above n 5, sch 1.
35 See OFA, above n 1, cl 4; or for a short summary see Office of Native Title, 'Fact sheet: Ord Final Agreement', Department of Premier and Cabinet, Perth, 2009, http://www.nativetitle.wa.gov.au/uploadedFiles/Agreements/Ord_Final/ord_final_fact_sheet.pdf, accessed 22 May 2013.
36 However, see K Guest, *The promise of comprehensive native title settlements: the Burrup, MG-Ord and Wimmera Agreements*, AIATSIS Research Discussion Paper, no. 27, AIATSIS, Canberra, 2009, http://www.aiatsis.gov.au/research/docs/dp/DP27.pdf, accessed 22 May 2013.
37 See Office of Native Title, above n 35.
38 OFA, above n 1, cl 19.3(1).
39 Ibid., cl 22.
40 Ibid., cl 20.8(3).
41 Ibid., cl 26.
42 Ibid., cl 30 and also see Kimberley Devlopment Commission (KDC), 'Ord Enhancement Scheme', http://www.kdc.wa.gov.au/The-Commission/KDC-Structure/Ord-Enhancement-Scheme, accessed 22 May 2013.
43 Kimberley Land Council (KLC), 'Ord Stage 1: fix the past, move to the future, an Aboriginal social and economic impact assessment of the Ord River Irrigation Project Stage 1', unpublished report by the KLC, Broome, 2004.
44 Western Australia Legislative Assembly Estimates Committees Supplementary Information B17, 22–25 May 2006.
45 OFA, above n1, cl 37.7.
46 Ibid., cl 37.7(2).
47 Ibid., cl 38.2(3).
48 MG Corporation n.d., 'Strategic Plan 2007–2012', http://www.mgcorp.com.au/index.php/component/content/article/21-main-category/news-a-projects/suggested-readings/45-strategic-plan-2007-2012, accessed 27 May 2013.
49 MG Corporation, above n 5.
50 Ibid., r 6.1.
51 Cl 20 of the OFA on MG Corporation's constitution involves 16 subclauses. See OFA, above n 1, cl 20.
52 MG Corporation, above n 5, r 6.
53 Ibid., r 10.1.
54 Ibid., r 2.1.
55 *MG (No. 1)*, above n 3, [2] and [4].
56 Some Gija people joined the native title claim as respondents and were eventually included in the determination. All groups recognised in the determination are represented by MG Corporation.

57 *MG (No. 4)*, above 4, [7].
58 Ibid., sch 5.
59 Ibid., [6].
60 MG Corporation, above n 5, r 2.1.
61 RM Berndt, 'The concept of the "tribe" in the Western Desert of Australia', *Oceania*, vol. 30, 1959, pp. 81–107; WEH Stanner, 'Aboriginal territorial organisation: estate, range, domain and regime', *Oceania*, vol. 36, no. 1, 1965, pp. 1–26.
62 I Keen, 'Metaphor and metalanguage: "groups" in NE Arnhem Land', *American Ethnologist*, vol. 22, no. 3, 1995, pp. 502–27.
63 MG Corporation, above n 5, sch 1.
64 For full text see MG#1 RNTBC, *Rules of the Miriuwung and Gajerrong #1 (Registered Native Title Prescribed Body Corporate) Aboriginal Corporation*, Miriuwung and Gajerrong #1 RNTBC, Kununurra, 2006, and MG#4 RNTBC, *Rules of the Miriuwung and Gajerrong # (Registered Native Title Prescribed Body Corporate) Aboriginal Corporation*, Miriuwung and Gajerrong #4 RNTBC, Kununurra, 2006.
65 MG Corporation, above n 5, r 21.1(b).
66 See above n 64.
67 MG Corporation, above n 5, r 17.1.
68 Ibid., r 14.1(c).
69 Ibid., r 15.
70 Ibid., r 14.1(a) and r 15.6(a).
71 Ibid., r 15.
72 Ibid., r 15.3.
73 Ibid., r 17.1(a).
74 Ibid., r 37.1.
75 See, for example, K Barber & H Rumley, *Gunanurang: (Kununurra) Big River: Aboriginal cultural values of the Ord River and wetlands, a study and report prepared for the Waters and Rivers Commission*, Water and Rivers Commission, 2003, pp. 16–17, http://www.water.wa.gov.au/PublicationStore/first/51768.pdf, accessed 20 June 2013.
76 MG Corporation, above n 5, r 2.1.
77 *Ward & Ors v Western Australia & Ors* [1998] FCA 1478
78 *MG (No. 4)*, above n 4, [7] (b).
79 For full text see MG#1 RNTBC, above n 62, and MG#4 RNTBC, above n 62.

Update: Miriuwung Gajerrong Corporation and Registered Native Title Bodies Corporate 2013

John Hughes

Since Chapter 6 was written, the Yawoorroong Miriuwung Gajerrong Yirrgeb Noong Dawang Aboriginal Corporation (MG Corporation), the umbrella corporation for two Registered Native Title Bodies Corporate (RNTBCs), Miriuwung and Gajerrong #1 (RNTBC) Aboriginal Corporation (MG#1 RNTBC) and the Miriuwung and Gajerrong #4 (RNTBC) Aboriginal Corporation (MG#4 RNTBC), has experienced a whirlwind of activity. MG Corporation has also established itself as a key participant in future economic planning for Kununurra in Western Australia and the surrounding region.

The Ord Final Agreement (OFA)[1] discussed in Chapter 6 sets up a framework to develop farmlands, including construction of irrigation canals and roads, and land clearing. MG Corporation negotiated and has been administering a multi-million dollar benefits package in relation to the first component of Ord Stage Two, for which consent to development was given by native title holders. This has involved the construction of 9000 hectares of irrigated farmlands beyond those released for agriculture before 1975, towards the Northern Territory border, on the Goomig area, formerly known as Weaber Plains. The benefits package includes scholarships and other social benefits contemplated by a proforma agreement set out in the OFA. Kimberly Agricultural Investments (KAI), a subsidiary of a Shanghai-based company, is the preferred farmer-developer of these Goomig farmlands. MG Corporation is now negotiating a benefits package with KAI as preferred developer of Knox Plains, an area of Western Australian land also covered by the OFA and seen as the natural extension of the Goomig irrigated farmlands development. On the Northern Territory side of Miriuwung and Gajerrong country, KAI wants to extend irrigated farmland further and then to develop a Brazil-sized large sugarcane processing plant.

With the benefit of substantial OFA foundation funding over 10 years and effective delivery of the benefits of the Goomig development package, MG Corporation was able to establish itself as a well-governed organisation with sufficient substance to qualify for significant funding from the Western Australian Government's Royalties for Regions fund and the Commonwealth – Western Australia East Kimberley Development Package. These funding arrangements have provided economic stimulus and substantial infrastructure improvements to the East Kimberley, including office premises for MG Corporation itself. The government grant in turn gave the corporation the opportunity to develop a reputation for safe management of publicly funded programs.

Governance

In 2009, a number of changes were made to MG Corporation's 2006 rule book.[2] Of particular significance is halving the number of *dawang* representatives from 32 to 16 representative members (one per *dawang*) to constitute a Dawang Council (see Figure 6.3) and the establishment of the Garralyel.[3]

The Dawang Council plays an intermediary role between native title holders and the board of MG Corporation. The role has aspects of the role of shareholder, as in other kinds of corporations, together with a director's right to be informed of the corporation's affairs more frequently. This arrangement is calibrated to protect *dawang* representatives from the legal liability of being 'shadow directors', while providing the greatest opportunity for their participation in MG Corporation's affairs. The Dawang Council has a decision-making role in relation to strategy and vision,[4] chooses the directors of the board and reviews board performance,[5] reviews the performance of the chief executive officer (CEO)[6] and approves some reserved board decisions.[7] Seeking to reflect as much as possible Miriuwung and Gajerrong traditional decision-making processes according to their laws and customs, the Garralyel comprises approximately 20 senior traditional owners with decision-making and advisory roles relating to native title, country, heritage, environmental issues, law, and culture and language.[8] Their ultimate authority is well recognised by the members.

While the reduction of the Dawang Council from 32 to 16 *dawang* representatives risked losing the feel of the community meeting, referred to in Chapter 6, this does not seem to have happened in the four years since the change came into effect. Under the current MG Corporation rule book, the Dawang Council meets as often as the board of directors require for the good functioning of the Dawang Council, but must in any case meet at least quarterly.[9] A quorum is nine of the 16 Dawang Council representatives.[10] In contrast, and in keeping with their more autonomous, traditionally conceived role, the Garralyel meet quarterly or more frequently, as they determine.[11] In practice, the quarterly meetings of the Dawang Council and

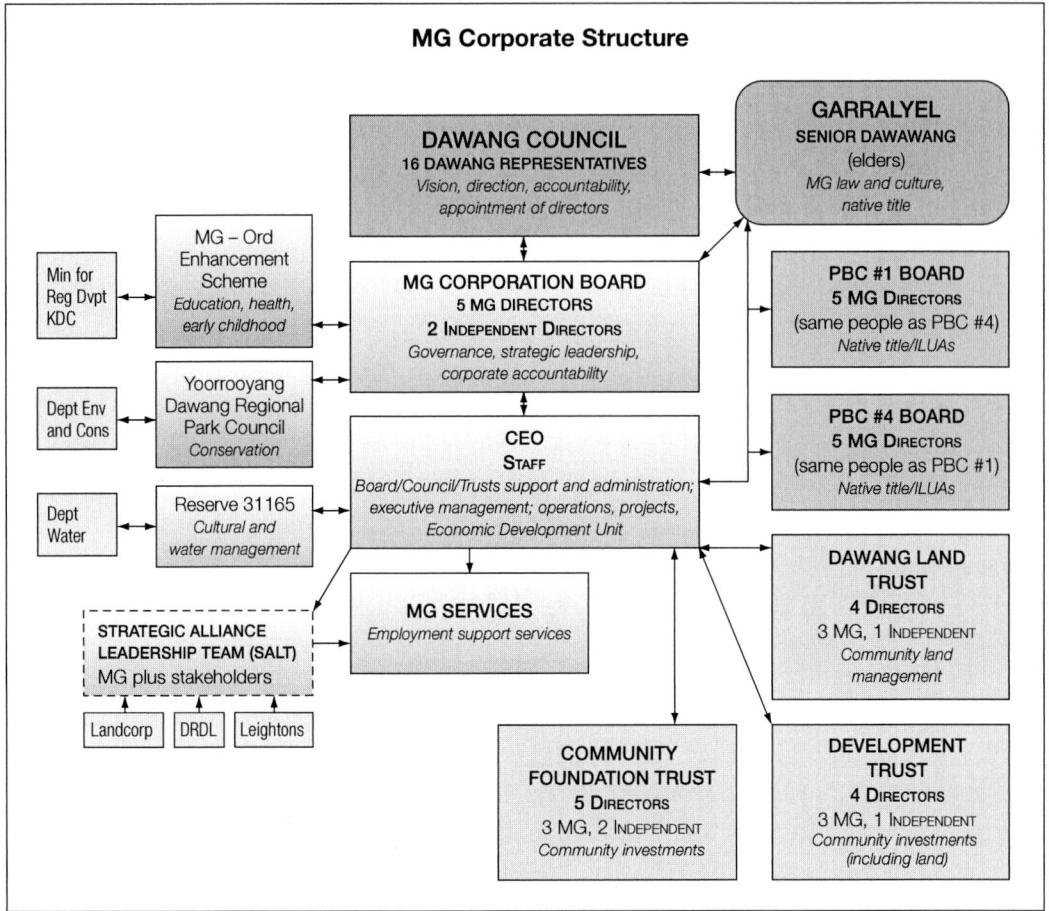

Figure 6.3 Corporate structure of MG Corporation in 2009, including MG#1 and MG#4 RNTBCs (shown here as 'PBC#1' and 'PBC#4')[12]. Diagram courtesy of MG Corporation

of the Garralyel are usually combined meetings, also alleviating a propensity for over-governance with too many meetings.

MG Corporation's board is comprised of seven directors, with a maximum of five Mirriuwung and Gajerrong directors and not more than two independent directors.[13] The CEO is appointed by the board of directors with Dawang Council approval and is accountable to the board of directors rather than the Dawang Council. Only meeting quarterly the Dawang Council does not observe CEO activities closely enough to supervise them, although it can dismiss the CEO. The CEO reports quarterly to the Dawang Council and to the Garralyel.[14] The management group in the 2006 rule book has been discontinued as another layer of governance, with more reliance on formal internal delegation, thus allaying Sullivan's concerns in Chapter 6 about the CEO being a member of the management group.

Eligibility for membership has been revised to include persons at least 15 years of age,[15] allocated to a class of youth membership less than 18 years.[16] Although there is no longer a requirement for the 16 Dawang Council members representing estates to be a combination of senior and junior and male and female representatives, there is some interest in reinstating this practice.

MG#1 and MG#4 RNTBCs share most of the MG Corporation's directors, but these do not include the two independent directors who are on MG Corporation's board. While under changes to the PBC Regulations[17] it is now possible for RNTBCs to have independent directors, the members of RNTBCs are unlikely to nominate these directors. This is because the directorship of the RNTBCs reflects traditional land ownership and laws and customs, and because the MG RNTBCs are able to rely on the MG Corporation for governance and financial management expertise, which are the main foci of MG Corporation's independent directors.

Dispute resolution procedures in the 2009 rule book set out a complicated combination of the involvement of directors, Dawang Council and the Garralyel, written submissions and attempts to settle in accordance with traditional laws and customs.[18] Recently this mechanism proved unable to respond to a fast-moving and multi-faceted dispute in a way that would deliver a ruling binding on disputants, and it requires revision.

The most significant governance issue relates to the efficient and effective involvement and representation of traditional owners. Corporate governance deals with the rules by which an individual CEO or other agent, or a small group of directors, with broad powers can legitimately make decisions binding on a larger body of member-shareholders. These rules reflect a cultural predisposition towards a certain kind of leadership which evolved in Western Europe and perhaps in all societies ruled by kings or emperors. In contrast, traditional Aboriginal decision-making will often be non-hierarchical, involving the widest possible participation of members. To reflect this requires a different kind of governance from mainstream corporations. Every method of communication needs to be employed to ensure that traditional owners all participate in a meaningful way to arrive at a consensus. An abundance of meetings is essential for decision-making accountabilities. Much of the coordination relies on the position of MG Corporation secretary, which requires a high level of organisational and technical skills, professionalism and an acute understanding of MG Corporation's complex governance structure.

Employment and business

The Western Australian Government–controlled LandCorp, the ultimate proponent undertaking the Goomig component of the Ord Stage Two development, engaged Leighton Contractors to achieve firm targets for the employment of native title holders and other Indigenous people (20 per cent of total workforce employed directly by Leighton or by its subcontractors) and a $6 million 'Indigenous business spend' target to engage Miriuwung Gajerrong contractors on the earthworks. Leighton has broadly attained these targets to MG Corporation's satisfaction, and this may be attributable to several factors. First, LandCorp insisted on scrutinising Leighton's reports on a monthly basis and devoting high-level LandCorp decision-makers to the achievement of the target. Secondly, LandCorp required Leighton to work with it in a four-party Strategic Alliance Leadership Team, also involving MG Corporation and the Western Australian Department of Regional Development. This focused the most senior Western Australian Leighton manager and counterparts in the other organisations on monthly problem-solving meetings to address barriers to satisfactory employment and business involvement. Thirdly, there are significant financial incentives linked to personal bonuses for key Leighton staff.

Leighton Contractors began major works on the Goomig component of Ord Stage Two in 2010. As MG Corporation's capacity for this was developed and demonstrated to LandCorp's satisfaction, MG Corporation assumed the role of recruiting, training, qualifying and mentoring employees to meet Leighton's targets, and of funnelling and providing business support to Miriuwung Gajerrong subcontractors. LandCorp provided for this with a multi-million dollar contract over two and a half years and MG Corporation contributed from relevant components of the Goomig benefits package. The resulting Employment and Business Division (the Division) saw staff of MG Corporation grow from a steady core of around six to 10 people, to 20 to 30 during the wet and dry seasons of 2012–13.

The Division is housed in a separate building from MG Corporation's main office. Owing to the pressing need to capture the potential of Leighton's employment and business commitment since 2010, the Division's employment and commercial engagement obligations have tended to overshadow the dominant objectives set out in MG Corporation's rule book, which concentrate on social goals, such as housing, cultural development and child care. The Division's sustained focus on employment outcomes has clearly revealed that poor and crowded housing and other social challenges which the corporation's dominant objectives seek to address are barriers to sustained employment.

The Western Australian Government has faithfully provided MG Corporation with the annual OFA implementation funding, but this is due to expire in 2015. While the OFA requires that the government must approve MG Corporation's operational budget, it has not applied a heavy hand through this mechanism, respecting MG Corporation's autonomy to run its own affairs. Nevertheless, it should be recognised that, in many ways, MG Corporation's dominant objectives align with the Western Australian Government's own agenda, particularly in terms of delivering employment and housing. Now that the implementation period is coming to a close, economic sustainability is a major concern. In spite of a number of economic development studies over several years, and some advanced commercial negotiations with potential business partners, the Economic Development Unit (EDU) funded through the OFA has not given rise to a sustainable independent commercial venture or other economic roles for MG Corporation. Losses due to a failed building products venture several years ago may have caused the membership and governance components of MG Corporation to be more risk averse. The relatively frequent replacement of CEOs over the years has also impacted the ability of MG Corporation to attend to medium and longer term opportunities with continuity. Nevertheless, there are a number of development and business opportunities being discussed, some of which may involve the relinquishing of native title rights.

In 2005 a separate multi-million dollar funding package was established as a form of compensation, partly for the flooding of Lake Argyle in Stage One referred to in Chapter 6. Over seven years this was administered by the Western Australian Kimberley Development Commission (KDC) as the Ord Enhancement Scheme (OES), under the direction of a committee comprising a key KDC official and Miriuwung Gajerrong members nominated by MG Corporation. The OES has funded local organisations to attend to educational, child-development, housing and other pressing needs of Miriuwung and Gajerrong people. This funding is largely fully spent, but the Western Australian Government has provided the balance to MG Corporation on trust for similar purposes.

The Western Australian Government's largesse in providing benefits beyond those in the OFA has made a remarkable difference. For example, in response to an offer by MG Corporation to contribute $1 million from the OES fund for houses on community living areas near Kununurra, roads and infrastructure improvements, the government provided $5 million from the Royalties for Regions fund and 10 houses have recently been built. This 2012 housing project appears to have departed markedly from apparent reluctance on the part of the Western Australian and Commonwealth governments to develop policy for small community living areas. MG Corporation was closely involved in this 2012 construction activity which has proved to be an opportunity to develop practical working relationships with government agencies to better service small Miriuwung and Gajerrong living areas. This includes officials of and contractors to the Commonwealth Department of Families, Housing, Community Services and Indigenous Affairs (FaHCSIA), which provides power, building maintenance and other essential services to living area residents. Co-contributions from the state government Royalties for Regions fund and from the federal government have also provided for four houses which are under construction in town, on MG Corporation land, for Indigenous tenants or buyers. Accommodation in Kununurra is scarce: it is a major problem for local Indigenous people and for staff of MG Corporation which the corporation will seek to address over the next few years.

The OFA gave rise to three cohorts of Miriuwung Gajerrong rangers: MG Corporation employs a small group to care for community living areas and other land under the corporation's control; the Western Australian parks authority employs another on jointly managed parks in the Kununurra area arising out of the OFA; and a third group works on conservation of water catchment land abutting Lake Argyle.[19]

Ord Stage Two to Ord Stage Three

In December 2012, a memorandum of understanding (MOU) was signed between the Western Australian, Northern Territory and Australian governments to begin the process of expanding the Ord River development to Miriuwung Gajerrong native title determination land in the Northern Territory. While the Territory government has yet to make a decision, the most likely preferred developer at the time of writing is KAI, the same company that the Western Australian Government identified in late 2012 as preferred developer and lessee of the Ord Stage Two areas in Western Australia, the Goomig and Knox Plains areas. KAI aspires to develop sufficient land on both sides of the Western Australian and Northern Territory border to justify construction of a large sugar-processing plant. In late 2013, KAI began to clear the Goomig area for farming, but the OFA requires it to enter a benefits package agreement in favour of MG Corporation before it can commence the 6000-hectare Knox Plains component of the Ord Stage Two irrigated farmlands expansion. The agreement must be negotiated with MG Corporation or arbitrated via Western Australian Government ministers.

Cross-border native title representation

MG Corporation aims to persuade Miriuwung Gajerrong native title holders, pursuant to determinations in the adjacent Northern Territory, that it is the organisation best placed to manage the business of RNTBCs established on the Northern Territory side of the border. If so, the nature of MG Corporation's role would depend on the regulations prescribed under the *Native Title Act 1993* (Cth) (NTA), as well as negotiations with the Northern Land Council which provided the legal team for the relevant determinations, but might be similar to that of a strata management company. MG Corporation aims to develop a model for efficient and effective RNTBC management through its experience with MG#1 and MG#4 RNTBCs and through economies of scale if acting for all Miriuwung Gajerrong native title holders.

Conclusion

MG Corporation is the creature of both its founding Miriuwung Gajerrong native title group members and of the OFA which, as noted in Chapter 6, mandated its incorporation. Stage-by-stage irrigated farmland development has given rise to a series of related but separate agreements which are sometimes very difficult to follow. The multiplicity of agreements may also have reduced capacity to concentrate on capturing the OFA's potential for economic sustainability, as has a turnover of key

staff and other factors which the OFA negotiators probably did not contemplate. Nevertheless, MG Corporation is conscious that it has a valuable reputation and a range of organisational options which allow it to aspire to a regional significance straddling the Western Australian and Northern Territory borders, and to building life options for its members in the economy of the future.

Endnotes

1. Western Australia, *Ord Final Agreement Variation #2* (OFA), State Solicitor's Office, State of Western Australia, Perth, 2006.
2. MG Corporation, *Rules of the Yawoorroong Miriuwung Gajerrong Yirrgeb Noong Dawang Aboriginal Corporation*, Yawoorroong Miriuwung Gajerrong Yirrgeb Noong Dawang Aboriginal Corporation (MG Corporation), Kununurra, 2006.
3. MG Corporation, *The rule book*, Yawoorroong Miriuwung Gajerrong Yirrgeb Noong Dawang Aboriginal Corporation (MG Corporation), Kununurra, 2009, sch 6.2(b).
4. Ibid., r 13.1.
5. Ibid.
6. Ibid., r 13.1(d)(ii).
7. Ibid., r 16.9.
8. Ibid., r 11.
9. Ibid., sch 6.9.1.
10. Ibid., sch 6.9.4.
11. Ibid., sch 7.3.1(a).
12. Derived from MG Corporation, 'MG corporation structure', http://www.mgcorp.com.au/index.php/about-us/board-of-directors-2/8-main-category/about-us/14, accessed 22 May 2013.
13. MG Corporation, above n3, r 14.1.2.
14. Ibid., r 12.2.
15. Ibid., r 7.2.2.
16. Ibid., r 7.4.
17. Native Title (Prescribed Bodies Corporate) Regulations 1999 (PBC Regulations).
18. MG Corporation, above n 3, r 27.1.
19. The reserves land mentioned here is 'Reserve 31165', location see OFA, above n 1, pt 38, and map 9, sch 2.

Chapter 7

Managing mixed Indigenous land titles — Cape York case studies

Paul Memmott and Peter Blackwood

Introduction

With a growing number of successful native title determinations under the *Native Title Act 1993* (Cth) (NTA), attention is increasingly turning to the administration of the rights and interests in land that flow from these determinations and the operations of Registered Native Title Bodies Corporate (RNTBCs), the entities which native title holders are obliged to incorporate to manage or hold those rights and interests. This paper is concerned with the effective design and operation of RNTBCs as well as other types of corporate bodies used by Indigenous groups in Queensland to hold the different forms of Aboriginal land title obtainable under state and Commonwealth legislation.

Native title exists in a complex legal, administrative and cultural environment of intersecting and sometimes conflicting rights, which tend to be viewed by the wider Australian public in terms of Indigenous versus non-Indigenous rights. What is less well appreciated is that many Aboriginal groups find themselves caught in this web, trying to integrate and reconcile their newly recognised native title rights with other forms of traditional and non-traditional Aboriginal landownership. This is especially the case in the area with which we are most familiar, remote Northern Australia where many Aboriginal groups have acquired land under a variety of titles as a result of state- and territory-based statutory land rights schemes introduced over the past 40 years, most significantly the *Aboriginal Land Rights (Northern Territory) Act 1976* (Cth) and the Queensland *Aboriginal Land Act 1991* (Qld) (ALA).[1] Much of this land is also now subject to native title claim, often by groups comprised of or including those who at the same time already hold, or in the future may hold, the same land under these other forms of title. What these forms of title have in common is that they attempt to draw systems of Aboriginal land tenure into the broader Australian system of landownership, while at the same time providing recognition to particular Aboriginal cultural connections to the land. But this transition has much potential to distort and rigidify the Indigenous system, in its description and in its practice, in order for it to 'fit' the legal requirements of the various statutory schemes and their requisite landowning corporations.[2]

This complexity offers both opportunities and challenges. In Queensland, native title claimants and the state government have introduced a 'tenure resolution' process to aid the resolution of native title claims. The land needs and land aspirations of Aboriginal people in a particular area may be settled through a combination of native title determination and the granting of Aboriginal freehold land under Queensland's ALA. In addition to Indigenous forms of tenure, these land settlements may also involve the granting of conventional tenure, including freehold, leasehold, trusteeship of reserves and joint management of protected natural areas. The challenge is to find ways of more effectively and efficiently integrating the ownership and management functions of the resulting multiple Aboriginal landholding entities.

This chapter extends and updates the findings of three earlier publications[3] based on research undertaken in 2001–02 into practical aspects of the ownership and management of native title and other forms of Indigenous landownership in the Wik and Coen Aboriginal regions of Cape York Peninsula, centred around the townships of Aurukun and Coen respectively[4] (see Figure 7.1). The research to date has focused on the options for rationalising and possibly combining Aboriginal land trusts and native title RNTBCs and models for cost-effective coordination of Aboriginal land management at a regional level.

This paper begins by briefly reviewing the forms of Aboriginal land tenure in Cape York. It then addresses structural options for integrating RNTBCs and other Indigenous landholding entities. This is followed by an analysis of the two case study regions, Wik then Coen, profiling the Indigenous and statutory land tenure systems and reviewing recent progress of the Aboriginal landholding entities in engaging with capitalist developments, as well as the integration of their aspirations for land and sea management.[5] Finally, the applications of the proposed land and sea management structures in the two study regions are re-evaluated.

Aboriginal land tenure on Cape York

Native title is one of several categories of Aboriginal-owned land on Cape York, each of which is associated with a particular corporate landholding entity. In 1991 a form of inalienable Aboriginal freehold title was introduced in Queensland under the ALA. It provides for land to be granted on the basis of either 'traditional affiliation' or 'historical association'.[6] Once granted, the land title is held by a land trust, generally comprised of a representative group of the beneficiaries of the grant. As of 2005, approximately five per cent of Cape York Peninsula was ALA Aboriginal

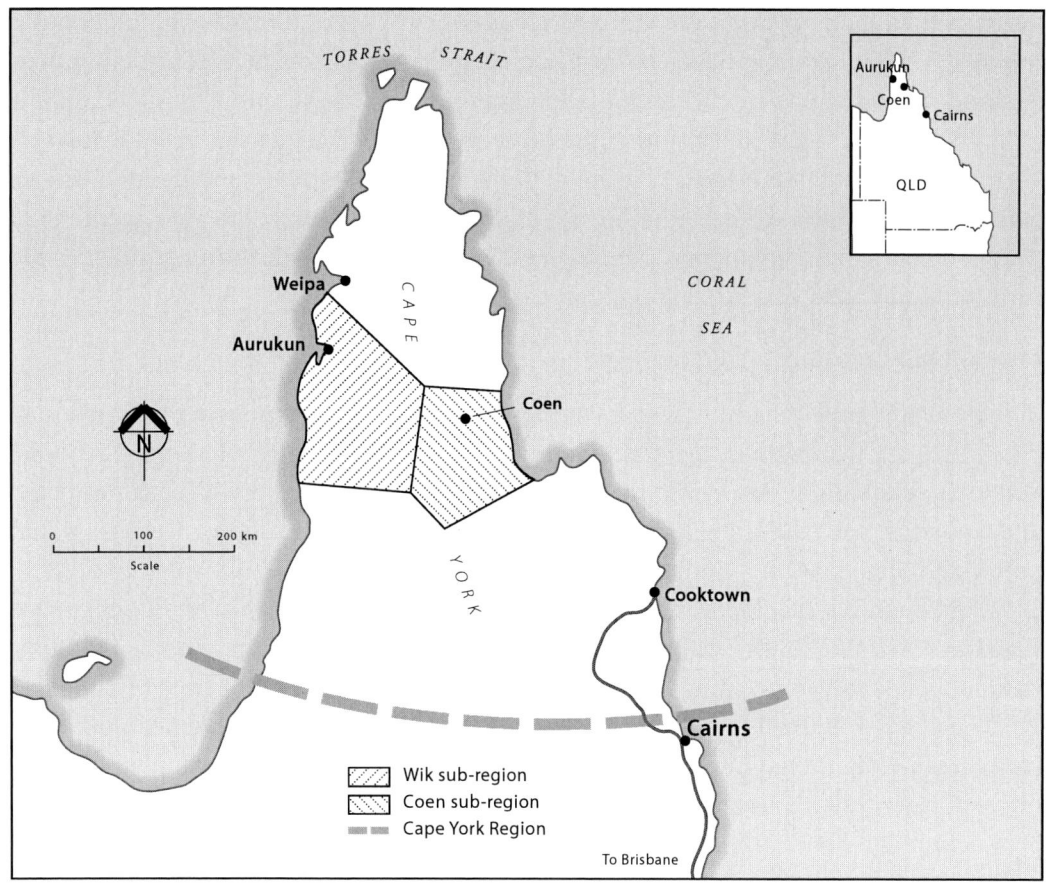

Figure 7.1 Map of Queensland showing Coen and Wik regions (here labelled sub-regions) in relation to the Cape York Land Council's Native Title Representative Body (NTRB) area. Map by Brenda Thornley for AIATSIS

freehold, held by 19 land trusts. This freehold may be granted as a result of either a claim process requiring claimants to prove their traditional or historical connection before a judicial tribunal, or by a more expedient administrative process referred to as 'transfer'. Both mechanisms rely on the government to make the land available by gazettal, and this provision has enabled some creative tenure resolutions to be negotiated between the Queensland Government and native title claimants. In time, ALA freehold will replace an earlier form of Aboriginal tenure known as Deed of Grant in Trust lands (DOGIT).[7]

A number of Aboriginal-owned pastoral leases also occur in each study region. The favoured structure for pastoral lease landholding entities is an Aboriginal corporation, formed under the *Corporations (Aboriginal and Torres Strait Islander) Act 2006* (Cth) (CATSI Act), as are RNTBCs.

Significantly for groups on Cape York, the NTA provides that any extinguishment of native title by the grant of previous land tenures must be disregarded over pastoral leases owned by native title holders as well as over DOGIT and Aboriginal freehold tenures. Demonstration by a claim group of ongoing native title connection over such areas may result in successful determinations. In these circumstances, native title groups will hold coexisting rights and responsibilities as native title holders with the owners of Aboriginal freehold under the ALA and/or leaseholders under conventional tenure. Under existing regulatory arrangements, the management of these overlapping interests necessitates the duplication of landholding entities in the form of land trusts and Aboriginal corporations, including RNTBCs.

Registered Native Title Bodies Corporate

The RNTBC is the effective face of a successful native title claim, being the corporate entity through which the native title community can interact with the wider economic and legal system, and providing the mechanism by which native title is both protected and managed. In 2007 new legislation covering the incorporation of RNTBCs and policy changes enabling Commonwealth funding of RNTBC administrative costs, either through Native Title Representative Bodies (NTRBs) or Native Title Service Providers (NTSPs) or directly to RNTBCs,[8] saw important changes in the operating environment and can be expected to have positive effects on the viability of RNTBCs.

The CATSI Act includes clauses relating to RNTBC functions designed to prevent conflicting obligations under the CATSI Act and the NTA. For example, it avoids imposing conflicting duties on directors, officers or employees of an RNTBC by providing that where they act in good faith to comply with the NTA they will not be in breach of any CATSI Act provisions. It allows for office holders to be elected for periods longer than one year and for 'rolling' appointments, such as two-year terms with half the office holders elected each year. The first of these features allows more flexibility for decision-making within the RNTBC, and assists directors in separating corporate governance responsibilities from native title management responsibilities. Longer tenure for directors should result in more continuity, better skill development among directors and less likelihood of RNTBC governance being dominated by individual or factional interests.

The CATSI Act distinguishes between 'small', 'medium' and 'large'[9] corporations according to the size of their operating income, assets[10] and number of employees, with 'small' and 'medium' having less onerous reporting and compliance requirements than 'large' corporations.[11] These easier reporting and compliance functions are likely to benefit the majority of RNTBCs on Cape York, which will fall into the 'small' category. They will only have to provide basic corporate details in their annual reports and not audited financial statements. These RNTBCs may apply to submit these reports at their annual general meetings (AGMs) only every second year.

In the short term, there is likely to be a need for external financial and organisational assistance from NTRBs and the Office of the Registrar of Indigenous Corporations (ORIC) for RNTBCs to meet the CATSI Act requirements. Lack of government funding to support the operations of established RNTBCs was highlighted as a significant constraint in the previous reports of this research as well as in other reviews, such as the 2006 *Report on the operation of Native Title Representative Bodies* by a parliamentary joint committee.[12] Under current funding guidelines, NTRBs can assist claimants to incorporate their RNTBCs prior to determination and are able to provide some ongoing financial support as well as ongoing legal, research and dispute resolution services for its members.

NTRBs and RNTBCs have applied to the Commonwealth Department of Families, Housing, Community Services and Indigenous Affairs (FaHCSIA) for funding for administration and day-to-day operational costs. Under the 2007–08 FaHCSIA guidelines, funding will normally not exceed $100,000 per corporation per year, and RNTBCs are encouraged to also seek funding from other government, industry and private sources.[13] The funding will be for recurrent costs of administration and compliance, specifically excluding employment and training, except where a real and ongoing need can be demonstrated, and funding will in any case be on an annual basis with no guarantee of continuity. At the time of writing it was too soon to make a meaningful assessment of how successful these initiatives have been for the viability of native title land management, either in the case study areas or elsewhere on Cape York, though it is known that FaHCSIA declined to fund at least one recently established RNTBC on Cape York for the 2007–08 financial year.

Structural options for RNTBCs in relation to land trusts and other Indigenous landholding entities

It is anticipated that eventually many parcels of Aboriginal-owned land on Cape York Peninsula will be held under at least two coexisting types of title, each with its associated landholding entity, namely:

- Aboriginal freehold and native title, with a land trust and an RNTBC
- DOGIT and native title, with a community or shire council and an RNTBC
- leasehold and native title, with an Aboriginal corporation and an RNTBC.[14]

As it is possible to lease land from the trustees on both DOGIT and Aboriginal freehold, there is potential for a third level of Aboriginal landholding entity on these tenures, each of which may have substantially the same membership of traditional owners — namely, a land trust, a native title PBC and an Aboriginal corporation or individual holding a lease.

The prospect of requiring both a land trust and an RNTBC to operate independently of each other over the same land is a source of concern and frustration to traditional owners, and has been recognised by the Queensland Government as one of a number of practical matters needing to be addressed in order to improve the articulation of the state and the Commonwealth legislation.[15] In the Coen region, for example, the RNTBC membership of three as yet undetermined native title claims will overlap with the membership of the six existing land trusts.[16] Given the importance of both the native title and ALA regimes to the traditional owners of Cape York Peninsula, there is a need to reconcile the practical day-to-day operations of the landholding and managing entities to reduce not only the confusion and frustration of traditional owners, but also that of external parties trying to engage with the landowners. It is expected that similar situations will occur in other Australian states and territories with their own forms of state land rights legislation.

Recent (2008) amendments to the Queensland ALA now enable an existing RNTBC to be appointed the grantee of 'transferred' Aboriginal freehold land and to act as a trustee in its own right.[17] This is a significant development, which allows the integration of native title and 'transferred' Aboriginal freehold within a single corporate ownership entity. For large-scale socio-geographic units, such as the language-based tribes in the case of the Coen region, such integration will not only simplify arrangements and reduce confusion but should also reduce the administration costs through a more effective (larger) scale of economy. Another option is the determination of a land trust as an RNTBC. On the face of it, this would likewise have the advantages of a single corporate entity holding both types of tenure. However, this option is not available without Commonwealth Government amendments to the Native Title Prescribed Bodies Corporate Regulations 1999 (PBC Regulations) and possibly further amendment to the ALA by the Queensland Government.[18] Because there are differences in the criteria for ALA land grants and for determination of native title, as well as differing legal responsibilities to be discharged by successful grantees on the one hand and native title holders on the other, combining the two sets of responsibilities into a single entity may not always be the preferred option because of the potential for members' conflicts of interest.

Where there are reasons for retaining both an RNTBC and a land trust as distinct entities, there are nonetheless mechanisms by which their operations may be streamlined and harmonised. One option is to appoint an RNTBC as the sole trustee of the land trust. In the past, the Queensland Government has declined to accept corporate entities as members of ALA land trusts. However, in 2007 for the first time it agreed to appoint a native title RNTBC as the sole trustee of an ALA land trust for the Eastern Kuku Yalanji people of south-east Cape York Peninsula, who in 2007 finalised a comprehensive set of Indigenous Land Use Agreements (ILUAs) which included both a native title determination and the grant of several Aboriginal freehold titles under the ALA.[19] The claim group formed two entities: the Jabalbina Yalanji Aboriginal Corporation as a trust type RNTBC to hold its native title, and the Jabalbina Yalanji Land Trust to hold title to the freehold grants. The rules of the land trust specify the RNTBC as its sole trustee, and the RNTBC rules include complementary clauses to enable both it and its officeholders to function as the land trust, as and when required.

Unlike the RNTBC as grantee model provided for in the recent ALA amendments (which results in a single corporate entity), the RNTBC as sole trustee model adopted for the Kuku Yalanji still entails the formation of two distinct corporate entities, each requiring careful drafting of rules to ensure they intermesh without conflict and unnecessary complexity. Table 7.1 sets out how two such entities may be harmonised within a single operational structure.

Table 7.1 Model of harmonised rules for an RNTBC as trustee of a land trust

Issue	Land trust rules	RNTBC (as grantee) rules
Objects	Objects are for purposes set out in the Aboriginal Land Regulations 1991 (Qld)	Objects to include acting as grantee/trustee of land trust and as an RNTBC
Membership	Limited to one grantee member, with the membership defined as the relevant RNTBC	Open to adult native title holders only
Committee	Provides for appointment of RNTBC board and officeholders as the committee and officeholders of the land trust	By election at AGM
Meetings	AGMs and general meetings to be held on the same day as RNTBC meetings and convened before, during or after the RNTBC meeting. Committee must meet quarterly	AGMs and general meetings (same day as for land trust). Committee meet as required by rules (at least quarterly)
Decision-making processes	As set out in rules and in accordance with code of 'permitted dealings' provisions in the ALA. To be identical to those of the RNTBC	Prescriptive decision-making processes set out in rules or as schedule to the rules. To be identical to those of the land trust
Administration	Separate accounts/audit annual statement to Land Claims Registrar	Separate accounts/audit reports to the Registrar of Indigenous Corporations

A final but more complex and potentially less workable option is for the RNTBC and land trust to operate as independent entities over the same land, coordinated through formal agreements, such as memoranda of understanding (MOUs), setting out their respective roles and responsibilities in relation to land use and consent. This option is the least efficient and provides the most scope for conflict and the fragmentation of Indigenous interests. However, it may remain the default option where 'claimed' rather than 'transferred' Aboriginal freehold is involved, or where there are differences in the membership of the native title group on the one hand, and traditional and/or historical owners of Aboriginal freehold on the other.

The Wik region

The Wik region (see Figure 7.2) contains an Aboriginal land lease held by the Aurukun Shire Council, where the township of Aurukun and a number of outstations, which are seasonally occupied by Wik families, are located. The region is occupied predominantly by the Wik-speaking peoples,[20] the majority of whom live in the Aurukun township and the Aboriginal DOGIT settlements of Pormpuraaw and Napranum, as well as the towns of Coen and Weipa which lie just outside the region. While there have now been native title determinations over areas of Crown land, the Aurukun Shire lease and some pastoral leases, determinations over several pastoral leases and areas of the bauxite mining leases were in 2008 yet to be achieved.

The building block of the Wik land tenure system[21] is the clan estate, and such estates can be aggregated into various types and levels of configuration, the most inclusive of which are 'large estate cluster' identity systems, including riverine groups, ceremonial groups and language groups. These are differentiated by particular principles of social and political organisation, totemic and religious geography, language, and land tenure.[22] Eight of these larger cluster groups comprising the Wik and Wik Way claim group are the social units on which the Wik RNTBC representative membership structure is based. Two representatives from each group make up an RNTBC Governing Committee of 16 members.[23]

As of 2006 there were at least 33 parcels of land of coexisting tenure within the native title claim area (see Figure 7.2). These included parcels of DOGIT land at Pormpuraaw and Napranum, the Aurukun Aboriginal land lease, pastoral leases under both Aboriginal and non-Aboriginal ownership, and areas under mining leases. Outside the claim area, but still potentially subject to future native title claims, were two large national parks which had been successfully claimed under the ALA (although not at that time granted), and further pastoral leases.

Wik interest in maintaining rights in country predates native title and is reflected through a history of decentralisation and land management initiatives. There is a mature outstation movement in the region, with some 24 or more outstations. Most are serviced from Aurukun, with the remainder serviced by an Aboriginal resource agency in Coen (Coen Regional Aboriginal Corporation which is discussed later). Almost all the outstation locations are on the Aurukun Shire lease or on Aboriginal-owned pastoral leases. Throughout the early and mid-2000s, the Aurukun Shire Council employed a land and sea management coordinator as well as between four and 10 Aboriginal rangers on the Community Development Employment Program (CDEP).

In 2001, to develop and implement land and sea management programs across the Wik traditional owners' lands, the Aurukun Shire Council proposed two resource centres known as Land and Sea Management Agencies (LSMAs). They were to provide a base for research into the environmental impacts of mining, and post mining rehabilitation, aimed primarily at generating real options for Indigenous people to gain economic and employment opportunities from lands impacted by bauxite mining. They were to become a training hub for a skilled Indigenous workforce that would build land management capacity across all Wik country.[24] By 2007 only one of these LSMAs had come to fruition, located to the south-east of Aurukun at Blue

Managing mixed Indigenous land titles — Cape York case studies

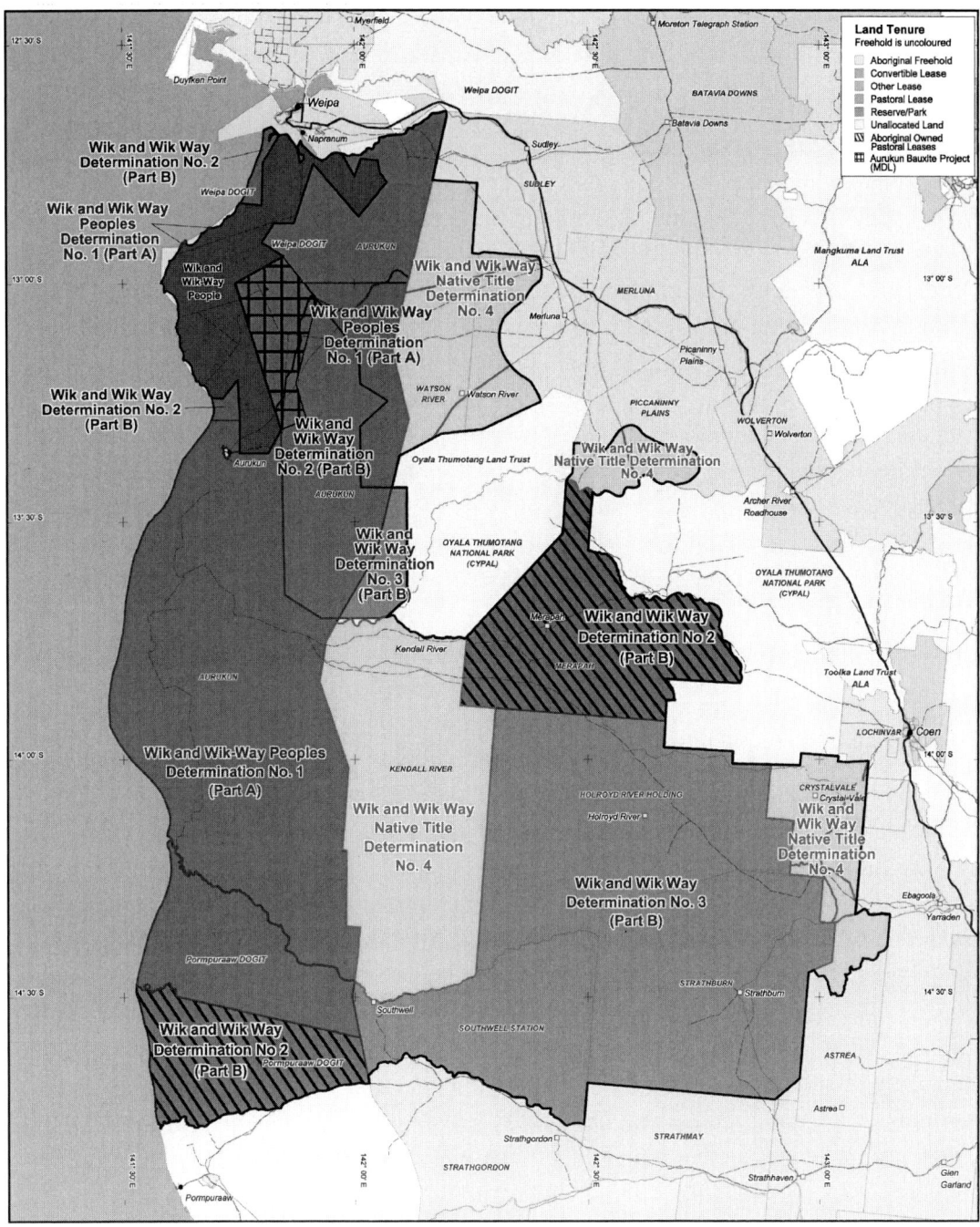

Figure 7.2 Map of Wik and Wik Way Native Title Claim in the Wik region, as at 2013.

Adapted from map ref. 20130207_QC94_3_QC01_31_Tenure_A3P.pdf, Geospatial Services, National Native Title Tribunal, 07/02/2013

Lagoon. It also functioned as an outstation resource centre. The second LSMA at Beagle Camp some 80 kilometres north of Aurukun was still on the drawing board, and awaiting funding.

Progress of the Wik RNTBC

The Wik established the Ngan Aak Kunch Aboriginal Corporation and registered it as their RNTBC in late 2002 (the Wik RNTBC).[25] The governing committee of the RNTBC has 16 appointed members comprising two members from each of the eight representative groups. Each representative group has native title rights and interests in its respective region and is affiliated to a ceremonial or language group.[26] The objects of the RNTBC clearly identify it as an agency and specify that it cannot make a native title decision unless authorised by the native title holders. The RNTBC is required by its rules to ascertain the identity of affected native title holders and ensure they understand the nature and purpose of proposed native title decisions as well as any associated liability.[27]

However, five years after its incorporation, the Wik RNTBC had conducted no training for its governing committee, had no office, had no financial capacity to hold AGMs, had no Australian Business Number (ABN),[28] had made no tax returns or annual returns for some years, and had no process for the distribution of any Aboriginal benefits. Since its establishment in 2002, it had held only two AGMs due to lack of resources to organise and transport participants spread over a wide region, and to administer proceedings. We suspect this lack of resources and capacity is much the same for many other RNTBCs in Australia,[29] and time will tell whether the recent changes to funding policy noted above will lead to improvements in the future.

The solicitor who negotiated the Wik native title settlement[30] has continued to provide limited pro bono services to the RNTBC. Although not receiving any fees from the RNTBC, he has been at times able to recoup fees from third parties who require the RNTBC's services for commercial activities. To date, these parties have comprised the Aluminium Corporation of China Ltd or 'Chalco', a bauxite mining company which tried to take up a mining lease in the region, and various other mining companies conducting exploration activities. The solicitor coordinates and provides secretarial support for occasional governing committee meetings and the RNTBC has signed an enormous number of legal agreements (for example, mining and future act agreements).

At the time of writing, the Wik RNTBC had accumulated about $40,000 of funds from exploration permits for minerals. An exploration permit provides capacity for a native title group to charge a mining company incremental fees. In the case of a voluntary contract, the size and timing of fee payments are controlled by what is stipulated in the contract. In the absence of a contract, standard form default conditions operate as set under the Queensland Native Title Protection Conditions

(NTPC), which are to satisfy requirements of the expedited procedures under s 237 of the NTA.

Under most agreements, including NTPC, the onus is on the native title group to raise a tax invoice. For these groups, one problem in issuing a tax invoice is the need for an ABN. Obtaining an ABN through website instructions may seem relatively easy for a computer-literate businessperson, but for an Aboriginal corporation with a board whose digital literacy skills are poor, this may be a difficult and intimidating task without appropriate professional assistance. Many native title groups and RNTBCs do not have an ABN, including the Wik.

Even the apparently basic step of opening a bank account for an RNTBC can be problematic. Fortunately, in the case of the Wik, a bank agency at Aurukun alleviated some of the problems of registering signatories. However, this process was prolonged because some members lived in other parts of the region. The solicitor has since been able to transfer accumulated money out of the Wik's trust accounts that he maintained into the RNTBC account.[31] The RNTBC, via its governing committee, should decide what happens to such monies. The Wik RNTBC has not had the capacity to do this yet. For example, five mining tenancies at Merapah Pastoral Station[32] have recently been generating a flow of fees to the RNTBC. This money should benefit the local families of an eastern subgroup of the Wik, but there is no administrative mechanism for its distribution.

The RNTBC thus consisted of a group of people, a corporation agreement and seal, a bank account of $40,000 and the human resource of a solicitor who had to retrieve his costs for any visit or meeting at Aurukun. In the first five years, the Wik RNTBC was barely able to sustain itself in a corporate sense and had, to a large extent, relied on the goodwill and guidance of its trusted professional outsider, the solicitor. This notion of the trusted outsider acting as a broker in the inter-ethnic field has received recent analytic attention in the literature on Aboriginal governance in Australia,[33] and is a point to which we shall return. However, a substantial achievement by the Wik RNTBC was Stage 1 of a mining agreement (with Chalco) that would allow leverage of a future, stable set of corporation resources once royalties and other benefits start flowing. This unique opportunity has been profiled in detail in a previous version of this chapter.[34]

Relation of the Wik RNTBC to the Chalco agreement

The RNTBC was a party to the ILUA to set up Stage 1 of the Aurukun bauxite mining project with Chalco. Stage 1 was to run for two years and incorporate a feasibility study with environmental and socio-economic impact assessment studies. In the Stage 1 agreement, there were no prescribed profits payable to specific people or entities, only an overheads budget to meet the actual costs of specific activities. A broad aim in Stage 1 was to prepare the Wik community and the RNTBC to take advantage of the opportunities presented by Stage 2, when the mine construction was to commence. The Wik solicitor indicated that the RNTBC had an ambition to set up a different Stage 2 contractual relation with Chalco, one that had the RNTBC taking a more integrated role in the project. It was expected that this would be discussed during the negotiations for Stage 2 implementation, with a view to seeking tangible benefits for the RNTBC. The ILUA also provided for an Indigenous Commercial Arrangement to give the Indigenous parties financial consideration. And a third fund, the Community Development Fund, was set up with state and Chalco contributions amounting to $500,000 over two years. It was up to the Aurukun Shire Council and the Wik and Wik Way native title holders to decide how to spend this funding, which could be used in part for preliminary RNTBC operations.[35]

With proper coordination, strong leadership and vision, it seemed likely that the Chalco mining project and its ILUA could have provided the basis for the following progressive steps for the Wik and the Wik Way:

- to re-establish a stable RNTBC administration with an office once a flow of benefits was in progress
- to establish the second Wik LSMA at Beagle Camp
- to provide long-term employment and training for Wik rangers in environmental management and cultural-awareness training.

The situation with Chalco is discussed further in the update following this chapter. The relation between the RNTBC, the LSMAs and the rangers is discussed later in the chapter.

The Coen region

The Coen region is on the east of Cape York Peninsula and contains the small service township of Coen as its regional centre as well as 10 Aboriginal outstations. Many of the traditional owners and native title holders live outside the Coen region in large Aboriginal communities, such as Lockhart River, Hopevale, Aurukun, and in the town of Cooktown. There are four language groups with native title interests in the Coen region: the Kaanju, Umpila, Lamalama and Ayapathu. These groups maintain their distinct linguistic identities and strong local affiliations to their respective language tribe territories. In this regard, the Coen region presents a more complex and heterogeneous cultural and administrative mix than the Wik region. Nonetheless, they share a system of traditional land tenure,[36] laws and customs which is regional in character[37] and they have a history of cooperation which is reflected in the success of joint land claims prosecuted over the past 15 years.[38] It is also reflected in the regional resource agency, the Coen Regional Aboriginal Corporation (see below), which has been supporting an outstation movement and providing planning, management, welfare and economic development support to all groups in the region throughout this period.

Aboriginal land tenure in the Coen region

There are substantial areas of Aboriginal freehold land held by six separate land trusts. These are listed in Table 7.2 (see also Figure 7.3). In addition there is one Aboriginal-owned pastoral lease (Geikie) and some areas of conventional freehold owned by Aboriginal groups. There are also two large national parks in the region that have been recommended for grant by the Land Tribunal following successful ALA hearings in 1994 and 1998.[39]

Table 7.2 Land trusts in the Coen region holding Aboriginal freehold land granted under the ALA, as at 2008[40]

Land Trust Name	Local Name	Area (Ha)	Incorporation Date
Wunthulpu Aboriginal Land Trust	Coen Aboriginal Reserve	11.769	4/06/1997
Yintjingga Land Trust	Port Stewart and Marina Plains	3,111.1	21/05/1992
Kulla Land Trust	Silver Plains	193,000	6/12/2000
Wathada Land Trust	Birthday Mountain	2,460	25/11/1997
Pu Pul Land Trust	Part of Lockhardt DOGIT	4,860	10/10/2001
Mangkuma Land Trust	Part of Lockhardt DOGIT*	349,262.7	10/10/2001

* Northern and eastern sections of the Mangkuma Land Trust lie outside the Coen region and are administratively linked to the Lockhart River Aboriginal Council.

In 2000 there were five native title claims in the region, but in the intervening years three have been withdrawn and a new one lodged, resulting (by 2007) in three active claims and at that time no native title determinations. The withdrawal of claims was partly on the basis of prior extinguishment, which would have meant prospects of success were very slight, but was also as a result of agreement with the state government over alternative tenure arrangements for claimants over parts of the original claims (see below).

The two remaining claims from the pre-2000 period are over substantial areas of timber reserve and Aboriginal freehold; both were lodged in the mid-1990s by

Table 7.3 Native title proceedings in the Coen region, as at 2008[41]

N.T. Application Name	Tribunal No.	Fed. Court No.	Approx. Area (sq. km)	Date Filed	Status	RNTBC Status
Kaanju/Umpila people	QC95/14	QUD6236/98	100,000	30/10/95	Active	Registered
Kaanju, Umpila, Lamalama, Ayapathu peoples #2	QC97/7	QUD6117/98	2,235.6045	12//03/97	Active	Not Registered
Ayapathu and Olkola peoples	QC03/012	QUD6012/03	1,211	8/10/03	Active	Registered

Kaanju/Umpila and Kaanju/Umpila/Lamalama/Ayapathu groupings respectively. In 2003, a third claim was lodged by a grouping of Ayapathu and Olkola (another language group from south of the Coen region), directly south of Coen and adjacent to the south-western boundary of the Kaanju/Umpila/Lamalama/Ayapathu claim.

Without a determination of native title in the region, no RNTBCs have been established. This apparent lack of progress is not so much a reflection on the merit of the claims as the outcome of sophisticated land tenure negotiations. A State Land Dealings project undertaken between the state government and the claimants, involving the Cape York Land Council, Balkanu Cape York Development Corporation (Balkanu) and the state's Cape York Tenure Resolution Task Force, has been running for several years. It involves the resolution of tenure on a number of properties in the region through negotiated ILUAs. For example, the Marina Plains Lamalama claim[42] was withdrawn in 2005 after a tenure settlement resulting in approximately 20 per cent of the claimed land being added to the existing holdings of the Yintjingga Land Trust at Port Stewart as Aboriginal freehold, and the remainder going into the adjacent Lakefield National Park.

The tenure resolution process is aimed at achieving practical tenure solutions that address conservation, economic and cultural factors while at the same time maximising Aboriginal participation as owners and managers of land in the region.[43]

The Coen Regional Aboriginal Corporation

The Coen Regional Aboriginal Corporation (CRAC) is an Indigenous service agency at the centre of regional planning for Indigenous land use and management.

In the absence of RNTBCs and operational land trusts, CRAC strives to provide support and to coordinate the resourcing of outstations and landowning bodies. It serves as a model of how a centralised land management agency might operate in a region characterised by numerous landowning corporations operating under different legislative regimes, and which are affiliated with different language or tribal groups and/or coalitions of groups. It is also an example of how organisations may develop income-generating enterprises which reduce their dependence on public funding and enable them to provide broader services to address the economic and social aspirations of Indigenous landholders.

CRAC was established in 1993 as a non-statutory corporation to administer CDEP. It has been structured to represent all Aboriginal people whose traditional lands lie in the region. From the start, it was viewed by its members as a means of re-establishing a presence on their own land.[44] Its composition is participatory, with

Figure 7.3 Map of existing and likely future Aboriginal land tenures in the Coen region, as at 2008.

Adapted from map 'Cape York Peninsula Claim Activity', Edition 10, 1/9/2007,
Queensland Department of Natural Resources and Water, courtesy of the Department

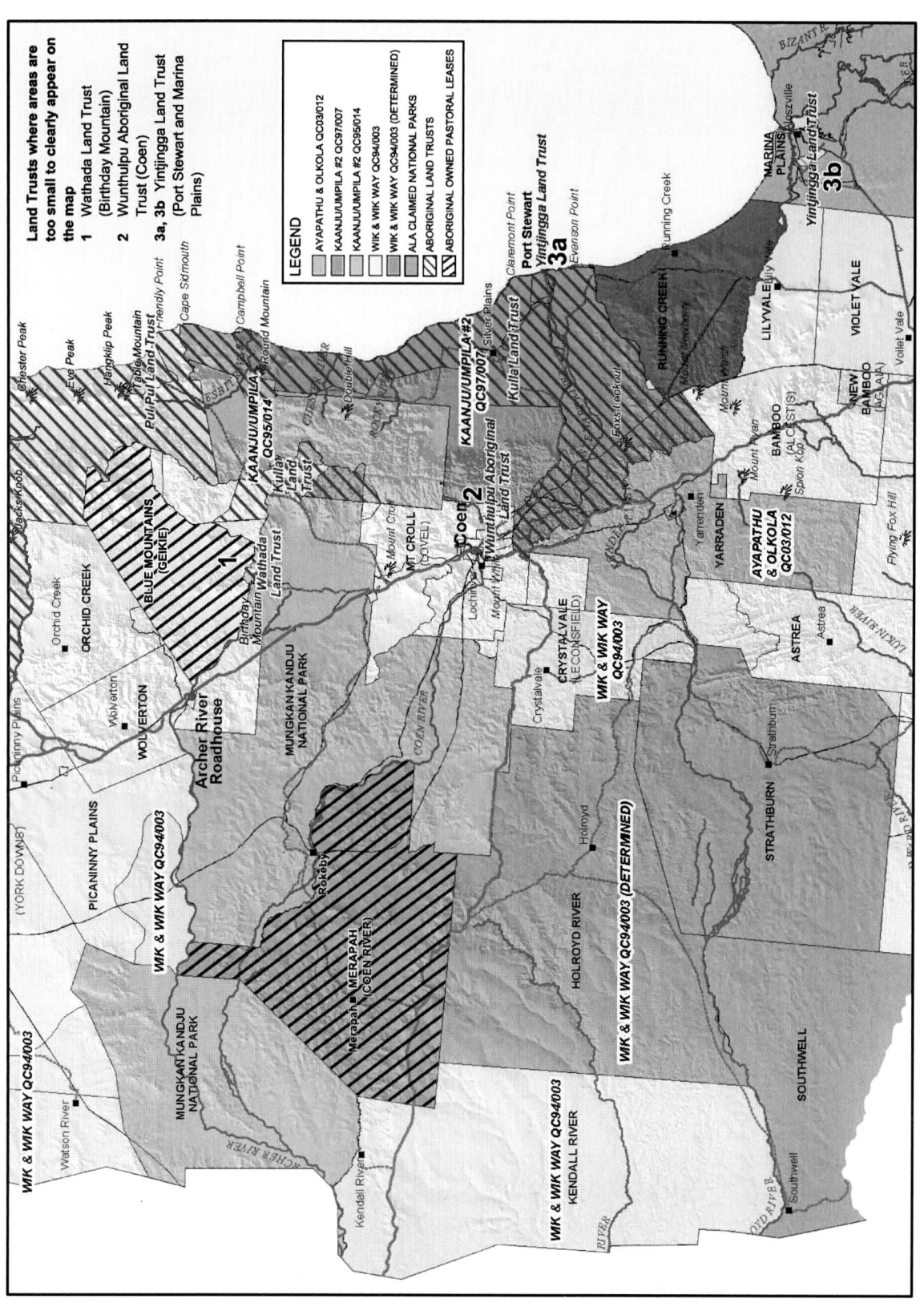

membership open to all Aboriginal residents of the region. However, its board is structured along representative lines,[45] with members nominated from each of six language groups associated with the different outstation communities and with the township of Coen. In addition to the four language groups mentioned above, there is also Wik Mungkan and Olkola representation through the affiliation of outstations on two Aboriginal-owned pastoral leases, Merepah and Glen Garland, which are outside the region but historically have relied on CRAC to provide administrative support.

CRAC derives its funding from three main sources. It receives core funding from the Commonwealth Government to cover its recurrent administrative costs; program funding from state, Commonwealth and other sources for housing, employment and training; and it generates its own income through a number of local enterprises developed between 2004 and 2008.[46] In recent years CRAC has deliberately moved to strengthen independent income sources by developing several commercial operations. In 2002 it formed Coen Business Enterprises (CBE) to put the organisation on a more sustainable footing and reduce its reliance on government grants. By establishing CBE as a private company, CRAC was able to preserve its status as a public benevolent institution (PBI),[47] and the taxation advantages this provides, such as competitive employee benefits. It will also ensure CRAC falls into the small or medium categories under the CATSI Act and will benefit from the resulting compliance and cost-saving advantages.

In this and other ways, CRAC has effectively leveraged its public funding base to build an enterprise and asset base that generates a growing income stream for the organisation by providing a range of services to both the Aboriginal and wider communities.[48] For example, CBE holds a Queensland Building Services Authority licence which enables it to tender for building and construction jobs in the region. Also under CBE's umbrella are a mechanical workshop, a catering business and a screen printing and art enterprise based in the CRAC-owned visitors centre at the southern entrance to Coen. In its first year of operation, CBE made less than $10,000 profit, the second year it made $32,000, and for 2006–07 it was expected to make over $100,000 profit, mainly from the building and catering businesses which were proving to be the most successful of its enterprises.[49]

Two of CRAC's main functions are to support outstations established on Aboriginal-owned land, and to act as a housing organisation for those living in the township and on outstations. For these purposes it receives various Commonwealth and state grants. CRAC services approximately a dozen residential outstations established on the various areas of Aboriginal land in the region, and assists the operations of several Aboriginal land trusts in the region. It has provided the foundation for a dramatic increase in the 'outstation' or 'homelands' movement in the region over the past decade. CRAC also employs about 100 people on CDEP. In the past, it administered the National Heritage Trust ranger program, a two-year grant to employ and train Indigenous rangers in the Coen area. In recent times, it has been funded by the Environmental Protection Agency to assist groups settling on land acquired through negotiation with the state government as part of the State Land Dealings project.

Recurrent funding for some outstations has come from FaHCSIA through the Indigenous Coordination Centre (ICC),[50] and in 2006 CRAC received just over $100,000 for an outstation coordinator and other outstation related services. It is able to use its work crew and plant to maintain access roads and provide trade services, such as plumbing and building. The CRAC Board usually determines the division of funds between the outstations. This money is for infrastructure only; there are no specific funds provided for outstation management or running costs. 'Bushlight', which installs solar power into remote area communities, is an example of a recent successful program negotiated by CRAC and funded through FaHCSIA on behalf of the outstations [but see update to this chapter].

Regional agency models for land use and management

The Wik RNTBC model

The Wik and Wik Way claimants have consistently expressed a strong preference for having all Wik people represented on a single RNTBC: 'All Wik people have spoken as one.'[51] Their preference was for an agency type RNTBC with participatory membership and a governing committee based on representation of the eight regional and ceremonial subgroups from across all Wik and Wik Way country. There was also a need to ensure that some of the committee representatives resided in each of the Coen, Napranum and Pormpuraaw communities to represent native title holders in these communities for the purposes of communication and feedback. Thus, the translation of customary membership into contemporary landholding corporations had to take into account post contact historical factors that have taken people away from their country.

A key feature of the Wik RNTBC design (see Figure 7.4) was that each of the represented groups would have the capacity to meet by themselves on occasions, in accordance with their customary methods of decision-making, to make decisions about critical events affecting native title in their respective regions. This aspect of the RNTBC is critical to ensuring that Wik and Wik Way law and custom are incorporated into decision-making on land and sea issues. However, this was also identified as a vulnerable aspect of the RNTBC design, with potential problems including the difficulty of individual groups having a viable meeting when key personnel may be dispersed, the need to raise funds for transport and the possibility of members being unable or disinclined to attend meetings.[52]

Decision-making within each of these Wik subgroups may still have to devolve to the clan or extended family level because these ceremonial and regional entities are not landholding units, nor are they units of political, social or economic action.

They do not correspond to corporate units within Wik society which are relevant to the operations of native title. 'Families' within each of the eight subgroups are the basic groupings in which discussions would be held.[53] It has never been proposed that any of the representational groups could be separately incorporated for business activities (as is the case for the four language-named tribes of the Coen region — see below). On the contrary, there is some concern about the likelihood of 'fissioning' or subdividing corporations if they were formed, as this is a common feature of political dynamics in the Wik universe, both socially and corporately.[54]

Whereas in our earlier reports we suggested that in the absence of RNTBC resources, it made sense for the Wik RNTBC to outsource administrative functions to the Aurukun Shire Council's LSMA,[55] it would seem with the likely advent of a mining company ILUA that the RNTBC could establish its own office with a manager and secretariat. This could be based in the mining company complex at Aurukun, particularly if it reverts to community control. The RNTBC's visiting consultants would be able to stay in the adjacent accommodation. Minimal administration services would be required.[56] In addition, the RNTBC could contract out a range of land and sea management services to the council's LSMA on behalf of the native title holders, including land and sea management planning; provision of outstation services; provision of rangers to monitor country and carry out management projects in country; cultural heritage assessments and socioeconomic impact studies prior to land developments; and employment of native title holders to participate in the range of land and sea management activities.

The Coen region model

In contrast to the Wik peoples, traditional owner groups in the Coen region expressed a preference for a structure that retains independent corporate vehicles for each of the four language-named tribes, while at the same time recognising the need for a centralised administrative agency for the region (see Figure 7.5). While some land trusts and existing native title claims comprise coalitions of language groups, within these structures there is a preference for each group retaining autonomy in relation to its territorial area and the management of that area, including appropriate representative structures within any landowning entities, whether RNTBCs or land trusts.

This model is structurally analogous to the relationship established between CRAC and the outlying outstation communities. The model has two key structural dimensions. The first is an overarching corporate structure, which brings together traditional owner and native title groups from the region to form a decision-making committee for common purposes, such as financial administration, regional land and sea management, resourcing outstations and liaising with national parks boards of management. Within this wider structure, separate traditional owner decision-making committees for each of the four tribal native title groups will act as trustees for their respective local land areas. These committees may have responsibility for making

Managing mixed Indigenous land titles — Cape York case studies

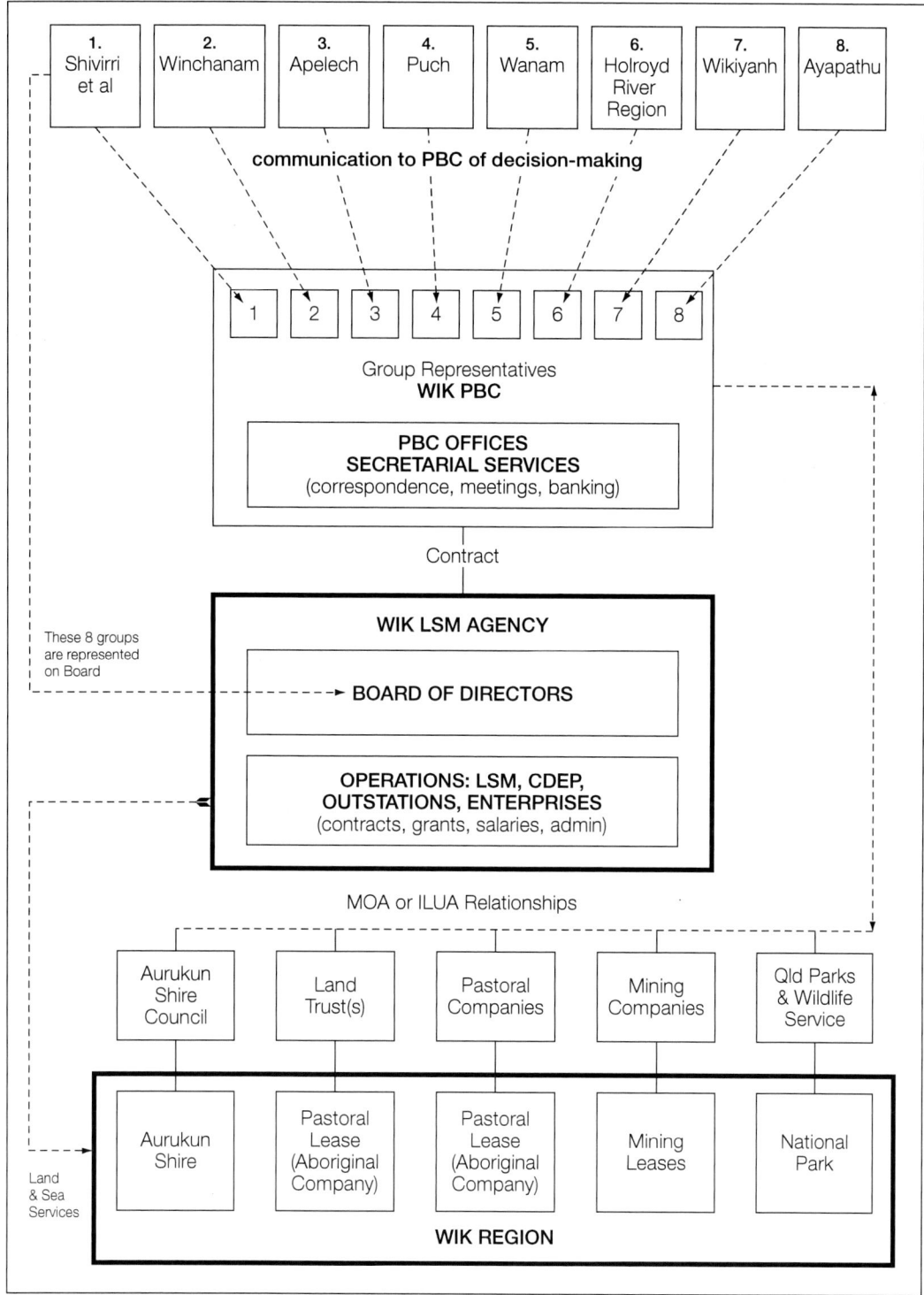

Figure 7.4 Wik region model showing the proposed structural relationship between the Wik RNTBC (here labelled PBC) and the Wik LSMA after the Chalco royalty flow allows a permanent RNTBC office to be established[57]

decisions about budget allocations for their own groups, use of local assets, businesses and so on, as well as RNTBC and relevant land trust matters, and overseeing land and sea management contracts on the group's traditional land. Eventually, this model should lead to the structural amalgamation of RNTBCs and land trusts for each tribal group, though this may still be some way off since it will depend on the resolution of the political and legal impediments discussed above.

There are persuasive arguments as to why there should be a central agency as a point of contact for the Coen region. One is to achieve economies of scale. Another is that it is already a requirement of most state and federal government agencies that funding goes through a regional organisation rather than to individuals, family or outstation groups. Further, while CRAC has historically acted as a de facto LSMA, there is a perceived need for the more formal recognition and funding of a separately mandated and dedicated unit.

The Coen region is economically 'poor' from the Indigenous perspective. While CRAC has had some success in spinning off enterprises and in using these to fund its wider operations, it continues to rely on government grants for most of its budget. Likewise, while there are small-scale cattle businesses on some outstations, currently they barely cover operating costs. Outstations, too, continue to rely on external funding for housing, basic infrastructure and members' personal incomes. While viable prospects for tourism, cattle herding, prawn farming and the like have been identified and form part of traditional owner aspirations, it is difficult to see these developing into a sustainable economic base without intensive external financial and administrative support. Further, there are no prospective mining or other development projects that could generate significant cash flows for landowners.

The right to negotiate and the ILUA provisions of the NTA provide a potential basis for negotiating benefits in return for access and use of native title lands, and in compensation for any extinguished or impaired native title resulting from land and sea developments. Mining and other development companies may also be legislatively obliged to carry out social and environmental impact assessments in relation to their projects. Through these, a range of economic activities that engage local Aboriginal groups can often be designed. The proposed gas pipeline from Papua New Guinea (PNG) is such a project, providing opportunities to the Kaanju and Ayapathu groups in the Coen region, who signed a pipeline ILUA in 2006. However, by 2007, the project had been mothballed with no definite prospects of being resuscitated.

Managing Aboriginal landholding entities at the regional level

Two key components common to the land management models for both regions are centralised LSMAs providing support to landholding entities, and a preference for the amalgamation of RNTBCs and land trusts. This arrangement is predicated on a desire to retain the traditional social organisation, land tenure and decision-making

Managing mixed Indigenous land titles — Cape York case studies

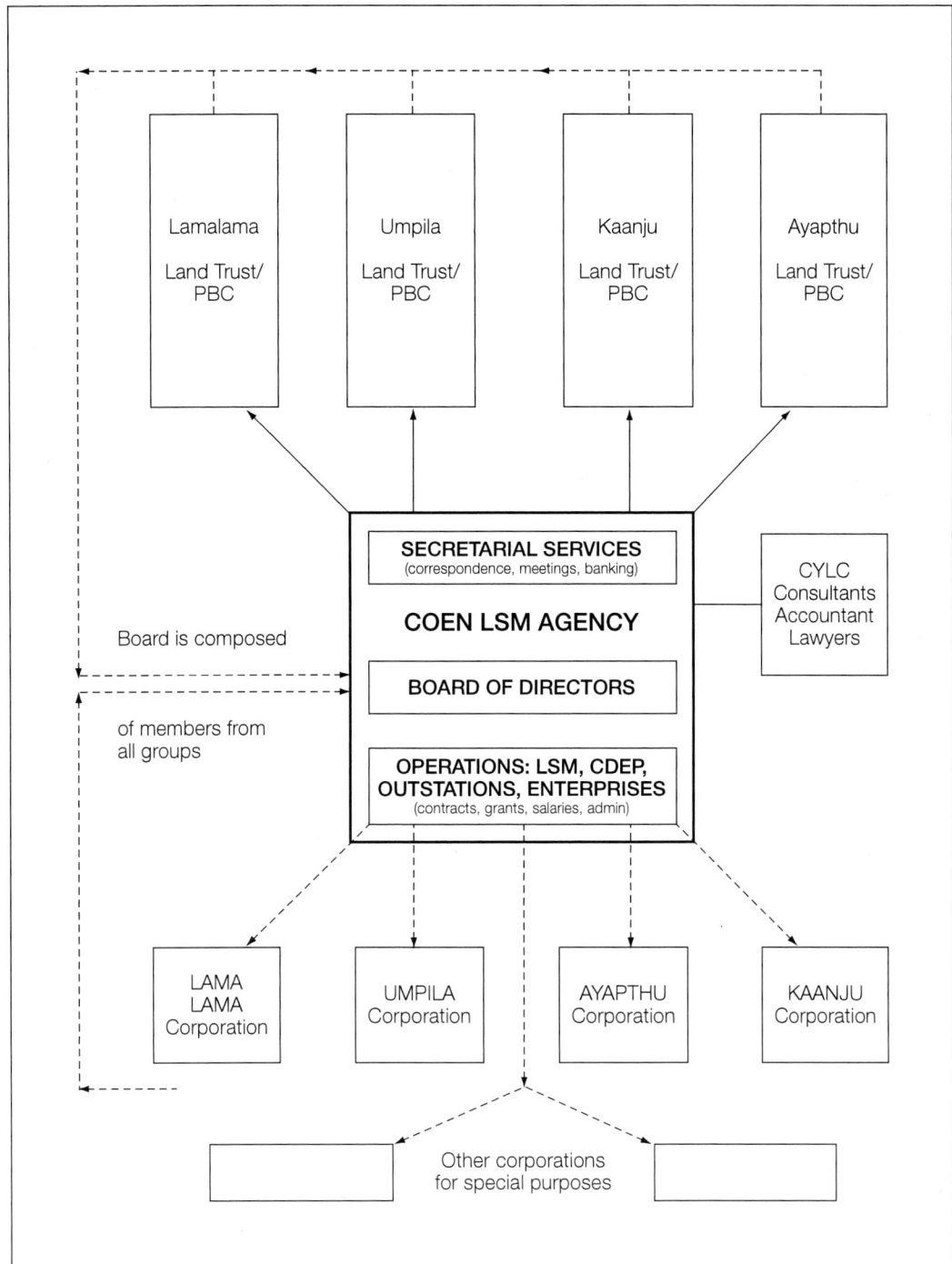

Figure 7.5 Coen region model illustrating the proposed Coen LSMA, a set of tribal PBCs which also serve as land trusts, and a set of four tribal corporations for day-to-day business in the Coen region. This would result from an amalgamation and rationalisation of all existing landowning corporations, RNTBCs (here labelled PBCs) and land trusts.[58]

systems among groups in each region. However, it is constrained by the need to incorporate traditional decision-making practices into organisations which will be economically sustainable and will comply with the legal and regulatory environment imposed by state and Commonwealth legislation.

Regional LSMAs should be able to deliver sufficient economies of scale for their affiliated title-holding bodies to be able to accommodate a more 'traditional' mode of operation. They would provide contracted secretarial services to RNTBCs, land trusts and lease-holding corporations. RNTBCs and land trusts might also outsource some of their functions; for example, the management of certain areas of native title land and issuing of entry permits to Aboriginal freehold land. The agencies' activities will intermesh with a range of the native title rights and interests being claimed in the region with respect to the general use of country: the erection and occupation of residences; hunting, fishing and collecting resources; management, conservation and care for the land; the right to prohibit unauthorised use of the land; and cultural, heritage and social functions.

In order to respond to consent requests for planning and development activities from other parties under the NTA, properly resourced consultation of native title holders needs to be ensured. Therefore, the development of satisfactory protocols for consultation and communication among landholding entities, the native title holders and the regional agencies is a critical design factor in the regional models.

A key problem for Indigenous landholding groups is to develop a capacity to independently fund their operational as well as their ongoing infrastructure costs. At the very least, a minimum income is required for a base secretarial and administration service to fulfil the legal compliance requirements of land trusts, RNTBCs and lease-holding corporations. Therefore, the ability to use ILUA agreements to finance not only title-holding bodies but also their regional service agencies will be vital, because ongoing grant funding is likely to become increasingly limited. The regional agency model allows income derived from compensation or other benefits, such as those negotiated under ILUAs, to be channelled through the RNTBC to the agency which can engage practically in a range of land-based operations, drawing on any available infrastructure, CDEP or 'Work for the Dole' employees, community rangers or consultants, on behalf of the native title holders.

The history of CRAC demonstrates the potential for an agency to develop associated income-generating enterprises and to integrate these with its core functions in such a way that it continues to benefit from the advantages of being a funded service organisation while at the same time loosening its dependence on public funding. In remote areas, such as Coen and Aurukun, there is significant scope for filling niche services not generally attractive to the private sector because of their small scale and remote location, but which are feasible for local organisations whose basic overheads are publicly funded. The RNTBC funding guidelines likewise encourage

RNTBCs to seek financial support from non-government sources. However, the reality is that for the foreseeable future, unless there are highly lucrative development projects in a region (for example, Chalco), Indigenous landholders and their service agencies will continue to require significant levels of public funding to cover their base operations and ensure their regulatory compliance. Funding will continue to be a critical limitation on the ability of Aboriginal landholders to derive real benefits from either native title or statutory land rights legislation in Queensland.

Traditional owners will need to agree on rules as to how monies coming into the regional agency will be distributed, to complement those set down for RNTBC and land trust income. This is particularly the case where a subgroup of native title holders has an established income stream from an ILUA or other agreement, but the other subgroups in the RNTBC do not. There is thus a need for an economic plan that allows, on the one hand, Aboriginal income into the region to be equitably spread to groups across the region for basic regional agency functions, but which at the same time recognises local native title rights in compensation outcomes and acknowledges local enterprise initiatives by individual groups.

A substantial dollar investment is required to maintain Aboriginal traditional connection to country through customary land tenure systems incorporated into contemporary corporate entities. Traditional land management does not necessarily equate to a cheaper alternative; indeed, because of its communal nature and a general tendency towards consensus decision-making through intra-community consultation, resources are required to run what might be termed the 'software' (that is, the recurrent administration) of traditional land management, as well as the 'hardware' (that is, the management operations). Funding bodies all too often fail to get this balance right, so that while there may be resources available for project implementation or program funding, there is little provision for maintaining the capacities of the organisation to function effectively over the longer term. The Commonwealth's belated decision to support RNTBCs financially through the NTRB network is a welcome step forward — one that is yet to be matched by the Queensland Government in relation to the land trust set up under its ALA legislation.

Conclusions — the sustainability of Aboriginal landholding entities under native title

This paper is based on ongoing research into the operations of RNTBCs and other Indigenous landholding entities on Cape York Peninsula. One object of the research has been to assess the possibilities within the existing Australian planning and legislative framework for rationalising and integrating the operations of RNTBCs, land trusts and other forms of Aboriginal landowning corporations so as to improve the outcomes from land acquired under a variety of tenures by Aboriginal groups on Cape York and elsewhere. A key to the models proposed has been to take a regional approach and, so far as possible, to pool resources and service landholding bodies on this basis.

In this paper we have reviewed developments in each of the Aurukun and Coen regions since the research began in 2001. Significant hurdles to the development of effective landholding bodies identified then were funding constraints and the differing legislative requirements for incorporation of landowning bodies under the Queensland ALA and the Commonwealth NTA. As the case of the Wik RNTBC shows, funding remains a constraint on the organisation's ability to fulfil even its basic legal responsibilities, let alone take on land management functions. Without short-term prospects of funding, the Wik RNTBC has been difficult to sustain. Fortunately it has been aided by a 'trusted outsider' professional who has acted as a broker in the inter-ethnic field, 'straddling the gap between administrative demands and local capacity',[59] and representing the RNTBC in future act and mining exploration negotiations.

While Queensland's legislative amendment enabling the amalgamation of RNTBCs into land trusts is a positive initiative, there is still no movement in the native title regulations at the Commonwealth level which would allow the alternative possibility of land trusts incorporated in Queensland to function as RNTBCs. On the other hand, the CATSI Act addresses some of the legal contradictions that previously impeded the incorporation of traditional decision-making processes into Aboriginal corporations.[60] Together with the changes to Commonwealth Government native title funding policy to allow NTRBs to provide ongoing assistance to RNTBCs, these are all positive, though limited, initiatives.

There have been further developments in the case study regions which give cause for optimism. Most notable is the mining project proposal at Aurukun, which offers the potential for the long-term prospects of the Wik RNTBC to become relatively secure, at least financially. A transition period is required until a royalty flow can support an administration service, secure premises and establish land and sea management services. However, most RNTBCs do not have the advantage of a multi-billion dollar mining project on their land. Such is the case in the Coen region where, other than domestic-scale cattle operations on the outstations, the opportunities for generating significant income remain limited. Though an ILUA has been signed for the proposed PNG gas pipeline, the project is yet to materialise and, in any case, will benefit only two of the Coen language groups.

On Cape York, RNTBCs are only one of a number of types of Aboriginal landholding bodies. While in the Aurukun region the RNTBC is poised to take a dominant role in land management, in Coen the scene is far more heterogeneous, with a variety of landholding and outstation organisations networked through a central non-government auspicing agency (CRAC) for the delivery of services, infrastructure, project funding and land management functions.

CRAC has grown to be a resilient and stable organisation; it is less dependent on particular individuals or 'trusted outsiders' than is often the case. However, its position in the regional constellation of landowning and residential groups in Coen is analogous to a 'trusted outsider' in the Wik RNTBC. CRAC's success as an organisation, and in particular its administration of CDEP and development initiatives over a 15-year period from 1993 to 2008, has been a predominant factor in establishing residential groups in outstations on their own land, at the same time providing the means for their engagement with wider economies.[61] The sustainability of these outstations largely depends on the strength of a centralised resource agency. In particular, CRAC demonstrates the long-term viability of a regional resource, and the potential for such organisations to not only harness multiple pools of public project funding on behalf of their landholding clients, but also to develop local enterprises which fulfil a need in the region, and have the potential to generate income and to provide training and employment.

Another key premise of our argument is that the cultural integrity of the native title holder community may be supported in the design of the RNTBC.[62] This can be done by giving primary consideration to elements of the local Aboriginal system of land tenure and its associated decision-making processes, rather than allowing these to be subordinated to legal and administrative convenience. However, in both the ALA and the native title claim processes, the structure of the title-holding corporation is often the last aspect to be considered. In our view, the preferred approach is to work with claimants from the outset on designing and establishing their RNTBCs and land trusts. This would shift the initial focus from the frustratingly lengthy and legalistic processes leading to a determination to consideration of the optimal corporate structures that will meet the long-term outcomes that Aboriginal communities wish to achieve from their native title.

A key principle is to inform the design process of RNTBCs, land trusts and other landholding corporations with an understanding of the social structure and decision-making dynamics of the autochthonous Aboriginal land tenure system. A successful RNTBC or land trust must operate to mediate the transition from the Aboriginal system of land tenure to the holding of title under a corporate, statutory entity, whose governing structures permit the replication of 'traditional' membership and decision-making processes into a corporate structure capable of articulating with a variety of non-Indigenous planning and land management entities. Major design challenges include maintaining the integrity of traditional decision-making processes while responding to the legal and administrative requirements of the various statutory regimes for Aboriginal land rights; structuring the membership to reflect traditional social organisational arrangements; and having a capacity to subsume any politicisation and power politics within the native title group.

The preferred models to emerge for each region have as a core structural element a centralised LSMA, providing administrative and other functions to the various

Aboriginal landholding entities in its region. In other respects, however, the models differ, reflecting the cultural, demographic and socio-geographic landscapes of each region. This can be seen in the case studies, which present almost two extremes. On the one hand there is a relatively homogenous tribal/cultural native title group, a limited number of overlapping tenures and good prospects for the generation of independent income. On the other hand, there is a region in which there are several distinct and very independent tribal groupings, a variety of overlapping and interweaving tenures, and ongoing land tenure negotiations without (as yet) successful native title determinations. Yet in both regions, for localised landholding groups to achieve their cultural and economic objectives, and to retain a desirable level of autonomy and control over land to which they have particular traditional connections, there is an awareness of the need to support and work through regional institutions.

The reality is that while the models presented in this chapter represent an ideal that each region is moving towards, and while there has been encouraging progress at local, state and Commonwealth levels, the RNTBCs and land trusts in both regions are under-resourced, under-supported and functionally dormant. In order to manage their traditional title, including responding to important economic opportunities such as Chalco and the PNG gas pipeline, they currently rely on minimal external support — in the Wik case from a lawyer in Brisbane and the Aurukun Council, and in the Coen case from CRAC, an auspicing non-governmental organisation. Based on these two case studies, it is not possible to say that RNTBCs and land trusts are effectively managing their own affairs through traditional decision-making.

Furthermore, while there have been local developments that have the potential to bring significant benefits to native title holders, to date their engagement with third parties has relied heavily on the external support and expertise of trusted outsiders and established organisations. It is unrealistic to expect that small, poorly resourced RNTBCs will ever be able to manage external relations involving ILUAs and complex commercial negotiations. However, a well-resourced regional LSMA would be able provide the management framework through which RNTBCs and land trusts might engage with third parties, NTRBs and other sources of expertise to assist them. While the changes to native title funding policy discussed above hold out the promise of placing RNTBCs on a more sustainable footing, the next logical step of establishing regional LSMAs to assist them to maximise economic opportunities has yet to be taken.

Endnotes

1 Western Australia is the exception; it is the only state without some form of Aboriginal land rights legislation.
2 Smith has elucidated a number of aspects of the complex and often uneasy relationship between Indigenous forms of knowledge, governance and land management in the Coen region of northern

Queensland with those of government and outside agencies seeking to incorporate Aboriginal perspectives into their operations. This complexity extends even to regional Aboriginal organisation. See BR Smith, 'Between places: Aboriginal decentralisation, mobility and territoriality in the region of Coen, Cape York Peninsula (Australia)', unpublished PhD thesis, London School of Economics and Political Science, 2000; BR Smith, *Decentralisation, population mobility and the CDEP scheme in central Cape York Peninsula*, CAEPR Discussion Paper, no. 238, Centre for Aboriginal Economic Policy Research, Australian National University, Canberra, 2002, http://caepr.anu.edu.au/sites/default/files/Publications/DP/2002_DP238.pdf, accessed 29 April 2008; and BR Smith, 'A complex balance: mediating sustainable development in Cape York Peninsula', *The Drawing Board: an Australian Review of Public Affairs*, vol. 4, 2003, pp. 99–115; and BR Smith, '"We got our own management": local knowledge, government and development in Cape York Peninsula', *Australian Aboriginal Studies*, vol. 2, 2005, pp. 4–15.

3 This chapter is based upon research begun in 2001 for the report P Memmott & S McDougall, *Holding title and managing land in Cape York: Indigenous land management and native title*, National Native Title Tribunal, Perth, 2003, http://www.nntt.gov.au/Mediation-and-agreement-making-services/Documents/Holding%20Title%20and%20Managing%20Land%20in%20Cape%20York.pdf, accessed 15 May 2013. Aspects of the research were also the subject of two previous papers: P Memmott, P Blackwood & S McDougall, 'A regional approach to managing Aboriginal land title on Cape York', in JF Weiner & K Glaskin (eds), *Customary land tenure and registration in Australia and Papua New Guinea: anthropological perspectives*, Asia-Pacific Environment Monograph 3, ANU EPress, Australian National University, Canberra, 2007, pp. 273–97, http://epress.anu.edu.au?p=99961, accessed 15 May 2013; and P Memmott & P Blackwood, *Holding title and managing land in Cape York — two case studies*, AIATSIS Research Discussion Paper, no. 21, Native Title Research Unit, AIATSIS, Canberra, 2008, http://www.aiatsis.gov.au/research/docs/dp/DP21.pdf, accessed 18 June 2013. Significant parts of this chapter were drawn from these earlier publications. The update was made possible by funding from AIATSIS.

4 Cape York Land Council, *Three year strategic plan 2001–2004*, Cape York Land Council, Cairns, 2001.

5 Building on Memmott & McDougall, above n 3, pp. 273–97.

6 The criteria for 'traditional affiliation' are that 'the members of the [claim] group have a common connection with the land based on spiritual and other associations with, rights in relation to, and responsibilities for, the land under Aboriginal tradition' (ALA, s 4.09(1)); those for 'historical association' are that 'the [claim] group has an association with the land based on them or their ancestors having, for a substantial period, lived on or used: (a) the land [under claim]; or (b) land in the district or region in which the land [being claimed] is located' (ALA, s 4.10(1)). Land may also be granted for 'economic' and 'cultural' reasons, but these provisions have so far not been used in Cape York where traditional affiliation as grounds for grant has taken precedence. See Memmott & McDougall, above n 3, for more detailed explication of the operation of the ALA.

7 Ibid., p. 24.

8 Department of Families, Housing, Community Services and Indigenous Affairs (FaHCSIA), 'Guidelines for support of Prescribed Bodies Corporate (PBCs)', FaHCSIA Land Branch Native Title Program, Canberra, 2007, p. 16, http://www.aiatsis.gov.au/ntru/docs/resources/rntbc/toolkits2011/FaHCSIAguidelines.pdf, accessed 15 May 2013.

9 *Corporations (Aboriginal and Torres Strait Islander) Act 2006* (Cth) (CATSI Act), pt 2.4, div 37.

10 For reporting purposes native title rights and interests are not included in determining the value of the RNTBC's assets. Thus corporations which only hold and/or manage native title rights and interests will not find themselves determined as 'large' for reporting purposes. See Office

of the Registrar of Aboriginal and Torres Strait Islander Corporations (ORATSIC), 'Fact sheet native title', ORATSIC, Canberra, 2010, http://www.oric.gov.au/html/publications/factsheets/Factsheet_Native-title_Jun2010.pdf, accessed 18 June 2013.
11 Ibid.
12 Parliamentary Joint Committee on Native Title and the Aboriginal and Torres Strait Islander Land Account (PJCNT), *Report on the operation of Native Title Representative Bodies*, Parliament of Australia, 2006, pp. 32–6, http://www.aph.gov.au/senate/committee/ntlf_ctte/rep_bodies/report/report.pdf, accessed 5 October 2007.
13 One of the criteria used to assess applications will be the availability of alternative funding. See FaHCSIA, above n 8, p. 16.
14 RNTBCs may hold leasehold land, and conversely, existing Aboriginal corporations set up to hold pastoral leases may, with appropriate rule amendments to their objects and membership clauses, be adapted to become RNTBCs.
15 Department of Natural Resources and Mines (DNRM), *Review of the Aboriginal Land Act 1991 (Qld)*, discussion paper, DNRM, Brisbane, March 2005, http://www.nrm.qld.gov.au, accessed 15 April 2008.
16 See Memmott & McDougall, above n 3, p. 93.
17 The *Aboriginal and Torres Strait Islander Land Amendment Act 2008* was passed by the Queensland parliament in May 2008. The relevant section is s 17. This provision applies only to 'transferable' land, not to Aboriginal freehold resulting from the ALA claim process. The authors do not know the reasons for changing one class of Aboriginal freehold but not the other.
18 Recognising similarities in the structure and intent of *Aboriginal Councils and Associations Act 1976* (Cth) (ACA Act) corporations and ALA land trusts, the Queensland Government recently canvassed the option of abolishing land trusts altogether and granting land directly to ACA Act Aboriginal corporations, which could include RNTBCs, thereby avoiding the duplication of organisations with almost identical functions. It also acknowledged that the integration of land trusts and corporations may be facilitated by allowing land trusts to be formed prior to the granting of the land. See DNRM, above n 15, pp. 33–4. Notably, neither of these options made their way into recent (May 2008) amendments to the ALA, which now enable transferred Aboriginal freehold land to be granted to RNTBCs.
19 The Jabalbina Yalanji Aboriginal Corporation RNTBC was incorporated under the 2006 CATSI Act. Its rules are available on the ORIC website, http://www.oric.gov.au/document.aspx?concernID=202074, accessed 5 May 2013. The Jabalbina Yalanji Land Trust was incorporated under the ALA regulations; land trust rules are not publicly available (see http://www.nrm.qld.gov.au/nativetitle/land/land_trusts.html#aboriginal_and_torres_strait_islander, accessed 5 May 2013).
20 See the following references for an ethnographic history of these peoples: D Thomson, 'Fatherhood in the Wik Monkan tribe', *American Anthropologist*, vol. 38, 1936, p. 374; U McConnel, 'Social organisation of the tribes of Cape York Peninsula, North Queensland [part 1]: distribution of tribes', *Oceania*, vol. 10, 1939, p. 62; P Sutton, 'Wik: Aboriginal society, territory and language at Cape Keerweer, Cape York Peninsula', unpublished PhD thesis, University of Queensland, St Lucia, 1978; J Von Sturmer, 'The Wik region: economy, territoriality and totemism in western Cape York Peninsula, North Queensland', unpublished PhD thesis, University of Queensland, St Lucia, 1978; D Martin, 'The "Wik" peoples of western Cape York', *Indigenous Law Bulletin*, vol. 4, no. 1, 1997, pp. 8–11; and D Martin, 'Autonomy and relatedness: an ethnography of Wik people of Aurukun, Western Cape York Peninsula', unpublished PhD thesis, Australian National University, Canberra, 1993.

21 The Wik peoples comprise a broad linguistic grouping sharing a range of cultural similarities, within which there are a number of identifiable linguistic subgroups, namely Wik Way, Wik Mungkan, Wik Ompom, Wik Iyanh or Mungkanhu, Wik-Ngencherr and Ayapathu (P Sutton, 'Wik native title: anthropological overview; The Wik Peoples native title determination application QC 94/3', manuscript for Wik Native Title Claim, Aldgate, SA, 1997, p. 36; A Chase, B Rigsby, D Martin, B Smith, M Winter & P Blackwood, *Mungkan, Ayapathu and Kaanju Peoples' land claims to Mungkan Kaanju National Park and Lochinvar Mineral Field*, unpublished claim book, Cape York Land Council on behalf of the claimants, Cairns, 1998, p. 59). The distribution of languages is often mosaic-like and language affiliation may be shared by clans with non-contiguous estates. Further, languages are not necessarily co-terminus with political or social groups such as riverine groupings and regional ritual groups in a given region. Commonality in language use does not necessarily correspond to a unity of political or social identity (see Sutton 1997, p. 33).

22 Sutton, above n 20, pp. 126–8, 140 and Sutton, above n 21, pp. 28–32.

23 Ngan Aak Kunch Aboriginal Corporation, 'Rules of Ngan Aak Kunch Aboriginal Corporation', Ebsworth and Ebsworth Lawyers, Brisbane, 2002, http://www.orac.gov.au/document.aspx?concernID=104097, accessed 29 April 2008.

24 Aurukun Shire Council, 'Wik Waya land and sea management centre', unpublished application for a project grant from the Natural Heritage Trust, Aurukun Shire Council, Aurukun, 2001.

25 Based on Philip Hunter, Ebsworth and Ebsworth Lawyers, interview with P Memmott, Brisbane, 24 July 2007, on the Aurukun RNTBC and the Chalco Development.

26 Ngan Aak Kunch Aboriginal Corporation, above n 23, pp. 10, 11.

27 Ibid., pp. 7–9.

28 An ABN is a unique 11-digit number used in Australia to identify businesses. While not compulsory, it is necessary if a business has sufficient turnover to require it to charge GST (the Australian Goods and Services Tax) and for other dealings with the Australian Taxation Office, http://www.business.gov.au/BusinessTopics/Registrationandlicences/Registerfortaxation/Pages/RegisterforanAustralianBusinessNumber%28ABN%29.aspx, accessed 22 July 2013.

29 The reader is referred to discussions on a range of case studies on PBCs that were canvassed in two AIATSIS workshops. See LM Strelein & T Tran, *Native Title Representative Bodies and Prescribed Bodies Corporate: native title in a post determination environment*, Native Title Research Report Report, no. 2, Native Title Research Unit, AIATSIS, Canberra, 2007, http://www.aiatsis.gov.au/ntru/documents/PBCReport.pdf, accessed 27 June 2013; T Bauman & T Tran, *First National Prescribed Bodies Corporate meeting: issues and outcomes, Canberra 11–13 April 2007*, Native Title Research Report, no. 3, Native Title Research Unit, AIATSIS, Canberra, 2007, http://www.aiatsis.gov.au/ntru/docs/researchthemes/pbc/PBCMeeting2007.pdf, accessed 27 June 2013.

30 Philip Hunter of Ebsworth and Ebsworth Lawyers, Brisbane.

31 At the time of writing, the RNTBC had only spent money on one occasion, for an air charter to a funeral.

32 In the central east of the claim area, shown as Area 5 in the claim map. See Memmott & McDougall, above n 3, Fig. 15.

33 See, for example, M Moran, 'Practising self-determination: participation in planning and local governance in discrete Indigenous settlements', unpublished PhD thesis, University of Queensland, St Lucia, 2006, pp. 256–8, 277.

34 See Memmott & Blackwood, above n 3.

35 State of Queensland, Ngan Aak Kunch Aboriginal Corporation, Council of the Shire of Aurukun, Aluminium Corporation of China Limited, A Kerindun, J Chevathun & A Woolla, *Aurukun bauxite project (feasibility study) agreement*, Aurukun, 2007.

36 The Aboriginal system of customary land tenure in this region has shifted from a predominantly patrilineal clan estate system towards cognatic descent groups and the 'language-named tribe' as the primary social structural units by which people identify with country and around which their traditional ownership of land, including native title, is organised and conceptualised (see Chase et al., above n 21, pp. 35–9). Thus, for example, the native title claims in the region are known by the names of the language tribes involved.

37 Ibid., p. 37.

38 Aboriginal Land Tribunal Queensland, *Aboriginal Land Claim to Lakefield National Park*, report to the Hon. the Minister for Natural Resources, Aboriginal Land Tribunal, Brisbane, 1996; and Aboriginal Land Tribunal Queensland, *Aboriginal land claims to Mungkan Kandju National Park and unallocated state land near Lochinvar Pastoral Holding*, report to the Hon. the Minister for Natural Resources and Mines, Department of Natural Resources and Mines, Brisbane, 2001.

39 Ibid.

40 From Memmott & Blackwood, above n 3, p. 25.

41 Ibid., p. 26.

42 Discontinued native title claim QC99/022; Q6021/99.

43 Cape York Land Council, *Cape York Land Council Aboriginal Corporation Newsletter*, vol. 1, no. 1, Cape York Land Council, Cairns, 2006.

44 Smith 2002, above n 2.

45 A participatory RNTBC model allows membership of all adult native title holders, thereby maximising the level of individual participation; representative RNTBCs, on the other hand, aim to keep the membership to the minimum required for the RNTBC to function and to provide an acceptable level of representation of the wider native title group (for example, by having an agreed number of representatives from each clan or descent group within the native title group). Although CRAC is not an RNTBC, these same principles apply to its membership and executive structures respectively.

46 Office of the Registrar of Aboriginal and Torres Strait Islander Corporations (ORATSIC), 'Document results for the Coen Regional Aboriginal Corporation', ORATSIC, Canberra, 2007, http://www.oric.gov.au/document.aspx?concernID=101725, accessed 22 July 2013.

47 Australian taxation law allows a range of tax advantages to organisations with PBI status. These include exemptions and concessions in relation to income tax, goods and services tax, and fringe benefits tax relating to employees. To qualify, an organisation must have as its dominant purpose the provision of services to people requiring benevolent relief and it must be non-profit. For further information, see the Australian Tax Office website, http://www.ato.gov.au/nonprofit/, accessed 15 May 2013.

48 See BR Smith, 2003, above n 2, pp. 99–115.

49 For further details about CRAC's property investments see Memmott & Blackwood, above n 3.

50 There are certain outstations which FaHCSIA will not acknowledge as outstations because they are without recognised services such as access to education, roads, water, transport and health. Ibid.

51 Statement made at a community consultation about the structure of a Wik RNTBC held at Aurukun, 25 July 2001. See Memmott & McDougall, above n 3, p. 96.

52 Ibid., p. 110.

53 David Martin, pers. comm. with Paul Memmott, February 2002.

54 Memmott & McDougall, above n 3, p. 111.

55 For example, Memmott et al., above n 3, p. 289.

56 See Memmott & Blackwood, above n 3, p. 32.

57 From Memmott et al., above n 3, p. 288. Original graphics by Aboriginal Environments Research Centre, University of Queensland.
58 Ibid., p. 291.
59 Moran, above n 33, p. 277.
60 See AIATSIS, *Review of the* Aboriginal Councils and Associations Act 1976: *final report*, AIATSIS, Canberra, 1996; C Mantziaris & D Martin, *Native title corporations: a legal and anthropological analysis*, The Federation Press, Sydney, 2000, pp. 183–232; Memmott & McDougall, above n 3, pp. 14–15.
61 Smith 2002, above n 2.
62 For discussion of RNTBC design options see Memmott & McDougall, above n 3, ch. 6 and Memmott & Blackwood, above n 3.

Update: Cape York Registered Native Title Bodies Corporate 2013

Paul Memmott and Peter Blackwood

Since the preceding chapter was completed in early 2008, there have been developments in the two case study regions that are relevant to the arguments we presented. Some of these developments, such as the outcome of ongoing tenure resolution negotiations in the Coen region, have continued along a trajectory already underway five years ago; others, such as the withdrawal of the Aluminium Corporation of China Ltd (Chalco) project, reinforce the need for the type of regional model and diversification of the economic bases for Registered Native Title Bodies Corporate (RNTBCs) and land trusts that we have advocated.

The Commonwealth Department of Families, Housing, Community Services and Indigenous Affairs (FaHCSIA) continued to provide annual funding for RNTBCs on Cape York in accordance with the policies discussed in Chapter 7; there are now eight RNTBCs on Cape York, though none to date in the Coen region. In a significant evolution of its support policy, in 2008–09 FaHCSIA agreed to fund, as a pilot project, a position for an RNTBC support officer in Cape York Land Council (CYLC). The person who holds the position has legal qualifications and provides administrative assistance as well as support with compliance, governance, training and sourcing funding. The objective is to ensure RNTBCs have the capacity to manage, comply with relevant laws and regulations, and adequately service their native title holders. This person also manages a future act unit within the land council which alerts native title holders and RNTBCs to development notifications, and the land council continues to assist with future act negotiations.[1]

While our model would ideally see such a person located in each region, it is unlikely to be financially feasible, at least in the present state of development on Cape York. In relation to *Aboriginal Land Act 1991* (Qld) (ALA) land trusts, CYLC has a policy of recognising partnerships with these and other Aboriginal organisations on the Cape and, though not funded directly to do so, provides limited assistance to land trusts and other landholding entities, particularly to ensure their legal and regulatory compliance, such as assisting to run annual general meetings (AGMs) and conducting elections.

Land Tenure in the Wik/Aurukun region

In October 2012 there were further native title determinations of the Wik and Wik Way claims, notably over the Rio Tinto bauxite mining lease (green in Figure 7.2) and the remaining areas of the claim over several pastoral leases (blue in Figure 7.2).[2]

Operations of Wik RNTBC

These additional areas of determined land have been added to the native title holdings of the established Wik RNTBC, Ngan Aak Kunch. Since 2008 there have been no additional RNTBCs, land trusts or other incorporated landholding entities established in the Aurukun region.

Since 2008, CYLC's RNTBC support officer has worked directly with Ngan Aak Kunch to respond to its increasing level of future act activity, particularly negotiating mining exploration agreements and meeting its compliance obligations under the *Corporations (Aboriginal and Torres Strait Islander) Act 2006* (Cth) (CATSI Act) (which includes regular AGMs and financial returns). Ngan Aak Kunch has obtained an Australian Business Number (ABN), a charitable income tax exemption, basic office equipment (but no office space) and a bank account now with upwards of $100,000, and is due to receive further income from the Community Development Fund set up by the Queensland Government and Chalco. However, the RNTBC has not obtained any substantial capacity building in the form of governance training or additional human resources.

Chalco

The termination of Chalco's development agreement with the State of Queensland in 2010 had major significance for Ngan Aak Kunch's vision and prospects. Chalco had been holding a five-year mineral development licence, which it received in 2007, with a works scope of a bauxite mine; a nearby port on west Cape York; and an alumina refinery on the east coast near Bowen. However, by 2009–10 the international value of bauxite and alumina had dropped to the point where the scope of the original development proposal was no longer economically feasible. Chalco argued to the state that it could restore viability to the project by omitting the Bowen refinery from the proposal and taking the bauxite ore directly to China for processing, but the state would not accept this, partly on the grounds that it could be sued by the others who tendered for the project. Chalco then decided it could not deliver according to the original scope of the licence, so the state terminated the development agreement. Chalco had spent over $100 million but had only produced a series of environmental impact assessments and feasibility studies.

The Wik and Wik Way people were very disappointed by this commercial setback. Their lawyer assisted them in writing a letter to the state in the hope of the decision being reconsidered, arguing that all the potential benefits for Aboriginal people had been embedded in the mine and the nearby port development, but that there would never have been any economic benefits for them from the proposed refinery at Bowen. The appeal was in vain. Nevertheless, tenders were recalled to develop the mining lease during 2013.

Land tenure in Coen

Negotiations have continued under the Queensland Government–funded State Land Dealings project, whereby CYLC and Balkanu Cape York Development Corporation (Balkanu) have facilitated negotiations between native title holders and the state government in tenure resolution initiatives designed to provide secure land tenure for local Aboriginal groups, and the protection of high-value conservation areas by the state. These negotiations are informed by and conducted within the framework of broader settlement agreements whose objective is to balance and reconcile land interests in each region of the Cape. This includes involving regional pastoral and conservation interests in land tenure negotiations and looks beyond purely native title outcomes towards the long-term economic and social aspirations of traditional owners.

In the Coen region this process has resulted in significantly more land being transferred to traditional owners as Aboriginal freehold under the ALA, and the creation of two new Aboriginal-owned and jointly managed national parks. Three additional land trusts have been created to hold these recently transferred lands, and two native title claims (Kaanju Umpila QC 95/14 and Kaanju/Umpila/Lamalama/Ayapathu QC 97/7) that were previously lodged over them have been discontinued.[3]

There is currently a single native title claim in the region (Ayapathu/Olkola QC 03/12), and no Prescribed Bodies Corporate (PBCs) have yet been registered.

Coen regional management

In late 2008 the Coen Regional Aboriginal Corporation (CRAC) went into administration and since then there has been a dramatic contraction in the services it has been able to provide to outstations and land trusts. It was forced to sell off assets to repay debt, including land and buildings in Coen, and its enterprise arm, Coen Business Enterprises (CBE), though itself a viable company, was also forced to close its doors.

Outstations and land trust organisations now deal directly with funding bodies and government agencies, such as the Queensland Department of Environment and Resource Management,[4] Commonwealth Department of Transport and Regional Services (DOTARs),[5] Indigenous Land Corporation (ILC)[6] and the Commonwealth Caring for our Country program,[7] as well as non-government organisations. Several programs put in place by CRAC, such as Bushlight,[8] have continued, and the

Cairns-based Balkanu provides development assistance. CRAC no longer employs work teams and the plant and equipment used to service outstations and the Coen township have either been sold or now mostly stand idle.

CRAC continues to exist as an organisation and the need for the sort of regional management it once provided remains. Its problems have been ones of internal management, not of structure or function. While to some extent its functions are being filled by Balkanu and various government departments, management at a regional level is now more atomised than it was four years ago, with more reliance on the skills and capacities of key leaders for each group. A consequence of this is a growing disparity in the level of development among the groups trying to establish themselves on their land; while some have thrived and have attracted significant funding, others are struggling without the local regional support once provided by CRAC, and run a greater risk of dysfunction and failure.

Endnotes

1 For a more detailed account of these developments as well as the progress of native title claims and land tenure developments in the two regions refer to the Cape York Land Council's annual reports for 2008–09 and 2009–10, http://www.cylc.org.au/index.php/resources/annual-reports/, accessed 15 May 2013.
2 *Wik and Wik Way Native Title Claim Group v State of Queensland* [2012] FCA 1096.
3 Details of these developments are:
   - Parts of the former Mt Croll pastoral lease east of Coen and the areas of the two withdrawn native title claims (pink and unhatched grey in Figure 7.3 in the preceding chapter) have become the Kulla McIlwraith National Park, owned and jointly managed by the existing Kulla Land Trust. See Department of National Parks, Recreation, Sport and Racing website, http://www.nprsr.qld.gov.au/parks/kulla-mcilwraith-range/, accessed 15 May 2013.
   - Lama Lama National Park has been created over part of the former Lilyvale pastoral lease, owned and jointly managed by a new Lama Lama Land Trust. See Department of National Parks, Recreation, Sport and Racing website, http://www.nprsr.qld.gov.au/parks/lama-lama/, accessed 15 May 2013. Another new land trust, Toolka, has been established for the Kaanju and Ayapathu people to hold other areas of recently transferred land at Mt Croll and Lilyvale. See map at Department of National Parks, Recreation, Sport and Racing website, http://www.nrm.qld.gov.au/nativetitle/land/pdfs/land_trusts_map.pdf, accessed 25 June 2013.
4 Following the 2012 Queensland state election, the department's functions were split among the departments of: Environment and Heritage Protection; National Parks, Recreation, Sport and Racing; Natural Resources and Mines; Energy and Water Supply; and Science, Information Technology, Innovation and the Arts. http://www.derm.qld.gov.au/, accessed 22 July 2013.
5 Now the Department of Infrastructure and Regional Development, http://www.infrastructure.gov.au/, accessed 4 November 2013.
6 See Indigenous Land Corporation, http://www.ilc.gov.au/, accessed 20 June 2013.
7 See Commonwealth Government's Biodiversity Conservation Division website, 'Caring for our Country 2008–13', http://www.nrm.gov.au/about/caring/index.html, accessed 15 May 2013.
8 See Centre for Appropriate Technology (CAT), 'Welcome to Bushlight', http://www.bushlight.org.au/, accessed 15 May 2013.

Chapter 8

Working with Indigenous and western corporate structures — the Central Arrernte case

Manuhuia Barcham

Introduction

Registered Native Title Bodies Corporate (RNTBCs) provide an opportunity for two laws — Australian and Aboriginal — to come together in what has elsewhere been referred to as the 'recognition space'.[1] In doing this, RNTBCs offer a space of interaction which, while created to satisfy the requirements of Australian law, provides an opportunity for Aboriginal law to be recognised by external stakeholders. RNTBCs also provide a space for the creation of new resources and meanings that may help Aboriginal groups more effectively undertake their roles in maintaining their own laws. These can even take the form of basic features, like providing increased support to cultural and language programs or improved and more appropriate health and education services for their communities. Although the recognition space is most often represented as the point of intersection of distinct Aboriginal and western laws, the reality is that the two are not so distinct and there is much interpenetration outside this space. Nevertheless, the recognition space can be a useful tool for analysis.

In exploring these issues, this chapter looks at the experiences of the three Central Arrernte[2] groups, Mparntwe, Irlpme and Antulye, which collectively hold native title in the Alice Springs region, as I observed them between 2007 and 2010.[3] The chapter opens with a discussion of the creation of the Lhere Artepe Aboriginal Corporation RNTBC for the three groups in the wake of the positive determination of their native title claim under the *Native Title Act 1993* (Cth) (NTA) in 1999[4] (see Figure 8.1), and the need for the RNTBC to be seen as legitimate by both the members of these groups and stakeholders, such as developers, local government and other Aboriginal people in the region. The next section looks at how the RNTBC, and related corporate bodies, may assist the three groups in their functions as custodians of the

Living with native title

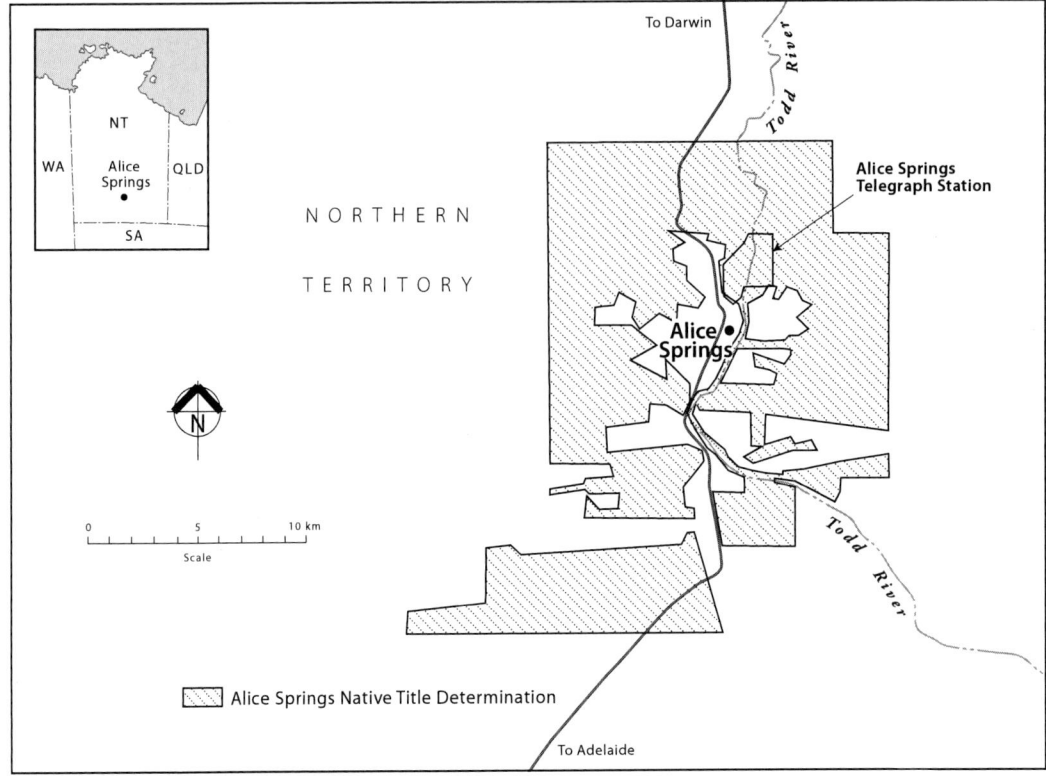

Figure 8.1 Alice Springs native title determination. Map by Brenda Thornley for AIATSIS

Altyerre (dreaming) in the Alice Springs region. I then consider how the RNTBC in pursuing economic development as an additional opportunity bolsters the ability of the three estate groups to fulfil their roles as custodians of the *Altyerre*. The chapter concludes with a brief discussion of some points of contention at the time of writing in 2010 that were confronting the RNTBC and related organisations as they worked to maintain the delicate balance between their 'internal' and 'external' legitimacy.

Gaining native title and establishing the Lhere Artepe RNTBC

The native title determination by the Federal Court in 1999 was the first determination over an urban area.[5] It ruled that three Central Arrernte estate groups — Mparntwe, Irlpme and Antulye — possess native title over Alice Springs and surrounds. In the ruling Justice Olney argued that:

> The persons who hold the common or group rights comprising the native title (the common law holders) are those Aboriginals who are descended from the original Arrernte inhabitants of the Mparntwe, Antulye and Irlpme estates who are recognised by the respective apmereke-artweye[6] and kwertengerle[7] of those

estates under the traditional laws acknowledged and the traditional customs observed by them as having communal, group or individual rights and interests in relation to such estates.[8]

Following the determination, the groups were required to establish an RNTBC to hold and manage the native title rights of the three estate groups and to register the body with the National Native Title Tribunal (NNTT). The Central Land Council (CLC), which had been acting as the Native Title Representative Body (NTRB) for the Lhere Artepe during the claim, called meetings for each of the groups to consider how the RNTBC was to be governed. It was decided that the three estate groups would each elect 10 members who would sit on the executive of the RNTBC. The 10 members would then each select a deputy chair from among their own numbers. The 30 members of the executive would choose one individual from the three deputy chairs to act as chairperson for the RNTBC. The elections would occur at the annual general meeting (AGM) and were in place at the time of writing in 2010–11. It was also decided that each of the three estate groups would be separately incorporated. It should be noted that the overall structure through which the RNTBC and the three estate groups interact with one another and the external community has changed under successive administrations as new functions have been added.

The name chosen for the RNTBC was Lhere Artepe. *Lhere Artepe* can be glossed in Central Arrernte as *alhere* = river or creek, and *artepe* = backbone. The name was chosen because the Todd River, which flows through the town of Alice Springs, also flows through and links all three estates. The RNTBC and the corporations representing the three estate groups (Mparntwe, Antulye and Irlpme Aboriginal corporations) were incorporated under the *Aboriginal Councils and Associations Act 1976* (ACA Act), and are now incorporated under its successor, the *Corporations (Aboriginal and Torres Strait Islander) Act 2006* (the CATSI Act).

Legitimising the RNTBC

In considering the creation of the RNTBC and its legitimacy, there is a need to address not only the western legal imperatives required under the NTA to create a corporate body in which native title rights can be vested; the various social and cultural imperatives motivating the native title holders as members of the RNTBC also need to be considered. This includes their different cultural roles as *apmereke-artweye* (glossed here as those linked patrilineally to an estate) and *kwertengerle* (glossed here as descendants of the women in the patriline) of the lands covered by the native title determination.

In one respect, then, I am referring to the issue of 'cultural match' as popularised by those who have worked in the Harvard Project on American Indian Economic Development (the Harvard Project) and further discussed in the Australian Indigenous

Community Governance Project.⁹ One of the underlying messages of the Harvard Project's work is that sovereignty matters. That is, the ability of an Indigenous group to successfully achieve economic development appears, from the empirical data, to be directly related to the ability of that group to exercise a degree of sovereignty over their own affairs. Cultural match, as one example of this exercise of sovereignty, is important in that it makes sure that the modern institutions and organisations Indigenous groups use to govern themselves and their interactions with external stakeholders are also based in their own cultural practices to ensure cultural legitimacy within the Indigenous community. In some respects, then, the current native title regime in Australia could be seen as being in opposition to the issue of cultural sovereignty, as the corporate structures Indigenous groups need to take on in the wake of a positive native title determination are strongly determined by the Australian Government in corporations legislation, such as the CATSI Act.

However, looking at the issue of cultural match through a slightly different lens, and putting to one side the fact that these structures are imposed by an external power, modern Indigenous groups by necessity must use hybrid structures which integrate western corporate requirements with their own cultural priorities in their interactions with both their members and external stakeholders. This is because the environment in which contemporary Indigenous groups and individuals operate is very different from where their cultural practices and modes of organisation have emerged.

This is not to say that the traditional practices and modes of organisation of modern Indigenous groups are necessarily no longer legitimate or effective. Rather, it is to make the claim that just as the environment in which Indigenous groups operate has changed, so too may the way in which members of the groups engage with each other and with members of other Indigenous groups, as well as with external stakeholders. The challenge for the RNTBC lies in maintaining a group's unique cultural and collective identity and the individual identities of its members and at the same time interacting effectively with external stakeholders, often through externally imposed organisational structures and processes.

In addressing these issues we need to look at the meanings of the terms *apmereke-artweye* and *kwertengerle* as they apply to the cultural machinations of the estate groups and which were central to the ruling of Olney J in the native title claim. To understand how the RNTBC may facilitate its effective performance, while at the same time providing a source of legitimacy for external stakeholders and resources, we also need to look at the roles associated with these terms and who has responsibility for them.

Apmereke-artweye, kwertengerle *and the* Altyerre

In the *Altyerre* (dreaming) of the region, the country in and around Alice Springs is a collection of ancestral bodies. As discussed above, the Todd River is the spinal column running north–south through Alice Springs, linking the three estates.[10] A number of stories overlay this, an important one being the *altyerre ayepe-arenye*. *Arenye* is a type of caterpillar that lives on the tar vine, which is one of the principal *Altyerre* of the Alice Springs region, crossing the region and leaving different parts of its body in the landscape. Depending on how balanced the country and people are, the *ayepe-arenye* has the effect of bringing either wellbeing or sickness to the country. The *apmereke-artweye* and *kwertengerle* from the three estate groups are said to work to maintain this balance and to keep the land and those who live on it healthy.

The word *apmereke-artweye* is taken from base words *apmere* (place) and *artweye* (ownership/belonging/relationship).[11] Thus, *apmereke-artweye* (as noted, usually estate owners in the patriline) are the holders of a particular estate or defined geographic area and have certain responsibilities for caring for that land. While *apmereke-artweye* can be identified as the owners of an estate, they care for the land in partnership with the *kwertengerle* (usually estate custodians who are the children of the women in the patriline, but see below). The *kwertengerle's* role includes taking the lead in discussions about certain estates and ensuring that *apmereke-artweye* look after an estate according to the dictates of the *Altyerre*.

For Arrernte, the strongest connections to estates are through patrilineal descent, particularly through the father's father's line. *Apmereke-artweye* links to particular estates are thus drawn through continuous patrilineal descent, whereas *kwertengerle* are generally descended from women who are patrilineally linked to a specific estate. In practice this means that *apmereke-artweye* have a notional degree of seniority over *kwertengerle* in the management of estates, although proper maintenance of *Altyerre* depends on the partnership between the roles. The importance of patrilineal descent also plays out in individual relationships and in the relationships of individuals to particular estates. An individual can simultaneously be *apmereke-artweye* to one estate and *kwertengerle* to another. This means that while *apmereke-artweye* have strong ties to the estate of their *arrenge* (father's father), they may also have *kwertengerle* roles and responsibilities for estates related to them through their *atyemeye* (mother's father). Others may be affiliated to various estates via their *aperle* (father's mother) and/or *ipmenhe* (mother's mother), some of whom may also be *kwertengerle*.

While various connections to particular estates may be held simultaneously, this does not necessarily mean that each role is held with the same level of commitment. Generally, one's strongest relationship is to the estate of one's father's father, next to the estate of one's mother's father, then one's mother's mother and father's mother. However, these relationships can vary, depending on factors such as the estate where an individual resides, his or her degree of knowledge of the country in various estates, the level of individual seniority within a family, and the nature of roles that may have been attributed through participation in various rituals. Roles and membership of estate groups do not necessarily depend on biological descent from particular ancestors. In Arrernte law, children whose fathers were not Arrernte, but whose mothers subsequently married Arrernte men, may be adopted by these

Arrernte men and given the same rights and responsibilities as the natural-born children of Arrernte men.[12]

Two laws and the role of the RNTBC

In looking at the roles of members of the three estate groups as *apmereke-artweye* and *kwertengerle*, we need to consider two meanings of the term *Altyerre*, which is often translated as 'dreaming' but which also means 'law'. In this respect, the *Altyerre* is a system of rules and regulations by which people define their rights and interests. The *Altyerre* and the common law are thus conceptually similar,[13] but nevertheless unequal. In addressing this issue we can usefully draw on Diane Austin-Broos's discussion of Western Arrernte's engagement with Christianity and early mission encounters at Hermannsburg or Ntaria. She uses the motif of 'two laws' to explore the way in which Arrernte accounts 'look for an exchange of laws or knowledge… that suggests a continuous world between the Aranda and Europeans'.[14] She contrasts the Arrernte understanding of these two laws as 'equal' to the Lutheran view of 'two laws' which stood 'in a hierarchical fashion'.[15] This hierarchical understanding of 'two laws' is mirrored in the modern understanding in the Australian legal system of the relationship between the common law and the law(s) of various Aboriginal and Torres Strait Islander groups, including the *Altyerre* of the Central Arrernte.

This concept of 'two laws' provides an interesting conceptual apparatus to explore the issue raised above of the need for Indigenous groups to maintain a degree of cultural legitimacy in their modes of governing themselves. This is necessary in order, at the very least, for them to maintain the cultural integrity of who they are as a group of first peoples, and as individuals, while simultaneously engaging with external stakeholders, such as governments and developers, who operate under a different set of laws. The issue, as noted by Austin-Broos, is that unfortunately those who operate under Australian law generally tend to see their law as superior to other law(s) in Australia, including to the *Altyerre*, rather than seeing them as different laws which deserve respect as equal yet different ways of viewing one's role and place in the world.[16]

In an earlier discussion of the Western Arrernte, Austin-Broos argued that 'the Aranda negotiation of two laws comes in the face of a European power that will not allow the assimilation of its knowledge to Arandic conditions'.[17] In one respect the recognition of the three estate groups as holding continuing native title over large areas of what is now known as Alice Springs, and the creation of the RNTBC as a corporate body in which those rights are vested, provides an opportunity of bringing together these two laws to provide a more effective way to engage with both traditions. Thus, the RNTBC may facilitate *apmereke-artweye* and *kwertengerle* maintenance of the *Altyerre* with all that entails, not only in relation to the land and the three estate groups, but also for the benefit of those individuals who now reside on this land and who are not members of these three estate groups. This includes both Aboriginal and non-Aboriginal people.

In arguing this, however, the recognition by Olney J that the three estate groups are *apmereke-artweye* and *kwertengerle* of the Alice Springs region does not imply that the resulting RNTBC is the key body for the maintenance of the *Altyerre* in this region. Nonetheless, this new corporate body and the fulfilment of these functions may be usefully intertwined. In some ways the new RNTBC represents external recognition of the roles played by the three estate groups in the maintenance of the *Altyerre*. So, too, the creation of the RNTBC can be seen as providing an opportunity for increased resources to be mobilised to assist these groups to fulfil their roles as *apmereke-artweye* and *kwertengerle* more effectively.

One immediate way in which the RNTBC may help improve the ability of the members of the three estate groups to fulfil their roles as *apmereke-artweye* and *kwertengerle* is to provide a point of organisational engagement with the Alice Springs Town Council, the Territory and Commonwealth governments and other external stakeholders, including Aboriginal organisations such as the CLC and Tangentyere Council. While the members of the three estate groups would argue that they have always performed the roles of *apmereke-artweye* and *kwertengerle*, and while this was affirmed by the Federal Court in its native title determination, the inflow to Alice Springs of large numbers of Aboriginal and non-Aboriginal people who do not belong to the three estate groups has seriously challenged their ability to do so. The reality is that the capacity of the three groups to effect change within Alice Springs over the years has been marginal. A notorious example of this was the construction of Barrett Drive in 1983, prior to the NTA, and which is discussed in the next section.[18]

Broken Promise Drive

The Mparntwe group holds the *Altyerre* in which the *ayepe-arenye* (tar vine caterpillars), after leaving their home at Anthwerrke (Emily Gap), swarmed along the eastern side of the Todd River. One of the important *Altyerre* sites created by the movement of the *ayepe-arenye* was Ntyarlkarle Tyaneme, a small ridge running east–west on the eastern side of the Todd River. The ridge signified the point where the *ayepe-arenye* crossed the river to the western side.

In 1983 the Northern Territory Government began constructing a road on the eastern side of the river to facilitate access to the new casino. Ntyarlkarle Tyaneme was identified as standing in the planned path for the new road. As the site was registered under the *Aboriginal Sacred Sites Amendment Act 1983* (NT), a negotiated agreement would be necessary to resolve this apparent impasse. A number of options were suggested, including a slight deviation in the road and building up both sides of the ridge so that the road could pass over the site without disturbing it. The government agreed to halt construction while the Mparntwe considered these options.

However, at Christmas time in 1983 and before a negotiated decision could be reached, a Mparntwe person walking near Ntyarlkarle Tyaneme where vehicle access to the site was blocked as part of the construction process saw that the tail of the caterpillar was missing. The government, tired of the delays in constructing the road, had taken advantage of the relative quiet of the holiday period and dynamited and bulldozed the site. While charges were laid against the Minister for Lands and others responsible under the *Aboriginal Sacred Sites Amendment Act 1983* (NT), they were dropped when it was found that the legislation was not binding on the Crown.[19] Despite the government's acknowledged acceptance of members of the Mparntwe group as custodians of Ntyarlkarle Tyaneme, their rights and interests were eventually ignored in the interests of the 'development' of Alice Springs.

In situations such as 'Broken Promise Drive', as Barrett Drive is colloquially named by the Central Arrernte, the RNTBC, established as a legitimate corporation within the Australian legal system, may provide increased leverage and support for the three estate groups in pursuing their native title rights and interests.

Protocols for visiting Alice Springs

The need to moderate the disruptive behaviour of Aboriginal visitors to Alice Springs who are not members of the three estate groups is an example of an issue where the RNTBC could provide leverage for the groups' cultural priorities. The debate about this issue while I was in Alice Springs highlighted the role of the RNTBC as representative of native title holders of the town.

Members of the RNTBC noted that in the past, Aboriginal people from elsewhere would occasionally pass through what is now Alice Springs for ceremony or to visit family, but only with the acceptance of local Central Arrernte owners and custodians. They said that visitors could expect violent repercussions from the custodians if they did not observe certain levels of decorum. They also noted that the Central Arrernte language has three ways of describing the types of relationships that characterise visiting arrangements, or in Aboriginal English 'keeping company', which also apply to how members of the three estate groups should engage and live with each other. The relationships are:

- *irlkwatherre* — to keep someone's company in a formal way observing protocols
- *yatyarre* — informal keeping company for a short time, to visit for an afternoon or a day trip
- *tantye* — keeping someone company while they do something, very informal and relaxed.[20]

Each of the three types of 'keeping company' is accompanied by specific principles and actions which define how the interactions should occur. However, in the wake of colonisation and the growth of the Alice Springs town, including the influx of Aboriginal and non-Aboriginal residents, the protocols associated with the three types of relationships no longer held force. The estate groups did not have the power to effectively police or enforce them, or, to put it another way, they no longer held sovereignty over the region.

Under the auspices of the RNTBC, its Lhere Artepe members, as the owners and custodians of Alice Springs, began to be more vocal about the need for those coming from elsewhere to respect the norms and values of Central Arrernte, especially in relation to *irlkwatherre*, *yatyarre* and *tantye*. Working with both the federal and state governments, at the time of field work the RNTBC was developing protocols to address 'anti-cultural' behaviour in the Alice Springs region, based on these three forms of relationships. It was hoped that these protocols would help reduce antisocial behaviour in the town, including 'humbugging' (which in the town environment can be glossed as 'begging') and disrespectful behaviour around a number of sacred sites. However, the issue of enforcement of the protocols remained uncertain, and was yet to be addressed by the RNTBC. Nevertheless, the legitimacy of the RNTBC as an organisation to be taken seriously in the town provided a focal point where the antisocial behaviour could be discussed and where actions to address it might begin to be formulated.

Economic development and revised corporate structures

The RNTBC also legitimated the interests of the three estate groups it represented in the eyes of external developers, because it provided the groups with increased economic leverage and the developers with a formal partner with whom they could negotiate.

One of the key issues confronting native title holders is how they can convert their native title rights into a resource base for development. Associated with this is a high degree of mistrust in the broader business community regarding the reliability and dependability of native title corporations. This mistrust prevails despite the overarching CATSI Act which strictly regulates RNTBCs, and despite the fact that some of the Central Arrente with whom I spoke during field work identified the CATSI Act as paternalistic and as providing opportunities for the Australian Government, through the Office of the Registrar of Indigenous Corporations (ORIC), to impose particularly onerous reporting constraints and compliance costs. In turn, this has the potential to negatively impact an Aboriginal corporation's ability to engage with private enterprise in the pursuit of entrepreneurial activity, particularly as private enterprise might be concerned about business-in-confidence being revealed to ORIC.

As with some other Aboriginal and Torres Strait Islander groups and indigenous groups in other parts of the globe, the Central Arrernte tend to mistrust corporations and their structures generally. Related to this is the way in which corporations can be captured by individuals or family groups as vehicles for their own interests as opposed to the interests of the members of the corporation as a whole. Some members of the three Alice Springs estate groups were also concerned about the mechanisms for dealing with decision-making in what they saw as an introduced structure, foreign to their ways and needs.

Nonetheless, native title rights will continue to be held by RNTBCs, and one of the key issues facing Indigenous groups is the need for corporate governance structures where private companies and governments feel they can safely invest resources and do deals but which also satisfy members that decision-making processes are legitimate, transparent and representative of their cultural interests.

The RNTBC brought together the three estate groups under a single corporate structure. As noted above, given the distinctive make-up of the three groups, three additional corporate structures were established to provide a mechanism to give each of the estate groups a voice in the operation of the RNTBC. The question remained, however, as to how these groups could satisfy their internal constituents, in their roles as *apmereke-artweye* and *kwertengerle* of the *Altyerre* of the Alice Springs region, as well as satisfying potential joint investment partners of their capacity to engage in entrepreneurial activity.

In 2008 a new corporate structure was agreed (see Figure 8.2). The three estate groups continued as distinct corporate bodies under the CATSI Act, providing a mechanism for decisions made by each of the groups to be fed into decision-making processes at the RNTBC level. Decisions by the three estate groups about native title matters were relayed to the RNTBC through the groups' representatives who sat on the RNTBC executive committee. This was seen to ensure that the RNTBC would

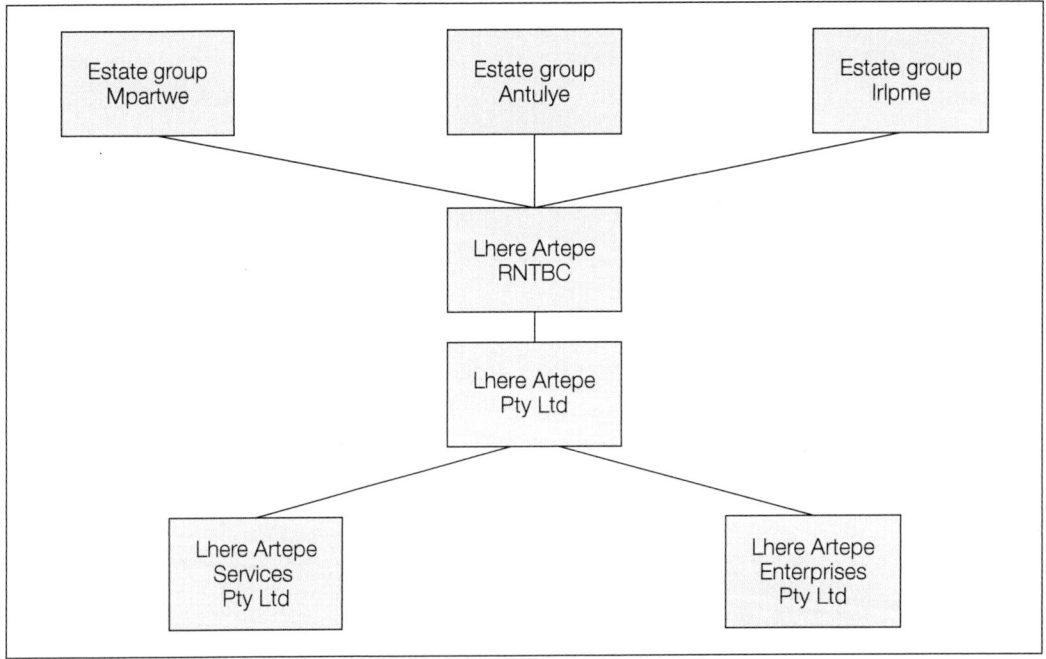

Figure 8.2 Lhere Artepe corporate structures, 2008

have to take the concerns of the *apmereke-artweye* and the *kwertengerle* seriously in its actions, for example, in pursuing economic development opportunities.

In addition to the four corporations set up under the CATSI Act (the RNTBC and the three separate estate corporations), three other corporate structures were established under the *Corporations Act 2001* (Cth) (Corporations Act), which is not subject to ORIC control. One of these was to operate as the key investment body for the three estate groups (Lhere Artepe Enterprises Pty Ltd) and the second was to be the main social services provider for the group (Lhere Artepe Services Pty Ltd). The third (Lhere Artepe Pty Ltd) was designed to act as the peak governing body for the two corporations above, with part of the executive from the native title holding body sitting on its board in addition to independent non-member directors.

This new structure was designed to quarantine risk associated with the corporations established under the CATSI Act from the operations of those incorporated under the Corporations Act. The rationale for this was that the potential power of ORIC, alluded to above, to access records of private business concerns engaging with the RNTBC could be detrimental to the operations of the corporate structures established to promote the group's economic and social interests. Private business entities may not want their operations made public. While this can sometimes be interpreted as evidence of corrupt activity and a lack of transparency, in maintaining a market edge there is often a need for confidentiality in business deals. The quarantining of risk also works in reverse, ensuring that bad business decisions made through the corporations under the Corporations Act do not cause the collapse of the RNTBC and the associated estate corporations.

The new corporations under the Corporations Act were thus able to satisfy the interests of a range of stakeholders, both external and internal to the three estate groups. Without becoming overly complicated, these interconnected corporate structures provided a way for the three estate groups to engage with external stakeholders through recognisably robust 'mainstream' corporate structures. At the same time, they ensured that their internal constituency was convinced of the legitimacy of any decisions, since they were informed by the decision-making processes of the three estate groups in the operations of their own corporations.

Under these new corporate structures, Lhere Artepe has operated a number of commercial deals including the Mount John property development ($20 million) and the Sterling Heights property development ($2 million). At the time of writing, it was also administering a number of other Indigenous Land Use Agreements (ILUAs) and a land release agreement. These include, though not necessarily in chronological order, the Simpson's Gap National Park Extension ILUA, the Emily and Jessie Gaps Nature Park ILUA, the Heavitree Range Extension ILUA, and Kuyunba Conservation Reserve 1 ILUA. The fifth ILUA, the Larapinta ILUA of 2004 between Lhere Artepe and the Northern Territory Government, was the first in Australia to release land in an urban area for residential development. Another

ILUA was made between the CLC, the Northern Territory of Australia and Lhere Artepe to clarify the future title and management of the Alice Springs Telegraph Station Historical Reserve.

Ongoing corporate change

The concerns of members of the RNTBC about the relationship of the RNTBC to the other corporations, particularly about the role of the RNTBC in native title specific issues, led to the redesign of the structure in 2010. There was now a more direct link between the three estate groups and the structures incorporated under the Corporations Act and it would ensure that the RNTBC could remain focused on native title issues.

Under the new structure Lhere Artepe Pty Ltd, Lhere Artepe's key corporation, was owned by discretionary trusts. These trusts were established for each of the three estate groups in 2005 for the first distribution of funds by the RNTBC but were not directly linked to the membership. The three estate groups also link to form the executive council of 30, the key governance mechanism for the RNTBC discussed above, but the RNTBC is no longer directly connected to Lhere Artepe Pty Ltd (see Figure 8.3).

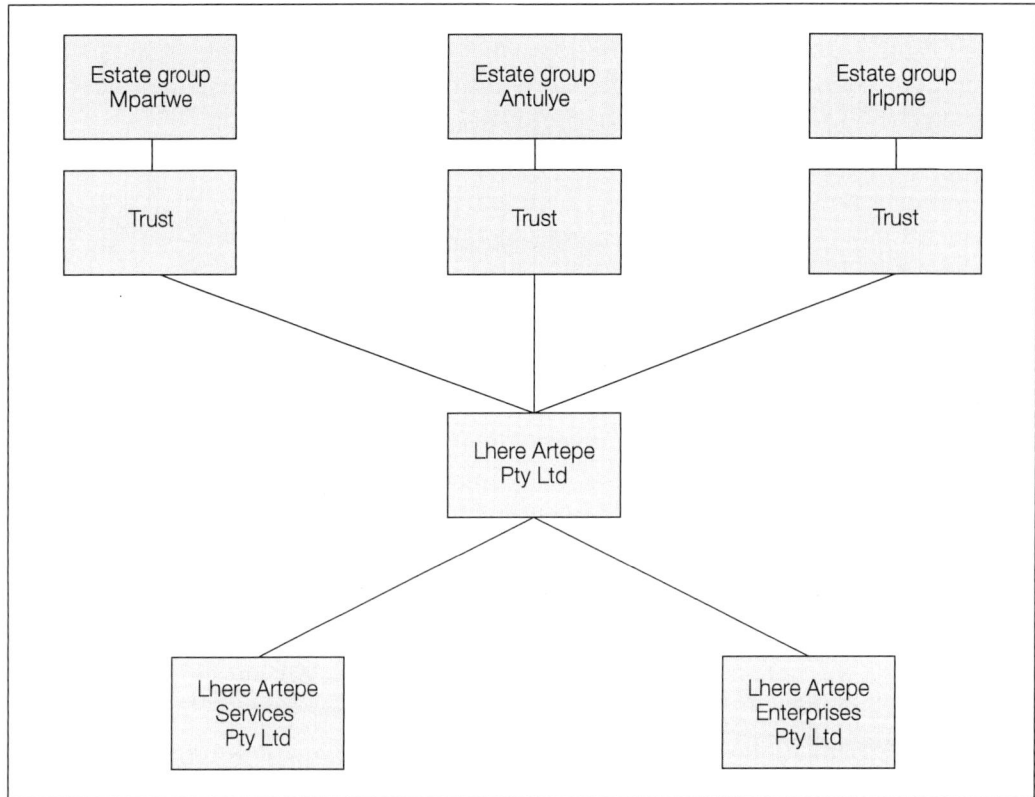

Figure 8.3 Lhere Artepe corporate structures, 2010

Lhere Artepe Enterprises Pty Ltd and Lhere Artepe Services Pty Ltd are owned by Lhere Artepe Pty Ltd. The directors for Lhere Artepe Pty Ltd are drawn from the three estate groups, four from each group, but there is no direct link between this group and the executive council. The directors of the investment body (Lhere Artepe Enterprises Pty Ltd) and service delivery body (Lhere Artepe Services Pty Ltd) are independently sourced but also include some native title holders as well as individuals with specific expertise, such as legal and financial expertise, relevant to the activities of the corporations they oversee.

Lhere Artepe Enterprises Pty Ltd profits will be distributed to the organisations within the network through the following breakdown:

- 50 per cent to remain with Lhere Artepe Enterprises Pty Ltd
- 10 per cent to the Mparntwe estate group's corporate structure
- 10 per cent to the Irlpme estate group's corporate structure
- 10 per cent to the Antulye estate group's corporate structure
- 10 per cent to the RNTBC
- 10 per cent to Lhere Artepe Services Pty Ltd.

These arrangements were to ensure that distribution of profits to the Lhere Artepe members involves investment in their community rather than them receiving 'cash along the finger', although the three estate groups are able to distribute the funds in the manner they feel most appropriate for their members. They avoided distribution direct to members because of the negative experience of Native American and Canadian groups on reserves receiving per capita payments which did not contribute to the development of the community as a whole, and which in some communities had led to a decline in wellbeing.[21] Lhere Artepe had also learned some hard lessons from an RNTBC commercial enterprise in 2005 concerning Stirling Heights and related per capita payments (see below). They did not want to repeat their mistakes.

New economic opportunities

Under this new structure (in Figure 8.3), the three estate groups, through Lhere Artepe Enterprises Pty Ltd, have undertaken their largest initiative to date, the Mount John development. Lhere Artepe Enterprises Pty Ltd took a new approach in pursuing the Mount John opportunity as a commercial venture.

In 2005, as part of a broader settlement package, the Northern Territory Government arranged the return and sale of a parcel of land at Stirling Heights in Alice Springs to the Lhere Artepe RNTBC. The three estate groups agreed to extinguish native title in the area in return for some of the land in a fee simple form of title. This package was brought to the table by the government because Alice Springs was growing at a rapid rate and there was an ongoing housing shortage. As part of the package, half the land was to be given to Lhere Artepe Aboriginal Corporation

(RNTBC) and the other half was to be sold by the government. At that point, the Lhere Artepe RNTBC agreed also to sell their half of the land and to receive a monetary compensation package. The money from the sale of this land was then distributed across the estate groups. Neither the RNTBC nor the corporations held by the three estate groups retained any of the capital for investment. As a result, the long-term impact of these monies in the community has been negligible, although it did fund consumer items for community members, such as cars and alcohol.

When a similar opportunity presented itself to the three estate groups in 2008–09, the groups chose a different path. As with the Stirling Heights deal, the parcel of land at Mount John was to be split, with half going to Lhere Artepe Aboriginal Corporation (RNTBC) and the other half to be sold by the Northern Territory Government in return for the native title holders agreeing to extinguish native title. However, rather than immediately on-selling the land, the Lhere Artepe RNTBC negotiated a number of different deals.

As a first step, they asked for first right of refusal on the land owned by the government. They then established a business plan for the development of the land they were to receive and which would then be sold as individual parcels of developed land. They took the plan to their bank, which agreed to provide a multi-million dollar line of credit for the development, with the land as security. At the time of writing all the sites had been pre-sold and the development was scheduled to begin in late 2010. The monies from this transaction were then to be used to purchase the land owned by the government as well as to provide seed capital for Lhere Artepe Enterprises Pty Ltd. Some funds would be directed to Lhere Artepe Services Pty Ltd for work within the community.

The explicit aim of this new approach in Mount John in contrast to what happened with the Stirling Heights development was voiced at a directors' meeting of the three estate groups in 2010. That is, this time 'money won't go into cars, grog and the casino'. Instead, the monies were to be used to provide long-term development opportunities for the community, in areas such as education, health and language, and in assisting the estate groups to effectively undertake their roles as *apmereke-artweye* and *kwertengerle* for the *Altyerre* in the Alice Springs region.

Overcoming concerns

The land dealings and changes to the corporate structure that have occurred have not been achieved without some conflict within the community over the direction the RNTBC and related corporations are taking. At the time of writing there are two key issues that directly impact the ongoing success of the RNTBC. The first relates to membership and who the members of each of the three estate groups are; and the second relates to the use of native title and its extinguishment for commercial purposes.

Firstly, the issue of membership is complicated by the fact that the list of native title holders in the native title determination does not necessarily include all those individuals and families who have connections to the lands covered by the decision.[22] Secondly, at the time of writing, the membership rolls and genealogies of the three estate groups used by the CLC during the prosecution of the native title case had not been made available to the RNTBC.[23] This meant that the three estate groups had to return to their members and compile new membership rolls, which is a time- and resource-intensive exercise.

Establishing genealogies and membership qualifications are the sites of much contestation, especially as the possibility of large amounts of money begin to become more real for the estate groups. Unfortunately, disagreements focused around attempts by individuals and families to exclude other families and individuals from estate group membership. In some cases, the disputes were public and heated. One particularly troublesome issue was the exclusion of those who claimed affiliation by adoption, although as noted earlier, Arrernte ways of being would usually not distinguish between adopted and natural-born children in the assumption of the roles of *apmereke-artweye* and *kwertengerle*.

The second point of contention faced by the RNTBC and the three estate groups was the extinguishment of native title on areas where the estate groups had been awarded native title. This alienation of land through extinguishment was a key factor in the economic development strategy being pursued by the RNTBC in locating start-up capital for Lhere Artepe Enterprises Pty Ltd. However, for some members of the estate groups, the hard battle they fought for the recognition of native title and the eventual positive determination meant that they would not agree lightly to the extinguishment of native title. Others argued that they were and always would be the *apmereke-artweye* and *kwertengerle* of the *Altyerre* in the Alice Springs region regardless of any Australian court ruling concerning native title, including changes in the legal status of the land to enable resources for community development.[24]

At the time of writing, these tensions were not derailing the development of the RNTBC and related corporate structures, but they were creating a dynamic and pressure that needed to be managed to ensure that the corporations continued to be seen as being representative of the interests of the three estate groups. While this may not necessarily mean that all members of the groups have to agree with all the actions of the RNTBC and the other corporations, there is a need for a critical level of agreement that all the corporations owned by Lhere Artepe Aboriginal Corporation (RNTBC) represent the groups' interests as a whole. To date, the various corporations owned by the Lhere Artepe Aboriginal Corporation (RNTBC) have managed to maintain this representative legitimacy with their own members — including a degree of internal cultural legitimacy — as well as with external stakeholders. Lhere Artepe's ongoing success in these issues will depend on maintaining this balance in the wake of a changing environment.

Conclusion

The members of the three Central Arrernte estate groups, Mparntwe, Irlpme and Antulye, are *apmereke-artweye* and *kwertengerle* for the *Altyerre* in the Alice Springs region and see themselves as such since time immemorial. However, the successful native title determination in 1999 provided the three groups with an opportunity to have these roles legitimised by external stakeholders. The RNTBC and related corporations, such as Lhere Artepe Pty Ltd, have thus provided a point of interaction which, while created to satisfy the requirements of Australian law, also provides an opportunity for Central Arrernte law to be recognised by external stakeholders. In addition, the operation of the RNTBC provides a space for the creation of new resources, such as money and external organisational legitimacy, which may help the *apmereke-artweye* and *kwertengerle* of the three estate groups to undertake their roles in maintaining the *Altyerre* in the Alice Springs region more effectively.

A pressing issue confronting the three estate groups in the operation of their RNTBC and related corporations was how they could ensure that these organisations were seen as legitimate: not only by their own members in terms of how the organisations accounted for cultural priorities in governing themselves, but also by external stakeholders who sought corporate legitimacy and integrity from the RNTBC and associated corporations. Maintaining this balance between what I have represented as 'two laws' provides a space for significant opportunities for the three estate groups. But it is also a precarious balance which the groups will need to continue to address to ensure that they are able to use their organisational structures in their roles as *apmereke-artweye* and *kwertengerle* of the *Altyerre* in the Alice Springs region.

Endnotes

1. M Mantziaris & D Martin, *Native title corporations: a legal and anthropological analysis*, The Federation Press, Sydney, 2000; D Martin, T Bauman & J Neale, *Challenges for Australian native title anthropology: practice beyond the proof of connection*, AIATSIS Research Discussion Paper, no. 29, AIATSIS, Canberra, 2011, http://www.aiatsis.gov.au/research/documents/DP29NTRU2011.pdf, accessed 3 June 2013.
2. Throughout this chapter the spelling 'Arrernte' is used following contemporary spelling conventions – although in quoting earlier authors, the chapter maintains their spellings such as 'Aranda' and 'Arunda'. For further discussion see J Henderson & V Dobson, *Eastern and Central Arrernte to English dictionary*, IAD Press, Alice Springs, 1994, p. 8.
3. Field work was undertaken at various points from 2007 through to 2010.
4. *Hayes* v *Northern Territory* [1999] FCA 1248.
5. Ibid., p 2. This chapter does not focus on the specific characteristics that an urban native title ruling may have on the progress of an RNTBC, as that would require an explicitly comparative study. However, some of the opportunities afforded to the three estate groups are a result of them having native title over an urban area. These include economic opportunities of some scale, in this case in the low tens of thousands, derived through their proximity to consumer

markets. The 2011 Census counted 25,186 residents in Alice Springs. See Australian Bureau of Statistics (ABS) website, http://www.censusdata.abs.gov.au/census_services/getproduct/census/2011/quickstat/7001?opendocument&navpos=220, accessed 22 July 2013.
6 *Apmereke-artweye* are usually seen as estate owners linked patrilineally to ancestors of the estates. See J Morton, 'Arrernte', in R Lee & R Daly (eds), *The Cambridge encyclopedia of hunters and gatherers*, Cambridge University Press, Cambridge, 1999, p. 332.
7 *Kwertengerle* are usually seen as estate custodians who are descended from women in the patriline and may be referred to as matrifiliates. See ibid., p. 332.
8 *Hayes* v *Northern Territory*, above n 4, p 2.
9 The key issue at stake here is that a 'cultural match' between the institutions and organisations of governance used by a group and their cultural priorities in organising themselves can lead to increased legitimacy in a group. This includes the ways in which their modern organisations operate and which directly impact on their sustainability and success. For a good overview of the key ideas of the Harvard Project on American Indian Economic Development and the issue of cultural match see M Jorgensen (ed.), *Rebuilding native nations: strategies for governance and development*, University of Arizona Press, Tucson, 2007. How these ideas have played out in research in the Australian context is discussed in J Hunt, D Smith, S Garling & W Sanders (eds), *Contested governance: culture, power and institutions in Indigenous Australia*, CAEPR Monograph, no. 29, ANU EPress, Australian National University, Canberra, 2011.
10 In examining the meanings of terms such as *apmereke-artweye*, *kwertengerle* and the *Altyerre* I am aware that there are complexities that I have not discussed. For the purposes of analysis in this chapter, I use the primary meanings of the terms and am not applying an anthropological analysis.
11 See Henderson & Dobson, above n 2, for further discussion.
12 In practice there appears to be an age cut-off for these forms of adoption. They generally seem to apply to children under the age of five at the time of adoption. They thus would not apply to the grown children of a woman who later in life marries an Arrernte man. This would make sense, in that older children would not be 'growed up' by the man and so would not acquire the necessary knowledge to act as *apmereke-artweye* and *kwertengerle* of their adoptive father's estates.
13 John Borrows' recent book provides a useful exposition of the ways in which different Indigenous legal systems within settler countries, such as Australia and Canada, are equivalent to introduced systems, such as the common law. J Borrows, *Canada's Indigenous constitution*, University of Toronto Press, Toronto, 2010.
14 D Austin-Broos, 'Narratives of encounter at Ntaria', *Oceania*, vol. 65, no. 2, 1994, p. 147.
15 Ibid.
16 Ibid.
17 Ibid., p. 148; for further discussion on this topic and for a more comprehensive view of Arrernte agency in the light of the operation of Australian law, see D Austin-Broos, *Arrernte present, Arrernte past: invasion, violence and imagination in Indigenous Central Australia*, University of Chicago Press, Chicago, 2009, pp. 16–20.
18 My description of this particular event draws heavily on an account described in D Brooks, *A town like Mparntwe*, Jukurrpa Books, Alice Springs, 2003, pp. 16–20.
19 For more on this case, see PN Grabosky, *Wayward governance: illegality and its control in the public sector*, Australian Institute of Criminology, Canberra, 1989, ch. 14, http://www.aic.gov.au/publications/previous%20series/lcj/1–20/wayward/ch14.html, accessed 23 July 2013.
20 C Franks & B Curr, *Keeping company: an inter-cultural conversation: Irlkwatherre, Yatyarre, Tantye/rtantye, Ngapartji-ngapartji, Kepenhe, Janku-janku*, Centre for Indigenous Development Education and Research, University of Wollongong, 1996.

21 There are some members who would prefer to receive the money directly. However, at the time of writing the groups had decided that they would not proceed with per capita payments.
22 These concerns are raised to demonstrate how things have not all been 'plain sailing' in the development of the RNTBC and related organisational structures since the positive determination in 1999. Specific issues will not be discussed in this chapter, but see R Morgan & H Wilmot, *Written proof: the appropriation of genealogical records in contemporary Arrernte society*, Native Title Research Unit Issues paper, vol. 4, no. 5, AIATSIS, Canberra, 2010, http://www.aiatsis.gov.au/ntru/docs/publications/issues/IPv4n5.pdf, accessed 3 June 2013.
23 Ibid. There are a number of implications in the increasing use of genealogical material by Arrernte people as a new form of objectified authority to assert connections to land. This was leading to a notable increase in disputes over membership claims that purported to be 'proven' by reference to genealogical records.
24 It should be noted that under the *Native Title Act 1993* (Cth), governments ultimately have the power of compulsory acquisition for such developments should they wish to proceed in that direction.

Update: Lhere Artepe Registered Native Title Body Corporate 2013

Francesca Merlan

Since 2010, when Manuhuia Barcham completed the field work for his Central Arrernte case study, the Lhere Artepe Registered Native Title Body Corporate (RNTBC) has encountered a number of challenges and has been going through a period of instability and learning.

A working relationship between Indigenous and western corporate structures has been challenged in a number of ways. While there is a general acceptance that the three estate groups, Mparntwe, Irlpme and Antulye, have been recognised in the native title determination as together holding native title rights and interests over Alice Springs,[1] there have been difficulties in ensuring equitable decision-making powers and benefit in relation to the town area for all members of the three groups. There is still also some contention over membership, and work to be done to update genealogies and the membership list. Any membership list will need to be related to the genealogies prepared for the native title determination and present views.

The situation is further complicated by the fact that some of the people who are genealogically clearly central to the native title case as presented, and recognised as such, play little role in the RNTBC, including not attending meetings. Busy with other interests, they, along with most of the other members, have been confounded by the formation of the complex corporate structures described in the case study, the involvement of only a few people in financial dealings and their inability to own or impact decisions. Although the complex corporations and trusts structures may have been established, as the case study suggests, to quarantine native title from the possible risks of commercial dealings, this has had other impacts. Together with the sudden onset of wealth and assets to be managed, these structures present complexities which many members have not been able to fully grasp. There is at least a perceived lack of transparency or line of sight from native title holders through to corporate decisions.

In contrast, there has been some enthusiasm for small-scale business ventures, such as — at one time — a proposed acquisition of the kiosk at the Alice Springs Telegraph Station Reserve, which could provide employment and a management regime more readily under the control of native title holders. However, with the commercial realities and complexities forced on it through developments such as Mount John discussed in the case study, the RNTBC has not had the option of starting with a small project and building capacity. These complex governance structures were established in response to complicated financial deals, particularly where settlements were not a simple compensation payout and also involved the extinguishment of native title rights. The RNTBC looked to deriving significant benefits in negotiating settlements including development opportunities that would be realised over time through the private sector dealings. It was hoped this would ensure a larger settlement base because it is more affordable to government to shift benefits to future budgets or to the private sector. However, the Lhere Artepe case study reveals some of the risks and challenges of such settlements. While the case study talks about dual accountability, the RNTBC in focusing on western corporate priorities appears to have fallen short in its internal accountability.

Although the case study foreshadowed that the RNTBC might play a greater role in the town, signified through the acknowledgment of Lhere Artepe on signs at the airport and road entrances to Alice Springs, other expectations — such as the establishment of behavioral standards for the many Aboriginal visitors to Alice Springs — have proved a daunting task, as has been the case in other urban areas. With the assistance of the Central Land Council (CLC), Lhere Artepe obtained some funds from the Department of Families, Housing, Community Services and Indigenous Affairs (FaHCSIA) for the establishment of senior men's and women's groups, in part to undertake this role. However, there seems little prospect that these groups will be able to effectively set protocols for behaviour that will be followed.

So far, then, the expectations in the case study concerning the RNTBC as a point of interaction between Indigenous and western laws appears not to have been realised. Some native title holders have not seen the organisation as speaking to them or as representing their interests. There have also been other challenges since the case study, with several changes in chief executive officers and difficulties in keeping the Lhere Artepe office open. The RNTBC has been assisted by the CLC which acquired a small amount of tide-over funding from FaHCSIA.

Nevertheless, many members of the Lhere Artepe RNTBC are resilient and committed to a strong future and there are grounds for cautious optimism, as the RNTBC finds ways of progressing, learning from past mistakes and dealing with significant change. There is a need to see beyond the native title case to subsequent organisational formation and to work consistently to set the conditions for it, including how to establish quasi-independent corporate structures and manage complex financial dealings in western corporate models not only in legal and commercial terms, but also in terms of human capacity. The RNTBC needs to work closely and consistently with its members, in ways that reflect the nature of members' interests, including their preferred forms of participation.

Endnotes

1 *Hayes* v *Northern Territory* [1999] FCA 1248.

Chapter 9

Registered Native Title Bodies Corporate and mining agreements: capacities and structures

Ciaran O'Faircheallaigh

Introduction

This chapter addresses a requirement faced by many Registered Native Title Bodies Corporate (RNTBCs) that hold native title rights and interests in trust or manage them as agents for the common law native holders; that is, the need to deal with rights, obligations and benefits arising from agreements with companies developing resources on native title land. This requirement arises from the fact that almost all new mining and other resource projects in Australia are developed within the framework of a contractually binding agreement negotiated between the developer and native title claimants or holders under the provisions of the *Native Title Act 1993* (Cth) (NTA). At the time of writing in 2010, only a minority of agreements have been signed by RNTBCs, but this will change as more determinations of native title are made and external stakeholders seek to enter into agreements with the native title holders. In addition, many existing agreements provide that if and when a determination of native title occurs, the obligations of the Indigenous entity that entered into the agreement, referred to here as the Native Title Party (NTP) and comprising, for instance, a number of individual native title claimants or an Aboriginal corporation, will or may pass to the RNTBC established as a result of the determination.

To clarify, in this chapter the term 'RNTBC' refers to the organisational entity that holds native title rights and interests on behalf of the common law native title holders, referred to here as the Native Title Group (NTG). RNTBCs are playing a variety of roles in relation to agreements. In some cases they may directly adopt obligations or rights previously exercised by the NTG; for instance, the right to exercise options regarding purchase of shares in a project. RNTBCs may consent to development projects on behalf of NTGs, and may facilitate the involvement of certain members of the NTG in project management; for example, the participation of senior custodians in site protection regimes. RNTBCs may monitor and if necessary enforce agreement provisions designed to benefit the NTG as a whole; for instance, through the creation of education and employment opportunities. They may also facilitate consensus within the NTG about distribution of benefits among the individuals, families and subgroups that constitute the NTG. In total, RNTBCs will play a key role in ensuring that the NTG complies with obligations imposed by agreements, and that the potential benefits promised by agreements are realised.

Giving added urgency and importance to the role of RNTBCs, research from both Australia and Canada shows that agreements between mining companies and Indigenous groups often suffer from serious implementation problems.[1] For example, Indigenous training programs may be ineffective; employment targets are often not met; business development opportunities are not fully exploited; structures to maintain communication between project operators and Indigenous communities are ineffective or fall into disuse; or systems for protecting cultural heritage do not operate effectively. Limited Indigenous organisational skills and capacities are one of the factors that explain the widespread failure to implement agreements fully and effectively, and RNTBCs must be able and resourced to identify and apply the requisite skills and capacities if the 'implementation deficit' is to be addressed.

There is considerable literature on the processes involved in agreement-making,[2] and on the content of agreements,[3] and an emerging literature on the implementation of agreements.[4] Little research has been conducted on the role of RNTBCs in the management and implementation of agreements, and this chapter is exploratory in nature. The first section of this paper identifies the sorts of rights and obligations RNTBCs are dealing with, by examining the major provisions of a mining agreement negotiated in 2007 that are typical of many recently negotiated in Australia,[5] and discusses the capacities and skills required to manage them effectively. The following section outlines one possible structure within which an RNTBC might develop and apply the necessary skills and capacities, and identifies options in addressing some key aspects of governance and organisational design. These include flows of authority and accountability, the appropriate organisational location for different sorts of decisions and the grouping of functional responsibilities. Here the objective is not to offer a detailed analysis of underlying organisational issues, but rather to introduce some concrete proposals that can provide a starting point for discussing options available to RNTBCs.

The chapter focuses on the specific context of resource development agreements. However, many of the skills and capacities discussed will also be required by RNTBCs in a wide variety of other situations, and similar issues of governance and organisational design are also likely to face most RNTBCs.

Rights and obligations arising from mining agreements

Recent agreements signed between Aboriginal companies and mining companies in Australia typically contain provisions in seven broad areas that may or will require actions or responses by RNTBCs.[6] These relate to financial benefits; education, training and employment opportunities; business development; cultural heritage protection and access to land; environmental management; project consent and support; and communication, liaison and implementation. These issues are generally addressed in separate sections of agreements and are dealt with separately here. It is recognised that in reality some of them (for instance cultural heritage protection and environmental management) are closely related.

Financial benefits

Agreements contain a variety of clauses providing for financial payments to native title parties. The agreement in question provides for a one-off payment on the signing of the agreement; an ongoing royalty stream based on the gross value of minerals shipped from the project; an issue of shares in the company operating the mine; and an option to take ownership of certain assets (for example, a shipping facility, camp accommodation) for a nominal cost at the end of the project life. With a determination of native title, the income streams, shares and assets may or will accrue to the RNTBC.

Effective management of these financial resources requires a range of skills and capacities, including the ability to make decisions:

- regarding allocation of income streams between current uses and building a capital fund for the future, a key consideration especially where projects have a short life
- on how to invest financial assets
- on whether to retain or sell shares
- on what assets the RNTBC may wish to take over when the project ends.

It is unlikely that many RNTBCs will have the specialist expertise to address these issues 'in house', and so a key challenge is to appreciate this limitation; to locate appropriate technical expertise at least possible cost; and to ensure that this expertise is applied within a clear policy framework established by the RNTBC. In the absence of such a framework, experts may end up making key decisions, rather than ensuring that decisions taken by the RNTBC and the NTG are fully informed.

A critical issue involves the ongoing allocation of project benefits between individuals, families and subgroups (for instance native title holders who have a particular connection to the part of the native title determination area where the project is located). Many mining projects in Aboriginal Australia have seen conflicts and tensions around distribution of benefits,[7] and a critical role for RNTBCs is to provide mechanisms through which conflicts can be avoided, defused or managed. In this regard key capacities include helping to negotiate initial allocations that have broad political support within the NTG, and monitoring benefit flows to ensure that policy decisions taken by the NTG are not undermined. They also involve identifying, establishing and monitoring legal and institutional structures that can give effect to policy decisions in a manner that maximises income, in part by being tax effective;[8] and providing dispute resolution mechanisms where conflict arises.

A final issue involves the increasing tendency of NTGs to use agreement revenues to establish or expand what might generally be described as community services, in areas such as education, youth, aged care, health, and housing and recreational facilities.[9] This trend raises complex issues in relation, for instance, to the entitlements of NTG members to government service provision; issues which cannot be addressed here. The key point to note is that effective use of agreement payments in this way requires skills in policy development, strategic planning, and program implementation and evaluation.

Education, training and employment

All recent mining agreements in Australia contain provisions designed to enhance education, training and employment opportunities for affected Aboriginal people. The agreement in question includes targets for Aboriginal employment; a commitment by the parties to develop and implement an employment strategy; and a process for jointly setting a budget for employment and training programs. It also involves a commitment by the project operator to ensure that contractors provide employment and training opportunities; provision for a minimum number of Aboriginal traineeships and construction of a training centre; and a requirement for the project operator to report to the Australian Stock Exchange on its performance relative to agreement goals. The agreement explicitly requires the cooperation of the NTP with the project operator in pursuit of Aboriginal employment objectives.

In this area, the RNTBC would need to participate effectively in the development of an employment strategy and monitor progress towards employment goals and contractor compliance with Aboriginal employment policies. It should be able to contribute to the effective operation of the training centre; and, more broadly, undertake a range of activities required to ensure that members of the NTG maximise the employment opportunities available to them. These activities could include advertising training and employment opportunities in the group; lobbying government to enhance the provision of education and training services; fostering a commitment to educational achievement among group members; and managing any conflicts that arise within the NTG regarding access to employment and training opportunities.

The RNTBC would thus require capacity in contract monitoring; in developing programs and policies in the field of employment and training; in engagement with private companies and government; in communication, both within the NTG and to external stakeholders; and in dispute resolution.

Business development

Agreements usually provide opportunities for Aboriginal businesses to become involved in providing goods and services to the mining project, which in turn creates opportunities to generate jobs and incomes for Aboriginal people, and opportunities to develop business skills that can be applied in other areas. RNTBCs can play two distinct roles in relation to business development.

The first relates to implementation of agreement provisions designed to create business development opportunities for members of the NTG. For instance, in our sample agreement the parties undertake to develop a business development strategy. The project operator commits to notifying the NTP of forthcoming contracting opportunities; to favourably consider tenders that have meaningful participation by businesses owned by the NTP or members of the NTG; and to include performance indicators relating to involvement of NTG businesses in assessing tenders for major contracts. The RNTBC needs a capacity to develop appropriate strategies; communicate information on contract opportunities to the NTG; and monitor the project operator's compliance with relevant provisions.

The second way in which an RNTBC can become involved is by owning and operating businesses that supply goods and services to the project. It is likely that in relation to major contracts in particular, individual families or subgroups of the NTG would lack the required organisational and financial capacity, and the RNTBC might wish to establish a business corporation, owned by the NTG, to pursue these opportunities. A critical issue here is to ensure that such a corporation, while established in a way that reflects the RNTBC's broad policy goals, is able to operate on business principles. If it is to be sustainable it must not, for instance, have its competitiveness undermined by having to provide sinecures to influential NTG members or subsidised goods or services to the NTG or subgroups within it. This requirement should be considered in designing an organisational structure for the RNTBC, by ensuring a clear separation between the setting of broad policy goals by the NTG and the RNTBC and the management of day-to-day operational matters by functional units reporting to a chief executive officer (CEO) (see 'A proposed RNTBC governance structure' below).

Cultural heritage protection and land access

A key component of mining agreements involves measures to protect physical manifestations of Aboriginal culture and sites or areas of cultural and/or spiritual importance and to ensure respect for Aboriginal cultural values. Protective measures frequently involve 'one off' cultural heritage surveys of areas intended for mining or related facilities; measures for dealing with heritage materials or sites identified through these surveys; and ongoing systems for dealing with cultural heritage whose existence is revealed by exploration or mining activity (for instance, burial sites), and for surveying additional areas for mine expansion. Provisions may also deal with cross-cultural training for the project workforce; support for cultural activities; and measures to enhance recognition of and respect for Aboriginal people and their culture. The agreement referred to here includes provisions for:

- establishment of exclusion areas around known sites, where mining or related activities or visitation by mineworkers is prohibited
- surveys of proposed mining areas
- procedures for dealing with archaeological material that may be an Aboriginal site, and for avoiding or mitigating any damage to such sites
- a commitment by the project operator to refrain from seeking approval under state cultural heritage legislation to damage or destroy a site without the approval of the NTP
- appointment of Aboriginal heritage rangers to perform a range of duties related to cultural heritage
- provision of cultural awareness training to all employees, contractors and consultants, including extended training for directors and senior managers
- opportunities for traditional owners to access the mining lease area on a regular basis.

In this case the RNTBC requires a capacity to monitor the company's compliance with exclusion provisions and, if necessary, enforce the prohibition through use of state heritage legislation. It needs to facilitate traditional owner access to the mine site and to oversee the conduct of surveys, the recruitment and activities of cultural heritage rangers and the delivery of cultural awareness training. It will also have to deal with any disputes arising from cultural heritage or site protection measures under the agreement, either within the NTG or between the NTG and the project operator.

Environmental management

A related and equally important aspect of recent mining agreements involves provisions dealing with environment management. While almost all recent agreements in Australia contain provisions in this area, the extent to which they allow substantial Aboriginal participation in environmental management varies greatly.[10] The agreement under discussion has substantive measures in this area, including:

- a general obligation on the mining company to consult with the native title party on environmental matters related to the project, and on any significant changes to the project that may have environmental implications
- a contractual commitment by the company to the NTP to comply with all relevant legislative obligations and government permit conditions. This provides

the NTP with a potential legal remedy if it believes that the project operator is not in compliance and that government is failing to act to remedy the breach
- a right for the NTP to access, review and comment on all environmental reports, plans, operating licences, permits and other documents relevant to environmental management of the project
- funding by the project operator for the NTP to obtain independent environmental advice
- participation by the NTP in development of closure plans
- a process for dealing with situations in which the NTP believes that environmental damage has occurred or may occur as a result of project operations
- a requirement for the project operator to maintain insurance to cover the cost of repairing any material environmental damage caused by the project.

These provisions create considerable potential for an RNTBC to be involved in environmental management and planning, and to take action if it believes that the project has or may create environmental damage. Critically, however, virtually all of them involve the project operator providing *opportunities* for participation or action; whether these opportunities are realised depends on the capacity of and action by the RNTBC. In particular, it requires the ability to:

- monitor the environmental impacts of the project
- review relevant documentation and respond where appropriate
- take legal action if it believes there has been a failure to comply with legislation or permit conditions
- activate and pursue the relevant process under the agreement if it believes that damage has or may occur
- identify, recruit and effectively manage specialist environmental expertise
- take the action required to activate the insurance clause, and ensure that the full costs of any environmental damage are recovered.

These are demanding requirements, involving the application of considerable technical, legal and administrative expertise. Given this, there may be a strong argument for a number of RNTBCs to pool resources in this area, or for an RNTBC to subcontract elements of the work involved to a Native Title Representative Body (NTRB) or other regional body, especially if the RNTBC is dealing with only one or two projects and agreements. I return to this point below.

Project consent and support

Virtually all mining agreements involve the provision of consent by the NTG to the grant of specific interests and the conduct of activities required for a project to proceed. It is largely in response to this consent that project operators provide economic benefits and opportunities, and offer measures beyond those required by law to minimise cultural and environmental impacts of mining.

A critical and demanding role for an RNTBC is to ensure that NTG members have access to the information they need to make an informed decision as to whether to grant their consent and support, either to the initial project proposal or to subsequent project expansions or alterations where these are not covered by the original agreement. Information needs to be comprehensive and conveyed in a manner that makes it intelligible and relevant within the cultural and social context of the NTG, and sufficient time must be available to absorb and weigh it. In addition, the RNTBC must ensure that the decision-making system employed to consider proposed projects or expansions reflects the values of the NTG; provides all of the NTG with the opportunity to influence the outcome; and allows an opportunity to negotiate outcomes that have broad support in a situation where there is a diversity of views in relation to the desirability of the project.

For major projects this will demand extensive information dissemination and consultation exercises, similar for instance to the community-controlled economic and social impact assessments used in Cape York in the 1990s,[11] or to the process organised by the Kimberley Land Council (KLC) to identify potential sites for a natural gas processing facility on the Kimberley Coast during 2008–09.[12] To undertake such approaches RNTBCs require the ability to raise and manage substantial funds; retain and effectively use expert advisers; communicate effectively with their members; engage with stakeholders that hold relevant information; and undertake the major logistical efforts usually involved in bringing NTG members together to consider project proposals. The scale of the effort involved will be more modest for small to medium-sized projects. But the capacity required will essentially be the same, particularly given that projects that are smaller in economic terms can still have major cultural and environmental impacts depending, for instance, on their location and the nature of the mining process involved.

Once an agreement has been signed, two additional issues can arise in relation to consent and support. The first is that agreements usually require the RNTBC to bind all of its members to the agreement. If members of the NTG subsequently seek to challenge the agreement — for example, by litigation or direct action — the RNTBC may be required to negate such activity. To my knowledge this situation has not occurred to date, but divisions certainly exist within some native title groups in relation to major resource projects. It seems only a matter of time before an RNTBC is faced with a situation where some of its members threaten to undermine commitments it has made in a mining agreement. This will require the application of skills in dispute resolution, negotiation and, as a last resort, litigation.

The second issue arises from the fact that mining agreements typically require undertakings by the NTP that, if individuals or groups not party to original agreements are recognised as having native title rights in relation to the project area, these individuals and groups must undertake to observe the terms of the agreement. The inclusion of additional individuals or groups is likely to require some reallocation of benefits under an agreement, particularly if those included are not initially supportive of a project. Again, this will require the application of dispute resolution and negotiation skills.

Liaison, communication, review and amendment

While agreements mark the conclusion of a process of negotiation, they also mark the starting point of an ongoing relationship that must be maintained throughout project life, in part by reviewing and amending agreements as circumstances change and the parties learn from experience about the utility of particular provisions. Typically, agreements provide for the creation of 'implementation', 'coordination' or 'liaison' committees, with members nominated by the project operator and the NTP or RNTBC. These bodies usually have the responsibility to maintain communication between the parties; monitor performance of the agreement; and undertake periodic reviews of its efficacy and appropriateness. They may also recommend amendment to an agreement, where required, and deal, at least initially, with any disputes between the parties. Subcommittees may be established to deal with specific components of the agreement, such as Aboriginal employment and training, or cultural heritage protection.

The effective operation of these structures is vital to the capacity of the NTG to maximise the benefits it derives from agreements. In their absence, operational problems are likely to go unaddressed; tension and bad feeling between the parties may develop; underlying problems with an agreement are likely to be ignored; and opportunities to enhance agreement outcomes may be missed. To ensure such structures operate effectively, RNTBCs require a substantial capacity to monitor the operation and outcomes of agreements; to engage effectively with the project operator; to communicate with NTG members, both to collect data on the performance of an agreement and to keep them informed of agreement outcomes; and to promote the NTG's interests in review and amendment processes.

A proposed RNTBC governance structure

This section outlines some options in relation to governance structures through which an RNTBC could deal with its obligations under mining agreements and derive maximum advantage from them, while at the same time maintaining the cultural and social values of the NTG. 'Governance structures' refers to institutional arrangements and processes through which goals and priorities are established, decisions are made, resources are allocated, and relevant initiatives are implemented and evaluated.

Given the diversity of Indigenous Australia, there is no single governance model that can achieve the required accommodation between effective implementation of commercial agreements and maintenance of cultural and social values. The intention is not therefore to try to identify a 'best possible' governance structure. Rather, as indicated in the introduction, it is to suggest some concrete options that can provide a starting point for discussion.

Figure 9.1 offers an overview of one possible structure for an RNTBC, which highlights broad roles and lines of authority and accountability but leaves room for a number of different approaches to key governance and organisational issues. This structure would comprise the common law native title holders (the NTG); a board of directors; a number of functional units responsible for management of different aspects of the RNTBC's business, including its engagement with external stakeholders (for example, government and commercial interests); and a CEO, responsible to the board for overall management and coordination of the functional units.

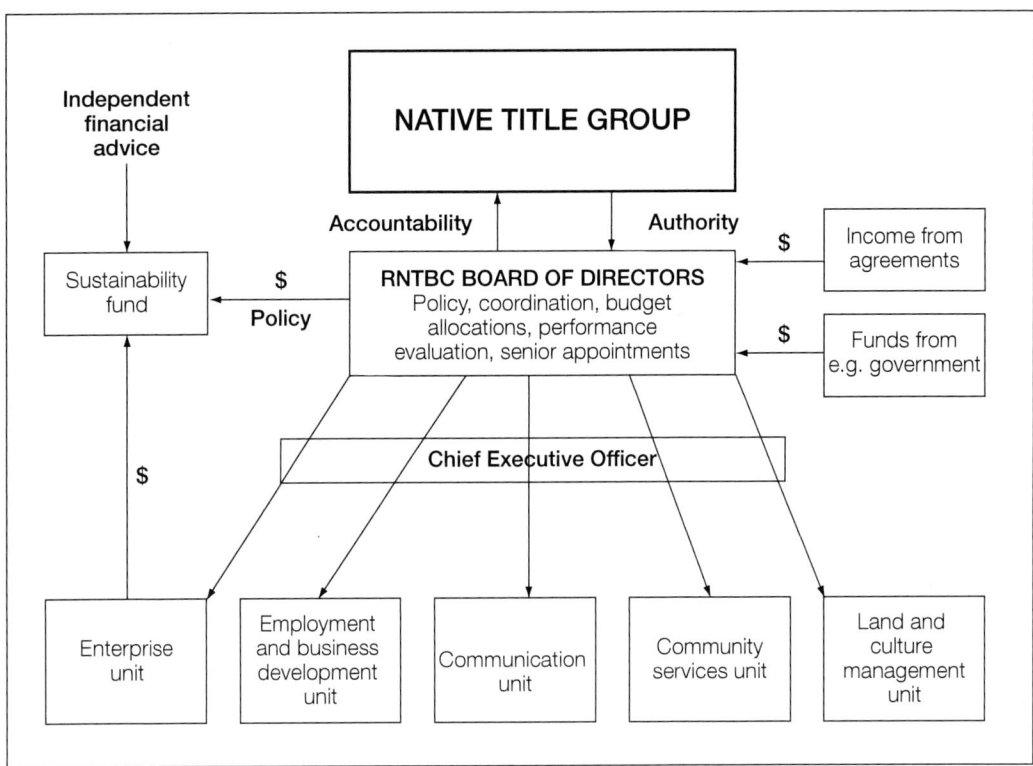

Figure 9.1 Possible structure for a 'mining agreement' RNTBC

The RNTBC board of directors could be chosen and constituted in a number of different ways, depending on the cultural values and practices of the NTG. Some options are:

- election of the board through a ballot of members, with members voting as a single constituency, and with the individuals receiving the largest number of

votes appointed. For example, if 16 people stand for election and there are 12 seats, the 12 people polling the largest number of votes will be elected
- appointment of members on the basis of family groups, with each group electing the same number of members. If, for example, there are six groups, each would select two members, using selection mechanisms determined by each group
- a mix of both approaches, designed to ensure that each family group is guaranteed some representation but that the board also reflected numerical support for particular candidates. For instance, again assuming six groups and a board of 12, six could consist of family representatives, with the remainder chosen in an 'open' election
- the addition to any of the alternative systems outlined above of a 'ward' system similar to that which operates in some local government systems in Australia. Under this system the claim area would be divided into a number of wards, with the traditional owners of land and sea country in each ward having particular rights and responsibilities for that area, including for dealing with mining projects and agreements that fall within it.

A key governance issue, and one whose resolution is critical to the effective operation of any organisation, involves the sorts of decisions that would be taken at different levels of the RNTBC. Lack of clarity on this point can lead to internal conflict as individuals and organisational units compete for control. It can also be a serious barrier to effective implementation of agreements, because lack of clarity on the locus of decision-making and on allocation of responsibilities can result in failure to take actions required to comply with obligations or to grasp opportunities. One possible approach is that the NTG would be responsible for fundamental decisions related to land, native title and culture; for instance, on actions that might affect native title rights, the basis on which mining agreements are concluded, and core principles for benefits management and distribution. Decisions would be based on the participation of the entire group. Decision-making authority would flow from the NTG to the board of directors, which would be responsible for implementing these fundamental decisions, and accountability would flow in the other direction.

Within the framework established by the NTG, the board has responsibility for setting strategic directions, including establishing policy guidelines, allocating budgets, monitoring expenditure and making senior staff appointments. In specific areas (for instance, annual budget allocations) a majority of at least three-quarters of board members, or a majority that includes at least one representative from each family group, might be required. For decisions of a more administrative nature (for example, filling managerial positions), a simple majority could suffice. If a ward system was introduced, board decisions related specifically to mining projects and agreements within that ward might be made by board members for that ward, or require the support of a majority of ward members.

To fulfil its role, the board will need to focus on providing strategic directions and on policy development. This can only occur if it is not preoccupied with detailed administrative matters, and if its members have the requisite skills. In relation to the former, the CEO can play a key role in 'filtering out' matters that do not require the board's attention, while at the same time ensuring that board members receive the information they need to fulfil their responsibilities and are fully appraised of issues that are of strategic importance. In terms of skills, RNTBC board members may need educational or training opportunities, not just in the formal aspect of directors' responsibilities but in the policy development, implementation and evaluation skills required to deal effectively with issues arising from agreements. For example, programs on agreement-making currently offered to staff of NTRBs could be modified, as could intensive short courses in policy analysis designed by a number of Australian universities for state and Commonwealth public servants. Board members could also develop specialist skills 'on the job' if they are allocated 'portfolio' areas which they take responsibility for (for example, land management and culture, health and housing, commercial development).

As indicated in the previous section, RNTBCs have to manage a wide range of activities, issues and resources arising from agreements. The approach suggested in Figure 9.1 is that units with considerable operational flexibility, and operating under the policy direction of the board and the day-to-day management of the CEO, would manage key activity areas and related issues. There would be five broad areas in relation to mining agreements, which are listed below. The unit titles are only illustrative and are used here as a device suggesting how responsibility for managing specific issues arising from agreements could be allocated.

- *Land and culture management unit*: potential impacts of projects and agreements on land and sea country and on culture; traditional owner participation in land management; fostering cultural values
- *Employment and business development unit*: training, employment and business development initiatives designed to maximise the ability of NTG members to take up employment and business opportunities associated with the resource projects and more broadly
- *Enterprise unit*: commercial opportunities available to the RNTBC as an entity, as opposed to economic opportunities available to individual NTG members or businesses they operate. This distinction is important because, as mentioned earlier, this area would have to be driven by commercial considerations within a broad policy framework established by the RNTBC
- *Community services unit:* planning, management and delivery of 'social services' such as education, housing, health and community infrastructure, arising from specific agreement provisions or from initiatives funded from agreement revenues

- *Communication unit*: communication and liaison within the NTG, to other parties to the agreement, and to stakeholders whose cooperation is important in ensuring agreement implementation.

Two important points should be made about the concept of 'functional units'. First, the scale of involvement will vary greatly, depending on the size of the NTG and the RNTBC and the number of mining projects and agreements they must deal with. At one extreme, a small NTG with one agreement for a medium-sized project might combine education, training, employment and business development functions in the hands of one individual. The communication function in relation to an agreement might be handled by an individual whose duties encompass the full range of communication, media and liaison functions for the RNTBC. At the other extreme, an RNTBC dealing with a natural gas processing precinct with turnover in the billions of dollars might have separate 'departments' with multiple employees for each function. Regardless of scale, it is important to identify the functions discussed above separately to ensure that all the tasks and issues critical to the successful management of agreements are addressed.

The second point, also related to issues of scale, involves the possibility that a number of smaller RNTBCs that are signatories to agreements might pool their resources and hire staff or consultants that could perform the same functions for multiple projects. This is especially important in areas such as environmental management where the skills required can be highly specialised, difficult and expensive to obtain. Another option is to 'subcontract' specific roles to existing regional or specialist organisations. For instance, an RNTBC keen to establish an educational initiative might engage an Aboriginal education service to undertake this work on its behalf, or an NTRB with extensive experience in negotiating and monitoring agreements could be contracted to undertake a scheduled review and recommend areas where amendments would be beneficial.

Finally, Figure 9.1 assumes that the RNTBC may wish to establish a sustainability or long-term investment fund, which would receive a regular allocation from agreement revenues and would build a capital fund designed to sustain the activities of the RNTBC and the NTG, especially if and when income from a project declines. It is assumed that this fund would operate under the policy direction of the board of directors and ultimately of the NTG, but would also draw on independent financial advice to ensure that decisions by the board and the NTG on investment and use of funds are fully and appropriately informed.

Conclusion

This chapter illustrates the wide range of skills and capacities RNTBCs require to fully exploit the opportunities and address the obligations created by mining agreements.

They include the need to manage and apply financial resources effectively in pursuit of both short- and long-term goals, and to adjudicate the allocation of resources between individuals, families and subgroups within the NTG. RNTBCs must also ensure that employment, training and business development opportunities are maximised so as to help overcome the economic disadvantage faced by many NTG members, and that cultural heritage and environmental management provisions are used to protect the native title rights and interests they hold in trust for the NTG. RNTBCs must ensure that their members have the information and advice they need to make complex decisions regarding the provision of native title consent for resource projects, the terms on which consent may be provided and the allocation of benefits arising from development. The required skills and capacities can only be developed and applied through governance structures that blend the requirement for effective management of commercial activity with promotion of the social and cultural values of the NTG.

Few if any RNTBCs will possess, at least early in their lives, the full range of skills and capacities required to deal with complex mining agreements. This has three major policy implications. First, in negotiating agreements, RNTBCs should be aware of the capacity constraints they are likely to face in seeking to manage and implement them. This may mean, for instance, that agreements should contain funds to assist capacity building in key areas, and that RNTBCs should focus their bargaining power on winning favourable agreement provisions in areas they are confident they can deal with effectively. Second, RNTBCs should systematically consider agreements they sign or 'inherit', determine the capacities, skills and structures that will be most important in dealing with them, and focus on development or acquisition of these skills. Third, except for the largest RNTBCs operating in resource-rich regions, gaining access to relevant skills and capacities is likely to involve a judicious mix of 'in house' skills in core, strategic areas, extensive resource 'pooling' with other RNTBCs and subcontracting functions to specialist service delivery organisations or NTRBs.

Endnotes

1. C O'Faircheallaigh, *A new model of policy evaluation: mining and Indigenous people*, Ashgate Press, Aldershot, 2002; C O'Faircheallaigh, 'Implementation: the forgotten dimension of agreement-making in Australia and Canada', *Indigenous Law Bulletin*, vol. 5, no. 20, 2002, pp. 14–17; New Economy Development Group Inc. (NEDGI), *Evaluation of the Golden Patricia Agreement*, NEDGI, Ottawa, 1993.
2. See, for example, C O'Faircheallaigh, *Negotiating major project agreements: the 'Cape York model'*, Research Discussion Paper, no. 11, AIATSIS, Canberra, 2000, http://www.aiatsis.gov.au/research/docs/dp/DP11.pdf, accessed 3 June 2013; V Weitzner, *'Dealing full force': Lutsel K'e Dene first nation's experience negotiating with mining companies*, North South Institute and Lutsel K'e Dene First Nation, Ottawa, 2006, http://www.nsi-ins.ca/wp-content/

uploads/2012/10/2006-Dealing-full-force-Lutsel-ke-Dene-first-nations-experience-negotiating-with-mining-companies.pdf, accessed 3 June 2013.

3 See, for example, C O'Faircheallaigh, 'Evaluating agreements between Indigenous peoples and resource developers', in M Langton, M Tehan, L Palmer & K Shain (eds), *Honour among nations? Treaties and agreements with Indigenous people*, Melbourne University Press, Melbourne, 2004, pp. 303–28; C O'Faircheallaigh & T Corbett, 'Indigenous participation in environmental management of mining projects: the role of negotiated agreements', *Environmental Politics*, vol. 14, no. 8, 2005, pp. 629–47, http://fennerschool-people.anu.edu.au/richard_baker/SRES3028/lectures_and_tutorials/week10/Indigenous%20Mgmt%20&%20Mining.pdf, accessed 3 June 2013; SA Kennett, *A guide to impact and benefits agreements*, Canadian Institute of Resources Law, University of Calgary, Calgary, 1999; Public Policy Forum, *Sharing the benefits of resource developments: a study of first nations — industry impact benefits agreements*, Public Policy Forum, Ottawa, 2006, http://www.ppforum.ca/sites/default/files/report_impact_benefits-english.pdf, accessed 3 June 2013.

4 O'Faircheallaigh, *A new model of policy evaluation*, above n 1; O'Faircheallaigh, 'Implementation: the forgotten dimension of agreement making', above n 1; P Crooke, B Harvey & M Langton, 'Implementing and monitoring Indigenous Land Use Agreements: the western Cape communities co-existence agreement', in M. Langton, O Mazel, L Palmer, K Shain & M Tehan (eds), *Settling with Indigenous people*, The Federation Press, Sydney, 2006, pp. 95–114.

5 The agreement is not identified for reasons of confidentiality. In its range and scope it is similar to many other agreements signed in north Australia during the last decade.

6 These areas and the range of provisions found in relation to them are discussed in detail in O'Faircheallaigh, above n 3, pp. 303–28.

7 See, for example, J Altman & D Smith, *The economic impact of mining moneys: the Nabarlek Case, Western Arnhem Land*, CAEPR Discussion Paper, no. 63, Centre for Aboriginal Economic Policy Research, Australian National University, Canberra, 1994, http://caepr.anu.edu.au/sites/default/files/Publications/DP/1994_DP63.pdf, accessed 3 June 2013; O'Faircheallaigh, *A new model of policy evaluation*, above n 1, pp. 153–79.

8 For a discussion of relevant taxation considerations and of alternative organisational structures see A Levin, *Improvements to the tax and legal environment for Aboriginal community organisations and trusts: discussion paper*, Jackson McDonald Lawyers, Perth, 2007, http://www.aiatsis.gov.au/ntru/docs/researchthemes/developmenttax/taxation/LevinDiscussionPaper.pdf, accessed 2 July 2013; LM Strelein, *Taxation of native title agreements*, Native Title Research Monograph, no. 1, Native Title Research Unit, AIATSIS, Canberra, 2008.

9 See, for example, Gelganyen Trust, Kilkayi Trust, *Gelganyen Trust, Kilkayi Trust: annual report April 2005 – June 2006*, Kununurra, 2006, http://www.gelganyem.com.au/reports/pdf/GelganyemAnnualReport2006.pdf, accessed 3 June 2013.

10 O'Faircheallaigh & Corbett, above n 3, pp. 629–47.

11 O'Faircheallaigh, above n 2.

12 W Bergmann & F Davey, 'North west gas precinct agreement', paper presented at the National Native Title Conference 2009, Melbourne, 5 June 2009.

Update: Registered Native Title Bodies Corporate and mining agreements 2013

Ciaran O'Faircheallaigh

Developments since 2010 highlight the growing importance of work related to exploration and mining agreements for Registered Native Title Bodies Corporate (RNTBCs); the critical role that RNTBCs will play in shaping the impact of agreements on Native Title Groups (NTGs); the necessity for RNTBCs to develop and exercise the capacities identified in Chapter 9; and the need to identify organisational structures that will support RNTBCs in doing so.

The growing importance of RNTBCs is highlighted by the recognition of native title over large areas of Australia during the period 2010–13, including those rich in mineral resources. For example, in 2011 the Federal Court made a determination in relation to the Wanjina Wunggurr Uunguu native title claim, finding that the claimants hold exclusive possession native title rights to some 26,000 square kilometres in the north Kimberley.[1] Also in the Kimberley in the same year, there was a similar outcome in relation to the Wanjina Wunggurr Dambimangarri claim, covering some 28,000 square kilometres.[2] At the other end of Australia in Victoria, the Gunaikurnai people, whose ancestral lands include a number of potential areas for oil and gas development, achieved recognition of their native title in October 2010.[3] The RNTBCs that will hold native title as a result of these and other native title determinations will have to address the issues, and exercise the skills and capacities, identified in Chapter 9.

The significance of the task facing RNTBCs is also highlighted by the continuing proliferation of native title agreements in Australia, many of them dealing with exploration and mining. For example, the Agreements, Treaties and Negotiated Settlements Project at the University of Melbourne added some 140 agreements to its database negotiated in 2012 alone, and the project captures only a proportion of the agreements actually negotiated.[4]

Another important development is that agreement provisions discussed in Chapter 9 and until recently confined to agreements in north Australia have started to appear in other parts of the country. For example, a review of agreements negotiated in the decade to 2005 revealed that few outside northern Western Australia, the Northern Territory and Cape York contained revenue sharing or royalty-type payments.[5] Yet a review of recent oil and gas development agreements in Victoria and South Australia shows that revenue-sharing provisions are now regularly included.[6] This indicates that the RNTBCs involved will need to exercise the capacities for financial management and for mediating disputes regarding revenue distribution and management discussed in the 'Financial benefits' section of Chapter 9.

Finally, agreements negotiated since 2010 have continued to extend the range of rights and powers that native title signatories to agreements can exercise in relation to matters discussed in Chapter 9. For example, the agreements for the proposed Kimberley Browse Liquefied Natural Gas (LNG) Precinct extend the role of traditional owners in environmental management. For instance, they confer on them, via state legislation, the power to decide whether further LNG processing facilities for offshore gas will be constructed on the Kimberley coast, and give them the right, which can be exercised unilaterally, to require the proponent to construct a desalination plant to provide water for the LNG precinct if traditional owners believe that use of groundwater would create unacceptable environmental impacts.[7] The ability to exercise the rights and exploit the opportunities provided by such agreement provisions will depend in large measure on the ability of RNTBCs to effectively exercise the capacities identified in Chapter 9.

Endnotes

1 *Goonack v State of Western Australia* [2011] FCA 516. See also Robert McClelland, 'Wanjina-Wunggurr Uunguu native title recognition, 23 May 2011', http://robertmcclelland.com.au/2011/05/23/wanjina-wunggurr-uunguu-native-title-recognition/, accessed 22 July 2013.

2 *VB (deceased) v State of Western Australia* [2011] FCA 518. See also 'Native title claim determined in Kimberley, 26 May 2011', *Sydney Morning Herald*, http://news.smh.com.au/breaking-news-national/native-title-claim-determined-in-kimberley-20110526-1f5q8.html, accessed 22 July 2013.

3 *Mullett on behalf of the Gunai/Kurnai People v State of Victoria* [2010] FCA 1144.

4 Agreements, Treaties and Negotiated Settlements Project, Melbourne, http://www.atns.net.au/search.asp, accessed 17 July 2013.

5 C O'Faircheallaigh, 'Aborigines, mining companies and the state in contemporary Australia: a new political economy or "business as usual"?', *Australian Journal of Political Science*, vol. 41, no. 1, 2006, pp. 16–17.

6 Confidential review conducted by the author for an RNTBC.

7 C O'Faircheallaigh, 'Extractive industries and Indigenous peoples: a changing dynamic?', *Journal of Rural Studies*, vol. 30, 2013, pp. 20–30.

RNTBC selected reading list

Aboriginal and Torres Strait Islander Social Justice Commissioner (ATSISJC) 2005, *Social justice report 2005*, Australian Human Rights Commission, http://www.humanrights.gov.au/publications/social-justice-report-2005-recommendations-and-follow-actions, accessed 31 July 2013.

——2010, 'Consultation, cooperation, and free, prior and informed consent: the elements of meaningful and effective engagement', in ATSISJC, *Native title report 2010*, Australian Human Rights Commission, Sydney, 2010, pp. 57–102, http://www.humanrights.gov.au/publications/native-title-report-2010, accessed 30 July 2013.

——2012, 'Prescribed Bodies Corporate — an example of effective Indigenous governance over lands, territories and resources?', in ATSISJC, *Native title report 2012*, Australian Human Rights Commission, Sydney, pp. 94–127, http://www.humanrights.gov.au/publications/native-title-report-2012, accessed 29 July 2013.

Allbrook, M & Jebb, MA 2004, 'Implementation and resourcing of native title and related agreements', National Native Title Tribunal, Perth, http://www.nntt.gov.au/Mediation-and-agreement-making-services/Documents/Implementation%20and%20resourcing%20of%20native%20title%20and%20related%20agreements.pdf.

Attorney-General's Department Steering Committee (AGDSC) 2006, *Structures and processes of Prescribed Bodies Corporate*, AGDSC, Canberra, copy available online at AIATSIS webpage, http://www.aiatsis.gov.au/ntru/docs/researchthemes/pbc/Guidelines2007.pdf, accessed 29 July 2013.

Australian Charities and Not-for-profits Commission (ACNC) website, 'Not-for-profits (NFP) reform', ACNC, http://www.acnc.gov.au/ACNC/About_ACNC/NFP_reforms/Reform_agenda/ACNC/Edu/NFP_Agenda.aspx, accessed 1 August 2013.

Bauman, T 2005, *Whose benefits? Whose rights? Negotiating rights and interests amongst Indigenous native title parties*, Land, Rights, Laws: Issues of Native Title, vol. 3, no. 2, Native Title Research Unit, AIATSIS, Canberra, <http://www.aiatsis.gov.au/ntru/docs/publications/issues/ip05v3n2.pdf>, accessed 30 July 2013.

——2006a *Final report of the Indigenous Facilitation and Mediation Project July 2003 – June 2006: research findings, recommendations and implementation*, Report no. 6, AIATSIS, Canberra, http://www.aiatsis.gov.au/ntru/docs/researchthemes/negmedfac/ifamp/IfampReport.pdf, accessed 30 July 2013.

——2006b 'Nations and tribes "within": emerging Aboriginal "nationalisms" in Katherine', *The Australian Journal of Anthropology*, vol. 17, no. 3, pp. 322–36.

———2006c *Waiting for Mary: process and practice issues in negotiating native title Indigenous decision-making and dispute management frameworks*, Land, Rights, Laws: Issues of Native Title, vol. 3, no. 6, Native Title Research Unit, AIATSIS, Canberra, <http://www.aiatsis.gov.au/ntru/docs/publications/issues/ip06v3n6.pdf>, accessed 30 July 2013.

——— & Ganesharajah, C 2009, *Second national Prescribed Bodies Corporate meeting: issues and outcomes, Melbourne 2 June 2009*, Native Title Research Report, no. 2, Native Title Research Unit, AIATSIS, Canberra, <http://www.aiatsis.gov.au/ntru/docs/researchthemes/pbc/PBCMeeting2009.pdf>, accessed 29 July 2013.

——— & Pope, J (eds) 2009, *Solid work you mob are doing: case studies in Indigenous dispute resolution and conflict management in Australia*, National Alternative Dispute Resolution Advisory Council, Barton, ACT.

——— & Tran, T 2007, *First national Prescribed Bodies Corporate meeting: issues and outcomes Canberra 11–13 April 2007*, Native Title Research Report, no. 3, Native Title Research Unit, AIATSIS, Canberra, <http://www.aiatsis.gov.au/ntru/docs/researchthemes/pbc/PBCMeeting2007.pdf>, accessed 29 July 2013.

——— & Williams, R 2011, *The business of process: research issues in managing Indigenous decision-making and disputes in land*, AIATSIS Research Discussion Paper, no. 13, AIATSIS, Canberra, <http://www.aiatsis.gov.au/research/docs/dp/DP13.pdf>, accessed 30 July 2013.

———, Haynes, C & Lauder, G 2013, *Pathways to the co-management of protected areas and native title in Australia*, AIATSIS Research Discussion Paper, no. 32, AIATSIS Research Publications, Canberra.

Behrendt, L & Kelly, L 2008, *Resolving Indigenous disputes: land conflict and beyond*, The Federation Press, Sydney.

Black, W 2000, 'Transferring native title to a body corporate under the *Native Title Act 1993* — can CGT arise?', *Journal of Australian Taxation*, March/April, pp. 155–61.

Campbell, D & Hunt, J 2010, *Community development in Central Australia: broadening the benefits from land use agreements*, CAEPR Topical Issue, vol. 7, no. 201, Centre for Aboriginal Economic Policy Research, Australian National University, Canberra.

Claudie, D 2007, 'We're tired from talking: the native title process from the perspective of Kaanju people living on homelands, Wenlock and Pascoe Rivers, Cape York Peninsula', in BR Smith & F Morphy (eds), *The social effects of native title: recognition, translation, coexistence*, CAEPR Research Monograph, no. 27, Centre for Aboriginal Economic Policy Research, Australian National University, Canberra, pp. 91–115.

Crooke, P, Harvey, B & Langton, M 2006, 'Implementing and monitoring Indigenous Land Use Agreements in the minerals industry: the Western Cape communities co-existence agreement', in M Langton, O Mazel, L Palmer, K Shain & M Tehan (eds), *Settling with Indigenous people*, The Federation Press, Sydney, pp. 95–114.

Day, R 2004, 'Ten years since Mabo — native title at Mer', *Journal of Indigenous Policy*, no. 45.

Deloitte Access Economics 2013, *Review of the roles and functions of native title organisations — June 2013*, discussion paper, Deloitte Access Economics, Sydney, http://www.aiatsis.gov.au/ntru/documents/BillGrayJeffHarmerRicSimes.pdf, accessed 9 September 2013.

Department of Families, Housing, Community Services and Indigenous Affairs (FaHCSIA) 2008, *Optimizing benefits from native title agreements*, Australian Government discussion paper, FaHCSIA, Canberra, http://www.fahcsia.gov.au/sites/default/files/documents/05_2012/native_title_discussion_paper_0.pdf, accessed 23 August 2013.

———2011, *Native Title (Prescribed Bodies Corporate) Amendment Regulations 2011 information sheet*, FaHCSIA, Canberra, http://www.fahcsia.gov.au/sites/default/files/documents/08_2012/native_title_2011.pdf, accessed 31 July 2013.

——2012 'Native title organisations review', FaHCSIA website, December, http://www.fahcsia.gov.au/our-responsibilities/indigenous-australians/programs-services/native-title-organisations-review-0, accessed 31 July 2013.

——2013 *Guidelines for basic support funding for Prescribed Bodies Corporate*, Land Programs Branch, FaHCSIA, Canberra, June, http://www.nativetitle.org.au/documents/FaHCSIA_PBCBasicSupportGuidelines2013.PDF, accessed 31 July 2013.

Department of the Treasury 2010, *Native title, Indigenous economic development and tax*, consultation paper, Australian Government, Canberra, http://www.treasury.gov.au/~/media/Treasury/Consultations%20and%20Reviews/2010/Native%20Title%20Indigenous%20Economic%20Development%20and%20Tax/Key%20Documents/PDF/CP_Native_Title_IED_and_Tax.ashx, accessed 1 August 2013.

Dodson, P 2012, 'Time for a new doctrine: the Yawuru experience', in T Bauman & L Glick (eds), *The limits of change: Mabo and native title 20 years on*, AIATSIS, Canberra, pp. 386–9.

Duff, N and Weir, J 2013, *Weeds and native title — law and assumption*, Rural Industries Research and Development Corporation, no. 13/078, Canberra, https://rirdc.infoservices.com.au/downloads/13-078, accessed 9 September 2013.

Edgar, J 2011, 'Indigenous Land Use Agreement — building relationships between Karajarri traditional owners, Bidyadanga Aboriginal Community La Grange Inc. and the Government of Western Australia', *Australian Aboriginal Studies*, no. 2, pp. 50–63.

Elvin, R 2009, *Local government reform in the Northern Territory: reforming the governance of service delivery and the view from the Barkly*, DKCRC Working Paper, no. 41, Desert Knowledge CRC, Alice Springs, http://www.nintione.com.au/sites/default/files/resource/DKCRC-Working-paper-41_Local-government-reform-in-the-Northern-Territory.pdf, accessed 27 September 2013.

Expert Mechanism on the Rights of Indigenous Peoples 2010, *Progress report on the study on Indigenous peoples and the right to participate in decision-making*, report to the Human Rights Council, 15th session, UN Doc A/HRC/15/35, http://www2.ohchr.org/english/bodies/hrcouncil/docs/15session/A.HRC.15.35_en.pdf, accessed 30 July 2013.

Flanagan, F 2002, *Pastoral access protocols: the corrosion of native title by contract*, Land, Rights, Laws: Issues of Native Title, vol. 1, no. 2, Native Title Research Unit, AIATSIS, Canberra.

Frith, A 2009, 'Postcolonial action or continuing colonisation? The role of a Gubbah lawyer in the formation of hybrid Indigenous corporations', *Sortuz, Oñati Journal of Emergent Socio-legal Studies*, vol. 3, no. 2, pp. 28–51, http://www.sortuz.org/content/pdfs2009dic/frith.pdf, accessed 8 August 2013.

——& Foat, A 2008, *The 2007 amendments to the* Native Title Act 1993 *(Cth): technical amendments or disturbing the balance of rights?*, Native Title Research Monograph, no. 3, Native Title Research Unit, AIATSIS, Canberra.

Guest, K 2009, *The promise of comprehensive native title settlements: the Burrup, MG-Ord and Wimmera agreements*, AIATSIS Research Discussion Paper, no. 27, Native Title Research Unit, AIATSIS, Canberra, http://www.aiatsis.gov.au/research/docs/dp/DP27.pdf, accessed 22 May 2013.

Glaskin, K 2007a, 'Claim, culture and effect: property relations and the native title process', in BR Smith & F Morphy (eds), *The social effects of native title: recognition, translation, coexistence*, CAEPR Research Monograph, no. 27, ANU Epress, Australian National University, Canberra, pp. 59–77, http://epress.anu.edu.au/caepr_series/no_27/pdf/whole_book.pdf#page=71, accessed 29 July 2013.

——2007b, 'Outstation incorporation as a precursor to a Prescribed Body Corporate', in L Hiatt (ed.), *Customary land tenure and registration in Australia and Papua New Guinea, anthropological perspectives*, ANU Epress, Australian National University, Canberra, http://epress.anu.edu.au/apem/customary/mobile_devices/ch10.html, accessed 29 July 2013.

Hill, R 2011, 'Towards equity in Indigenous co-management of protected areas: cultural planning by Miriuwung-Gajerrong people in the Kimberley, Western Australia', *Geographical Research*, vol. 49, no. 1, pp. 72–85.

——, Wallington, T, Robinson, T, Westcott, CJ, Stevenson, B, Davies, J & Walsh, F 2011, *Biodiversity planning — capturing multiple values in decision-making: a framework for research 2011–2015*, Marine and Tropical Sciences Research Facility Transition Project Final Report, Reef and Rainforest Research Centre Limited, Cairns, https://publications.csiro.au/rpr/download?pid=csiro:EP112042&dsid=DS2, accessed 26 September 2013.

Hunt, J, Smith, DE, Garling, S & Sanders, W (eds) 2008, *Contested governance: culture, power and institutions in Indigenous Australia*, CAEPR Research Monograph, no. 29, Centre for Aboriginal Economic Policy Research, Australian National University, Canberra.

Joint Working Group on Indigenous Land Settlements 2009, *Guidelines for best practice, flexible and sustainable decision making*, Joint Working Group on Indigenous Land Settlements, Canberra, August, http://www.aiatsis.gov.au/ntru/docs/researchthemes/agreement/agreements/GuidelinesForBestPractice.pdf, accessed 5 June 2013.

Jorgensen, M (ed.) 2007, *Rebuilding native nations: strategies for governance and development*, University of Arizona Press, Tucson.

Kimberley Land Council 2011, *Bardi Jawi Governance Project newsletter*, Kimberley Land Council, Broome, http://www.aiatsis.gov.au/ntru/documents/BJGOVNEWSLETTER1sm.pdf, accessed 16 July 2013.

Langton, M & Mazel, O 2012, 'The resource curse compared: Australian Aboriginal participation in the resource extraction industry and distribution of impacts', in M Langton & J Longbottom, *Community futures, legal architecture: foundations for Indigenous peoples in the global mining boom*, Routledge, London.

Levin, A 2007, *Improvements to the tax and legal environment for Aboriginal community organizations and trusts*, discussion paper, Jackson McDonald Lawyers, Perth, http://www.aiatsis.gov.au/ntru/docs/researchthemes/developmenttax/taxation/LevinDiscussionPaper.pdf, accessed 2 July 2013

Macklin, J & McClelland, R 2010, *Leading practice agreements: maximising outcomes from native title benefits*, discussion paper, July, the Attorney-General and the Minister for Families, Housing, Community Services and Indigenous Affairs, http://www.fahcsia.gov.au/our-responsibilities/indigenous-australians/publications-articles/land-native-title/leading-practice-agreements-maximising-outcomes-from-native-title-benefits, accessed 30 July 2013.

Mantziaris, C 1999a, 'Problems with Prescribed Bodies Corporate', *Indigenous Law Bulletin*, vol. 4, no. 22, pp. 21–2.

——1999b, 'The dual view theory of the corporation and the Aboriginal corporation', *Federal Law Review*, vol. 27, pp. 283–321.

——& Martin, DF 2000, *Native title corporations: a legal and anthropological analysis*, The Federation Press, Sydney.

Martin, DF 2003, *Rethinking the design of Indigenous organisations: the need for strategic engagement*, CAEPR Discussion Paper Series, no. 248, Centre for Aboriginal Economic Policy Research, Australian National University, Canberra, <http://caepr.anu.edu.au/sites/default/files/Publications/DP/2003_DP248.pdf>, accessed 29 July 2013.

——2004, 'Designing institutions in the "recognition space" of native title', in S Toussaint (ed.), *Crossing boundaries: cultural, legal, historical and practice issues in native title*, Melbourne University Press, Melbourne, pp. 244–55.

——2005a, 'Governance, cultural appropriateness, and accountability', in G Macdonald & D Austin-Broos (eds), *Culture, economy and governance in Aboriginal Australia*, Sydney University Press, Sydney, pp. 189–201.

——2005b, 'Rethinking Aboriginal community governance: challenges for sustainable engagement', in P Smyth, T Reddel & A Jones (eds), *Community and local governance in Australia*, University of New South Wales Press, Sydney, pp. 108–27.

——2009, 'The governance of agreements between Aboriginal people and resource developers: principles for sustainability', in JC Altman and DF Martin (eds), *Power, culture, economy: Indigenous Australians and mining*, CAEPR Research Monograph, no. 30, Centre for Aboriginal Economic Policy Research, Australian National University, Canberra, pp. 99–126.

——, Bauman, T & Neale, J 2011, *Challenges for Australian native title anthropology: practice beyond the proof of connection*, AIATSIS Research Discussion Paper, no. 29, Native Title Research Unit, AIATSIS, Canberra.

Martin, F 2007, 'Prescribed Bodies Corporate under the *Native Title Act 1993* (Cth): can they be exempt from income tax as charitable trusts?', *UNSW Law Journal*, vol. 30, no. 3, pp. 713–30.

——2010a, 'Local government rates exemptions for Indigenous organisations: the complexities of a state-by-state system', *Australian Indigenous Law Review*, vol. 14, no. 1, pp. 35–45.

——2010b, 'Native title payments and their tax consequences: is the Federal Government's recommendation of a withholding tax the best approach?', *UNSW Law Journal*, vol. 33, no. 3, pp. 685–713.

——2012, 'An Indigenous economic development corporation: how does this compare to a charity?', *Indigenous Law Bulletin*, vol. 7, no. 30, pp. 12–16.

McDonald, E 2007, 'The Torres Strait Regional Authority: is it the answer to regional governance for Indigenous people?', *Australian Indigenous Law Review*, vol. 11, no. 3.

McGrath N, Moran, M & Anda, M 2010, *The boundaries of representation: exploring the bordering of Martu governance in Australia*, DKCRC Working Paper, no. 70, Desert Knowledge CRC, Alice Springs.

McLean, J 2012, 'From dispossession to compensation: a political ecology of the Ord Final Agreement as a partial success story for Indigenous traditional owners', *Australian Geographer*, vol. 43, no. 4, pp. 339–55.

——2013, 'Still colonising the Ord River, northern Australia: a postcolonial geography of the spaces between Indigenous peoples' and settlers' interests', *The Geographical Journal*, 9 May, pp. 1–13, http://onlinelibrary.wiley.com/doi/10.1111/geoj.12025/abstract, accessed 8 August 2013.

McLean, K 2013, 'Healthy country, healthy people: an Australian Aboriginal organisation's adaptive governance to enhance its social–ecological system', *Geoforum*, vol. 45, March, pp. 94–105, http://www.sciencedirect.com/science/article/pii/S0016718512002059, accessed 26 September 2013.

Memmott, P, Blackwood, P & McDougall, S 2007, 'A regional approach to managing Aboriginal land title on Cape York', in JF Weiner & K Glaskin (eds), *Customary land tenure and registration in Australia and Papua New Guinea: anthropological perspectives*, Asia-Pacific Environment Monograph 3, ANU EPress, Australian National University, Canberra pp. 273–97, http://epress.anu.edu.au?p=99961, accessed 15 May 2013.

Morgan, R & Wilmot, H 2010, *Written proof: the appropriation of genealogical records in contemporary Arrernte society*, Land, Rights, Laws: Issues of Native Title, vol. 4, no. 5, Native Title Research Unit, AIATSIS, Canberra, http://www.aiatsis.gov.au/ntru/docs/publications/issues/IPv4n5.pdf, accessed 3 June 2013.

Murphy, A 2002, 'Prescribed Bodies Corporate in the post determination landscape', *Balayi: Culture, Law and Colonisation*, vol. 5, pp. 162–65.

National Native Title Tribunal (NNTT) 2009, *Working with native title: linking native title and local government processes*, 3rd edn, NNTT website, http://www.nntt.gov.au/News-and-Communications/

Publications/Documents/Booklets/Working%20with%20native%20title.pdf, accessed 8 August 2013.

Native Title Research Unit 2010, submission to FaHCSIA on the draft Native Title (Prescribed Bodies Corporate) Amendment Regulations, AIATSIS, Canberra, http://www.aiatsis.gov.au/ntru/docs/2010pbcamendment.pdf, accessed 8 August 2103.

Native Title Services Victoria (NTSV), 'Prescribed Bodies Corporate', NTSV website, http://ntsv.com.au/prescribed-body-corporates/, accessed 28 July 2013.

O'Faircheallaigh, C 2000, *Negotiating major project agreements: the 'Cape York model'*, AIATSIS Research Discussion Paper, no. 11, AIATSIS, Canberra, http://www.aiatsis.gov.au/research/docs/dp/DP11.pdf, accessed 3 June 2013.

——2002, 'Implementation: the forgotten dimension of agreement-making in Australia and Canada', *Indigenous Law Bulletin*, vol. 5, pp. 14–17.

——2004, 'Evaluating agreements between Indigenous peoples and resource developers', in M Langton, M Tehan, L Palmer & K Shain (eds), *Honour among nations? Treaties and agreements with Indigenous people*, Melbourne University Press, Melbourne, pp. 303–28.

——2007, 'Native title and mining negotiations: a seat at the table, but no guarantee of success', *Indigenous Law Bulletin*, vol. 6, no. 26, pp. 18–20.

——& Corbett, T 2005, 'Indigenous participation in environmental management of mining projects: the role of negotiated agreements', *Environmental Politics*, vol. 14, no. 8, pp. 629–47, http://fennerschool-people.anu.edu.au/richard_baker/SRES3028/lectures_and_tutorials/week10/Indigenous%20Mgmt%20&%20Mining.pdf, accessed 3 June 2013

Office of the Registrar of Aboriginal Corporations (ORAC) 2004, *Report — Forum on risk issues for programs funding Indigenous corporations*, ORAC, Australian Government, Canberra.

Office of the Registrar of Indigenous Corporations (ORIC) 2013, *Remuneration: a report benchmarking the salaries of Aboriginal and Torres Strait Islander corporations*, ORIC, Canberra, http://www.oric.gov.au/html/publications/other/remuneration-report_f.pdf, accessed 29 July 2013.

Parliamentary Joint Committee on Native Title and the Aboriginal and Torres Strait Islander Land Account 2006, *Report on the operation of Native Title Representative Bodies*, Australian Parliament, Canberra.

Phillips, A 2013, 'Compensation covenants for mining activities run with the land: a win for successive landowners', *Australian Property Law Bulletin*, vol. 27, no. 4, pp. 56–8, http://eprints.qut.edu.au/58260/, accessed 26 September 2013.

Redmond, A 2007, 'Some initial effects of pursuing and achieving native title recognition in the northern Kimberley', in BR Smith & F Morphy (eds), *The social effects of native title: recognition, translation, coexistence*, CAEPR Research Monograph, no. 27, Centre for Aboriginal Economic Policy Research, Australian National University, Canberra, pp. 79–90.

Right People for Country Project Committee 2011, *Report of the Right People for Country Project Committee*, Department of Planning and Community Development, Melbourne, http://www.dpcd.vic.gov.au/aboriginal-affairs/projects-and-programs/right-people-for-country, accessed 30 July 2013.

Riley, M 2002, 'Winning' native title: the experience of the Nharnuwangga, Wajarri and Ngarla People, Land, Rights, Laws: Issues of Native Title, vol. 1, no. 2, Native Title Research Unit, AIATSIS, Canberra.

Ritter, D 2002, 'So, what's new? Native Title Representative Bodies and Prescribed Bodies Corporate after Ward', *Australian Mining and Petroleum Law Journal*, vol. 21, pp. 303–10.

——2009a, *Contesting native title: from controversy to consensus in the struggle over Indigenous land rights*, Allen & Unwin, Crows Nest, NSW.

——2009b, *Native title market*, University of Western Australia Press, Crawley, WA.

Sanders, W & Arthur, WS 2000, 'Assessing compensation for native title: a valuation perspective', *Pacific Rim Property Research Journal*, vol. 6, no. 1, pp. 43–56.

Smith, BR 2005, '"We got our own management": local knowledge, government and development in Cape York Peninsula', *Australian Aboriginal Studies*, vol. 2, pp. 4–15.

——2007, 'Towards an uncertain community? The social effects of native title in central Cape York Peninsula', in BR Smith & F Morphy (eds), *The social effects of native title: recognition, translation, coexistence*, CAEPR Research Monograph, no. 27, Centre for Aboriginal Economic Policy Research, Australian National University, Canberra, pp. 117–34.

—— & Morphy, F (eds) 2007, *The social effects of native title: recognition, translation, coexistence*, CAEPR Research Monograph, no. 27, Centre for Aboriginal Economic Policy Research, Australian National University, Canberra.

Smith, DE 2001, *Valuing native title: Aboriginal, statutory and policy discourses about compensation*, CAEPR Research Discussion Paper, no. 222, Centre for Aboriginal Economic Policy Research, Australian National University, Canberra, http://caepr.anu.edu.au/sites/default/files/Publications/DP/2001_DP222.pdf, accessed 21 August 2013.

—— & Hunt, J 2008, 'Understanding Indigenous Australian governance: research, theory and representations', in J Hunt, DE Smith, S Garling & W Sanders (eds), *Contested governance: culture, power and institutions in Indigenous Australia*, CAEPR Research Monograph, no. 29, ANU Epress, Australian National University, Canberra, pp. 1–23, http://epress.anu.edu.au?p=97361, accessed 29 July 2013.

Stacey, C & Fardin, J 2011, *Housing on native title lands: responses to the housing amendments of the Native Title Act*, Land, Rights, Laws: Issues of Native Title, vol. 4, no. 6, Native Title Research Unit, AIATSIS, Canberra.

Stewart, M 2010, 'Native title and tax: understanding the issues', *Indigenous Law Bulletin*, vol. 7, no. 21, 2010.

Strelein, LM 2008, *Taxation of native title agreements*, Native Title Research Monograph, no. 1, Native Title Research Unit, AIATSIS, Canberra.

——2009, *Compromised jurisprudence: native title cases since Mabo*, 2nd edn, Aboriginal Studies Press, Canberra.

——2012, 'Native title agreements, taxation and economic development in Australia', in M Langton & J Longbottom (eds), *Foundations for Indigenous peoples in the global mining boom*, Routledge, London, pp. 181–95.

—— & Tran, T 2007, *Native Title Representative Bodies and Prescribed Bodies Corporate: native title in a post determination environment*, Native Title Research Report, no. 2, Native Title Research Unit, AIATSIS, Canberra, http://www.aiatsis.gov.au/ntru/documents/PBCReport.pdf, accessed 29 July 2013.

Sullivan, P 1996, 'The needs of Prescribed Bodies Corporate under the *Native Title Act 1993* and Regulations', in AIATSIS (ed.), *Final report: Review of the* Aboriginal Councils and Associations Act 1976, vol. 2: supporting material, AIATSIS, Canberra.

——1997, *A sacred land, a sovereign people, and an Aboriginal corporation: Prescribed bodies and the Native Title Act,* North Australian Research Unit Report Series, no. 3, North Australian Research Unit, National Centre for Development Studies, Research School of Asia and Pacific Studies, Australian National University, Casuarina.

——2000, book review of *Guide to the design of native title corporations*, *Indigenous Law Bulletin*, vol. 4, no. 30, p. 42.

Taylor, J, Doran, B, Parriman, M & Yu, E 2012, *Statistics for community governance: the Yawuru Indigenous population survey of Broome*, CAEPR Working Paper, no. 82, Centre for Aboriginal

Economic Policy Research, Australian National University, Canberra, http://caepr.anu.edu.au/sites/default/files/Publications/WP/CAEPR%20WP82%20Tayloretal.pdf, accessed 8 August 2013.

Tran, T, Strelein, LM, Weir, LK, Stacey, C & Dwyer, A 2013, *Native title and climate change: changes to country and culture, changes to climate: strengthening institutions for Indigenous resilience and adaptation*, National Climate Change Adaptation Research Facility, Gold Coast.

Tsey, K, McCalman, J, Bainbridge, R & Brown, C 2012, 'Improving Indigenous community governance through strengthening Indigenous and government organizational capacity', Resource Sheet no. 10, produced for the Closing the Gap Clearinghouse, Australian Institute of Health and Welfare, Australian Institute of Family Studies, Canberra and Melbourne, http://www.aihw.gov.au/closingthegap/documents/resource_sheets/ctgc-rs10.pdf, accessed 29 July 2013.

Turner, P & Bauman, T 2012, 'Reflections on the 20th anniversary of Mabo', in T Bauman & L Glick (eds), *The limits of change: Mabo and native title 20 years on*, AIATSIS, Canberra, pp. 310–21.

Walker, BW, Porter, D & Marsh, I 2012, *Fixing the hole in Australia's heartland: how government needs to work in remote Australia*, Desert Knowledge Australia, Alice Springs.

Weir, JK 2007, 'Native title and governance: the emerging corporate sector prescribed for native title holders', Land, Rights, Laws: Issues of Native Title, vol. 3, no. 9, http://www.aiatsis.gov.au/ntru/docs/publications/issues/ip07v3n9.pdf, accessed 10 September 2013.

——2012, 'Country, native title and ecology', in JK Weir (ed.), *Country native title and ecology*, ANU EPress, Canberra, 2012, pp. 1–20.

Weir, JK, Stone, R & Mulardy, M 2012, 'Water planning and native title: a Karajarri and government engagement in the West Kimberley', in JK Weir (ed.), *Country, native title and ecology*, ANU EPress, Australian National University, Canberra, pp. 81–104.

Wensing, E & Taylor, J 2012, *Secure tenure options for financing home ownership and economic development possibilities on Aboriginal land subject to native title: the case of Aboriginal Lands Trust reserve lands in Western Australia*, AIATSIS Research Discussion Paper, no. 31, AIATSIS, Canberra.

Yu, P & Bauman, T 2012, 'Reflections on the 20th anniversary of Mabo', in T Bauman & L Glick (eds), *The limits of change: Mabo and native title 20 years on*, AIATSIS, Canberra, pp. 322–35.